Irving Howe was born in New York City in 1920. A graduate of the College of the City of New York, he is the author of *The UAW and Walter Reuther* (with B. J. Widick), *Sherwood Anderson: A Critical Biography, William Faulkner: A Critical Study,* and *Politics and the Novel.* Together with Eliezer Greenberg, he edited *A Treasury of Yiddish Stories,* and he is also the author, along with Lewis Coser, of *The American Communist Party: A Critical History,* which has recently been published by the Beacon Press.

Modern Literary Criticism

Modern Literary Criticism

An Anthology

Edited with an introduction 801.08

by IRVING HOWE

Beacon Press   Beacon Hill   Boston

A Word to the Reader

The main purpose of this anthology is to provide, both for the general public and for students of literature, a sampling of modern American and English literary criticism. I have tried to choose essays that are interesting and valuable in their own right, not because they happen to illustrate the method or approach of a critical "school." The stress has been upon practical criticism rather than esthetics or theorizing about criticism.

Important critics have been omitted: some, like Van Wyck Brooks, because their writings are available in popular editions, and others, like Newton Arvin, because their best work appears in books from which it is hard to obtain self-sufficient extracts. On the other hand, it has been pleasant to be able to include a number of critics who have done good work but have not yet won major reputations.

The essays are roughly divided into four groups: general literary discussions, studies of fiction, studies of poetry, and book reviews. But within these groups there is no particular order and each essay must be read in its own right.

Finally, a word about the Introduction. I have probably raised more questions than could reasonably be handled in an essay of this length or kind; but if so, that may be helpful to the reader in stimulating him to read fuller and more systematic expositions. I should also remark that the opinions expressed in the Introduction sometimes clash with those held by many of the critics who appear in this book. But that is in the nature of things, at least whenever men can think and write freely.

I. H.

Contents

CONTENTS   viii

Modern Literary Criticism

Modern Criticism: Privileges and Perils

Irving Howe

I

Few facts about the life of our culture are more striking than the recent growth of literary criticism in both extent and prestige. Not very long ago the province of journalists, casual impressionists, and academic humanists, literary criticism has become fiercely professional, an "institution" as well as a discipline, a self-contained world as well as a secondary branch of humane letters.

Perhaps for the first time in American experience, young men have elaborately and solemnly prepared themselves for careers as critics: not poets or novelists who also write criticism, but critics pure and complex. The honor available to the critic in the American intellectual community has sharply increased. Among certain sections of our "educated classes" there has been a tendency to look upon literary criticism as a genre peculiarly suited to their spiritual needs. Most literary scholars have begun to accept critics as their colleagues in the universities. And even where critics are treated with hostility, as in certain mass-circulation weeklies, one also finds an undercurrent of grudging respect.

This is not to imply that life has become a featherbed for critics. With one or two exceptions, their books sell poorly. Few of them are welcomed to the pages of the major review supplements. Not half a dozen could feed their children if they tried to live by their writing. Yet the word of the critics is today regarded as significant, and their audience turns to them not merely for knowledge but also for a kind of wisdom.

Why this should be so, is a question that lends itself to no easy or certain answer. I propose to speculate, in the hope that the reader will thereby be helped to "place," understand, and judge the essays that follow in this book.

The kind of literature called modern is almost always difficult; indeed, that is a sign of its modernity. To the established guardians of culture, the modern writer seems willfully inaccessible. He works with new and unfamiliar forms; he chooses subjects that disturb the audience and lead it to suppose that he is trying to violate its most cherished feelings; he provokes traditionalist critics to such epithets as "unwholesome," "coterie," and "decadent."

At certain points in the development of a culture, usually points of dismay and restlessness, writers find themselves *affronting* their audience, and not from decision or whim but from some deep moral and psychological necessity. Such writers may not even be aware that they are challenging crucial assumptions of their day, yet their impact is revolutionary; and once this comes to be recognized, the *avant garde* has begun to cohere as a self-conscious and combative group. As Paul Goodman observes:

. . . there are these works that are indignantly rejected, and called not genuine art, but insult, outrage, blague, fumiste, wilfully incomprehensible. . . . And what is puzzling is not that they are isolated pieces, but some artists persistently produce such pieces, and there are schools of such "not genuine" artists. What are they doing? In this case, the feeling of the audience is sound—it is always sound—there *is* insult, wilful incomprehensibility, experiment; and yet the judgment of the audience is wrong—it is often wrong—for this is a genuine art.

Why does this clash arise? Because, for one thing, the modern writer can no longer accept the formal claims of society. When he does try to acquiesce in the norms of the audience, he finds himself depressed or outraged. The usual morality seems to him counterfeit; taste, a genteel indulgence; tradition, a wearisome fetter. It becomes a condition of being or remaining a writer that he rebel, not merely and sometimes not at all against received opinions, but, more significantly, in the way he does his work.

It is now, in moments of extreme tension between writers and audience, that criticism takes on a unique importance. To indulge in a useful simplification: the more problematic modern literature seems, the more does criticism need to rehearse the nature of the problem. And that, in response to the growth during the present century of a distinctively modern literature, is what criticism has for the most part been doing.

Some of the critics, usually the younger ones, welcome the new writers and become their champions. In the battle of books (really a battle over styles of life) that now begins to take shape, these critics try to establish articles of war that will help the underdog. And because the new writing seems so difficult and exciting, it becomes profitable to burrow into texts, to quarrel over their meanings, to scrutinize them line by line with a fervor that must strike some observers as both preposterous and threatening.

These younger critics have as their main purpose the exploration of a new sensibility, and with time they become the mediators between the modern writers and that section of the public which is able, perhaps a bit too late, to respond to such writers. Far from being, like certain older critics, *arbitres elegantium* who journey at leisure among established masterpieces registering fine variations in weight and value, the younger critics band together as a dedicated group seeking to overturn the established standards of literary opinion and perhaps the established relations of literary power. To further their cause, they make commando raids, usually taking prisoners, on the literary past. Whole periods of literary history take on a new brilliance, even glamor; other periods wilt and suffer. It is inevitable, interesting, and, for a while, valuable.[1]

Started early in the present century, this process had come to an end by the mid-fifties. The *avant garde* has now disappeared almost entirely, and the enormous impetus—the zest, animation, and self-

---

[1] Some critics, to be sure, respond primarily to the "newness" of the new writing, as some readers of these critics respond primarily to discussions of the *idea* of newness. American culture is troubled by a ceaseless quest for novelty—which helps explain its abrupt discontinuities and recurrent excitements; and it would be unreasonable to expect that literary criticism could for long resist this impulse.

At the very worst, then, the audience for modern criticism may sometimes have substituted explications of the new literature for reading and experiencing it: even Kenneth Burke is occasionally less difficult than *Finnegan's Wake*. The mistaken notion could arise that criticism has a value in its own right, without reference to works of literature. And given our facility at absorbing new fashions, the insurgent critics often had a way of quickly becoming entrenched critics. None of this, however, should deflect us from the fact that modern criticism has confronted and grappled with serious problems.

confidence—it had imparted to criticism has also largely disappeared. Criticism, to be sure, had been written before the recent upsurge of the *avant garde* and seems likely to be written long after its total demise; but if criticism now finds itself in a state of uncertainty and perhaps even exhaustion, one reason must surely be that it has lost the buoying sense of purpose that had come from the *avant garde* experience.

Most discussions of modern criticism, I should hasten to add, do not follow this line of argument. The warmer partisans of modern criticism often regard its development as a self-contained progress from a pulpy impressionism in the magazines and a club-footed scholasticism in the universities to a blaze of analytic glory by critics uniquely gifted at close reading. But even if one were to accept this description, it would still seem plausible to say that for an understanding of the peculiar influence of modern criticism, inner shifts of critical doctrine have been less important than the common task of confronting the *avant garde* poetry and fiction of our time. To the extent that it did this, literary criticism took on an aura of dedication and excitement, and thereby captured the imagination of a significant audience. The reader turning to the little magazines in the twenties or thirties could feel that some of the criticism they printed not only gave him insight and information but might actually modify the values by which he tried to live.

Meanwhile, as the challenge of the *avant garde* gave edge and fire to modern criticism, the threat of commercialized mass culture brought a sense of peril. The preservation of standards of taste in a time of mass-produced vulgarity; the defense of literacy against its systematized public abuse; a restatement of faith in the power of the private imagination—these were among the tasks that modern critics set for themselves.

Few literary critics, as it happens, tried seriously to analyze the elusive new phenomenon that we call mass culture. Some dismissed it as beneath discussion; others tried to assimilate it to the cultural debasements of the past; still others contented themselves with hurling curses at the advancing barbarians. But if the critics contributed little to the study of mass culture, it was largely the standards of value implicit in their best work that made possible whatever stringent analysis we do have. And frequently the work of the critics would take on a tone of urgency, even of combative exhilaration, from their awareness that they were writing at a time when, as it seemed, the tradition of high culture was both in question and in danger.

At its best modern criticism has always been an "engaged" criticism. It has found itself caught up in a desperate struggle over the nature and quality of our culture. It could take almost nothing for granted, the very act of reading a poem having itself become highly self-conscious and problematic. Nor could the modern critic relax, as we like to suppose Dr. Johnson could, with the assumptions of his age and speak in terms of easy assurance to the "common reader." No matter how condescending T. S. Eliot and his followers might be toward Matthew Arnold, it was the threat described by Arnold—the threat from the massed ranks of Philistines and Barbarians—which also haunted the modern critics.

Had the purpose of modern criticism been merely to establish the currency of certain names, to make the reading of *Ulysses* and *The Waste Land* fashionable in the universities, there would by now be no further need for it. But clearly this was not the central purpose. The struggle for Joyce and Eliot mattered only as and if it was a struggle for literary standards; the defense of Joyce and Eliot was a defense not merely of modern innovation but also of the traditional culture which could no longer be assumed as a "given" and which nevertheless was a source of the best aspects of modern innovation. Seen in these terms criticism could become more than a craft: it could become a passion and a calling.

In the universities, too, the critics were caught up in conflict. For some decades into the twentieth century there had been a strong feeling among literary men that the American universities had taken over the external forms of German scholarship without adapting them to our needs. This complaint is seldom heard these days, but a few decades ago it was commonly charged that the scholarship of many professors of English came to no more than an arid accumulation of historical data that bore only the faintest relevance to an understanding of literature.

Even if such charges were too sweeping, there was enough truth in them to cause anxiety among some of the scholars; and the critics, sensing this, were quick to press their advantage. Relations between scholars and critics were, for a time, somewhat frosty, each group feeling threatened by the other because each could generally do what the other could not or could generally not do what the other was supposed to. The baiting of professors became standard sport among critics; the dismissal of critics as mere journalists, a routine academic retaliation. But then, with surprising suddenness—partly because of a decline in self-confidence among the scholars, partly because of a tremendous growth in the American universities after the Second World War—the English departments not only made room for critics but in some instances welcomed and surrendered to them. Thus, both the struggle against a sterile academicism and, a bit later, a partial triumph within the academy served to give the modern critics a sense of mission and assurance.[2]

There remains still another reason for the growing importance of literary criticism in our culture, and since it can hardly be discussed without indulging in speculation I have left it for last.

The best critics of our time have been oppressively aware that they were writing in a moment of extreme cultural dislocation. (Even the few who might deny this had to spend so much combative energy upon their denials that the effect was not notably different from an affirmation.) Certain persistent themes in modern criticism—one thinks, for example, of T. S. Eliot's preoccupation with the terrors of nihilism, I. A. Richards' early concern with the relation between poetry and science, Allen Tate's philippics against positivism—now interest us not merely for what they declare but as responses to and perhaps symptoms of cultural distress.

The dominant formal claim of modern criticism has been an insistence upon defining and limiting its enterprise, upon treating literature

---

[2] Certain results of the recent academic alliance between critics and scholars have obviously been desirable: a new *élan* among younger teachers, a new dedication among the more serious students. If this dedication has sometimes been accompanied by a naïve pride in possessing "the" critical method and, more important, by a loss of historical knowledge, it may be that the price has been worth paying. But I think that the growing fraternization between scholars and critics is likely to be most profitable if it does not end in a merger. Each can learn from and needs the other, if only to quarrel with; but only rarely should one try to assume the task of the other.

There is a sense, to be sure, in which it is desirable that scholars be distinguished critics and critics, expert scholars—the sense in which it is desirable that all of us remain forever handsome, charming, and young. But in the course of actual life, becoming a good critic or scholar is hard enough, and the talents needed for one are seldom the same as for the other. A blurring of distinctions could easily bring out the worst in both disciplines: as witness the academic journals where traditional scholarship is being replaced by routine exercises in the analysis of poetic structure. Dull scholarship can be useful; dull criticism rarely.

as self-contained and autonomous. The main actual circumstance for the writing of modern criticism has been the constant pressure to which it has been subjected by numerous extra-literary commitments. (One of the most interesting recent books of criticism is called *On the Limits of Poetry,* and a good part of it keeps breaking past the proclaimed limits.) It is no paradox to say that, because the most serious modern critics were so admirably devoted to the independent status and value of literature, they could seldom keep their extra-literary interests from entering and, at times, suffusing their criticism. At least since Matthew Arnold found that reflecting upon the place of poetry in an industrial society led him to worrying about "a girl named Wragg," the most influential critics have assumed the role of cultural spokesman, pundit, prophet—call it what you will. And it has been the clash between a desire for coherence within a formal discipline and an impulse to relate literature to human experience that has been the source of the best, as well as the worst, in modern criticism. The temptation to make criticism into a wide-ranging vehicle for humanist discourse has been recurrent and inescapable, both its chief privilege and most insidious peril.

In his day Matthew Arnold foresaw a related possibility:

More and more mankind will discover that we have to turn to poetry to interpret life for us, to console us, to solace us. Without poetry, our science will appear incomplete; and most of what passes for religion and philosophy will be replaced by poetry.

Certain modern critics have sharply dissented from this passage, insisting that Arnold's treatment of religion is frivolous and that poetry, because it has its own ground for existence, should not be regarded as a surrogate for philosophy or religion. Yet at least for the intellectual segments of our society, Arnold's statement has proved to be an accurate prediction. And what he wrote about poetry has also come to hold for criticism as the mediating agent between literature and the cultivated public.

Some critics, particularly those with a yearning for the "unity of belief" they locate in the Christian past, insist that the intellectual chaos which Arnold found in religion and philosophy has also seeped into criticism; they are fond of noting that modern criticism is troubled by the absence of common standards and assumptions. No doubt; a sense of certainty is hard to come by in our time, and literary criticism, like most other activities of the human mind, often does resemble a Tower of Babel. But it might also be remarked that a readiness to accept this condition, to take the disorder of modern life as something perhaps to be regretted but not soon to be remedied, can make for a criticism alive with the quality of risk and attractive for its candor and modesty.

To the extent that modern criticism does command such qualities, it has won for itself a quite unprecedented loyalty—not despite but because of our fracture of belief. For literary criticism has come to seem one of the few areas of discourse in which it is still possible for the human intelligence to move freely and disinterestedly.

The most intense moment in the history of modern criticism, the moment of its greatest hold upon the imagination of serious young people, has probably just come to an end. This was a moment in which the sense of the collapse of received beliefs had become unusually acute. One generation had been wounded by the debris of political ideologies; another had come to feel that public life was inherently repulsive. Religion seemed for a time to claim the minds of a good many literary people, but most of these apparently felt that a genuine conversion placed demands upon their energy and credulity which they could not meet. As a result, religion tended to become a *literary* experience, and the study of myth as the buried foundation of literature became a fascinating strategy for approaching religion without yielding to it.

In an age where intellectuals were both unusually sophisticated and unusually susceptible to social malaise, it began to seem that literature retained a purity and good faith which few other experiences could provide. *Literature alone had not betrayed modern man, literature alone could not betray him*—so, one suspects, many people have felt during the past few decades.

To the extent that this feeling led to a cult of literature, a solemn praise for the sanctity of the "creative," one can say that an evasive impulse had come into play, an impulse to escape the pain and sordidness of our time. With such a charge I am prepared to go a little way; but no more than a little. For how could any cultivated person deny the strain of truth in the assertion that literature could "interpret" and "console" our lives as nothing else? Most of the prevalent commitments had turned out to be deceptions, and none could preserve the sense of the human as could literature in an inhuman age.

Criticism, in turn, became the vehicle through which a cultivated elite not only exercised its powers of perception but reflected upon its sense of the human condition in the middle of the twentieth century: a sense that came through most significantly in the literature of our time but which seemed also to need the partial conceptualizing that criticism could provide. The critic became a guardian of taste, a priest of values, a protector of the undefiled word. And in some ways he seemed even more accessible to the audience than the poet or novelist, for the critic talked directly about the problems which the poet or novelist presented imaginatively.

Criticism thus seemed to be one of the last humane disciplines in which it was still possible to take a "total view." Critics might become specialists in the sprung verse of Hopkins or the techniques of Faulkner, but even those who were most insistent upon formal limits could not avoid touching larger issues that soon took them beyond literature. They could not help it: literature itself forced them to. And as long as some men still wished to reflect not merely upon subjects but also upon themselves as reflecting men, literary criticism would continue to exert its attraction.

I am aware that this picture is somewhat of an ideal one and may omit the usual touches of the ridiculous that mar any human enterprise. But this should not disturb us, since what matters at the moment is to discover the essential needs and motives behind the writing and reading of criticism.

The usual touches of the ridiculous are not, in any case, hard to find. Young critics expatiating upon the importance of their subject and smugly explaining that one has to read the poem *qua* poem—this could be infuriating. The claim to limitation that might seem to be one of the more modest traits of modern criticism could itself become a source and symptom of fanaticism. At its stuffy and pompous worst, criticism suffered from the defects of its virtues: it became a department of letters in which one could make oneself foolish in an astonishingly large number of ways, from counting images in an Elizabethan play or reading Kafka's novels as cabalistic notations on homosexuality, to declaiming about the ache at the heart of the universe.

Our involvement with criticism led to still other difficulties. Momentary turns of the *Zeitgeist* had a way of insinuating themselves all too easily into the minds of critics, who took them as the fruits of an ultimate and timeless wisdom. The extraordinary reputation enjoyed by Lionel Trilling during the past fifteen years was in part a deserved tribute to a critic of stature; but in part it was also the result of Trilling's capacity for expressing, in the vocabulary of traditional English liberalism, the new and barely acknowledged conservative moods that had begun to entice American intellectuals. Had Trilling's disciples been aware of what was happening, there might have been no great harm in this; but because of the enormous prestige that had accrued to criticism, such awareness was slow and hard in coming.

Yet in any final reckoning one hopes that the efflorescence of modern criticism will be regarded as among the more estimable attempts to salvage the tradition of humanism and recreate the idea of the human. At least a small portion of mankind found itself, as Arnold had foreseen, turning "to poetry to interpret life for us, to console us, to solace us." That some even turned to poetry or criticism to "save" us Arnold would also have understood: for it is an error which, if born in desperation, can grow into generosity.

II

Something should now be said about the development of recent American criticism, though the reader must be warned that what follows is neither a condensed history nor even a sketch for such a history. Major critical groups and tendencies go unmentioned; there is no pretense at evaluating the work of individual critics; my only intention is to note a few central problems and directions.

The beginnings of a distinctly "modern" criticism in America can be dated with fair precision: 1915, the year Van Wyck Brooks published *America's Coming-of-Age*. During and after the Second World War Brooks was to abandon most of his youthful beliefs and to lapse into a rosy, soft-spirited outlook upon life and literature; but the early Brooks, though not himself contributing very much to the small stock of distinguished criticism written by Americans, led the way toward arousing a desire and creating some of the conditions for a serious criticism.

Brooks lashed out against the "genteel tradition," that cluster of decayed inhibitions and pieties which seemed to him responsible for so much of the evasiveness and deceit in American culture. He poured forth his contempt upon American commercialism and materialism, not merely because they were so dreary in their own right but because he saw them as a cause of the collapse that so frequently broke the careers of promising American writers. Like Emerson before him, Brooks worried the problem of what it meant to be an American, and not merely as being an American was a social fact but also as it was a spiritual possibility. He provided his followers with a rough yet ready criterion for evaluating both experience and literature—the criterion of "reality"—which soon came to signify an eagerness to break past the bland surfaces of American life and to discover the animating values of the American tradition as these have been embodied in the work of our major writers.

This approach could not, by itself, provide critics with clear guidance at either the practical or the theoretical level; it gave them a cultural rhetoric but not a critical technique; it failed to indicate how, in twentieth-century America, one might go about the job of criticizing a particular novel or poem. Yet the work of Brooks and his colleagues (Randolph Bourne, Waldo Frank, Lewis Mumford) was important to American criticism, if only because it prepared the way for achievements greater than their own. Perhaps more than anyone else, they brought into being an atmosphere in which the problems of literature and criticism could be regarded as vital to the future of our civilization.

The excitement that bubbled through the work of Brooks and his friends had a good many sources: it drew upon the insurgent spirit of early twentieth-century American radicalism, it had some connection with the gradual discovery in this country of the European *avant garde,* and it was greatly influenced by a number of revolutionary systems of thought about man and society which had been drifting across the Atlantic. From our immediate point of view, the most important of these were Freudianism and Marxism, both of which, though never designed as methods of literary criticism, were soon appropriated by eager disciples intent upon "applying" them to literature.

While it would survive into and no doubt beyond the fifties, the psychoanalytic vogue in criticism had its most exciting and popular moment during the twenties. Most of the pioneering Freudian criticism is now likely to seem excessively crude, but at the time it had, at least, the strength that comes from unqualified commitment. Later psychoanalytic critics, more cautious and sophisticated, learned from the mistakes of such beginners as Ludwig Lewisohn and Joseph Wood Krutch—but with this qualification: the more their work approached the flexibility and sensitiveness one looks for in criticism, the more their rigid Freudianism tended to melt away and become one element among others in the usual kind of critical intelligence.

On the face of it, the discoveries of psychoanalysis should have turned out to be enormously valuable to literary criticism. Psychoanalysis insists upon the primacy, and devotes itself to the buried drama, of individual life—a major theme in modern literature. Psychoanalysis sees human personality in highly dynamic terms, with the self becoming a kind of battlefield upon which fierce struggles rage between impulse and regulation, desire and convention—a vision surely close to the scrutiny of inner motives that is so frequent in nineteenth- and twentieth-century writing. Psychoanalysis not only confronts the critic with the task of exploring both the representations and the effects of the unconscious in literature but seems also to offer him a brilliant technique for doing it. Psychoanalysis presents its interpretation of dreams through a series of signs that themselves require close interpretation— a procedure not unlike that of many recent critics. Psychoanalysis is peculiarly sensitive to the way language is seized and twisted by the imagination, the concept of "condensation," for example, being quite similar to the assumptions behind many recent studies of wit and paradox in poetry. Psychoanalysis seeks to break past the façade of personality and discover the implicit motifs of behavior—which again is closely related to a dominant concern of modern literature: the search for realities of the self behind social masks. And in its stress upon the unavoidable pains and costs of repression, psychoanalysis offers a somber view of human destiny, one that in grandeur and depth approaches the "tragic sense" which has been so recurrent a topic in modern criticism.[3]

Yet these contributions to criticism have thus far proved mainly theoretic, a promise unfulfilled. I do not say this for the reason that such judgments are usually advanced: that the Freudian approach to literature fails to issue in evaluations of the poem or novel. It is true that the Freudian approach, like any other variety of "extrinsic" criticism, cannot by itself provide literary valuation; but then even its most fanatical defenders do not claim that it can. What they do assert is that it makes possible a deeper or better understanding of a good many works of literature.

Nor is my point merely that the Freudian approach frequently

[3] I leave aside the most questionable aspect of psychoanalytic speculation about art: the notion that a poem or picture is a "substitute gratification." (See, on this, Lionel Trilling's excellent essay, "Art and Neurosis," p. 94.) For even if one rejects out of hand this simplistic theory, one can still grant the possibility that the Freudian approach will help us to understand the particular work of literature or to grasp the dominant outlook of a particular writer or to discover why readers react as they do to various poems and novels.

proves reductive, a means of clamping the richness and variety of litera-ture into a tight system. This complaint is valid enough, and a de-cidedly serious one too. But the problem is finally to decide whether the Freudian approach is necessarily or inherently reductive, whether greater experience and skill might not remove most of the crudeness from psychoanalytic criticism. And here, I think, we reach a difficulty that *may* be inherent in the Freudian approach to literature.

Psychoanalysis is devoted to an investigation of the individual's inner life, but as long as we employ it primarily upon the conceptual level and are not closely involved in a clinical situation, the individual postulated by the Freudians must necessarily remain abstract. Few critics, when turning to particular poems or novels, have been able, so to speak, to individualize the Freudian image of the individual, to melt the Freudian concepts into a vital apprehension of specific character or event. Somewhat similarly, psychoanalysis may place a heavy stress upon the inherent dynamism of human personality, but this concept itself must also remain static. The psychoanalyst finds in it valuable tips for the practice of therapy, for setting into motion the clinical rela-tionship: a relationship that, despite the possibility of certain kinds of prediction, remains a unique interchange between two human beings. In dealing with the work of literature, however, the critic has no equiva-lent to the insights provided the analyst by the specific clinical situation.

The tendency of Freudian criticism must therefore be to treat the poem or novel as if it were a case study—at best, a marvelously rich case study—without the experience of analysis behind it; that is, as a report for which the analyst had no enriching and complicating history of struggle and affection with the patient. And this, I think, must be as unsatisfactory in regard to literature as it would be in therapy. Given a limitation so severe, Freudian critics have been tempted to regard the work of literature (I quote Arnold Hauser) as if it were "no more than a mere puzzle, whose meaning can in no case be comprehended directly" and to treat "its symbols as abstract, rigid, conventional signs, with an explanation that may be looked up, as it were, in a diction-ary. . . ."

Even in such relatively careful studies as Ernest Jones' essay on Hamlet or Ernest Kris' on Prince Hal, psychoanalytic criticism fre-quently courts the danger of becoming a mere sequence of predictable correlations, a sectarian allegory in which the events and figures of the

plays are "translated" into the fixed categories of a system. The Freud-ian constants, which in a well-conducted analysis quickly lead to and become interwoven with the materials of a particular human history, usually remain frozen when applied to a work of literature. And the main reason for this, I think, is not the ineptitude or inexperience of the Freudian critics but the fact that the characters of a novel or a play cannot "talk back" or engage in free association or modify previous revelations, as a patient in therapy can. The Freudian critic is therefore inclined to concentrate upon recurrent human types rather than indi-vidual representations as they appear in novels or plays. But at its best criticism must soon go beyond the notation of archetypes and seek to discover why certain embodiments of them are so much more valuable than others, why, for example, Hamlet is so much more engaging than any number of other figures in literature with whom he shares the Oedipus complex.

A related difficulty stems from the fact that few critics who employ the Freudian terms and categories can really be said to have mastered them—indeed, it is questionable whether these critics, as long as they remain critics primarily, *can* master them. At the most, they have read carefully and pondered upon the Freudian literature, but few have been able to apply the Freudian concepts in the only setting in which these concepts take on full, dynamic meaning: the clinical setting. On the other hand, when practicing psychoanalysts try to write criticism, their expertness in handling the Freudian system ends precisely at the point where they cease being analysts and start becoming critics. As critics, however, they have neither a larger nor a smaller claim upon our atten-tion than other amateurs bearing theories, and they are not necessarily a bit more skillful than the Freudian literary men at applying psycho-analytic concepts to the criticism of literature.

None of this is to deny that there have been a number of dis-tinguished achievements in Freudian criticism: studies describing the temperaments of certain writers (Saul Rosenzweig on Henry James, William Troy on Stendhal) or explications of works that bear a startling resemblance to the texture of dreams (Selma Fraiberg on Kafka). What I have been saying may come to no more than an account of how diffi-cult it is to write psychoanalytic criticism. And since the difficulties may be due to the youthfulness of psychoanalysis, which makes it hard even for sympathetic critics fully to absorb its ideas, this critique of the psychoanalytic approach to literature may prove not to be "fundamen-

tal." But if my description of the difficulties is reasonably accurate, then the immediate outlook for the practice of psychoanalytic criticism is rather dim.

Though a small part of the social, or sociological, criticism that flourished in the thirties was considerably better than most Freudian criticism, the great bulk of it was probably worse. A small part was better because the social approach, if used with restraint, lent itself to a more fruitful and intimate relationship with certain literary texts than did psychoanalytic criticism. The great bulk was worse because in the thirties social criticism usually degenerated into the kind of "Marxist" apologetics that served primarily to advance the Communist movement.

Even the most rigid Freudian was usually his own man, and when he did mangle a poem or novel it was the result of disinterested zeal. A good part of what passed for Marxist criticism in the thirties, however, was not at all disinterested, as can be seen in the now familiar record of Stalinist publications habitually praising a writer who seemed politically friendly and then damning him once he had become a "renegade." [4]

Like almost any other significant trend in modern thought, Marxism could prove useful to a literary critic, particularly if he regarded his commitment with a certain skepticism or at least reserve, and if he were not so innocent as to suppose that Marxism could by itself constitute a critical method. The power of Marxism as an analytical instrument for a critic dealing, say, with the nineteenth-century novel could be enormous—indeed, the trouble was likely to be that the tool was too powerful for the critic to control. And if he wrote as a friend of the Communist movement, his work was likely to be crippled by an inquisitorial narrowness of spirit and a form of intellectual presumption that has been described as taking upon oneself "the conceit of history."

The "vulgar Marxism" of the thirties, like vulgar Freudianism and other reductive schools of thought, had a special fascination for the kind of critic who in a time of chaos enjoyed the *idea* of intellectual tidiness and whose dominant interest in literature was to provide systematic statements about its historical significance—which in practice often meant statements about its relation to Communist needs. It would

[4] Cf. the chapter entitled "The Intellectuals Turn Left," in *The American Communist Party: A Critical History* by Irving Howe and Lewis Coser. A few sentences in the present text are adapted from this source.

therefore be quite beside the mark to discuss most left-wing criticism of the thirties by trying to estimate the possible strengths and weaknesses of a Marxist approach to literature. The reality of the thirties was not a pure-spirited effort to develop a distinctive kind of criticism, but a relationship of power: the relationship between Communist ideology as embodied in a political apparatus and a flock of sympathetic critics.

Yet it is also important to remember that there were some critics, men free of organizational control and devoted to their craft, who wrote from a conviction that Marxism—or some social perspective in which it played a part—could help us to apprehend both large-scale trends of literary history and certain individual works. Most notable among such critics was Edmund Wilson, but there were others, such as Newton Arvin, Philip Rahv, F. O. Matthiessen, and Harold Rosenberg, who used Marxist categories with restraint and intelligence.

Many claims have been made for a sociological approach to literature, and these claims do not necessarily depend upon an acceptance of Marxism. Here, for example, is a passage from Henry Bamford Parkes, a critic hostile to Marxism:

Every writer . . . grows up as a member of a particular society, and the structure of his personality, his view of life and his emotional conflicts and consummations are conditioned by social factors. He is likely, moreover, to be generally receptive to those broad currents of thought and feeling which are shared by the other members of his society. For this reason the content of his work, including its deeper emotional quality as well as its subject-matter, cannot be explained without reference to his social background. In revealing himself the writer also reflects his society; he indicates what type of personality and what forms of emotional experience may develop within that society, and this reflection may often be most significant when it is least deliberate.

There are other claims: The social approach (for our purposes often the same as what is called the historical approach) can show how apparently autonomous developments in literary history have been shaped by the pressure of historical events, e.g., how the rise of both the periodical essay and the novel in eighteenth-century England depends on the growth of new reading publics. The social approach can help us to grasp the world-outlook, or, as critics now like to say, the vision of a writer, by analyzing the component parts of his belief and thought. This approach can also help us locate the social coordinates of a work of literature, those references and implications that help bind it together and must be understood if the work is not to seem inaccessible.

Some of these claims have an obvious plausibility. Since literature exists within history yet has a history of its own, there is likely to be some value in serious efforts to account for changes in the content, themes, and perhaps even forms of literature by correlating them with events co-extensive in time. For the criticism of such genres as the novel, and particularly such sub-genres as the realistic novel, the social approach can be very fruitful—it is often employed even by those critics who scorn it in principle. There would seem to be no other way of grasping the significance of dominant patterns of conduct portrayed in such novels: Can one really appreciate decisive parts of *Bleak House* without a knowledge of early nineteenth-century English life or, at the very least, an awareness of what the Industrial Revolution meant for the great English cities? Can one fully respond to *Middlemarch* unless one sees the way in which George Eliot has employed characteristic ideas of her time and given them imaginative embodiment in her novels? Nor is this merely—it is hardly at all—a matter of what scholars call "background material." The use of social and ideological categories is as relevant to a literary judgment of *Middlemarch* as the analysis of devices of rhetoric and patterns of form to a literary judgment of *The Waste Land:* that is, both are necessary and neither is sufficient.

There is a counter-argument which merits attention, the counter-argument which says in effect: yes, your social or historical approach may be of some use in the writing of literary history but it is of almost no use in literary criticism. For even if it does help illuminate the inner world of a novel, it cannot yield judgments of literary value, it cannot tell us why *Middlemarch* is so much better than many other nineteenth-century novels.

The argument is familiar and, up to a point, valid; but it is not quite so valid as is commonly supposed. For I would suggest that any approach to literature which accurately describes or genuinely illuminates what is happening within a poem or novel has already taken a long step toward the goal of evaluation. If, for example, the social approach really can give us a rounded and supple description of *Middlemarch,* then it has provided us with at least some of the materials that validate a literary judgment. Surely it is an error to suppose that a mature critic separates the act of analysis from that of evaluation; surely an error to suppose that there is some sacred moment of judgment which can be strictly differentiated from earlier analysis of the work of literature. And it is equally an error, I think, to suppose that in trying to rationalize or validate our judgments of literary works we do not regularly employ "extra-literary" criteria that deeply involve our beliefs and values.[5]

Yet, all this granted, I find myself increasingly skeptical as to the uses of the social approach to literature—particularly if it is regarded as a self-sufficient way of reading novels or poems. The social approach may work well if we are trying to examine large curves of literary history, but it becomes stiff when we turn to specific literary problems. You can use it to explain the rise of the periodical essay in the eighteenth century, but it will not help much if you want to study the genesis and characteristics of Addison's style. It may illuminate George Eliot's mastery of the social world of *Middlemarch,* but it contributes very little toward describing a major quality of that novel: the way in which epigrammatic comment is woven into the action. The social approach helps as a preliminary in those instances where the poem or novel is concerned with large social topics, but it can seldom take us very far toward defining the particular quality of a writer or a work. It is simply too coarse for the requirements of literary criticism, and there are too many areas of poetry and fiction about which it has almost nothing to say.

Nonetheless, in the twentieth century the social approach to literature probably has to its credit a greater body of competent work than does the psychoanalytic. For one thing, the social approach extends farther back in time, so that it has been able to develop a fuller tradition and to shed its more extreme claims. The principle of "historicity" to which it is committed permits a more complex and flexible awareness than does the psychoanalytic approach. And paradoxically, the quality of whatever social or Marxist criticism has been written in recent years may well have risen just because it had become so decidedly unfashion-

---

[5] The criteria of judgment proposed by Austin Warren and René Wellek, two authoritative spokesmen for "formalist" criticism, include "coherence and complexity," of which at least the second and perhaps also the first are bound up with the beliefs and values held by intellectuals in our time. Coherence and complexity have, no doubt, interested critics in other times as well, but it seems reasonable to suppose that the particular bent of meaning we give such terms has a great deal to do with whatever is unique or special in contemporary ways of thought.

able. Once a critical approach is no longer burdened with group fanaticism or self-seeking, its most valuable insights can be fruitfully absorbed even by its opponents. A good many Marxist procedures are today frequently employed by non-Marxists, often with greater skill than by the Marxists themselves. A critic like Allen Tate, despite his principled opposition to the social or historical approach, writes essays that are rich in historical materials and observations; indeed, they would be inconceivable apart from the imprint of his strong historical sense. Almost any critic worth reading soon transcends the categories he employs.

It would be a pity if these remarks were taken as an attack upon the claim that Freudianism and Marxism can be useful to some critics. I have been concerned mainly to delimit their area of relevance; to suggest that they not be regarded as self-sufficient methods; and to conclude that, like other branches of modern thought, they are most useful to criticism when they cease being rigid ideologies and become modes or elements of our thought.

By the late thirties both psychoanalytic and social criticism had lost much of their *élan,* and many of the younger critics, indifferent to the ideological battles that both of these schools encouraged, turned for guidance to a group that has since come to be known as the New Critics.

The work of such New Critics as John Crowe Ransom, Allen Tate, Robert Penn Warren, and R. P. Blackmur extended back into the twenties, when some of them had led a group of Southern writers (the "Fugitives") who were sharply aware of their estrangement from modern life and committed somewhat quixotically to an "agrarian" politics, while others, like Blackmur, had begun to print close criticism of poetry in the literary magazine *Hound and Horn.* Their moment of decisive influence within the literary world did not really come, however, until both Freudian and Marxist criticism began to fade. To say that the prestige of the New Critics in the forties and fifties was merely a function of the collapse of their opponents would be gratuitously to disparage these gifted men. But it would also be naïve to deny that their recent success has had much to do with shifts in the *Zeitgeist,* most notably with the large-scale reaction among intellectuals against psychological experimentalism, literary bohemia, and social radicalism.

The roots of the New Criticism, to be sure, extend farther back. Its chroniclers have traced a number of doctrines and attitudes to Coleridge (literary psychology), Rémy de Gourmont (theories of style), Henry James (techniques of fiction), Ezra Pound (close analysis of verse), and I. A. Richards (speculations about the place of poetry in a scientific age). These and other influences deserve to be noted, but by far the most significant is that of T. S. Eliot, whom the New Critics saw as their living guide and exemplar.

Eliot's importance as a critic derived, first of all, from his achievement as a poet, since his poetic practice helped to create a view of English literature that would soon revolutionize the taste of the age. In his literary essays Eliot has been concerned to make possible and justify his own kind of poetry; and as his poetry has shifted from early evocations of the malaise of modern life to efforts in both reflective verse and poetic drama at reestablishing the Christian vision, so has his criticism shifted from early studies in the formal characteristics of individual writers to a series of attempts at using the analysis of literature for a Christian critique of our culture.

Much of the work the New Critics were to do consisted in applying —sometimes merely systematizing—the hints and notions that Eliot had advanced in his essays. Like many other critics less sympathetic to his outlook, they found in Eliot a mind that was capable, through a skilled use of the exact epithet, the neat comparison, and the apt quotation, of capturing the particular quality of a writer. They found in Eliot a critic who possessed an impressive awareness of literature as a historical tradition, yet who could also make the poets of the seventeenth century seem like vibrant contemporaries. ("The historical sense," wrote Eliot, "compels a man to write not merely with his own generation in his bones, but with a feeling that the whole literature of Europe from Homer and within it the whole of his own country has a simultaneous existence. . . .")

Eliot was a critic with a flair for coining, borrowing, and dramatizing critical catch-phrases—the objective correlative, the dissociation of sensibility, the impersonality of poetry, the uses of tradition—which scholars and critics might later call into question, but which nonetheless had the immediate effect of provoking thought and speculation. He had an enviable capacity for elevating the unformed concerns of his audience into explicit issues, as in his repeated reflections upon the "problem of belief" (whether, in an age of clashing world-outlooks, a reader must share the religious or ideological convictions of a writer in order fully to enjoy his work). And perhaps most important, Eliot seemed a model of serious and disinterested devotion to the criticism of literature—and in his earlier phase, to the criticism not of literature as it might affect or promote some other activity but of literature as something to be valued and cherished in its own right.

In recent years, as the New Critics have begun to seem a bit uneasy with their disciples, they have been inclined to deny that there ever was an identifiable tendency or a coherent body of ideas warranting the label of New Criticism. And indeed, there can be no question that differences of outlook and stress have, with the passage of time, become quite sharp among the New Critics. The severe moralistic judgments which Yvor Winters brings to bear upon a poem have little in common with John Crowe Ransom's interest in the local wit, the niceties of observation and diction, which for him constitute the "texture" of a poem. There is an equally great distance between R. P. Blackmur's semantic dissections and Allen Tate's concern with discovering whether some large unifying mode of belief is resident in the total work of a poet. Yet it would seem reasonable to suppose that the identification of these and other critics as part of a loose tendency is not merely fortuitous and has some basis in reality. What that basis is, has been suggested by Allen Tate in his remark that the New Criticism has been distinguished by "a hostility to, or neglect of, the 'historical method.'" This hostility or neglect will obviously be greater in the work of some New Critics than others, and in one or two it is barely visible; but for defining the central characteristic of a critical *tendency* Tate's remark is very useful, not least so because it can be accepted by the opponents of the New Criticism as readily as it is advanced by Tate himself.

In their zeal, often a fiercely defensive zeal, to proclaim and celebrate the integrity of literature, the New Critics declared that, unlike the "positivists" and "historicists," their purpose was to study poetry *as poetry* and not as a version or reflection of anything else. Literature was to be regarded as an autonomous mode of utterance, an independent category of experience. The work of literature could become accessible to *literary* description and judgment only if the critic employed terms referring to its inner characteristics. Where all "extrinsic" schools of criticism proposed some measure of "correspondence" to one or another aspect of (or idea about) human experience, the "intrinsic" approach of the New Criticism favored "coherence," the inner unity and propriety of the parts of the poem, as a basis for analysis and judgment.[6]

Poetry, wrote John Crowe Ransom, gratifies not a "practical" but a "perceptual impulse." Unlike science, which erects abstract cognitive structures, poetry presents the particular and concrete; it apprehends what Ransom, in a striking phase, has called "the World's Body." Ransom even drove this distinction into poetry itself, expressing a sharp distaste for "Platonic poetry," by which he meant a poetry of ideas as it approaches the condition of expository prose.

In the eyes of a good many New Critics it was a mistake to suppose that the value of poetry which presents "the World's Body" can be judged primarily by reference to the world as known and experienced. With one or another degree of purism, they resisted the "doctrine of relevance," as Tate called it—the notion that "the subject-matter of a literary work . . . must be tested (on an analogy to scientific method) by observation of the world that it 'represents.' " The historical method, charged Tate, "will not permit us to develop a critical instrument for dealing with works of literature as existent objects," for it is a method that insists upon regarding works of literature as "expressive of substances beyond themselves." [7]

Hoping to free literature from what they apparently regarded as the pressure and competition of science, the New Critics tried to establish poetry as something quite apart from any pragmatic rationale. Poetry, in Allen Tate's words, is "an independent form of knowledge, a kind of cognition equal to the knowledge of the sciences at least, perhaps superior." [8] Poetry provides a "presentational" kind of truth, and any

[6] Again, not all the New Critics. But most would probably agree with Cleanth Brooks and William Wimsatt in their *Short History of Literary Criticism* that "Poetry is truth of 'coherence,' rather than truth of 'correspondence,' as the matter is sometimes phrased nowadays."

[7] Such remarks are extreme versions of the opinions held by many New Critics; they were first advanced in a polemical context, when Tate was waging war against both "positivism" and the tendency of graduate schools to dissolve literature in a solution of historical fact. In practice, Tate's criticism has rarely satisfied the impossible conditions set forth in his literary theorizing, and is all the better for it.

[8] Except as indices of preference, it is difficult to make out the meaning of "equal" and "superior." For if Tate really intended to suggest that poetry and science are distinct disciplines, each with its own aims, characteristic procedures, and modes of convention, then a comparison using terms like "equal" and "superior" is probably meaningless. How can such terms be used if it is

criticism that would avoid the taint of the pragmatic must, in Tate's view, refrain from dissolving poetry into something else.

Though some New Critics might wish to qualify the above position, there was concurrence of a kind in the practical criticism they wrote. What the New Critics wanted primarily was to put an end to the absorption of the poem in a massive background of social and historical forces, or the absorption of the poem in some impressionistic account of the emotions it aroused. Their ideal program posited—and in practice they sometimes achieved—a close and patient description of what the poem is: a description in which an effort would be made to connect the paraphrase the critic provided of the poem's content with those technical devices, patterns of form, and strategies of rhetoric through which meaning is realized in literature. A central doctrine of the New Critics asserted that content and form are inseparable—that the content of a poem could be located only in the specific dynamics of the form.

Very often this critical outlook involved a strong emphasis upon devices of rhetoric. The New Critics became keen at detecting the way in which a subtle qualifier might enrich a whole passage, a series of recurrent images might form a substructure of bias, an ambiguous use of key words could create a tension of discordant or incongruous materials to lend a poem its unexpected complexity. And since most critics, even those committed in principle to formal analysis, must have some hierarchy of preference guiding their choice of problems to investigate, individual New Critics were likely to stress certain elements (ambiguity, irony, paradox, tension) to the virtual exclusion of other formal properties or thematic materials. In fiction the New Critics stressed such matters as the "point of view" through which a novelist authenticates his material, the realization of themes through a coherent structure, and the metaphoric use of language even in realistic contexts.

Cleanth Brooks, perhaps the main codifier of the New Criticism, has formulated certain other principles of the school:

---

acknowledged in advance that the functions of science and poetry are different in kind? Suppose that instead of poetry and science Tate had spoken of the lyric and physics: would there be any point in saying that the lyric is a kind of cognition equal to the knowledge of physics at least, perhaps superior?

For that matter, if Tate really did mean to suggest that science and poetry are two independent categories of experience, then much of the talk encouraged by the New Criticism about the threat of science to poetry becomes meaningless. It could only be a social or literary *situation* involving a certain use or misuse of science that threatened poetry.

. . . the primary concern of criticism is with the problem of unity—
the kind of whole which the literary work forms or fails to form,
and the relation of the various parts to each other in building up
this whole.

. . . form is meaning.

. . . literature is ultimately metaphorical and symbolic.

The "formalist critic," wrote Brooks, "because he wants to criticize
the work itself, makes two assumptions":

1) he assumes that the relevant part of the author's intention is
what he actually got into his work; that is, he assumes that the
author's intention *as realized* is the "intention" that counts, not
necessarily what he was conscious of trying to do. . . . And 2)
the formalist critic assumes an ideal reader: that is, instead of focusing on the varying spectrum of possible readings, he attempts to
find a central point of reference from which he can focus upon the
structure of the poem or novel.

In addition to these formal concerns, the New Critics, being men of
our time and men deeply involved in the troubles of our time, shared a
number of cultural attitudes which greatly affected their work, often in
ways of which they were not quite aware. They were much concerned
with what they regarded as the fracturing of the modern mind into
utilitarian and esthetic sectors, a fracturing that has resulted in a steady
diminution of power and confidence since the time of the Renaissance;
and they looked upon poetry (except when looking upon religion) as
the one possibility for restoring wholeness and unity. They were concerned with the decay of tradition, both in the social and in the literary
senses of the term: the decay of those inherited assumptions of value
which, beneath the surface of consciousness, give order and meaning to
human experience. And as a result of these preoccupations, they kept
returning, often with a genuine perceptiveness, to the "problem of
belief," which in the final analysis involved nothing less than whether it
was still possible in our time to have a disinterested response to works
of literature.

The achievements of the New Criticism are by now quite familiar,
a matter of public record. Even those who question its theory of literature as knowledge or its anti-romanticist bias or its actual procedures in
analyzing a poem must acknowledge that it has done a distinct service
in asserting the integrity of the work of art at a time when that integrity
was under systematic assault and in creating an awareness that the

primary task of criticism is to examine poems and novels in their own right. Some of the pioneer New Critics, men like Ransom, Tate, Blackmur, and Winters, have made solid contributions to American letters. And if there is reason to be impatient with their more slavish followers, it should also be recognized that in the long run a major contribution of the New Criticism will have been to force its opponents into a revaluation of their own methods, a refinement of critical sensibility that might otherwise not have taken place.

At this point, however, it might be profitable to glance at some of the objections that critics and scholars have made to the New Criticism, so that the reader who proceeds to the essays in this book can form his own estimates.

Most traditional literary scholars have regarded the New Criticism with suspicion, in some instances out of a feeling that they were being threatened by high-powered analysts with whom they could not compete, and in other instances because they felt that the New Criticism failed adequately to consider the historical context of works of literature. Critics like Empson and Brooks, it was charged, elaborated their complexities of interpretation by ignoring or being ignorant of the limits of meaning imposed by history. If there are certain advantages in regarding a text as though it were contemporaneous and anonymous, there are very grave disadvantages as well, since language is neither static nor stable but has an inner development of its own and is subject to the shifting pressures of the whole historical process. Not merely is it necessary to know the meaning or meanings of words as they were used at the time a poem was written, but one must try to command the complex of historical and ideational associations that accrued to the word at a given time. Thus, charged the traditional literary scholars— and at times with some justice—certain of the ingenious ambiguities or paradoxes noted by the New Critics were really read into the poems, violating the limits of possibility in behalf of modernist complexities. It may be that these are incidental blemishes on the bright face of the New Criticism; but it may also be that, if the New Critics heeded such cautions systematically, a good part of their brilliance would be dimmed.

The historical objection can be enlarged beyond the scholar's argument. When the New Critics describe their methods as "intrinsic" and other methods as "extrinsic"—and impart a strong normative flavor to their description—they may be stacking the cards a bit too strongly in their own behalf. For if one believes that an understanding of the historical context or the underlying ideas or the psychological patterns of a work of literature is essential—not, be it noted, equivalent—to the act of criticism, that is only because such an understanding seems really to help one penetrate the work, that is, practice a kind of "intrinsic" criticism.

As one reads the polemics of the New Criticism against "extrinsic" approaches, one wonders what will be left after all experiential references have been stripped away. Presumably the work of literature itself. But since literature is founded in language and language contains unavoidable relationships to possible events in experience, can the meaning of the work be apprehended without some implicit and (one hopes) subtle use of such experiential disciplines as history and morality? There is, of course, always the danger of reducing a poem or novel to an abstract schema; but this can be the consequence of *any* critical approach. To withdraw a work of literature from historical context can be as much a reduction as to abandon it to the historical context, for in both instances the possible richness of meaning is threatened.

It is noteworthy that the criteria for literary judgment offered by such theorists of the New Criticism as René Wellek and Austin Warren —for example, coherence and complexity—are heavily weighted with value associations taken over from such non-literary domains as history, logic, and psychology. Is there any evaluative term not so weighted, and must not any attempt to find purely "intrinsic" terms of evaluation bog down in sterile descriptives? Wellek and Warren question T. S. Eliot's evaluative term, "maturity," but in critical practice it is very hard, for critics old or new, to do without it.

Somewhat similar observations have been made by Lionel Trilling, and made so well that it is economical to quote him:

[The New Critics] in their reaction from the historical method forget that the literary work is ineluctably a historical fact, and what is more important, that its historicity is a fact in our esthetic experience. . . .
The New Critics exercised their early characteristic method almost exclusively upon lyric poetry, a genre in which the historical element, although of course present, is less obtrusive than in the long poem, the novel and the drama. But even in the lyric poem the factor of historicity is part of the esthetic experience. . . . It is part of the *given* of the work, which we cannot help but respond to. The New Critics imply that this situation *should* not exist, but it cannot help existing.

These objections to the New Criticism assert an insufficiency in what its practitioners do or believe they should do. But another class of objections needs also to be noted, that which asserts a deficiency in the typical practice of the New Critics.

Because some of the New Critics tend to erect a rigid or "monist" principle of rhetorical analysis (irony, ambiguity, tension) which is assumed to be grounded in the very nature of poetry and to be almost equally applicable to poetry of all kinds and times, they find themselves engaged, not in flexible observations of the variety of elements and the various ways in which these elements can be arranged in the poem, but in an almost exclusive scrutiny of diction.[9] Isolated from a consideration of such matters as the poem's theme, historical implications, genre, and structure, even the most exacting analysis of diction can prove misleading.

Some of the New Critics, especially when dealing with poetry of unusual complexity, have also been inclined to provide monolithic readings that stiffen the poem into a moral allegory.[10] Why this should be so I am not quite sure, but let me suggest that it may be related to the fact that the New Critics are torn in two directions: their theory requires them to be dispassionate technicians of literary analysis while their experience makes them into passionate moral philosophers. As they proliferate "levels" or ambiguities of meaning in their study of a poem, they naturally seek a counter-principle of unity, one that will bind together the disparities and incongruities they have discovered and lend some principle of order to their serried interpretations. And since they are also deeply involved in the modern quest for values, it becomes a natural temptation—one by no means confined to their

[9] This point is cogently developed by Elder Olson, a leading spirit in the Neo-Aristotelian school of critical theorists at the University of Chicago: ". . . the profundity and complexity in poetry which so much interests William Empson is due primarily to action and character, which cannot be handled in grammatical terms, rather than to diction, which can. . . . Shakespeare's profoundest touches are a case in point. 'Pray you, undo this button' and 'The table's full' are profound, not as meaningful verbal expressions but as actions permitting an extraordinary number of implications. . . . We shall not explain them by jumbling the dictionary meanings of 'button' and 'table,' but by asking, among other things, why Lear requested the unfastening of a button and why Macbeth thought the table was full. This is true even in lyric poetry; the 'Once more' of *Lycidas*, for instance, has no profound verbal meaning; it is affecting because it implies the repeated suffering of bereavement."
[10] This observation has been made to me by J. V. Cunningham, though I do not know whether he would accept the use to which I have put it.

school of criticism—to regard the poem as ultimately possessing the rigor, certainty, and completeness of allegory.

For the most part, the New Critics have minimized the significance of literary genres, and this has led them both to a tendency to treat all works of literature as if they were lyric poems and to an undervaluation of what some critics would call the "mimetic" and others the "realistic" or "experiential" aspect of the poem. Particularly when turning to the criticism of fiction (an area in which they have been least successful), the New Critics have often indulged in an extreme overemphasis upon symbolism, sometimes to the point where every represented object or character seems to become absorbed into an abstract symbolic scheme. And for all that they have in theory counterposed poetry to science, their whole practice has tended to encourage the dubious notion that criticism can or should become an impersonal technique approaching the precision of science: as witness the unhappy accumulation of pseudotechnical jargon ("ontological density," "heresy of paraphrase," "poetry of the will," "affective fallacy," etc.).

We have been assuming all the while that the New Critics habitually practice what they preach, but, like any other group of critics committed to a method or an approach, they have never found this entirely possible. The truth is that they have often mixed (or contaminated) close analysis of texts with oracular pronouncements of a sort that might be described as moralistic impressionism. A major charge that could be brought against a good many New Critics is not that they are limited in their approach but that they stray, often unawares, past the limits they have set for themselves.

In our day it is very hard for a serious critic to avoid coloring his work with one or another ideological bias, and surely the best way of minimizing this danger is to be acutely sensitive to it (which then, by the way, makes it possible to transform the danger into an advantage). The New Critics have, to their credit, succeeded in making a good many other critics sensitive to it; but they have shown a startling lack of awareness that they too, even as they seem to be going through the procedures of close reading, can be promoting theological and political notions.

Consider the peculiar prestige which terms like "orthodox," "tradition," and "Original Sin" enjoy among many New Critics. "Orthodox" is, properly speaking, not a literary term at all, since it pertains to matters of religious or other belief rather than to critical judgment.

"Original Sin" is a category of a particular theology. The word "tradition" is somewhat more tricky, since it has legitimate uses in both literary and moral-ideological contexts. What happens, however, in much contemporary criticism—the New Critics are not the only sinners —is that these two contexts are taken to be one or to be organically related, so that it becomes possible to assume that a sense of the literary tradition necessarily involves and sanctions a "traditional" view of morality. There is a powerful inclination to forget that the literary tradition has never been a unitary one but has consisted of competing tendencies, and that it can be fruitfully regarded as a series of revolts, literary but sometimes more than merely literary, of generation against generation, one age against another. There is an equally powerful inclination among the New Critics to take for granted in their work the beneficent presence of a neo-orthodox theology and a conservative politics. Opposed though they are in principle to confusing literary and ideological categories, they have seldom troubled to examine their own work in order to inquire whether this confusion has afflicted them even as it has afflicted other mortals.

There is a sense in which these remarks about modern criticism have been systematically unjust—perhaps unjust to the extent that they have been systematic. For it has been necessary to discuss the various critical approaches as if they were actually as internally consistent as their defenders sometimes claim, while in the reading of criticism what matters is precisely the individual variations, the touches of private sensibility. Any critic who is more than a robot seldom stays very long within one approach. The social critics may favor some version of "correspondence" as a criterion of judgment and the formalist critics some version of "coherence"; but in practice, when confronted with the task of elucidating "Sunday Morning" or *Light in August,* no critic of any intelligence has had any choice but to bring both criteria into play.

Literary criticism at its best is a personal art in which the power of insight counts far more than allegiance to a critical theory or position. When one reads Newton Arvin on Melville, one cannot easily place his book in any of the usual categories—indeed, so fine and just a book merits an appreciation much more generous than any act of "placing" could be. When one reads the criticism of Edmund Wilson, it may be possible to notice that he was at various times influenced by

Freud and Marx, but what really matters is his skill at grasping the outlines of a work, his gift for evoking its essential quality, his zest before the experience of reading. His work suggests no image of blackboard and chalk, he does not add to the dreariness of the scene by proposing still another "system" or catalogue of jargon; each of his essays is his and his alone, the revelation of a unique and cultivated sensibility.

The methods critics use must obviously affect the nature and quality of their work, but they are not finally decisive. Perhaps there has recently been too much talk about critical method—a "searching," as Gide once wrote, "for criteria without wishing to go to the trouble of acquiring taste"—and not nearly enough about critical tone and breadth and insight. The best method could not make a mediocre man into a good critic; the worst can do a sensitive critic harm but not, I think, suppress his gifts indefinitely. And no method can give the critic what he needs most: knowledge, disinterestedness, love, insight, style. "The only method," Eliot once wrote, "is to be very intelligent." He might have added that it is also the hardest method.

III

American criticism has fallen upon quiet days. A vast production of critical books and articles continues from one season to the next, but there has been an ebbing of the disputatious passions of a decade ago, when literary people could work themselves into arguments about the New Criticism. I think it a reasonable guess to say that by the mid-fifties there were fewer American critics than at any time during the past thirty years who cared to identify themselves with a "school" or an "approach." This is due partly to a general slackening of American intellectual life; partly to the remarkable capacity of our culture for assimilating and devitalizing all ideas, so that nothing fades more quickly than yesterday's cultural innovation; partly to the fact that the New Criticism, at least for the moment, has exhausted itself through over-assertiveness; and partly to a growing opinion that the disputes among estheticians and critics of critics have rather little to do with the problems of writing criticism.

The result must obviously be a rather dull literary "atmosphere"—one that will not make good copy or send polemics rattling through the air. The gifted and independent critics, as they grow older, find themselves valuing serious opponents more than pedestrian disciples; and besides, the actual differences in performance between, say, a formalist and a social critic often prove to be less significant than one might suppose from an abstract comparison of their theories. But despite—or perhaps because of—this drop in polemical temperature, it is likely that during the next decade or two there will be a considerable amount of distinguished criticism written by men who have profited from the risks of their elders and are content to be eclectics rather than pioneers. If this prospect of isolated achievements seems unexciting, we should beware of dismissing it too easily. Books continue to be written by solitary persons, not teams or tendencies.

These observations find some support in recent works of criticism that cannot easily be labeled with the tags of any "school" yet are thoroughly grounded in the ideas, both literary and otherwise, which have concerned intellectuals during the past few decades. I have in mind—other examples could be found—a book such as Ian Watt's study of the eighteenth-century English novel, *The Rise of the Novel,* a first-rate work of criticism that would surely have been impossible without the crossing influences of the various recent schools of criticism, yet is admirably free from the sectarian dogmatism that has disfigured most of them. Traditional literary scholarship, psychoanalysis, the functional school of modern sociology, Marxism, the close analysis of texts —these and more come into play in Mr. Watt's book, but as elements that have been absorbed by his sensibility rather than as "methods" applied with programmatic intent. Even as one sees this complex of influences behind Mr. Watt's criticism, it remains a criticism firmly disciplined, secure, and single-voiced. When, for example, he discusses *Robinson Crusoe* as an economic myth he inevitably turns to Marx, but not in order to "use" Marxism as still another device in the critical repertoire. He has read Marx, learned what he could, kept his head, and gone his way, so that the insights borrowed from Marx become his own possession. As a result, the usual chatter about critical approaches tends to become irrelevant; what matters—it is the only thing that finally does matter in criticism—is watching a superior mind at work, sharing in its discoveries and enjoying the privilege of disagreement.

If, then, the immediate prospect is for a sophisticated and perhaps somewhat relaxed eclecticism; if we can expect a consolidation of certain gains (no serious critic is likely to return to the more blatant kinds of impressionism) and a decline of fanatical excess and partisan narrowness (few critics, even if they wished to, could follow the more extreme paths charted in the later writings of Kenneth Burke and William Empson); and if it becomes a generally accepted premise that critics, though they can hardly avoid discussing a good many non-literary topics, should not be expected to do the work of the philosophers, theologians, and politicians—then one may hope for a certain settling of opinion as to the place and function of literary criticism. Not, I hasten to add, a settling of opinion as to critical estimates and procedures: there is every reason to hope that debate about these matters will continue indefinitely. But perhaps there will be a modest amount of agreement as to the possibilities, which almost means the limitations, of literary criticism: for example, that the very desire for a binding monistic method fruitful on all critical occasions is a violation of the tacit assumptions of freedom, variety, and spontaneity upon which the literary life depends.[11] One sympathizes with the message that Randall Jarrell has directed to modern critics:

Write so as to be of some use to a reader—a reader, that is, of poems and stories, not of criticism. Vary a little, vary a little! Admit what you can't conceal, that criticism is no more than (and no less than) the helpful remarks and the thoughtful and disinterested judgment of a reader, a loving and experienced and able reader, but only a reader. . . . At your best you make people see what they might never have seen without you; but they must always forget you in what they see.

Mr. Jarrell would probably not want us to take these strictures completely to heart, for then not only the excesses but the triumphs that often seem inseparable from the excesses of modern criticism would be lost. Yet there is good reason to hope that, if the critics of tomorrow prove as brilliant, learned, and expert as ideally they should, their work will come to us as somewhat more tentative in its claims, somewhat more humanly vulnerable and disarmed, than recent criticism has generally supposed itself to be.

The complaint lodged against the New Critics by Lionel Trilling

[11] Is there a critic alive who at some time has not felt uneasy after reading a massive critique in which an esthetician exposes the jumble of vague and perhaps contradictory notions that lie behind most critical writing? Why should a critic try to do the job with his bare hands when here, ready and eager, stands someone equipped with the most modern machinery?

Only after the esthetician has tried *his* hand at a piece of practical criticism does one feel somewhat reassured. And then one resigns oneself, happily enough, to the idea that criticism is an art which requires talent, knowledge, and fortune, but a minimum of machinery.

—that *"they try too hard"*—seems to me a very cogent one; but it is a complaint that could just as well be made against many other modern critics, certainly against those with a formidable battery of social or mythic or psychoanalytic concepts. One rarely finds in modern criticism the tone of lively conversation, of relaxed and cultivated dialogue, that is to be savored in critics like Virginia Woolf and E. M. Forster. The point I am making here can easily degenerate into a genteel sort of anti-intellectualism, particularly if it appears in articles by English *littérateurs* who like to judge new books as if they were old wines. The special charms, to say nothing about the special talents, of the Bloomsbury group (Woolf, Forster, Fry, Keynes, etc.) are not easily acquired by American critics: I don't suppose they can be *acquired* at all. But then it might as well be admitted that the gains which American criticism has made in exegetic power have been paid for with a loss of literary ease and assurance.

Too much of modern criticism—and for this there can be no excuse—is an aggrandizement at the expense of the writer: a demonstration of the critic's virtuosity rather than of the values of the poem or novel he is discussing. Only seldom does one find in modern criticism the capacity for pleasure, the human desire to share in good and beautiful things which ought to be a motive for writing about literature. Louis Kronenberger has put the matter sharply but well: "Too much current criticism sees literature as a form of testimony rather than of talent, as something that explains far more than it enriches; as, in other words, education rather than culture." And somewhat unexpectedly T. S. Eliot, in the ripeness of age, buttresses this judgment with a few remarks about what he calls "the lemon-squeezer school of criticism":

If in literary criticism, we place all the emphasis upon *understanding*, we are in danger of slipping from understanding to mere explanation. We are in danger even of pursuing criticism as if it was a science, which it never can be. If . . . we over-emphasize *enjoyment*, we will tend to fall into the subjective and impressionistic. . . . Thirty-five years ago, it seems to have been the latter type of criticism, the impressionistic, that had caused [us] annoyance. . . . Today it seems to me that we need to be more on guard against the purely explanatory.

But the problem comes to more than merely guarding against zealous extremes. If one can say in good spirit that one has profited from R. P. Blackmur's examination of Wallace Stevens' exotic diction or from Cleanth Brooks' close reading of *The Waste Land,* then one should be ready to grant that the seemingly casual remark in an essay by Virginia Woolf comparing Jane Austen to the Greek tragedians— "she, too, in her modest everyday prose, chose the dangerous art where one slip means death"—may provide as much insight into the purpose and pattern of *Emma* as several book-length studies speckled with the word "irony." This is not to deny that the highly personal and impressionist criticism of Virginia Woolf can become as routinized as the image-probing of American professors: that fate threatens pearl-divers as much as lemon-squeezers. It is to suggest, however, that at present American critics might find it peculiarly valuable to recognize how often Mrs. Woolf, happily free of either terminology or apparatus, does come up with the right insight and judgment.

If during the next few years our criticism turns out to be at all similar to what I have been supposing—a break-up of critical "schools," a turn toward eclecticism, a consolidation of recent achievements, and a relaxation in manner and tone—the result may help bring the best American critics a little closer to American literature itself. And for this, the need is very great.

By a curious turn of history, a criticism generated primarily by concern with the "modern" has recently become extremely conservative in its habits and temper, thereby losing a good part of the intimate contact it once enjoyed with the best poets and novelists of the time. Few young or middle-aged critics could now claim the kind of relationship Waldo Frank once had with Hart Crane and Sherwood Anderson; or Edmund Wilson with Fitzgerald and Dos Passos; or John Crowe Ransom with the group of Southern writers known as the Fugitives. The virtual disappearance of literary bohemias and the dispersion of writers and critics to the loneliness of suburbs and the routine of universities have made such relationships increasingly difficult.

Very few of the better American critics care, or are in a position, to do regular reviewing of new fiction and poetry. Nor do many of them trouble to discuss contemporary writing in any sort of rounded fashion. The complaint made by scholars against critics—that they do not know enough about English literature written before 1800 and therefore lack a sense of its historical depth—is sometimes valid; but then so is another complaint—that the modern writers who continue to absorb the attention of our critics seldom can still be called contemporary. And the result is that, despite the enormous amount of criticism being written, very little of it helps, or checks, or enters any sort of vital relationship with living writers. Nor do many critics try to perform what in our society must be one of their main tasks: to intervene in the current discussions of books and cultural issues in order to defend literary standards. This can admittedly be a wearying and time-consuming task; but it is a necessary one.

Now these are genuine difficulties, not to be solved with a phrase or a blow; and it would be malicious to attribute them to the doctrines or pride of one or another group of critics. A small part of the trouble does seem to stem from the fact that many of the older critics naturally remain most engaged with the work done by writers of their own generation. In itself there would be no harm in this, but the influence of the older critics upon the younger ones remains so enormous that the latter continue doggedly to follow in their masters' footsteps. For Allen Tate to write the Introduction to Hart Crane's *White Buildings* in 1926 or for R. P. Blackmur a few years later to write one of the earliest essays on Wallace Stevens constituted an act of independent judgment; but few of the younger critics seem similarly inclined to strike out on their own.

In saying this I may be unjust. Twenty years from now it may seem quite clear that the critics who will then matter *were* striking out on their own during the late forties and fifties. At the moment, however, it is a little hard to see this.

There is, to be sure, no group of poets or novelists who are today quite as challenging as were the *avant garde* writers of a few decades ago; but precisely because there does seem to be so much uncertainty of direction in current American writing, a friendly yet stringent criticism could be particularly valuable. Valuable to the writers themselves; to the critics, who are becoming muscle-bound from going through the same motions; and to literate readers, who can at present turn to no periodical for sustained and serious criticism of new fiction and poetry.

Another reason, also subsidiary, for the increasing distance between critics and writers is the contempt that has been cultivated in some critical circles for "mere journalism." It is too easily forgotten that the most influential, and probably most distinguished, criticism of our time —the early essays of T. S. Eliot—first appeared as reviews in English newspapers and magazines. Today critics seem to feel—at least some of them do—that they are taking too much of a *risk* with their time and prestige if they write of anyone but the safely and greatly dead.

There are other ways in which critics help bring about their isolation from contemporary American writing: not least of all, by the fondness some of them display for a pseudoscientific jargon and a pretentious style which, to all but the initiated, is likely to seem a needless barrier. Yet none of the reasons I have cited comes near to being decisive: the critics, for good or bad, do not have that much control over their public destinies. If, as was remarked earlier, they have gained a considerable influence during recent years, that is an influence largely confined to intellectual circles. In the world where reviews significantly affect the opinions of a large public or the sales of a new novel, the serious critics remain severely limited in influence, perhaps even more limited than they were three or four decades ago.

The truth is that in the United States today there are very few possibilities for writing respectable literary journalism—that is, for the kind of topical comment which may not call upon a critic's deepest gifts yet allows him to do honest work and is useful to the health of a culture. If, as is so often noted with alarm, most of our critics are now tucked away in universities, that is primarily for lack of any decent alternative. Many of them would be delighted if they could so much as survive by writing serious literary journalism. But this seems less and less possible. The level of popular and middlebrow reviewing is abominable, as anyone can see who troubles to compare the not-very-good work done in the major review supplements of thirty years ago with the drab and listless work, often coming to no more than mere puffs, done today.

Those who direct the mass media resist serious literary criticism, not so much from principle (that might have some virtue to it), but from a tight repressive instinct which prompts them to feel hostile toward severe standards of taste, closely reasoned judgments, precise discriminations. And in a sense these people are right. Between their enterprise and the values of serious literary criticism there can be no lasting or genuine peace.

Nothing that the critics might try to do seems likely to change this situation in a fundamental way. Yet it would be useful if they acknowledged the losses that result from it, losses ranging from a stiffness of style and stuffiness of manner to an inability to affect the taste and thought of large numbers of people. It would be very useful if they also recognized that a criticism without a lively auxiliary journalism soon runs the danger of becoming both estranged and eviscerated.

Literary criticism demands skills that few people can acquire in a lifetime; yet it is rarely done well by those who devote their attention exclusively to acquiring those skills. The critic should have a deep knowledge not only of literature but also of many other things; yet none of these will ultimately suffice, he cannot rest or depend upon them, he remains one reader trying to persuade others to credit certain observations he has made about works of literature and ultimately about human life as well. Secondary though it always is to the work itself, fragmentary and transient as it almost always turns out to be, criticism offers seemingly endless possibilities for the discrimination of values, the sharing of insights, the defense of a living culture. Criticism may indulge in one or another stress, chart one or another part; but if it is to survive, it must remain the work of solitary men, private readers who reflect upon the poem or novel in its own right and as a part of our culture. To say that machines will never be invented for the writing of criticism seems, at the moment, somewhat rash. But here at least one can feel confident that the machine will never be able to do what the thinking and responsive man can do: the thinking and responsive man as he confronts the work of art.

The Function of Criticism

T. S. Eliot

I

Writing several years ago on the subject of the relation of the new to the old in art, I formulated a view to which I still adhere, in sentences which I take the liberty of quoting, because the present paper is an application of the principles they express:

"The existing monuments form an ideal order among themselves, which is modified by the introduction of the new (the really new) work of art among them. The existing order is complete before the new work arrives; for order to persist after the supervention of novelty, the *whole* existing order must be, if ever so slightly, altered; and so the relations, proportions, values of each work of art toward the whole are readjusted; and this is conformity between the old and the new. Whoever has approved this idea of order, of the form of European, of English literature, will not find it preposterous that the past should be altered by the present as much as the present is directed by the past."

I was dealing then with the artist, and the sense of tradition which, it seemed to me, the artist should have; but it was generally a problem of order; and the function of criticism seems to be essentially a problem of order too. I thought of literature then, as I think of it now, of the literature of the world, of the literature of Europe, of the literature of a single country, not as a collection of the writings of individuals, but as "organic wholes," as systems in relation to which, and only in relation to which, individual works of literary art, and the works of individual artists, have their significance. There is accordingly something outside of the artist to which he owes allegiance, a devotion to which he must surrender and sacrifice himself in order to earn and to obtain his unique position. A common inheritance and a common cause unite artists consciously or unconsciously: it must be admitted that the union is mostly unconscious. Between the true artists of any time there is, I believe, an unconscious community. And, as our instincts of tidiness imperatively command us not to leave to the haphazard of unconsciousness what we can attempt to do consciously, we are forced to conclude that what happens unconsciously we could bring about, and form into a purpose, if we made a conscious attempt. The second-rate artist, of course, cannot afford to surrender himself to any common action; for his chief task is the assertion of all the trifling differences which are his distinction: only the man who has so much to give that he can forget himself in his work can afford to collaborate, to exchange, to contribute.

If such views are held about art, it follows that *a fortiori* whoever holds them must hold similar views about criticism. When I say criticism, I mean of course in this place the commentation and exposition of works of art by means of written words; for of the general use of the word "criticism" to mean such writings, as Matthew Arnold uses it in his essay, I shall presently make several qualifications. No exponent of criticism (in this limited sense) has, I presume, ever made the preposterous assumption that criticism is an autotelic activity. I do not deny that art may be affirmed to serve ends beyond itself; but art is not required to be aware of these ends, and indeed performs its function, whatever that may be, according to various theories of value, much better by indifference to them. Criticism, on the other hand, must always profess an end in view, which, roughly speaking, appears to be the elucidation of works of art and the correction of taste. The critic's task, therefore, appears to be quite clearly cut out for him; and it ought to be comparatively easy to decide whether he performs it satisfactorily, and in general, what kinds of criticism are useful and what are otiose. But on giving the matter a little attention, we perceive that criticism, far from being a simple and orderly field of beneficent activity, from which impostors can be readily ejected, is no better than a Sunday park of contending and contentious orators, who have not even arrived at the articulation of their differences. Here, one would suppose, was a place for quiet co-operative labour. The critic, one would suppose, if he is to justify his existence, should endeavour to discipline his personal prejudices and cranks—tares to which we are all subject—and compose his differences with as many of his fellows as possible, in the common pursuit of true judgment. When we find that quite the contrary prevails, we begin to suspect that the critic owes his livelihood to the violence and extremity of his opposition to other critics, or else to some trifling oddities of his own with which he contrives to season the opinions which men already hold, and which out of vanity or sloth they prefer to maintain. We are tempted to expel the lot.

Immediately after such an eviction, or as soon as relief has abated our rage, we are compelled to admit that there remain certain books, certain essays, certain sentences, certain men, who have been "useful" to us. And our next step is to attempt to classify these, and find out whether we establish any principles for deciding what kinds of book should be preserved, and what aims and methods of criticism should be followed.

II

The view of the relation of the work of art to art, of the work of literature to literature, of "criticism" to criticism, which I have outlined above, seemed to me natural and self-evident. I owe to Mr. Middleton Murry my perception of the contentious character of the problem; or rather, my perception that there is a definite and final choice involved. To Mr. Murry I feel an increasing debt of gratitude. Most of our critics are occupied in labour of obnubilation; in reconciling, in hushing up, in patting down, in squeezing in, in glozing over, in concocting pleasant sedatives, in pretending that the only difference between themselves and others is that they are nice men and the others of very doubtful repute. Mr. Murry is not one of these. He is aware that there are definite positions to be taken, and that now and then one must actually reject something and select something else. He is not the anonymous writer who in a literary paper several years ago asserted that Romanticism and Classicism are much the same thing, and that the true Classical Age in France was the Age which produced the Gothic cathedrals and—Jeanne d'Arc. With Mr. Murry's formulation of Classicism and Romanticism I cannot agree; the difference seems to me rather the difference between the complete and the fragmentary, the adult and the immature, the orderly and the chaotic. But what Mr. Murry does show is that there are at least two attitudes toward literature and toward everything, and that you cannot hold both. And the attitude which he professes appears to imply that the other has no standing in England whatever. For it is made a national, a racial issue.

Mr. Murry makes his issue perfectly clear. "Catholicism," he says, "stands for the principle of unquestioned spiritual authority outside the individual; that is also the principle of Classicism in literature." Within the orbit within which Mr. Murry's discussion moves, this seems to me an unimpeachable definition, though it is of course not all that there is to be said about either Catholicism or Classicism. Those of us who find ourselves supporting what Mr. Murry calls Classicism believe that men cannot get on without giving allegiance to something outside themselves. I am aware that "outside" and "inside" are terms which provide unlimited opportunity for quibbling, and that no psychologist would tolerate a discussion which shuffled such base coinage; but I will presume that Mr. Murry and myself can agree that for our purpose these counters are adequate, and concur in disregarding the admonitions of our psychological friends. If you find that you have to imagine it as outside, then it is outside. If, then, a man's interest is political, he must, I presume, profess an allegiance to principles, or to a form of government, or to a monarch; and if he is interested in religion, and has one, to a Church; and if he happens to be interested in literature, he must acknowledge, it seems to me, just that sort of allegiance which I endeavoured to put forth in the preceding section. There is, nevertheless, an alternative, which Mr. Murry has expressed. "The English writer, the English divine, the English statesman, inherit no rules from their forbears; they inherit only this: a sense that in the last resort they must depend upon the inner voice." This statement does, I admit, appear to cover certain cases; it throws a flood of light upon Mr. Lloyd George. But why *"in the last resort"*? Do they, then, avoid the dictates of the inner voice up to the last extremity? My belief is that those who possess this inner voice are ready enough to hearken to it, and will hear no other. The inner voice, in fact, sounds remarkably like an old principle which has been formulated by an elder critic in the now familiar phrase of "doing as one likes." The possessors of the inner voice ride ten in a compartment to a football match at Swansea, listening to the inner voice, which breathes the eternal message of vanity, fear, and lust.

Mr. Murry will say, with some show of justice, that this is a wilful misrepresentation. He says: "If they (the English writer, divine, statesman) dig *deep enough* in their pursuit of self-knowledge—a piece of mining done not with the intellect alone, but with the whole man—they will come upon a self that is universal"—an exercise far beyond the strength of our football enthusiasts. It is an exercise, however, which I believe was of enough interest to Catholicism for several handbooks to be written on its practice. But the Catholic practitioners were, I believe, with the possible exception of certain heretics, not palpitating Narcissi; the Catholic did not believe that God and himself were identical. "The man who truly interrogates himself will ultimately hear the voice of God," Mr. Murry says. In theory, this leads to a form of pantheism which I maintain is not European—just as Mr. Murry maintains that "Classicism" is not English. For its practical results, one may refer to the verses of *Hudibras*.

I did not realise that Mr. Murry was the spokesman for a considerable sect, until I read in the editorial columns of a dignified daily that "magnificent as the representatives of the classical genius have been in England, they are not the sole expressions of the English character, which remains at bottom obstinately 'humorous' and nonconformist." This writer is moderate in using the qualification *sole,* and brutally frank in attributing this "humorousness" to "the unreclaimed Teutonic element in us." But it strikes me that Mr. Murry, and this other voice, are either too obstinate or too tolerant. The question is, the first question, *not* what comes natural or what comes *easy* to us, but what is right? Either one attitude is better than the other, or else it is indifferent. But how can such a choice be indifferent? Surely the reference to racial origins, or the mere statement that the French are thus, and the English otherwise, is not expected to settle the question: which, of two antithetical views, is *right?* And I cannot understand why the opposition between Classicism and Romanticism should be profound enough in Latin countries (Mr. Murry says it is) and yet of no significance among ourselves. For if the French are *naturally* classical, why should there be any "opposition" in France, any more than there is here? And if Classicism is not natural to them, but something acquired, why not acquire it here? Were the French in the year 1600 classical, and the English in the same year romantic? A more important difference, to my mind, is that the French in the year 1600 *had already a more mature prose.*

III

This discussion may seem to have led us a long way from the subject of this paper. But it was worth my while to follow Mr. Murry's comparison of Outside Authority with the Inner Voice. For to those who obey the inner voice (perhaps "obey" is not the word) nothing that I can say about criticism will have the slightest value. For they will not be interested in the attempt to find any common principles for the pursuit of criticism. Why have principles, when one has the inner voice? If I like a thing, that is all I want; and if enough of us, shouting all together, like it, that should be all that *you* (who don't like it) ought to want. The law of art, said Mr. Clutton Brock, is all case law. And we can not only like whatever we like to like but we can like it for any reason we choose. We are not, in fact, concerned with literary *perfection* at all—the search for perfection is a sign of pettiness, for it shows that the writer has admitted the existence of an unquestioned spiritual authority outside himself, to which he has attempted to *conform*. We are not in fact interested in art. We will not worship Baal. "The principle of classical leadership is that obeisance is made to the office or to the tradition, never to the man." And we want, not principles, but men.

Thus speaks the Inner Voice. It is a voice to which, for convenience, we may give a name: and the name I suggest is Whiggery.

IV

Leaving, then, those whose calling and election are sure and returning to those who shamefully depend upon tradition and the accumulated wisdom of time, and restricting the discussion to those who sympathise with each other in this frailty, we may comment for a moment upon the use of the terms "critical" and "creative" by one whose place, on the whole, is with the weaker brethren. Matthew Arnold distinguishes far too bluntly, it seems to me, between the two activities: he overlooks the capital importance of criticism in the work of creation itself. Probably, indeed, the larger part of the labour of an author in composing his work is critical labour; the labour of sifting, combining, constructing, expunging, correcting, testing: this frightful toil is as much critical as creative. I maintain even that the criticism employed by a trained and skilled writer on his own work is the most vital, the highest kind of criticism; and (as I think I have said before) that some creative writers are superior to others solely because their critical faculty is superior. There is a tendency, and I think it is a whiggery tendency, to decry this critical toil of the artist; to propound the thesis that the great artist is an unconscious artist, unconsciously inscribing on his banner the words Muddle Through. Those of us who are Inner Deaf Mutes are, however, sometimes compensated by a humble conscience, which, though without oracular expertness, counsels us to do the best we can, reminds us that our compositions ought to be as free from defects as possible (to atone for their lack of inspiration), and, in short, makes us waste a good deal of time. We are aware, too, that the critical discrimination which comes so hardly to us has in more fortunate men flashed in the very heat of creation; and we do not assume that because works have been composed without apparent critical labour, no critical labour has been done. We do not know what previous labours have prepared, or what goes on, in the way of criticism, all the time in the minds of the creators.

But this affirmation recoils upon us. If so large a part of creation is really criticism, is not a large part of what is called "critical writing" really creative? If so, is there not creative criticism in the ordinary sense? The answer seems to be, that there is no equation. I have assumed as axiomatic that a creation, a work of art, is autotelic; and that criticism, by definition, is *about* something other than itself. Hence you cannot fuse creation with criticism as you can fuse criticism with creation. The critical activity finds its highest, its true fulfilment in a kind of union with creation in the labour of the artist.

But no writer is completely self-sufficient, and many creative writers have a critical activity which is not all discharged into their work. Some seem to require to keep their critical powers in condition for the real work by exercising them miscellaneously; others, on completing a work, need to continue the critical activity by commenting on it. There is no general rule. And as men can learn from each other, so some of these treatises have been useful to other writers. And some of them have been useful to those who were not writers.

At one time I was inclined to take the extreme position that the *only* critics worth reading were the critics who practised, and practised well, the art of which they wrote. But I had to stretch this frame to make some important inclusions; and I have since been in search of a formula which should cover everything I wished to include, even if it included more than I wanted. And the most important qualification which I have been able to find, which accounts for the peculiar importance of the criticism of practitioners, is that a critic must have a very highly developed sense of fact. This is by no means a trifling or frequent gift. And it is not one which easily wins popular commendations.

The sense of fact is something very slow to develop, and its complete development means perhaps the very pinnacle of civilisation. For there are so many spheres of fact to be mastered, and our outermost sphere of fact, of knowledge, of control, will be ringed with narcotic fancies in the sphere beyond. To the member of the Browning Study Circle, the discussion of poets about poetry may seem arid, technical, and limited. It is merely that the practitioners have clarified and reduced to a state of fact all the feelings that the member can only enjoy in the most nebulous form; the dry technique implies, for those who have mastered it, all that the member thrills to; only that has been made into something precise, tractable, under control. That, at all events, is one reason for the value of the practitioner's criticism—he is dealing with his facts, and he can help us to do the same.

And at every level of criticism I find the same necessity regnant. There is a large part of critical writing which consists in "interpreting" an author, a work. This is not on the level of the Study Circle either; it occasionally happens that one person obtains an understanding of another, or a creative writer, which he can partially communicate, and which we feel to be true and illuminating. It is difficult to confirm the "interpretation" by external evidence. To any one who is skilled in fact on this level there will be evidence enough. But who is to prove his own skill? And for every success in this type of writing there are thousands of impostures. Instead of insight, you get a fiction. Your test is to apply it again and again to the original, with your view of the original to guide you. But there is no one to guarantee your competence, and once again we find ourselves in a dilemma.

We must ourselves decide what is useful to us and what is not; and it is quite likely that we are not competent to decide. But it is fairly certain that "interpretation" (I am not touching upon the acrostic element in literature) is only legitimate when it is not interpretation at all, but merely putting the reader in possession of facts which he would otherwise have missed. I have had some experience of Extension lecturing, and I have found only two ways of leading any pupils to like anything with the right liking: to present them with a selection of the simpler kind of facts about a work—its conditions, its setting, its genesis—or else to spring the work on them in such a way that they were not prepared to be prejudiced against it. There were many facts to help them with Elizabethan drama: the poems of T. E. Hulme only needed to be read aloud to have immediate effect.

Comparison and analysis, I have said before, and Rémy de Gourmont has said before me (a real master of fact—sometimes, I am afraid, when he moved outside of literature, a master illusionist of fact), are the chief tools of the critic. It is obvious indeed that they *are* tools, to be handled with care, and not employed in an inquiry into the number of times giraffes are mentioned in the English novel. They are not used with conspicuous success by many contemporary writers. You must know what to compare and what to analyse. The late Professor Ker had skill in the use of these tools. Comparison and analysis need only the cadavers on the table; but interpretation is always producing parts of the body from its pockets, and fixing them in place. And any book, any essay, any note in *Notes and Queries,* which produces a fact even of the lowest order about a work of art is a better piece of work than nine-tenths of the most pretentious critical journalism, in journals or in books. We assume, of course, that we are masters and not servants of facts, and that we know that the discovery of Shakespeare's laundry bills would not be of much use to us; but we must always reserve final judgment as to the futility of the research which has discovered them, in the possibility that some genius will appear who will know of a use to which to put them. Scholarship, even in its humblest forms, has its rights; we assume that we know how to use it, and how to neglect it. Of course the multiplication of critical books and essays may create, and I have seen it create, a vicious taste for reading about works of art instead of reading the works themselves, it may supply opinion instead of educating taste. But *fact* cannot corrupt taste; it can at worst gratify one taste—a taste for history, let us say, or antiquities, or biography— under the illusion that it is assisting another. The real corrupters are those who supply opinion or fancy; and Goethe and Coleridge are not guiltless—for what is Coleridge's *Hamlet:* is it an honest inquiry as far as the data permit, or is it an attempt to present Coleridge in an attractive costume?

We have not succeeded in finding such a test as any one can apply; we have been forced to allow ingress to innumerable dull and tedious books; but we have, I think, found a test which, for those who are able to apply it, will dispose of the really vicious ones. And with this test we may return to the preliminary statement of the polity of literature and of criticism. For the kinds of critical work which we have admitted, there is the possibility of co-operative activity, with the further possibility of arriving at something outside of ourselves, which may provisionally be called truth. But if any one complains that I have not defined truth, or fact, or reality, I can only say apologetically that it was no part of my purpose to do so, but only to find a scheme into which, whatever they are, they will fit, if they exist.

Emotion of Multitude

William Butler Yeats

I have been thinking a good deal about plays lately, and I have been wondering why I dislike the clear and logical construction which seems necessary if one is to succeed on the Modern Stage. It came into my head the other day that this construction, which all the world has learnt from France, has everything of high literature except the emotion of multitude. The Greek drama has got the emotion of multitude from its chorus, which called up famous sorrows, long-leaguered Troy, much-enduring Odysseus, and all the gods and heroes to witness, as it were, some well-ordered fable, some action separated but for this from all but itself. The French play delights in the well-ordered fable, but by leaving out the chorus it has created an art where poetry and imagination, always the children of far-off multitudinous things, must of necessity grow less important than the mere will. This is why, I said to myself, French dramatic poetry is so often a little rhetorical, for rhetoric is the will trying to do the work of the imagination. The Shakespearean Drama gets the emotion of multitude out of the sub-plot which copies the main plot, much as a shadow upon the wall copies one's body in the firelight. We think of King Lear less as the history of one man and his sorrows than as the history of a whole evil time. Lear's shadow is in Gloster, who also has ungrateful children, and the mind goes on imagining other shadows, shadow beyond shadow till it has pictured the world. In *Hamlet,* one hardly notices, so subtly is the web woven, that the murder of Hamlet's father and the sorrow of Hamlet are shadowed in the lives of Fortinbras and Ophelia and Laertes, whose fathers, too, have been killed. It is so in all the plays, or

From *Essays* by William Butler Yeats. Reprinted by permission of The Macmillan Company.

all but all, and very commonly the sub-plot is the main plot working
'f out in more ordinary men and women, and so doubly calling
_efore us the image of multitude. Ibsen and Maeterlinck have on
the other hand created a new form, for they get multitude from the
Wild Duck in the Attic, or from the Crown at the bottom of the
Fountain, vague symbols that set the mind wandering from idea to
idea, emotion to emotion. Indeed all the great Masters have understood, that there cannot be great art without the little limited life of
the fable, which is always the better the simpler it is, and the rich,
far-wandering, many-imaged life of the half-seen world beyond it.
There are some who understand that the simple unmysterious things
living as in a clear noon-light are of the nature of the sun, and that
vague many-imaged things have in them the strength of the moon.
Did not the Egyptian carve it on emerald that all living things have
the sun for father and the moon for mother, and has it not been said
that a man of genius takes the most after his mother?

Notes on Writing a Novel

Elizabeth Bowen

Plot.—Essential. The Pre-essential.

Plot might seem to be a matter of choice. It is not. The particular plot for the particular novel is something the novelist is driven to. It is what is left after the whittling-away of alternatives. The novelist is confronted, at a moment (or at what appears to be the moment: actually its extension may be indefinite), by the impossibility of saying what is to be said in any other way.

He is forced towards his plot. By what? By "what is to be said." What is "what is to be said"? A mass of subjective matter that has accumulated—impressions received, feelings about experience, distorted results of ordinary observation, and something else—*x*. This matter is *extra* matter. It is superfluous to the non-writing life of the writer. It is luggage left in the hall between two journeys, as opposed to the perpetual furniture of rooms. It is destined to be elsewhere. It cannot move till its destination is known. Plot is the knowing of destination.

Plot is diction. Action of language, language of action.

Plot is story. It is also "a story" in the nursery sense—lie. The novel lies, in saying that something happened that did not. It must, therefore, contain uncontradictable truth, to warrant the original lie.

Story involves action. Action towards an end not to be foreseen (by the reader) but also towards an end which, having *been* reached, must be seen to have been from the start inevitable.

Action by whom? The Characters (see CHARACTERS). Action in view of what, and because of what? The "what is to be said."

From *Collected Impressions* by Elizabeth Bowen. Reprinted by permission of Alfred A. Knopf, Inc.

What about the idea that the function of action is to *express* the characters? This is wrong. The characters are there to provide the action. Each character is created, and must only be so created, as to give his or her action (or rather, contributory part in the novel's action) verisimilitude.

What about the idea that plot should be ingenious, complicated—a display of ingenuity remarkable enough to command attention? If more than such a display, what? Tension, or mystification towards tension, are good emphasis. For their own sakes, bad.

Plot must further the novel towards its object. The non-poetic statement of a poetic truth.

Have not all poetic truths been already stated? The essence of a poetic truth is that no statement of it can be final.

Plot, story, is in itself un-poetic. At best it can only be not anti-poetic. It cannot claim a single poetic licence. It must be reasoned—only from the moment when its none-otherness, its only-possibleness has become apparent. Novelist must always have one foot, sheer circumstantiality, to stand on, whatever the other foot may be doing. (N.B.—Much to be learnt from story-telling to children. Much to be learnt from the detective story—especially non-irrelevance. [See RELEVANCE.])

Flaubert's *"Il faut interesser."* Stress on manner of telling: keep in mind, "I will a tale *unfold*." Interest of watching a dress that has been well packed unpacked from a dress-box. Interest of watching silk handkerchief drawn from conjuror's watch.

Plot must not cease to move forward. (See ADVANCE.) The *actual* speed of the movement must be even. *Apparent* variations in speed are good, necessary, but there must be no actual variations in speed. To obtain those apparent variations is part of the illusion-task of the novel. Variations in texture can be made to give the effect of variations in speed. Why are *apparent* variations in speed necessary? (a) For emphasis. (b) For non-resistance, or "give," to the nervous time-variations of the reader. Why is actual evenness, non-variation, of speed necessary? For the sake of internal evenness for its own sake. Perfection of evenness = perfection of control. The evenness of the speed should be the evenness inseparable from tautness. The tautness of the taut string is equal (or even) all along and at any part of the string's length.

Characters.

Are the characters, then, to be constructed to formula—the formula pre-decided by the plot? Are they to be drawn, cut out, jointed, wired, in order to be manipulated for the plot?

No. There is no question as to whether this would be right or wrong. It would be impossible. One cannot "make" characters, only marionettes. The manipulated movement of the marionette is not the "action" necessary for plot. Characterless action is not action at all, in the plot sense. It is the indivisibility of the act from the actor, and the inevitability of *that* act on the part of *that* actor, that gives action verisimilitude. Without that, action is without force or reason. Force-less, reasonless action disrupts plot. The term "creation of character" (or characters) is misleading. Characters pre-exist. They are *found*. They reveal themselves slowly to the novelist's perception—as might fellow-travellers seated opposite one in a very dimly-lit railway carriage.

The novelist's perception of his characters takes place *in the course of the actual writing of the novel.* To an extent, the novelist is in the same position as his reader. But his perceptions should be always just in advance.

The ideal way of presenting character is to invite perception.

In what do the characters pre-exist? I should say, in the mass of matter (see PLOT) that had accumulated before the inception of the novel.

(N.B.—The unanswerability of the question, from an outsider: "Are the characters in your novel invented, or are they from real life?" Obviously, neither is true. The outsider's notion of "real life" and the novelist's are hopelessly apart.)

How, then, is the pre-existing character—with its own inner spring of action, its contrarieties—to be made to play a pre-assigned role? In relation to character, or characters, once these have been contemplated, *plot* must at once seem over-rigid, arbitrary.

What about the statement (in relation to PLOT) that "each character is created in order, and only in order, that he or she may supply the required action"? To begin with, strike out "created." Better, the character is *recognised* (by the novelist) by the signs he or she gives of unique capacity to act in a certain way, which "certain way" fulfils a need of the plot.

The character is there (in the novel) for the sake of the action he or she is to contribute to the plot. Yes. But also, he or she exists *outside* the action being contributed to the plot.

Without that existence of the character outside the (necessarily limited) action, the action itself would be invalid.

Action is the simplification (for story purposes) of complexity. For each one act, there are an x number of rejected alternatives. It is the palpable presence of the alternatives that gives action interest. Therefore, in each of the characters, while he or she is acting, the play and pull of alternatives must be felt. It is in being seen to be capable of alternatives that the character becomes, for the reader, valid.

Roughly, the action of a character should be unpredictable before it has been shown, inevitable when it has been shown. In the first half of a novel, the unpredictability should be the more striking. In the second half, the inevitability should be the more striking.

(Most exceptions to this are, however, masterpiece-novels. In *War and Peace, L'Education Sentimentale* and *La Recherche du Temps Perdu,* unpredictability dominates up to the end.)

The character's prominence in the novel (pre-decided by the plot) decides the character's range—of alternatives. The novelist must allot (to the point of rationing) psychological space. The "hero," "heroine" and "villain" (if any) are, by agreement, allowed most range. They are entitled, for the portrayal of their alternatives, to time and space. Placing the characters in receding order to their importance to the plot, the number of their alternatives may be seen to diminish. What E. M. Forster has called the "flat" character has no alternatives at all.

The ideal novel is without "flat" characters.

Characters must *materialise*—i.e., must have a palpable physical reality. They must be not only see-able (visualisable); they must be felt. Power to give physical reality is probably a matter of the extent and nature of the novelist's physical sensibility, or susceptibility. In the main, English novelists are weak in this, as compared to French and Russians. Why?

Hopelessness of categoric "description." Why? Because this is static. Physical personality belongs to action: cannot be separated from it. Pictures must be in movement. Eyes, hands, stature, etc., must appear, and only appear, *in play*. Reaction to physical personality is part of action—love, or sexual passages, only more marked application of this general rule.

(Conrad an example of strong, non-sexual use of physical personality.)

The materialisation (in the above sense) of the character for the novelist must be instantaneous. It happens. No effort of will—and obviously no effort of intellect—can induce it. The novelist can *use* a character that has not yet materialised. But the unmaterialised character represents an enemy pocket in an area that has been otherwise cleared. This cannot go on for long. It produces a halt in plot.

When the materialisation *has* happened, the chapters written before it happened will almost certainly have to be recast. From the plot point of view, they will be found invalid.

Also, it is essential that for the reader the materialisation of the character should begin early. I say begin, because for the *reader* it may, without harm, be gradual.

Is it from this failure, or tendency to fail, in materialisation that the English novelist depends so much on engaging emotional sympathy for his characters?

Ruling sympathy out, a novel must contain at least one *magnetic* character. At least one character capable of keying the reader up, as though he (the reader) were in the presence of someone he is in love with. This not a rule of salesmanship but a pre-essential of *interest*. The character must do to the reader what he has done to the novelist— magnetise towards himself perceptions, sense-impressions, desires.

The unfortunate case is, where the character has, obviously, acted magnetically upon the author, but fails to do so upon the reader.

There must be combustion. Plot depends for its movement on internal combustion.

Physically, characters are almost always copies, or composite copies. Traits, gestures, etc., are searched for in, and assembled from, the novelist's memory. Or a picture, a photograph or the cinema screen may be drawn on. Nothing physical can be *invented*. (Invented physique stigmatises the inferior novel.) Proust (in last volume) speaks of this assemblage of traits. Though much may be lifted from a specific person in "real life," no person in "real life" could supply everything (physical) necessary for the character in the novel. No such person could have just that exact degree of physical intensity required for the character.

Greatness of characters is the measure of the unconscious greatness of the novelist's vision. They are "true" in so far as he is occupied with poetic truth. Their degrees in realness show the degrees of his concentration.

Scene.—Is a Derivative of Plot. Gives Actuality to Plot.

Nothing can happen nowhere. The locale of the happening always colours the happening, and often, to a degree, shapes it.

Plot having pre-decided what is to happen, scene, scenes, must be so found, so chosen, as to give happening the desired force.

Scene, being physical, is, like the physical traits of the characters, generally a copy, or a composite copy. It, too, is assembled—out of memories which, in the first place, may have had no rational connection with one another. Again, pictures, photographs, the screen are sources of supply. Also dreams.

Almost anything drawn from "real life"—house, town, room, park, landscape—will almost certainly be found to require *some* distortion for the purposes of the plot. Remote memories, already distorted by the imagination, are most useful for the purposes of scene. Unfamiliar or once-seen places yield more than do familiar, often-seen places.

Wholly invented scene is as unsatisfactory (thin) as wholly invented physique for a character.

Scene, much more than character, is inside the novelist's conscious power. More than any other constituent of the novel, it makes him conscious *of* his power.

This can be dangerous. The weak novelist is always, compensatorily, scene-minded. (Jane Austen's economy of scene-painting, and her abstentions from it in what might be expected contexts, could in itself be proof of her mastery of the novel.)

Scene is only justified in the novel where it can be shown, or at least felt, to act upon action or character. In fact, where it has dramatic use.

Where not intended for dramatic use, scene is a sheer slower-down. Its staticness is a dead weight. It cannot make part of the plot's movement by being shown *in play*. (Thunderstorms, the sea, landscape flying past car or railway-carriage windows are not scene but *happenings*.)

The deadeningness of straight and prolonged "description" is as apparent with regard to scene as it is with regard to character. Scene must be evoked. For its details relevance (see RELEVANCE) is essential. Scene must, like the characters, not fail to materialise. In this it follows the same law—instantaneous for the novelist, gradual for the reader.

In "setting a scene" the novelist directs, or attempts to direct, the reader's visual imagination. He must allow for the fact that the reader's memories will not correspond with his own. Or, at least, not at all far along the way.

Dialogue.—Must (1) Further Plot. (2) Express Character.

Should not on any account be a vehicle for ideas for their own sake. Ideas only permissible where they provide a key to the character who expresses them.

Dialogue requires more art than does any other constituent of the novel. Art in the *celare artem* sense. Art in the trickery, self-justifying distortion sense. Why? Because dialogue must appear realistic without being so. Actual realism—the lifting, as it were, of passages from a stenographer's take-down of a "real life" conversation—would be disruptive. Of what? Of the illusion of the novel. In "real life" everything is diluted; in the novel everything is condensed.

What are the realistic qualities to be imitated (or faked) in novel dialogue? Spontaneity. Artless or hit-or-miss arrival at words used. Ambiguity (speaker not sure, himself, what he means). Effect of choking (as in engine): more to be said than can come through. Irrelevance. Allusiveness. Erraticness: unpredictable course. Repercussion.

What must novel dialogue, behind mask of these faked realistic qualities, really be and do? It must be pointed, intentional, relevant. It must crystallise situation. It must express character. It must advance plot.

During dialogue, the characters confront one another. The confrontation is in itself an occasion. Each one of these occasions, throughout the novel, is unique. Since the last confrontation, something has changed, advanced. What is being said is the effect of something that has happened; at the same time, what is being said *is in itself something happening,* which will, in turn, leave its effect.

Dialogue is the ideal means of showing what is between the characters. It crystallises relationships. It *should,* ideally, be so effective as to make analysis or explanation of the relationships between the characters unnecessary.

Short of a small range of physical acts—a fight, murder, love-making—dialogue is the most vigorous and visible inter-action of which characters in a novel are capable. Speech is what the characters *do to each other.*

Dialogue provides means for the psychological materialisation of the characters. It should short-circuit description of mental traits. Every sentence in dialogue should be descriptive of the character who is speaking. Idiom, tempo, and shape of each spoken sentence should be calculated by novelist, towards this descriptive end.

Dialogue is the first case of the novelist's need for notation from real life. Remarks or turns of phrase indicatory of class, age, degree of intellectual pretension, *idées reçues,* nature and strength of governing fantasy, sexual temperament, persecution-sense or acumen (fortuitous arrival at general or poetic truth) should be collected. (N.B.—Proust, example of this semi-conscious notation and putting to use of it.)

All the above, from *class* to *acumen,* may already have been established, with regard to each character, by a direct statement by the novelist to the reader. It is still, however, the business of dialogue to show these factors, or qualities, in play.

There must be present in dialogue—i.e., in each sentence spoken by each character—*either* (a) calculation, *or* (b) involuntary self-revelation.

Each piece of dialogue *must* be "something happening." Dialogue *may* justify its presence by being "illustrative"—but this secondary use of it must be watched closely, challenged. Illustrativeness can be stretched too far. Like straight description, it then becomes static, a dead weight—halting the movement of the plot. The "amusing" for its *own* sake should above all be censored. So should infatuation with any idiom.

The functional use of dialogue for the plot must be the first thing in the novelist's mind. Where functional usefulness cannot be established, dialogue must be left out.

What is this functional use? That of a bridge.

Dialogue is the thin bridge which must, from time to time, carry the entire weight of the novel. Two things to be kept in mind—(the bridge is there to permit *advance,* (b) the bridge must be stro enough for the weight.

Failure in any one piece of dialogue is a loss, at once to the continuity and the comprehensibility of the novel.

Characters should, on the whole, be under rather than over articulate. What they *intend* to say should be more evident, more striking (because of its greater inner importance to the plot) than what they arrive at *saying.*

Angle.

The question of *angle* comes up twice over in the novel.

Angle has two senses—(a) visual, (b) moral.

(a) *Visual Angle.* This has been much discussed—particularly I think by Henry James. Where is the camera-eye to be located? (1) In the breast or brow of *one* of the characters? This is, of course, simplifying and integrating. But it imposes on the novel the limitations of the "I"—whether the first person is explicitly used or not. Also, with regard to any matter that the specific character does not (cannot) know, it involves the novelist in long cumbrous passages of cogitation, speculation and guesses. E.G.—of any character other than the specific (or virtual) "I" it must always be "he appeared to feel," "he could be seen to see," rather than "he felt," "he saw." (2) In the breast or brow of a succession of characters? This is better. It *must,* if used, involve very careful, considered division of the characters, by the novelist, in the *seeing* and the *seen.* Certain characters gain in importance and magnetism by being only *seen:* this makes them more romantic, fatal-seeming, sinister. In fact, no character in which these qualities are, for the plot, essential should be allowed to enter the *seeing class.* (3) In the breast or brow of omniscient story-teller (the novelist)? This, though appearing naïve, would appear best. The novelist should retain right of entry, at will, into any of the characters: their memories, sensations and thought-processes should remain his, to requisition for appropriate use. What conditions "appropriateness"? The demands of the plot. Even so, the novelist must not lose sight of point made above —the gain in necessary effect, for some characters, of their remaining *seen*—their remaining closed, apparently, even to the omniscience of the novelist.

The cinema, with its actual camera-work, is interesting study for the novelist. In a good film, the camera's movement, angle and distance have all worked towards one thing—the fullest possible realisation of the director's idea, the completest possible surrounding of the subject. Any trick is justified if it adds a statement. With both film and novel, plot is the pre-imperative. The novelist's relation to the novel is that of the director's relation to the film. The cinema, cinema-going, has no doubt built up in novelists a great authoritarianism. This seems to me good.

(b) *Moral Angle*. This too often means pre-assumptions—social, political, sexual, national, aesthetic and so on. These may all exist, sunk at different depths, in the same novelist. Their existence cannot fail to be palpable; and their nature determines, more than anything else, the sympatheticness or antipatheticness of a given novel to a given circle of readers.

Pre-assumptions are bad. They limit the novel to a given circle of readers. They cause the novel to act immorally *on* that given circle. (The lady asking the librarian for a "nice" novel to take home is, virtually, asking for a novel whose pre-assumptions will be identical with her own.) Outside the given circle, a novel's pre-assumptions must invalidate it for all other readers. The increasingly bad smell of most pre-assumptions probably accounts for the growing prestige of the detective story: the detective story works on the single, and universally acceptable, pre-assumption that an act of violence is anti-social, and that the doer, in the name of injured society, must be traced.

Great novelists write without pre-assumption. They write from outside their own nationality, class or sex.

To write thus should be the ambition of any novelist who wishes to state poetic truth.

Does this mean he must have no angle, no moral view-point? No, surely. Without these, he would be (a) incapable of maintaining the *conviction* necessary for the novel, (b) incapable of *lighting* the characters, who to be seen at all must necessarily be seen in a moral light.

From what source, then, must the conviction come? and from what morality is to come the light to be cast on the characters?

The conviction must come from certainty of the validity of the truth the novel is to present. The "moral light" has not, actually, a moral source; it is moral (morally powerful) according to the strength of its power of revelation. Revelation of what? The virtuousness or non-virtuousness of the action of the character. What is virtue in action? Truth in action. Truth by what ruling, in relation to what? Truth by the ruling of, and in relation to, the inherent poetic truth that the novel states.

The presence, and action, of the poetic truth is the motive (or motor) morality of the novel.

The direction of the action of the poetic truth provides—in fact, is—the moral angle of the novel. If he remains with that truth in view, the novelist has no option as to his angle.

The action, or continuous line of action, of a character is "bad" in so far as it runs counter to, resists or attempts to deny the action of the poetic truth. It is predisposition towards such action that constitutes "badness" in a character.

"Good" action, or "goodness" in the character from predisposition towards such action, is movement along with, expressive of and contributory to, the action of the poetic truth.

If the novelist's moral angle is (a) decided by recognition of the poetic truth, and (b) maintained by the necessity of stating the truth by showing the truth's action, it will be, as it should be, impersonal. It will be, and (from the "interest" point of view) will be able to stand being, pure of pre-assumptions—national, social, sexual, etc.

(N.B.—"Humour" is the weak point in the front against pre-assumptions. Almost all English humour shows social [sometimes, now, backed by political] pre-assumptions. [Extreme cases—that the lower, or employed, classes are quaint or funny; that aristocrats, served by butlers, are absurd.] National pre-assumptions show in treatment of foreigners.)

Advance.

It has been said that plot must advance; that the underlying (or inner) speed of the advance must be even. How is this arrived at?

(1) Obviously, first, by the succession, the succeedingness, of events or happenings. It is to be remembered that *everything* put on record at all—an image, a word spoken, an interior movement of thought or feeling on the part of a character—is an event or happening. These proceed out of one another, give birth to one another, in a continuity that must be (a) obvious, (b) unbroken.

(2) Every happening cannot be described, stated. The reader must

be made to feel that what has not been described or stated has, none
the less, happened. How? By the showing of subsequent events or
happenings whose source *could* only have been in what has not actually
been stated. Tuesday is Tuesday by virtue of being the day following
Monday. The stated Tuesday must be shown as a derivative of the
unstated Monday.

(3) For the sake of emphasis, time must be falsified. But the
novelist's consciousness of the subjective, arbitrary and emotional nature
of the falsification should be evident to the reader. Against this falsification—in fact, increasing the force of its effect by contrast—a clock
should be heard always impassively ticking away at the same speed.
The passage of time, and its demarcation, should be a factor in plot.
The either concentration or even or uneven spacing-out of events along
time is important.

The statement "Ten years had passed," or the statement, "It was
now the next day"—each of these is an event.

(4) Characters most of all promote, by showing, the advance of the
plot. How? By the advances, from act to act, in their action. By their
showing (by emotional or physical changes) the effects both of action
and of the passage of time. The diminution of the character's alternatives shows (because it is the work of) advance—by the end of a novel
the character's alternatives, many at the beginning, have been reduced
to almost none. In the novel, everything that happens happens either
to or *because* of one of the characters. By the end of the novel, the
character has, like the silk worm at work on the cocoon, spun itself out.
Completed action is marked by the exhaustion (from one point of view)
of the character. Throughout the novel, each character is expending
potentiality. This expense of potentiality must be felt.

(5) Scene promotes, or contributes to, advance by its *freshness*.
Generically, it is fresh, striking, from being unlike the scene before.
It is the new "here and now." Once a scene ceases to offer freshness,
it is a point-blank enemy to advance. Frequent change of scene *not*
being an imperative of the novel—in fact, many novels by choice, and
by wise choice, limiting themselves severely in this matter—how is
there to continue to be freshness? By means of ever-differing presentation. Differing because of what? Season of year, time of day, effects
of a happening (e.g., with house, rise or fall in family fortunes, an
arrival, a departure, a death), beholding character's mood. At the first
presentation, the *scene* has freshness; afterwards, the freshness must be

in the *presentation*. The same scene can, by means of a series of presentations, each having freshness, be made to ripen, mature, to actually advance. The *static* properties in scene can be good for advance when so stressed as to show advance by contrast—advance on the part of the characters. Striking "unchangingness" gives useful emphasis to change. Change should not be a factor, at once, in *both* scene and character: either unchanged character should see, or be seen, against changed scene, or changed character should see, or be seen, against unchanged scene. *Two* changes obviously cancel each other out, and would cancel each other's contribution to the advance of plot.

Relevance.

Relevance—the question of it—is the headache of novel-writing.

As has been said, the model for relevance is the well-constructed detective story: nothing is "in" that does not tell. But the detective story is, or would appear to be, simplified by having *fact* as its kernel. The detective story makes towards concrete truth; the novel makes towards abstract truth.

With the detective story, the question "relevant to *what*?" can be answered by the intelligence. With the novel, the same question must constantly, and in every context, be referred to the intuition. The intelligence, in a subsequent check over, may detect, but cannot itself put right, blunders, lapses or false starts on the part of the intuition.

In the notes on Plot, Character, Scene and Dialogue, everything has come to turn, by the end, on relevance. It is seen that all other relevances are subsidiary to the relevance of the plot—i.e., the relevance to itself that the plot demands. It is as contributory, in fact relevant, to plot that character, scene and dialogue are examined. To be perfectly contributory, these three must be perfectly relevant. If character, scene or dialogue has been weakened by anything irrelevant to *itself,* it can only be imperfectly relevant—which must mean to a degree disruptive—to the plot.

The main hope for character (for each character) is that it should be magnetic—i.e., that it should *attract* its parts. This living propensity of the character to assemble itself, to integrate itself, to make itself in order to *be* itself will not, obviously, be resisted by the novelist. The magnetic, or magnetising, character can be trusted as to what is relevant *to itself*. The trouble comes when what is relevant to the character is found to be not relevant to the plot. At this point, the novelist must adjudicate. It is possible that the character may be right; it is possible that there may be some flaw in the novelist's sense of what is relevant to the plot.

Again, the character may, in fact must, decide one half of the question of relevance in dialogue. The character attracts to itself the right, in fact the only possible, idiom, tempo and phraseology for *that* particular character in speech. In so far as dialogue is *illustrative,* the character's, or characters', pull on it must not be resisted.

But in so far as dialogue must be "something happening"—part of action, a means of advancing plot—the other half of the question of dialogue-relevance comes up. Here, the pull from the characters may conflict with the pull from the plot. Here again the novelist must adjudicate. The recasting and recasting of dialogue that is so often necessary is, probably, the search for ideal compromise.

Relevance in scene is more straightforward. Chiefly, the novelist must control his infatuation with his own visual power. No non-contributory image, must be the rule. Contributory to what? To the mood of the "now," the mood that either projects or reflects action. It is a good main rule that objects—chairs, trees, glasses, mountains, cushions—introduced into the novel should be stage-properties, necessary for "business." It will be also recalled that the well-set stage shows many objects *not* actually necessary for "business"—but that these have a right to place by being descriptive—explanatory. In a play, the absence of the narrating voice makes it necessary to establish the class, period and general psychology of the characters by means of objects that can be seen. In the novel, such putting of objects to a descriptive (explanatory) use is excellent—alternative to the narrator's voice.

In scene, then, relevance demands either usefulness for action or else explanatory power in what is shown. There is no doubt that with some writers (Balzac, sometimes Arnold Bennett) categoricalness, in the presentation of scene, is effective. The aim is, usually, to suggest, by multiplication and exactitude of detail, either a scene's material oppressiveness or its intrinsic authority. But in general, for the purposes of most novelists, the number of objects genuinely necessary for explanation will be found to be very small.

Irrelevance, in any part, is a cloud and a drag on, a weakener of, the novel. It dilutes meaning. Relevance crystallises meaning.

The novelist's—any writer's—object is to whittle down his meaning to the exactest and finest possible point. What, of course, is fatal is when he does not know what he does mean: he has no point to sharpen.

Much irrelevance is introduced into novels by the writer's vague hope that at least some of this *may* turn out to be relevant, after all. A good deal of what might be called provisional writing goes to the first drafts of first chapters of most novels. At a point in the novel's progress, relevance becomes clearer. The provisional chapters are then recast.

The most striking fault in work by young or beginning novelists, submitted for criticism, is irrelevance—due either to infatuation or indecision. To direct such an author's attention to the imperative of relevance is certainly the most useful—and possibly the only—help that can be given.

Character Change
and the Drama

Harold Rosenberg

*We have already seen Bernard change; passions
may come that will modify him still more.*
Gide, *The Counterfeiters*

I

An egg with an ancestry, developing, changing its form, maturing
—later, degenerating, dying, decaying, again changing its form—all in a
slow gradual way, with but few shocks like birth and death, such in
broadest outline is the career of the personality, the empirical ego, which
the organic point of view, expressed most often in those studies of mutation, biology, history, biography and associated subjects, finally presents
before us. Whatever unity an organism maintains at the base of its
transformations is something mysterious; an organism may be arranged
with reference to other organisms with which it sustains resemblances,
it may be classified, noted statistically, or subsumed under an imagined
archetype, but its individual unity can only be "felt." From the view-
point of the human person himself, his coherence is, as Herbert Read
has put it, "an organic coherence intuitively based on the real world of
sensation." [1]

On the other hand, the concepts of morality or social law, spe-
cializing in the human and ignoring any possible connection with
"things," tend to define the individual not as an enduring historical

This essay reprinted by permission of the author.
[1] "Personality in Literature," *The Symposium*, July, 1931.

entity but by what he has done in given instances. A special sequence of acts provokes a judgment, and this judgment is an inseparable part of the recognition of the individual. Here too there is no final comprehension of individuals; but whereas the historical approach, even when it reaches mechanistic conclusions, points toward the existence of individuals, who, however, can be grasped singly only by a nonrational operation, social legality acts as though it were unaware of them altogether except as they are completely defined by their "overt acts." If the law is not always satisfied with itself, it is not because it has at any time still to discover something about the nature of individuals, but for the reason that it realizes all at once that acts are being performed which it has no means of controlling.

The law pronounces, or should pronounce, its judgments and penalties with regard only to the acts of individuals and without recognition of the individuals as persons; its judgments are applied at the end of a series of acts. Thus the law creates a definite fiction, an individual who is identified by the coherence of his acts with a fact in which they have terminated (a crime or a contract, for example) and by nothing else. The judgment is the resolution of these acts; the law visualizes the individual as a sort of actor with a role, and its judgment relates him finally to the broader, more universal system of the legal code. This assertion that the individual is what we may call an identity in contrast with a personality, that is, one defined solely by the coherence of his action with an adjudged fact and not by the continuity of his being, is entirely contradictory to the biological or historical organism-concept, which visualizes action as serving for a clue to the existence and endurance of a thing *in esse* whose real definition can only be attained by an intuition.

The modern novel, which contains most of what we have today in the way of dramatic literature, has more in common with the historical or biological view of character than with the legal. Consider *Ulysses, The Magic Mountain,* or *Remembrance of Things Past:* in the growing and decaying of their characters, the portrayal of organic texture and change is of the essence of the attempt.

As for the legal definition, it seems at first glance to be far removed from the needs of literary fiction, since it stands ready with its systematic chopping-block to execute come who may on the basis of his most easily definable acts and without consideration of the finer points of his feeling or motive. Only action which is "relevant and material" to the fact to be judged can the party to a suit plead as bearing on his status. The law is forever fixed to that edge of individuality where the particular is caught in the web of the abstract and is shifted against its will into a position where it can only suffer and be tortured by the contradiction between its own direction and the rules of the place in which it finds itself. . . . Yet in the old tragedy, the individual was similarly menaced by an external organization with laws and habits of its own.

Even from this angle, however, there are distinctions to be made; social law is not dramatic law. The persons who appear before the bar of justice are identities, they can be seen to have obeyed and to be completely interpretable by the apparent logic of their crimes, only for the convenience of judicial pronouncement. In fact, however, a man who has committed a murder may not have acted in a manner which we recognize and condemn with all our hearts as murderous until that last moment when he pulled the trigger of his revolver. That he meant to kill at that moment satisfies the law's demand for premeditation and murderous intent; but since all the acts of the criminal person were not of a criminal quality, we are forced more or less to think of extenuating circumstances. All those puny, common details, small gestures in every way resembling our own, which may have preceded the murder, entering an automobile, stepping on the gas, obeying the traffic lights—and further back, receiving certain influences, being molded by certain values —and which go more to form part of the criminal, in the innocence or "alegality" of his mere endurance, than of the relevant *res gestate* of his crime, the law takes into account only for the purpose of filling in the scenic accompaniments of the last act and intent. So that in spite of the fact that social law deals with identities rather than with personalities, it can do so only by arbitrarily converting persons with histories into emblems of unified action of a given quality. In other words, the law, like its victims, suffers from the discrepancy between action and being, the failure of the individual to conform in every respect to his role. If this were not so, law and justice could be synonymous terms.

If, then, the old drama, as contrasted with biography (of actual or of fictitious personalities), succeeded, as has been asserted by ethical critics, in supplying a picture of action in which a kind of justice and a kind of law conform to each other, it must be because the dramatist started with identities. Like the judge he left aside personalities, their growths, and their structural peculiarities; like the judge he established the particularity of a character only on the basis of the coherence of all of his acts with a special fact; like the judge phenomena of character interested him not for themselves merely but only in so far as there were involved in them the means of reaching a decisive termination of the action. But unlike that of the judge, the dramatist's definition of the character was not an arbitrary superimposition which negates the horde of emotional, intellectual and mechanical characteristics of a person whose some one deed concerns the court; it constituted instead the entire reality of the character and, avoiding the ruinous abstractness of the law, determined in advance that his emotions, his thoughts and his gestures should correspond with and earn in every respect his special fate. . . . Of course, it is because the dramatist had created his characters that he could maintain the proportion between their emotions, their thoughts and their destinies; while those who confront the judge on his dais were, unfortunately, born.

This distinction, quietly implied by their modes of approach to the problem of the definition of the individual, between a personality and an identity, and the decision that the identity alone is of importance in the consideration of the status of individuals, is what the dramatic attitude has in common with the legal. The characters of biography and the biographical novel are persons with histories, but in the drama the characters are identities with roles. The distinction also entails a contrast in the purposes of biography and tragedy. Biography presents the picture of a life precisely enlarged and developed with that type of exactitude which is proper to history, to events visualized as successive in time. But drama, as a "poetical picture of life," is composed of events which, though apparently related sequentially and causally, are chosen with reference to a special type of judgment, to the application of specific laws; the conventional coherence of these events, the suggestion to the observer that such things may have happened in actuality and are at least within the range of rational possibility, is superficial, and, far from determining the outcome of a tragedy, serves merely as a link to connect in the mind of the audience the natural world of compulsive cause and accident with the dramatic world of judgment. Those psychological explanations of the motivations of dramatic figures which form so large a part of modern criticism apply to this layer of reasonable causality which is the outer form of dramatic movement; they have no reference to the dramatist's act of judging[2] which constitutes the sub-surface impulsion of the characters. Once the *rationality* of it has been established by psychology, the *sufficiency* of the motivation of a Macbeth or a Lear is to be referred not to the probable, nor even a possible, human equivalent, but to those laws of Shakespeare's world which criticism formulates as pivots for the action of his dramatic identities.

It is with respect to these laws, rather than by copying types, that drama is objective, that the dramatist's image has external application, that it comments on the lives of other people. "Natural" individuals may evade any system of justice, or seem to, but a dramatic identity is a creature in whom a judgment is involved at his birth; a judgment which instigates to a pathos and also gives meaning to it. And by this substitution for personalities, who erratically live and grow within the mystery of moral laws not yet discovered, of identities whose motor organs are judgments,[3] dramatic figures are rendered at once particular and general, and drama appears as "more philosophical" than history.

II

Religious experience also interprets the individual as an identity. In contrast with psychology, which concentrates upon his personality, religion looks to the judgment which will establish his eternal role. And upon the fixed operation of an identity mutations of the personality have no bearing. As in the bloody book and bitter letter of the law, there are in religion stark examples of this division between identity and personality. For instance, in demoniacal possession identities usurped personalities: the demon, in all respects a new being controlled

[2] Instead of the "dramatist's act of judging" we may refer to the "dramatist's act of seeing judgment as involved in and carried out by action." From the historical or the common-sense point of view, there is no judgment impressed upon action, and the presence of judgment in the drama must therefore be attributed to an act of the dramatist; but from the dramatic viewpoint there is no action that does not effect judgment, and the judgment is therefore projected, in Platonic fashion, into the real formula of the action, is said to be discovered by the dramatist, and not to be the result of an act of judgment. In any case, it is a judgment which is at the basis of the dramatic act and not a psychological cause.

[3] Of course the moral judgments of drama may not seem moral at all in the conventional sense. For example, the dramatist may rather choose to execute a character because he seems strong and is yet destructible than because he is wicked.

by the facts and laws of a supernatural world, subjected the individual to its own will.[4] The personality of the possessed remained intact. The demon was a character with a name of his own. His voice was heard from the mouth of a man—but he was not that man, any more than Hamlet was Barrymore. And he could be influenced only by special means fundamentally identical in all cases of possession. There was one law for all demons. Exorcism was applied, a contest between powers of a purely religious cosmos. The exorcist addressed the demon directly, and no attempt was made to alter the psychological texture of the possessed. It was irrelevant!

As we have seen, a character becomes an identity through the integration of his life about a single fact adjudged by the author of the identity, and this fact determines his position and the reconstitution of his existence as a role. It is by fixing his ideas and emotions around the particular fact that the character's limitations and his definition are concretely shown. In law and religion it is easy to isolate the character's identifying fact, the crime, the contract, the spirit or deity. In drama it is often more difficult, and we are led to speak of the theme of the play, which is nothing else than a vague description of the central fact of the protagonist's role (e.g., *Macbeth*—fair and foul Murder).

An identity is a constant thing. From the viewpoints which create them growth is impossible, and psychological mutation occurs above a rigid substratum. Dramatic reversal of situation depends for its effectiveness upon this persistence of identity. The mere possibility of a psychological adjustment to the new position would destroy the tragic irony, disperse the pathos, and render the imitation natural rather than dramatic.

The identity may be revealed more fully as a drama progresses; this is commonly called character development. The character's action rises or declines on the moral plane, without, however, altering the fact by which he is identified. E.g., Prince Henry's—*Henry IV, Part II*—abandoned

> Well, thus we play the fools with the time

belongs to the same "princely" identity as King Henry's—*Henry V*—conscientious

---

[4] The cases reported in the Middle Ages are the best examples. The reader who is not familiar with these may recall Socrates' description of poetical inspiration or possession in the *Ion*.

Our bad neighbour makes us early stirrers,
Which is both healthful and good husbandry.

This is also true of the sudden reversals of moral direction which appear
in the *crises de conscience* episodes of certain dramas; moral reversal
being merely a species of character development carried on at quick-
time.

Yet characters may change in a drama not through moral or psychological modification but by means of a change of identity. In genuine cases of change of identity a special process causes the central fact
which identifies the character to give place to another of a different type
and value, and the fact to which the character's action was previously
attached becomes powerless to motivate or explain him. His moral
situation may remain substantially the same, but the quality of his acts
is altered and his movements transpire on another level; he is a different
dramatic individual, and acts which before were in his probable range
are now no longer even seriously thinkable.

It is especially in the substitution of one identity for another, or
for a personality, that the type of coherence which marks the identity
is clarified, *since the change of identity takes place,* as we shall see, *all
at once, in a leap,* and is not, as in personality, the result of a continual
flow.

To begin with the legal instance: the fact of the crime interpreted
and limited (by determining their relevance) the acts of the criminal.
For the law, he lived by that fact alone. If it were suddenly discovered
that no crime had been committed, the coherence of action which had
led to the apparent fact would collapse, and the prisoner, having been
converted in an instant into the figure (hypothetical) of an innocent
man, would no longer exist under the eye of the court. But if there-
after he were charged with a different crime, his legal identity would
depend upon this new fact and would be entirely other when established
than the former one.

We may next indicate how the idea of identity and change of
identity has been treated by religions, and has even, one may say, been
made the dominant feature of their most significant and important
ceremonies. To use familiar material, this is Professor Guignbert's
version of the pagan taurobolium:

In the Phrygian cult of Cybele and Attis, but not in that alone,
for we find it in various other Asiatic cults and in that of Mithra,

a singular ceremony, called the *taurobolium*, took place. It formed part of the mysterious initiatory rites exclusively reserved for believers. [*Christianity*.]

Here follows a description of the rites and this explanation:

The pit signifies the kingdom of the dead, and the mystic, in descending into it, is thought to die; the bull is Attis, and the blood that is shed is the divine life-principle that issues from him; the initiate receives it and, as it were, absorbs it; when he leaves the pit he is said to be "born again" and milk, as in the case of a new-born infant, is given him to drink. But he is not born the mere man again he was before; he has absorbed the very essence of the god and, if we understand the mystery aright, he is in his turn become an Attis and is saluted as one.

Guignbert then draws attention to the resemblance between these rites and the Christian baptism and eucharist.

The change consists, then, in both the legal and religious instances in (1) the dissolution or death of the previous identity—this may involve the death of the individual, as with Ivan Ilych, abandoned by Tolstoy on the threshold of change, or it may be indicated by cancellation of the central fact of the identity,[5] or by a symbolic proximity to death; and (2) a re-identification, wherein the individual is placed in a new status, is "reborn," so to say, and given a new character and perhaps a new name.

Drama is no more religion or law than it is psychology, history or biography. But the fact that the phenomenon of religious conversion is the only one "in life" [6] which effects a change of identity, in which, through the touch of death, a course of action and valuation is completely annulled and another substituted without breaching the duration of the individual, relates religion and drama in a special way. To present the change objectively, to suggest the actual method of identity-replacement, the dramatist must make use of events indicating the character's experience of death. But drama speaks in terms of action

[5] That the purpose of the law in executing a criminal is to avenge itself upon him or to offer his fate as a deterrent has been denied by philosophers of the law. The logic of the law's act becomes clear when we understand the execution as an attempt to eliminate the criminal identity, and that the death of the criminal is incidental to this aim. Any means equally certain as death of accomplishing the dissolution of the criminal identity would be satisfactory, at least theoretically, even though it worked no harm to the criminal.

[6] The legal identity is a formal one.

alone, and it neither contradicts nor supports any explanation religious or psychological. Dramatic "death and regeneration" is no mystery.[7] There is the death-laden incident; and then occurs a coupling of two different identities under a figure presented as one, a change of the faces behind the mask.

To indicate the similarity and differences in the treatment of this type of change in drama, I have chosen examples from three literatures.

A very early account of identity-change is the life-story of the Biblical Jacob. From the moment he begins his career by outwitting his brother in the matter of the pottage his character is consistent with the trait described by his name. A tricky winner, he dreams but once, and his dream is of promised protection and prosperity . . . until the threat of death descends upon him in the form of the avenging Esau, victim of his precocious cunning. Then "greatly afraid and distressed" he calls on God to save him and schemes to be the last of his company to die. But alone behind the encampment he is met by the angel, who wrestles with him until dawn. During this contest he receives the sign of the dislocated thigh and his name is changed to Isra-el (Wrestler-With-God). In the morning he advances to meet his brother, whose fury has been unaccountably—on psychological grounds though not in regard to the symbolism of identity-change—transformed to love.

From that time, the lone adventurer, gatherer of property and wives, disappears; he has become the patriarch, and the interest shifts to his children. In the next episode, the seduction of Dinah, it is his sons who plot the vengeance and perform the treacherous action. The transformed Jacob, Israel, is busy with God and the erection of altars; his practical career is at an end.

This is an extremely simple picture of the process of identity-change as it appears in dramatic literature. There is a minimum of action-detail, only the death-threat and the change by divine contact and renaming.

In the next example a personality is transformed into a dramatic identity; it clarifies the contrast between the action of a personality,

[7] Death in the drama means only cessation of the character's action with the impossibility of taking it up again. In tragedy, when no change is present, death comprehends the destruction of the individual and mirrors natural death; in the "impostor" type of social comedy death applies to the false identity—the individual continues to live but through the exposure he cannot go on with his old act.

which is the expression of a psychological condition, and that of an identity, who always acts with reference to his role, who performs what is required of him by the plot, by the whole in which he is located. The fact that the hero at the outset is the image of a personality means that our example begins as a biography in dramatic form, and the fact that he changes into an identity means that from that point the biography-drama becomes a true drama.

In *Hamlet* there is an interfusion of two forms of interpretation, the psychological and the dramatic. The argumentative, self-analytical, naturalistic Hamlet of "non-action," describing himself in every speech and using speech as a substitute for deed, is very much the figure of a personality, of a being insufficient for, *because irrelevant to,* the dramatic role offered to him.[8]

> I do not know
> Why yet I live to say "This thing's to do,"
> Sith I have cause and will and strength and means
> To do 't.

Despite the views of psychological criticism, Hamlet has all the qualities required for action, the will and the strength; he lacks only the identity structure which would fit him to be a character in a drama, the identity which originates in and responds totally to the laws of his dramatic world. Thus he is contrasted or "paralleled" with Laertes,

> For by the image of my cause, I see
> The portraiture of his,

whose situation is equal to his own but whose identity is dramatic;[9] and he sets himself off in his helplessness against the drama of the visiting players. It is not a weakness of personality that cripples his action but the fact that he is a personality at all. His moves are cut off as by the Revolving Sword at that point where they would force an effective entry into the dramatic cosmos. He lives on a sort of middle ground between the natural world and the dramatic, a world of fantasy somewhat insane, because its laws are contradictory. He is inadequate

[8] In the customary psychological criticism, Hamlet's failure to act is laid to the preponderance of one trait or another, usually the reflective one. But interpreting the character in terms of dramatic identity, we relate his incapacity to a structural insufficiency, a defect which no psychological correction could remedy or even affect.

[9] Cf. IV, v: "Save yourself, my lord," etc. The scene belongs in all respects to the role of Hamlet.

to carry out the judgment which has been pronounced upon him because he has been permitted to retain a portion of himself. He thinks too much not because he is an intellectual, but because it is impossible for him to do anything else. The mystery which surrounds him consists in that he is neither an identity nor a personality wholly, but a combination of both, a being who has wandered by accident upon a stage.[10]

Clearly then, this character must be changed if the play is to become a tragedy, if it is not to go on like a naturalistic novel peeling him to expose his psychological layers. As he stands, his career can lead to no pathos or dramatic termination. Hamlet must be given an identity before the finish which will alter his status and fit him into the drama. And there is only one way of representing dramatically such a change.

So that until we meet him returned from the voyage to England, where he had been sent to his death and narrowly escaped in the grapple with the pirates, we have to do with the standard figure of Hamlet-criticism. But when we come upon him after this immersion in symbolic death,[11] we encounter a new character, a regenerated man. In his very next appearance on the stage, Hamlet discourses maturely on death. Also he has acquired a certainty with respect to his feelings and a capacity for action. This is I, he announces, as he leaps into the grave of Ophelia, Hamlet the Dane! Having named himself, he is at once fiercely attacked by Laertes, but he proclaims his dramatic equality with unexpected firmness.

> I prithee, take thy fingers from my throat;
> For, though I am not splenetive and rash,
> Yet have I something in me dangerous,
> Which let thy wisdom fear. Hold off thy hand!

This "something dangerous" in him is new and could not have been predicted; it refers directly, of course, to his ability to act. While about the emotion which had so disconcerted him earlier he says:

> Why, I will fight with him upon this theme. . . .
> I loved Ophelia. . . .

[10] "For he was likely, *had he been put on*,
   To have proved most royally."

[11] "High and mighty," he writes upon his return, "you shall know I am set naked in your kingdom." We need not, however, trace the symbolism of rebirth into the language but only to follow the course of the action. Acts are a firmer foundation than words for the acrobatics of interpretation.

To his mother this new self-assured identity is unrecognizable; her comment on his dramatics is a description applicable before the change.

> This is mere madness,
> And thus a while the fit will work on him.
> Anon, as patient as the female dove
> When that her golden couplets are disclosed,
> His silence will sit drooping.

But she is in error. For Hamlet had commenced to act with reference to his role of self-purifying vengeance, had taken up immutably his appropriate dramatic position, at that moment when aboard the ship bound for England he had read his sealed death-warrant. Then for the first time he had known immediately and with certainty what he had to do.

> Being thus be-netted round with villainies—
> Ere I could make a prologue to my brains,
> They had begun the play—

And now, this hero who had looked with such passionate envy upon passion is "constant in his purposes" toward the King. Some experience barely indicated ("Had I but time, O, I could tell you") has released his forces. His action hustles the play to its tragic close, and the apparently accidental character of his revenge serves to emphasize that he is controlled at the end not by the dualities of his ego but by the impulsions of the plot. Transformed from the image of a personality into that of a dramatic identity, he has found at last his place in the play.

The third example is from Dostoevsky's *Brothers Karamazoff* This author's handling of the subject follows more closely experience of typically religious change of identity than does that of the writers of the Old Testament or of Shakespeare. He tends to relate the phenomenon to Christian belief and emotions. Identity-change in his novel is connected with stimuli of the kind mentioned by religious psychologists

The "biographical notes" of Father Zossima set out two parallel cases of identity-change. First there is Markel, Zossima's brother, whose conversion is briefly stressed to furnish a ground for Zossima's own conversion which comes later and is developed in greater detail. After his brother's death, Zossima was sent to Petersburg to enter the Imperial Guard. From the house of his childhood, he records, he had brought none but precious memories of a religious import, but these grew dimmer in the cadet school and he became a "cruel, absurd, almost savage creature." . . . A disappointing love affair, an insult, and a challenge to a duel . . . "and then something happened that in very truth was the turning point of my life. . . ." The evening preceding the duel, he flew into a rage and struck his orderly so violently that his face was covered with blood. When Zossima awoke the following morning he went to the window and looked out upon the garden. The sun was rising. "It was warm and beautiful, the birds were singing." At that point the conversion began.

What's the meaning of it, I thought, I feel in my heart as it were something vile and shameful? Is it because I am going to shed blood? No, I thought, I feel it's not that. Can it be that I am afraid of death, afraid of being killed? No, that's not it, that's not it at all . . . And all at once, I knew what it was; it was because I had beaten Afanasy the evening before!

Then Zossima recalls his converted brother, the deceased Markel. On the field of honor, risking his companions' contempt, he halts the duel after his adversary has fired. A short time later he becomes a monk.

This incident contains the typical antecedent conditions listed by psychologists for cases of religious conversion; and it stages a death-danger, though fear of death is denied. It may be assumed that Dostoevsky had read books on the psychology of conversion. Yet Zossima's change leaves no suspicion that it is a psychological mutation disguising an orthodox conception of the descent of grace rather than a genuine dramatic happening.[12] The change takes place on the dramatic level; the psychological conditions described, while belonging to realistic literature, are equivalent to the legendary and picaresque adventures in transformation of the Bible and of *Hamlet*.

In our three examples, the process underlying the character's change remains the same, although the actions accompanying it vary, and the explanations for its occurrence range from angelic intervention to nostalgia and remorse. Besides the close danger of death common to all three, the same anxiety is present. In the terse account of Jacob's transformation he is "greatly afraid and distressed," Hamlet relates that

[12] Such as, for example, the *Madame Gervaisais* of the de Goncourt frères, in which, by means of a sequence of credible psychological episodes, a nominal conversion to Roman Catholicism was effected which, however, resulted in no change of identity manifest in dramatic conduct, but only in a psychopathological regression. Such a naturalistic representation of the degeneration of a personality has no bearing on the problem of identity-change.

> . . . in my heart there was a kind of fighting,
> That would not let me sleep,

while Zossima feels "something vile and shameful."

The so-called psychic states preceding conversion [says Sante de Sanctis] seem all to have this in common, that they dissolve the economy of the individual, and excite the soul, but cannot satisfy it or allay its disturbance. They are psychic states which propound questions, but do not answer them; they initiate, but do not complete. They provoke a suspension of the soul in which they are being experienced. [*Religious Conversion.*]

III

The forms of thought which conceive the individual as an identity have to do with action and with the judgment of actions. The concept of identity suggests that in this realm of action the multiple incidents in the life of an individual may be synthesized, by himself or by others, into a scheme that pivots on a single fact judged to be central to the individual's existence and which, governing his behavior and deciding his fate, becomes part of his definition, though it is external to him. Here unity of being becomes one with unity of the "plot," [13] and through the fixity of identity change becomes synonymous with revolution.

With this dramatic integration religious conversion of all actual conditions of the human individual supplies the most complete example, though it is only an example. Through conversion the individual gains an identity which revolves upon a fact which is both private in its unifying effect upon him yet extra-personal in its relation to his world. All converts are by no means, of course, converted to the same thing, their identities after the conversion are not identical, and with regard to each the moral question will receive a different answer. But in all there is that integration about some one thing which instigates their action in a coherent line susceptible of judgment which is the mark of

[13] Whether or not the identity exists and what it is are metaphysical questions. From the psychological view, identity may seem a fictitious unity inhibiting personality, just as the personality may seem from the religious view a fiction dissipating identity. This essay has been dealing with those forms of thought which uniformly interpret the individual as an identity. But even from the empirical view, the identity differs from such intellectual-repressive factors as "character." Its coherence is not necessarily the effect of a negation; its function is not inhibition but affirmation of a "new reality"; it has its own sentiments, emotions, sensibility—it may produce lyric poetry.

the dramatic character. To other individuals such unity may be attributed;[14] the convert openly asserts it of himself and compels his life to accord with his interpretation.

It is on the basis of identity and character-change that the fundamental connection is established between religious and dramatic thought which often permits the processes leading to the phenomena of religious life to suggest dramatic movement, and the vice versa. The identity which both of these attitudes recognize *as* the individual repeats itself to the satisfaction of an eternal judgment, symbolized by a role, and unaffected by any possibility of organic transformation. In drama the judgment is carried out by reversal of position and by a transposition of roles where the character survives. In religious thought the individual is judged by his situation in a hierarchy according to the consistency of his acts with the god-fact. In both instances he does not obey his own will but the rules of the location in which he finds himself. And in both, change can only be accomplished according to the same law, the dissolution of the identity and the reappearance of the individual in a "reborn state."

Dramatic and religious thought, then, retrace the steps which social legality overleaps; they reconstruct the entire individual to fit him into their schemes of justice. The law court receives the individual as he is and in judging him changes him. But dramatics and religion are creative methods, and they elaborate the means according to which the individual relates himself to law and receives justice from it.

[14] This is rarely done by biographers who stress the "human" aspects of a character. But see Prince Mirsky's biography of Lenin as a man who had almost no "personal life."

The Interactions of Words

I. A. Richards

There should be an ancient saying, "If you talk too much about words, your tongue will become a stone." More than once in this lecture you will see why. I have been minded again and again to change my title or dodge the topic, "Whereof we cannot speak, thereof we must be silent," remarked Ludwig Wittgenstein some twenty years ago, but men have gone on inventing languages in which to talk about that silence.

What are these words we talk with and talk so much about? Taking poetry to be an affair of the interaction of words, how far will we get in a discussion of poetry, if we are in real doubt about what words are and do?

This essay threatens thus to become an attempt to define "a word." I am extremely loath to inflict that upon you. The definition of "a word" has been a task from which the best authorities have rightly shrunk, an obligation which has made even psychologists into mystics and left the adepts in linguistics at a loss. But when the subject has been tactlessly raised, how are we to avoid it? How are we to conceive the interactions of words without forming as clear a conception as we can of the words themselves?

"As clear a conception as we can!" But what are these *conceptions* and how can they be *clear*? The implications of this word "conception," if we take it literally and thereby awaken it to full metaphoric liveliness, are a philosophy of poetic language—as Plato pointed out, in the *Phaedrus* (277). It is true he calls them "scientific words" there, but he was concerned with "the dialectic art" which I arbitrarily take here to

From *The Language of Poetry*. Reprinted by permission of the Princeton University Press.

have been the practice of a supreme sort of poetry—the sort which was to replace the poetry he banished from the Republic. Here is the passage. "Noble it may be to tell stories about justice and virtue; but far nobler is a man's work, when finding a congenial soul he avails himself of the dialectic art to sow and plant therein scientific words, which are competent to defend themselves, and him who planted them, and are not unfruitful, but bear seed in their turn, from which other words springing up in other minds are capable of preserving this precious seed ever undecaying, and making their possessor ever happy, so far as happiness is possible to man." Plato is fond of this sort of language. If you look for it you will find it everywhere in the *Republic,* used with a frankness which embarrassed his Victorian translators.

What are these conceptions through which words, by uniting, bring new beings into the world, or new worlds into being? A truly philosophic definition of "a word" would be, I suppose, an all-purpose definition. I am hoping for no such thing—only for a definition useful for our purpose: the study of the language of poetry. But limits to that are not easily set. However, I can escape some of the most dreadful parts of the undertaking by assuming frankly that our purposes are not those of psychology or of linguistics. Their troubles come in part from the uses for which they require their definitions of "a word." Poetics has a different set of purposes and needs a different sort of definition. If so, I can work at it without the tedious attempt to relate it to the other definitions that other studies need. Philosophically speaking, this leaves Poetics "up in the air"; but that is perhaps where, in the present state of philosophy, it will be safest.

But very likely someone will already be saying, "Wait a moment. Are these troubles real or only philosophic? Do we really need any definition poetic or otherwise? Are not most of us in fact clear enough about what poetry and words in general are and do? This marvelous, this miraculous thing we call our language works somehow for us and within us; the better, it may well be, for our not knowing too much about it. Our digestions, to take a humble parallel, do not depend, fortunately, on our knowledge of physiology. Don't our poetic difficulties also arise with particular instances only? Isn't this pretense that we never understand what we are saying or how we say it rather like witchcraft—an epidemic invented to give employment to specialists in its treatment?"

"I would meet you upon this honestly." Such questionings can be barren. To ask "What is a word and how does it work?" may do us no good. On the other hand, there is a sense in which this question is the very foundation, the source, the origin, the ἀρχή (to use Plato's word), the starting point and final cause of the intellectual life. But I do not know how, in *words,* to distinguish the idle from the vital question here.

In the philosophy of poetry this vital question is not a question of fact but one of choice or decision. In that, it is like the fundamental definitions of mathematics. Facts, by themselves, do not, in any simple direct way, settle what we should define "a word" to be. Facts, which we are aware of and can compare only through words, come later. None the less our definition must let the facts be facts. We do well to be humble here; this "What is a word?" is one of the founding questions—along with "What am I?" "What is a fact?" and "What is God?"—on which all other questions balance and turn. The art of entertaining such questions, and of distinguishing them from other questions which we might ask with the same sounds, is the dialectic study of poetry. And the founding questions—those that establish and maintain our state as men—are themselves poetic. But that might mean so many false things that I tremble as I say it.

Still, the other ways of saying it, and ways of guarding it, suffer equal danger. If I add, for example, that this poetic basis of ours is no matter of *mere make-believe,* well, we have the varying possible ways of understanding that richly mysterious phrase, "make-believe," before us. "Mere make-believe." Here is a notable example of the interaction of words. Just where do its disparaging or mocking implications come from? Are beliefs *not* to be made (i.e., forced)? Is *that* the point? Or is it the poor quality of the belief so made? Are beliefs which *we* make not genuine? Must the world, something not ourselves, make them for us? And if so, *which* world will we trust to do that? The world of tradition, of theology, of current public opinion, of science, or one of the worlds of poetry? Which will give us the beliefs we need? Is that the question, or is it the inferior quality of such beliefs which is being mocked, the immature craftsmanship, the inexperience which knows too little about either the materials or the purpose of the belief?

All this and more is to be considered in asking seriously if the poetic basis of our world is make-believe. This phrase, *make-believe,* like a good watch dog, warns us off sternly—if we have no proper business with these premises. But if we were their master, it would be silent. There is another possibility of course. In the Chinese story the stone-deaf visitor remarked, "Why do you keep your dog up so late? He did nothing but yawn at me as I came through the gate."

However, if we know what we are doing, and what the phrase "make-believe" is doing—and it has several senses which should alarm us for one which is safe because true—we may say that our world rests on make-belief or—to use a more venerable word—on faith. But it is *our* world, mind you, which so rests, our world in which we live as men, so different from the bullet's world, in which *it* travels. And yet our world includes the bullet.

I have been trying with all this to revive for you the sense of the word "maker," in which a poet may be seriously said to be a maker. This is the sense in which poetry matters because it is creative—not the sense in which we say it is "creative" because we feel it matters. The poet is a maker of beliefs—but do not give here to "belief" the first meaning that comes to mind, for it is as true that for other senses of "belief" poetry has nothing to do with them. What does the poet *make* and what does his work *create?* Himself and his world first, and thereby other worlds and other men. He makes through shaping and molding, through giving form. But if we ask what he shapes or molds or gives form to, we must answer with Aristotle that we can say nothing about that which has no form. There are always prior forms upon which the poet works, and how he takes these forms is part of his making. He apprehends them by taking them into forms of more comprehensive order. To the poet as poet, his world is the world, and the world is his world. But the poet is not always poet. All but the greatest poets in the most favorable societies seem to have to pay for being poets. Of recent poets, Yeats has put this best:

> The intellect of man is forced to choose
> Perfection of the life or of the work,
> And if it take the second must refuse
> A heavenly mansion, raging in the dark.
> When all that story's finished, what's the news?
> In luck or out, the toil has left its mark:
> That old perplexity, an empty purse
> Or the day's vanity, the night's remorse.

The work of the poet is the maintenance and enlargement of the human spirit through remaking it under changing circumstances; through molding and remolding the ever-varying flux. The molds are sets of words, interacting in manifold ways within a language. At first sight this old Platonic image of the mold looks crude. What could be less like a mold than a word—which endlessly changes its work with its company as we all may note if we care to look? But the mold metaphor—the dominant metaphor of the Greek invention of education—is there to shock us into thought. The poetic problem is precisely the maintenance of stability *within* minds and correspondence *between* them. It is *not* how to get the flux into molds supposed somehow to be fixed already; but how to recreate perpetually those constancies (as of sets of molds) upon which depend any order, any growth, any development—any changes, in fact, other than the chance-ridden changes of chaos.

It is through the interactions of words within a language that a poet works. In a sense all literary men are inquiring concretely into the detail of this in all their work, but let us try to take a more general and comprehensive view before going on to contrast two types of verbal interactions. If I can show you how I conceive words, the rest will be easier. First I spoke of the *question,* "What is a word?", not of any answer to it, as one of the founding forces, and as thereby poetic. Answers to it of many sorts can be contrived and offered. Linguistics and psychology in their different divisions have many very different answers and the debate between them, as studies aspiring to become sciences (in various senses of "science"), must be a long one. But these answers would answer different questions from my poetic "What is a word?" That question is nourished by awareness of them, but it is not reducible to them. It is not answered by an exhaustive dictionary or encyclopedia article on the word *Word.* That would answer only the set of historical, factual, linguistic, psychological, religious, metaphysical and other questions which I am trying—by these very odd means—to distinguish from the poetic question. With any of these questions, it would be shocking —would it not?—to suggest that its answer is one and the same with itself. But the poetic question has to be its own answer—as virtue is its own reward, to cite the wider rule of which this is an example. As an answer it is aware that it is a bundle of possibilities dependent on other possibilities which in turn it in part determines; as a question it is attempting through its influence on them to become more completely itself. It is growing as a cell grows with other cells. It is a conception. It is being "divided at the joints" and recombined. "Attempting" and "growing" are not metaphors here. A word, a question or its answer, does all that we do, since we do all that in the word. Words are alive as our other acts are alive—though apart from the minds which use them they are nothing but agitations of the air or stains on paper.

A word then by this sort of definition is a permanent set of possibilities of understanding, much as John Stuart Mill's table was a permanent possibility of sensation. And as the sensations the table yields depend on the angle you look from, the other things you see it with, the air, your glasses, your eyes and the light . . . so how a word is understood depends on the other words you hear it with, and the other frames you have heard it in, on the whole setting present and past in which it has developed as a part of your mind. But the interactions of words with one another and with other things are far more complex than can be paralleled from the case of the table—complex enough as those are. Indeed they are not paralleled anywhere except by such things as pictures, music or the expressions of faces which are other modes of language. Language, as understood, is the mind itself at work and these interactions of words are interdependencies of our own being.

I conceive then a word, as poetry is concerned with it, and as separated from the mere physical or sensory occasion, to be a component of an act of the mind so subtly dependent on the other components of this act and of other acts that it can be distinguished from these interactions only as a convenience of discourse. It sounds nonsense to say that a word is its interactions with other words; but that is a short way of saying the thing which Poetics is in most danger always of overlooking. Words only work together. We understand no word except in and through its interactions with other words.

Let me now come down to detail. I invite you to compare two very different types of the interactions of words in poetry: I will read the first twelve lines of Donne's *First Anniversary*.

AN ANATOMY OF THE WORLD
THE FIRST ANNIVERSARY
Wherein

By occasion of the untimely death of Mistress
Elizabeth Drury, the frailty and the decay of
this whole world is represented.

When that rich Soule which to her heaven is gone,
Whom all do celebrate, who know they have one,
(For who is sure he hath a Soule, unlesse

It see, and judge, and follow worthinesse,
And by Deedes praise it? hee who doth not this,
May lodge an In-mate soule, but 'tis not his.)
When that Queene ended her progresse time,

And, as t'her standing house to heaven did climbe,
Where loath to make the Saints attend her long,
She's now a part both of the Quire, and Song,
This world, in that great earthquake languished;
For in a common bath of teares it bled.

Let us compare with that the first stanza of Dryden's

ODE: *To the Pious Memory of the accomplished young*
lady, Mrs. Anne Killigrew, excellent in the two
sister arts of Poesy and Painting

Thou youngest virgin-daughter of the skies,
Made in the last promotion of the blest;
Whose palms, new pluck'd from Paradise,
In spreading branches more sublimely rise,
Rich with immortal green above the rest:
Whether, adopted to some neighboring star,
Thou roll'st above us, in thy wandering race,
Or, in procession fixt and regular,
Mov'd with the heaven's majestic pace;
Or, call'd to more superior bliss,
Thou tread'st with seraphims the vast abyss:
Whatever happy region is thy place,
Cease thy celestial song a little space;
Thou wilt have time enough for hymns divine,
Since Heaven's eternal year is thine.
Hear, then, a mortal Muse thy praise rehearse,
        In no ignoble verse;
But such as thy own voice did practice here,
When thy first-fruits of Poesy were given,
To make thyself a welcome inmate there;
While yet a young probationer,
        And candidate of Heaven.

In the Donne, I suggest, there is a prodigious activity between the words as we read them. Following, exploring, realizing, *becoming* that activity is, I suggest, the essential thing in reading the poem. Understanding it is not a preparation for reading the poem. It is itself the poem. And it is a constructive, hazardous, free creative process, a process of conception through which a new being is growing in the mind. The Dryden, I suggest, is quite otherwise. No doubt there are interactions between the words but they are on a different level. The words are in routine conventional relations like peaceful diplomatic communications between nations. They do not induce revolutions in one another and are not thereby attempting to form a new order. Any mutual adjustments they have to make are preparatory, and they are no important part of the poetic activity. In brief Dryden's poem comes before our minds as a mature creation. But we seem to create Donne's poem.

Donne's poem is called *The First Anniversary* because he wrote it a year after the death of Elizabeth Drury. He was going to write a similar poem every year but only wrote one other. His latest editor, Mr. John Hayward (in the Nonesuch Edition) says this "concluded the series of preposterous eulogies." Whether Mr. Hayward thinks them preposterous, whether they are eulogies, and whether, if we took them as such, they would be preposterous—are questions I leave till later.

Opinion about them has always been mixed. Ben Jonson is reported to have said that "they were prophane and full of blasphemies; that he told Mr. Donne if it had been written of the Virgin Marie it had been something; to which he answered that he described the Idea of a Woman, and not as she was." That is a helpful hint. It points to the Platonism in the poem. But Mr. Hayward comments: "However this may be, the subject of the two poems was a real woman, a child rather, who died in 1610 at the age of fifteen." Two things are worth a word here. Doubtless, in one sense, Elizabeth Drury is the subject; but in a more important sense, the subject of the poem, what it is about, is something which only a good reading will discover. That discovery here is the poetic process. Secondly, when Mr. Hayward says "a child rather," he is being twentieth century, not seventeenth century. A fifteen year old girl was a woman for the seventeenth century. In Donne's poem *Upon the Annunciation and the Passion* he writes of the Virgin Mary:

> Sad and rejoyc'd shee's seen at once, and seen
> At almost fiftie and at scarce fifteene.

For Donne the Annunciation came to Mary when she was "scarce fifteen." Elizabeth's youth is of course no bar—rather the reverse—to Donne's taking her very seriously as a symbol.

Dryden's *Ode* has long been an anthology piece. Dr. Johnson called it "the noblest Ode that our Language produced" and "the richest complex of sounds in our language." A modern critic has called this "a judgment then bold but now scarcely intelligible." There are seventy-five years between the poems.

Now let us consider the lines in detail and especially this question, "How closely should we be examining them in our reading?" I will take Dryden first. You may guess perhaps that even in taking him first here I am expressing a judgment between them.

How near should we come to the *Ode*? The only way to find out is by experimenting. Public declamation—the style of reading which the *Ode* suggests as right—does not invite close attention to the meaning. The façade of a public building is not to be studied with a handglass. Gulliver, you remember, thought nothing of the complexions of the Brobdingnagian ladies. Let us try looking a little closer.

> *Thou youngest virgin-daughter of the skies*

Why "youngest virgin-daughter"? "Youngest" may here mean "new-born"; but then, why *virgin*? New-borns are necessarily virgins. And why, then, "daughter of the skies"? Do we need especially to be reminded that daughters of the skies—in Christian mythology—as denizens of Paradise, are virgins? On earth she was a virgin, it is true. In Heaven, there is neither marriage nor giving in marriage. And there is no special relation to the Virgin. We gain nothing by such ponderings here. Again:

> *Whose palms, new pluck'd from Paradise,*
> *In spreading branches more sublimely rise,*
> *Rich with immortal green above the rest:*

Why *from* Paradise? Has she left it? Why not *in* Paradise? The answer might be in terms of resonance of the line.

But why should these palms of hers *more sublimely* rise? or be "rich with immortal green *above the rest*"? Do Paradisaic palms wilt and fade like florist's goods here on earth? Or does the row of palms get greener and greener, richer and richer, loftier and loftier, as we get further along the line from the first saints?

Clearly these questions and all others of the sort are quite irrelevant and out of place. We are looking too close, looking for a kind of poetic structure, an interaction of the words which is not there and is not needed for the proper purpose of the poem.

The same thing would appear if we questioned similarly Dryden's suggestions about what she is doing and where she is: on a planet, "in thy wandering race" or on a fixed star "in procession fixt and regular."

Or if we wondered whether "the vast abyss" so described seems a *happy* region. Or again if we ask whether she need really stop singing to listen to Dryden. Or again whether Dryden really, for a moment, considers her earthly verses to have been such as his own voice is practicing here? Of course, he doesn't. Or again, if we ask whether her *verses* could possibly make her welcome *in Paradise?* Or if they would advance her as a "candidate for heaven"? Or lastly if we asked why she is called an "inmate"? We shall see later that the same word in the Donne is packed with implications.

The outcome of all such close questioning is the same. Dryden's words have no such implications and we shall be misreading him if we hunt for them. In brief, this is not a poetry of Wit—in the technical sense of the word in which Donne's verses are, as Coleridge called them,

> Wit's fire and fireblast, meaning's press and screw.

On this question of wit, let us listen to Dr. Johnson a moment. He is talking about conversation and has been comparing styles of conversation with beverages. He says,

"Spirit alone is too powerful to use. It will produce madness rather than merriment; and instead of quenching thirst, will inflame the blood. Thus wit, too copiously poured out, agitates the hearer with emotions rather violent than pleasing; everyone shrinks from the force of its oppression, the company sits entranced and overpowered; all are astonished, but nobody is pleased." One might retort, "Please, why should we please?" Or, when he says, "It will produce madness rather than merriment," we might recall the link between poetry and madness that has been noted from Plato's time to Shakespeare's. Dr. Johnson had deep personal reasons for distrusting this connection. He would have replied that he was talking about conversation, social intercourse. "Instead of quenching thirst," he says, "wit will inflame the blood." Quenching thirst? "Do you converse, Sir, in order to have had enough of it?" But Dr. Johnson's prose here no more requires us to pursue such implications and interactions than Dryden's verses.

Turn now to the Donne. Let us see what minute reading brings out of that.

> *When that rich Soule which to her heaven is gone,*

rich: in two senses—possessing much (a rich man); giving much (a rich mine). Compare Coleridge:

> Oh lady, we receive but what we give
> And in our life alone does Nature live.

or Croce: "Intuition is Expression": we *have* only that which we can give out.

her heaven: again the double force; she possesses it and it possesses her, as with "her country," or "her place."

Whom all do celebrate, who know they have one;

celebrate: a new word then in the sense of "praise, extol, or publish the fame of." This would be its first occurrence in that sense. Prior to 1611 it means "commemorate or perform publicly and in due form (with a ritual—as in a celebration of the Eucharist) or solemnize." There is a very serious suggestion of participation or partaking or ritual imitation. Thus, all who know they have a soul partake of that rich Soule, in knowing that (i.e., in having a soul). Then follows Donne's gloss:

> *For who is sure he hath a Soule, unlesse*
> *It see, and judge, and follow worthiness;*

sure is more than "confident, without doubts about it"; it means "safe, firm, immovable," because seeing, judging and following worthiness are themselves the very possession of a soul, not merely signs of having one. To see and judge and follow worthiness is to have a soul.

worthiness: excellence in the highest of all senses. That use was going out in Donne's time (1617).

And by Deedes praise it

No verbal praise, but imitation of or participation in actual works;

> *hee who doth not this,*
> *May lodge an In-mate soule, but 'tis not his.*

in-mate: a word of very ill suggestions. We keep some of them in "an inmate of a penitentiary or an asylum." For Donne it suggests a lodger or a foreigner. Compare Milton:

> So spake the Enemie of Mankind, enclos'd
> In Serpent, Inmate bad, [*P.L.* ix, 495]

Who does not see and follow worthiness hasn't a soul but is possessed by something not truly him.

And so often with Donne, what seems a most farfetched conceit is no more than the result of taking a commonplace of language seriously. We say daily that a man is "not himself" or "beside himself" or "not his true self," and we do the same thing when we say he is "alienated" or call a psychopathologist an "alienist." Donne is just expanding such expressions, making their implications explicit, increasing their interaction, as heat increases chemical interaction. That is the technique of most "metaphysical poetry."

> *When that Queene ended here her progresse time,*
> *And, as t' her standing house to heaven did climbe,*

Here Donne's metaphor takes seriously the doctrine of the Divinity of Kings. The Ruler is to the body politic as the soul is to the body. Sickness or departure of the Ruler is sickness or death to the state. In fact he is just reversing the metaphor which created the doctrine of Divine Right. He adds a pun. A Queen made royal progresses through her dominions so that her subjects might come together and realize themselves as a State in her. But the soul, as in Bunyan, also makes a pilgrim's progress. Her "standing house" is where she *rests* at the end of her progress. Compare Augustine: "Thou has made us for Thyself and our souls are restless until they find their rest in Thee."

> *Where loath to make the Saints attend her long,*
> *She's now a part both of the Quire, and Song,*

A soul so conceived need not delay in joining the company of the Saints. *Quire:* How deep we could take this word you can see from Ruskin's note in *Munera Pulveris*. But the main point of the line is that the Soul becomes both a singer and the song. That goes to the heart of Aristotelianism—where the Divine thinking is one with the object of its thought. (*Metaphysics* 1075 a). It is itself that thought (or intellect) thinks, on account of its participation in the object of thought: for it becomes its own object in the act of apprehending it: so that thought (intellect) and what is thought of are one and the same. We come back here to our founding questions where the distinction between matter and activity vanishes—as it does for the modern physicist when his ultimate particles become merely what they do.

But to elucidate Donne's line it is better perhaps just to quote another poet: from the last verse of W. B. Yeats's "Among School Children" in *The Tower.*

O Chestnut tree, great rooted blossomer
Are you the leaf, the blossom or the bole?
O body swayed to music, O brightening glance,
How can we know the dancer from the dance?

or this from T. S. Eliot's *Burnt Norton:*

At the still point of the turning world . . . at the still point,
    there the dance is,
But neither arrest nor movement. And do not call it fixity . . .
                    Except for the point, the still point,
There would be no dance, and there is only the dance.

Donne's next line contains the word upon which, with the word
Soule—as on two poles—the entire interpretation of this poem turns, as
for that matter all philosophy must, the word *world.*

.   *This world, in that great earthquake languished;*

world: not of course this planet, the earth, but this present life as opposed to the other, the realm of departed spirits. Or more narrowly
"the pursuits and interests of the earthly life," as the *Oxford Dictionary*
puts it, with the note, "especially in religious use, the least worthy of
these." Donne was extremely fond of playing with the word "world."
It is one of the chief of his wonder workers. Compare *A Valediction
of Weeping:*

    On a round ball
A workman that hath copies by, can lay
An Europe, Afrique, and an Asia,
And quickly make that which was nothing, All,
        So doth each teare,
        Which thee doth weare,
A globe, yea world by that impression grow,
Till thy tears mixt with mine doe overflow
This world, by waters sent from thee, my heaven dissolved so.

That is metaphysical metaphor at its height. Philosophically it is
the age-old recognition that, as Blake put it, "The eye altering, alters
all." Donne, of course, plays throughout his poem on shifts between
the private solipsistic world and the general public world of mundane
interests. It is his general theme that both these worlds die, corrupt
and disintegrate in the absence of the Soule—as defined in the paren-
thesis of lines 3 to 6.

Is this extravagance? Is the poem a "preposterous eulogy"? Is it
not rather that Donne is saying something which if said in our every-

day style would seem so commonplace that we would not notice what we were saying? If so, what was he saying? To put it with our usual crude and unilluminating briefness, he was saying that Elizabeth Drury was an example, an inspiration, and would have been to all who knew her. That looks little enough to say, *if so said*. It took a Donne to expand the implications of those two words "example" and "inspiration" into the poem. But the more we look into the poem, the more we will discover that the understanding of those two words is an understanding of the whole Platonic Aristotelian account of the fabric of things. These words take their meaning, by participation, directly from the founding questions. The best witness will be the closing lines of *The Second Anniversary*:

>   nor would'st thou be content,
> To take this, for my second yeares true Rent,
> Did this Coine beare any other stampe, than his,
> That gave thee power to doe, me, to say this.
> Since his will is, that to posteritie,
> Thou should'st for life, and death, a patterne bee,
> And that the world should notice have of this:
> The purpose, and th'authoritie is his;
> Thou art the Proclamation; and I am
> The Trumpet, at whose voyce the people came.

To read the poem rightly would be to hear and come.

Art and Neurosis

Lionel Trilling

The question of the mental health of the artist has engaged the
attention of our culture since the beginning of the Romantic Movement. Before that time it was commonly said that the poet was "mad,"
but this was only a manner of speaking, a way of saying that the mind
of the poet worked in different fashion from the mind of the philosopher; it had no real reference to the mental hygiene of the man who
was the poet. But in the early nineteenth century, with the development of a more elaborate psychology and a stricter and more literal
view of mental and emotional normality, the statement was more
strictly and literally intended. So much so, indeed, that Charles Lamb,
who knew something about madness at close quarters and a great
deal about art, undertook to refute in his brilliant essay, "On the
Sanity of True Genius," the idea that the exercise of the imagination
was a kind of insanity. And some eighty years later, the idea having
yet further entrenched itself, Bernard Shaw felt called upon to argue
the sanity of art, but his cogency was of no more avail than Lamb's.
In recent years the connection between art and mental illness has been
formulated not only by those who are openly or covertly hostile to art,
but also and more significantly by those who are most intensely partisan to it. The latter willingly and even eagerly accept the idea that
the artist is mentally ill and go on to make his illness a condition of his
power to tell the truth.

This conception of artistic genius is indeed one of the characteristic
notions of our culture. I should like to bring it into question. To do
so is to bring also into question certain early ideas of Freud's and cer-

tain conclusions which literary laymen have drawn from the whole
tendency of the Freudian psychology. From the very start it was recognized that psychoanalysis was likely to have important things to say
about art and artists. Freud himself thought so, yet when he first addressed himself to the subject he said many clumsy and misleading
things. I have elsewhere and at length tried to separate the useful from
the useless and even dangerous statements about art that Freud has
made.[1] To put it briefly here, Freud had some illuminating and even
beautiful insights into certain particular works of art which made complex use of the element of myth. Then, without specifically undertaking
to do so, his "Beyond the Pleasure Principle" offers a brilliant and
comprehensive explanation of our interest in tragedy. And what is of
course most important of all—it is a point to which I shall return—
Freud, by the whole tendency of his psychology, establishes the *naturalness* of artistic thought. Indeed, it is possible to say of Freud that he
ultimately did more for our understanding of art than any other writer
since Aristotle; and this being so, it can only be surprising that in his
early work he should have made the error of treating the artist as a
neurotic who escapes from reality by means of "substitute gratifica-
tions."

As Freud went forward he insisted less on this simple formulation.
Certainly it did not have its original force with him when, at his
seventieth birthday celebration, he disclaimed the right to be called the
discoverer of the unconscious, saying that whatever he may have done
for the systematic understanding of the unconscious, the credit for its
discovery properly belonged to the literary masters. And psychoanalysis
has inherited from him a tenderness for art which is real although
sometimes clumsy, and nowadays most psychoanalysts of any personal
sensitivity are embarrassed by occasions which seem to lead them to reduce art to a formula of mental illness. Nevertheless Freud's early belief
in the essential neuroticism of the artist found an all too fertile ground
—found, we might say, the very ground from which it first sprang, for,
when he spoke of the artist as a neurotic, Freud was adopting one of
the popular beliefs of his age. Most readers will see this belief as the
expression of the industrial rationalization and the bourgeois philistinism of the nineteenth century. In this they are partly right. The nineteenth century established the basic virtue of "getting up at eight, shav-
ing close at a quarter-past, breakfasting at nine, going to the City at

[1] See "Freud and Literature."

ten, coming home at half-past five, and dining at seven." The Messrs. Podsnap who instituted this scheduled morality inevitably decreed that the arts must celebrate it and nothing else. "Nothing else to be permitted to these . . . vagrants the Arts, on pain of excommunication. Nothing else To Be—anywhere!" We observe that the virtuous day ends with dinner—bed and sleep are naturally not part of the Reality that Is, and nothing must be set forth which will, as Mr. Podsnap put it, bring a Blush to the Cheek of a Young Person.

The excommunication of the arts, when it was found necessary, took the form of pronouncing the artist mentally degenerate, a device which eventually found its theorist in Max Nordau. In the history of the arts this is new. The poet was always known to belong to a touchy tribe—*genus irritabile* was a tag anyone would know—and ever since Plato the process of the inspired imagination, as we have said, was thought to be a special one of some interest, which the similitude of madness made somewhat intelligible. But this is not quite to say that the poet was the victim of actual mental aberration. The eighteenth century did not find the poet to be less than other men, and certainly the Renaissance did not. If he was a professional, there might be condescension to his social status, but in a time which deplored all professionalism whatever, this was simply a way of asserting the high value of poetry, which ought not to be compromised by trade. And a certain good nature marked even the snubbing of the professional. At any rate, no one was likely to identify the poet with the weakling. Indeed, the Renaissance ideal held poetry to be, like arms or music, one of the signs of manly competence.

The change from this view of things cannot be blamed wholly on the bourgeois or philistine public. Some of the "blame" must rest with the poets themselves. The Romantic poets were as proud of their art as the vaunting poets of the sixteenth century, but one of them talked with an angel in a tree and insisted that Hell was better than Heaven and sexuality holier than chastity; another told the world that he wanted to lie down like a tired child and weep away this life of care; another asked so foolish a question as "Why did I laugh tonight?"; and yet another explained that he had written one of his best poems in a drugged sleep. The public took them all at their word—they were not as other men. Zola, in the interests of science, submitted himself to examination by fifteen psychiatrists and agreed with their conclusion that his genius had its source in the neurotic elements of his tempera-

ment. Baudelaire, Rimbaud, Verlaine found virtue and strength in
their physical and mental illness and pain. W. H. Auden addresses his
"wound" in the cherishing language of a lover, thanking it for the gift
of insight it has bestowed. "Knowing you," he says, "has made me
understand." And Edmund Wilson in his striking phrase, "the wound
and the bow," has formulated for our time the idea of the characteristic sickness of the artist, which he represents by the figure of Philoctetes, the Greek warrior who was forced to live in isolation because of
the disgusting odor of a suppurating wound and who yet had to be
sought out by his countrymen because they had need of the magically
unerring bow he possessed.

The myth of the sick artist, we may suppose, has established itself
because it is of advantage to the various groups who have one or
another relation with art. To the artist himself the myth gives some
of the ancient powers and privileges of the idiot and the fool, half-
prophetic creatures, or of the mutilated priest. That the artist's neurosis
may be but a mask is suggested by Thomas Mann's pleasure in representing his untried youth as "sick" but his successful maturity as sena-
torially robust. By means of his belief in his own sickness, the artist
may the more easily fulfill his chosen, and assigned, function of putting
himself into connection with the forces of spirituality and morality; the
artist sees as insane the "normal" and "healthy" ways of established
society, while aberration and illness appear as spiritual and moral
health if only because they controvert the ways of respectable society.

Then too, the myth has its advantage for the philistine—a double
advantage. On the one hand, the belief in the artist's neuroticism allows
the philistine to shut his ears to what the artist says. But on the other
hand it allows him to listen. For we must not make the common mistake—the contemporary philistine does want to listen, at the same time
that he wants to shut his ears. By supposing that the artist has an
interesting but not always reliable relation to reality, he is able to contain (in the military sense) what the artist tells him. If he did not
want to listen at all, he would say "insane"; with "neurotic," which
hedges, he listens when he chooses.

And in addition to its advantage to the artist and to the philistine,
we must take into account the usefulness of the myth to a third group,
the group of "sensitive" people, who, although not artists, are not
philistines either. These people form a group by virtue of their passive
impatience with philistinism, and also by virtue of their awareness of

their own emotional pain and uncertainty. To these people the myth of the sick artist is the institutional sanction of their situation; they seek to approximate or acquire the character of the artist, sometimes by planning to work or even attempting to work as the artist does, always by making a connection between their own powers of mind and their consciousness of "difference" and neurotic illness.

The early attempts of psychoanalysis to deal with art went on the assumption that, because the artist was neurotic, the content of his work was also neurotic, which is to say that it did not stand in a correct relation to reality. But nowadays, as I have said, psychoanalysis is not likely to be so simple in its transactions with art. A good example of the psychoanalytical development in this respect is Dr. Saul Rosenzweig's well-known essay, "The Ghost of Henry James." [2] This is an admirable piece of work, marked by accuracy in the reporting of the literary fact and by respect for the value of the literary object. Although Dr. Rosenzweig explores the element of neurosis in James's life and work, he nowhere suggests that this element in any way lessens James's value as an artist or moralist. In effect he says that neurosis is a way of dealing with reality which, in real life, is uncomfortable and uneconomical, but that this judgment of neurosis in life cannot mechanically be transferred to works of art upon which neurosis has had its influence. He nowhere implies that a work of art in whose genesis a neurotic element may be found is for that reason irrelevant or in any way diminished in value. Indeed, the manner of his treatment suggests, what is of course the case, that every neurosis deals with a real emotional situation of the most intensely meaningful kind.

Yet as Dr. Rosenzweig brings his essay to its close, he makes use of the current assumption about the causal connection between the psychic illness of the artist and his power. His investigation of James, he says, "reveals the aptness of the Philoctetes pattern." He accepts the idea of "the sacrificial roots of literary power" and speaks of "the unhappy sources of James's genius." "The broader application of the inherent pattern," he says, "is familiar to readers of Edmund Wilson's recent volume *The Wound and the Bow*. . . . Reviewing the experience and work of several well-known literary masters, Wilson discloses the sacrificial roots of their power on the model of the Greek

<hr>

[2] First published in *Character and Personality*, December, 1943, and reprinted in *Partisan Review*, Fall, 1944.

legend. In the case of Henry James, the present account . . . provides a similar insight into the unhappy sources of his genius. . . ."

This comes as a surprise. Nothing in Dr. Rosenzweig's theory requires it. For his theory asserts no more than that Henry James, predisposed by temperament and family situation to certain mental and emotional qualities, was in his youth injured in a way which he believed to be sexual; that he unconsciously invited the injury in the wish to identify himself with his father, who himself had been similarly injured—"castrated": a leg had been amputated—and under strikingly similar circumstances; this resulted for the younger Henry James in a certain pattern of life and in a preoccupation in his work with certain themes which more or less obscurely symbolize his sexual situation. For this I think Dr. Rosenzweig makes a sound case. Yet I submit that this is not the same thing as disclosing the roots of James's power or discovering the sources of his genius. The essay which gives Edmund Wilson's book its title and cohering principle does not explicitly say that the roots of power are sacrificial and that the source of genius is unhappy. Where it is explicit, it states only that "genius and disease, like strength and mutilation, may be inextricably bound up together," which of course, on its face, says no more than that personality is integral and not made up of detachable parts; and from this there is no doubt to be drawn the important practical and moral implication that we cannot judge or dismiss a man's genius and strength because of our awareness of his disease or mutilation. The Philoctetes legend in itself does not suggest anything beyond this. It does not suggest that the wound is the price of the bow, or that without the wound the bow may not be possessed or drawn. Yet Dr. Rosenzweig has accurately summarized the force and, I think, the intention of Mr. Wilson's whole book; its several studies do seem to say that effectiveness in the arts does depend on sickness.

An examination of this prevalent idea might well begin with the observation of how pervasive and deeply rooted is the notion that power may be gained by suffering. Even at relatively high stages of culture the mind seems to take easily to the primitive belief that pain and sacrifice are connected with strength. Primitive beliefs must be treated with respectful alertness to their possible truth and also with the suspicion of their being magical and irrational, and it is worth noting on both sides of the question, and in the light of what we have said about the ambiguous relation of the neurosis to reality, that the whole economy of the neurosis is based exactly on this idea of the *quid pro quo* of sacrificial pain: the neurotic person unconsciously subscribes to a system whereby he gives up some pleasure or power, or inflicts pain on himself in order to secure some other power or some other pleasure.

In the ingrained popular conception of the relation between suffering and power there are actually two distinct although related ideas. One is that there exists in the individual a fund of power which has outlets through various organs or faculties, and that if its outlet through one organ or faculty be prevented, it will flow to increase the force or sensitivity of another. Thus it is popularly believed that the sense of touch is intensified in the blind not so much by the will of the blind person to adapt himself to the necessities of his situation as, rather, by a sort of mechanical redistribution of power. And this idea would seem to explain, if not the origin of the ancient mutilation of priests, then at least a common understanding of their sexual sacrifice.

The other idea is that a person may be taught by, or proved by, the endurance of pain. There will easily come to mind the ritual suffering that is inflicted at the tribal initiation of youths into full manhood or at the admission of the apprentice into the company of journeyman adepts. This idea in sophisticated form found its way into high religion at least as early as Aeschylus, who held that man achieves knowledge of God through suffering, and it was from the beginning an important element of Christian thought. In the nineteenth century the Christianized notion of the didactic suffering of the artist went along with the idea of his mental degeneration and even served as a sort of countermyth to it. Its doctrine was that the artist, a man of strength and health, experienced and suffered, and thus learned both the facts of life and his artistic craft. "I am the man, I suffered, I was there," ran his boast, and he derived his authority from the knowledge gained through suffering.

There can be no doubt that both these ideas represent a measure of truth about mental and emotional power. The idea of didactic suffering expresses a valuation of experience and of steadfastness. The idea of natural compensation for the sacrifice of some faculty also says something that can be rationally defended: one cannot be and do everything and the wholehearted absorption in any enterprise, art for example, means that we must give up other possibilities, even parts of ourselves. And there is even a certain validity to the belief that the individual has a fund of undifferentiated energy which presses the harder upon what outlets are available to it when it has been deprived of the normal number.

Then, in further defense of the belief that artistic power is connected with neurosis, we can say that there is no doubt that what we call mental illness may be the source of psychic knowledge. Some neurotic people, because they are more apprehensive than normal people, are able to see more of certain parts of reality and to see them with more intensity. And many neurotic or psychotic patients are in certain respects in closer touch with the actualities of the unconscious than are normal people. Further, the expression of a neurotic or psychotic conception of reality is likely to be more intense than a normal one.

Yet when we have said all this, it is still wrong, I believe, to find the root of the artist's power and the source of his genius in neurosis. To the idea that literary power and genius spring from pain and neurotic sacrifice there are two major objections. The first has to do with the assumed uniqueness of the artist as a subject of psychoanalytical explanation. The second has to do with the true meaning of power and genius.

One reason why writers are considered to be more available than other people to psychoanalytical explanation is that they tell us what is going on inside them. Even when they do not make an actual diagnosis of their malaises or describe "symptoms," we must bear it in mind that it is their profession to deal with fantasy in some form or other. It is in the nature of the writer's job that he exhibit his unconscious. He may disguise it in various ways, but disguise is not concealment. Indeed, it may be said that the more a writer takes pains with his work to remove it from the personal and subjective, the more—and not the less—he will express his true unconscious, although not what passes with most for the unconscious.

Further, the writer is likely to be a great hand at personal letters, diaries, and autobiographies: indeed, almost the only good autobiographies are those of writers. The writer is more aware of what happens to him or goes on in him and often finds it necessary or useful to be articulate about his inner states, and prides himself on telling the truth. Thus, only a man as devoted to the truth of the emotions as Henry James was would have informed the world, despite his characteristic reticence, of an accident so intimate as his. We must not of course suppose that a writer's statements about his intimate life are equivalent to true statements about his unconscious, which, by definition, he doesn't consciously know; but they may be useful clues to the nature of an entity about which we can make statements of more or less cogency, although never statements of certainty; or they at least give us what is surely related to a knowledge of his unconscious—that is, an insight into his personality.[3]

But while the validity of dealing with the writer's intellectual life in psychoanalytical terms is taken for granted, the psychoanalytical explanation of the intellectual life of scientists is generally speaking not countenanced. The old myth of the mad scientist, with the exception of an occasional mad psychiatrist, no longer exists. The social position of science requires that it should cease, which leads us to remark that those partisans of art who insist on explaining artistic genius by means of psychic imbalance are in effect capitulating to the dominant mores which hold that the members of the respectable professions are, however dull they may be, free from neurosis. Scientists, to continue with them as the best example of the respectable professions, do not usually give us the clues to their personalities which writers habitually give. But no one who has ever lived observantly among scientists will claim that they are without an unconscious or even that they are free from neurosis. How often, indeed, it is apparent that the devotion to science, if it cannot be called a neurotic manifestation, at least can be understood as going very cozily with neurotic elements in the temperament, such as, for example, a marked compulsiveness. Of scientists as a group we can say that they are less concerned with the manifestations of personality, their own or others', than are writers as a group. But this relative indifference is scarcely a sign of normality—indeed, if we choose to regard it with the same sort of eye with which the characteristics of writers are regarded, we might say the indifference to matters of personality is in itself a suspicious evasion.

[3] I am by no means in agreement with the statements of Dr. Edmund Bergler about "the" psychology of the writer, but I think that Dr. Bergler has done good service in warning us against taking at their face value a writer's statements about himself, the more especially when they are "frank." Thus, to take Dr. Bergler's notable example, it is usual for biographers to accept Stendhal's statements about his open sexual feelings for his mother when he was a little boy, feelings which went with an intense hatred of his father. But Dr. Bergler believes that Stendhal unconsciously used his consciousness of his love of his mother and of his hatred of his father to mask an unconscious love of his father, which frightened him. ("Psychoanalysis of Writers and of Literary Productivity" in *Psychoanalysis and the Social Sciences*, vol. 1.)

It is the basic assumption of psychoanalysis that the acts of *every* person are influenced by the forces of the unconscious. Scientists, bankers, lawyers, or surgeons, by reason of the traditions of their professions, practice concealment and conformity; but it is difficult to believe that an investigation according to psychoanalytical principles would fail to show that the strains and imbalances of their psyches are not of the same frequency as those of writers, and of similar kind. I do not mean that everybody has the same troubles and identical psyches, but only that there is no special category for writers.[4]

If this is so, and if we still want to relate the writer's power to his neurosis, we must be willing to relate all intellectual power to neurosis. We must find the roots of Newton's power in his emotional extravagances, and the roots of Darwin's power in his sorely neurotic temperament, and the roots of Pascal's mathematical genius in the impulses which drove him to extreme religious masochism—I choose but the classic examples. If we make the neurosis-power equivalence at all, we must make it in every field of endeavor. Logician, economist, botanist, physicist, theologian—no profession may be so respectable or so remote or so rational as to be exempt from the psychological interpretations.[5]

[4] Dr. Bergler believes that there is a particular neurosis of writers, based on an oral masochism which makes them the enemy of the respectable world, courting poverty and persecution. But a later development of Dr. Bergler's theory of oral masochism makes it *the* basic neurosis, not only of writers but of everyone who is neurotic.

[5] In his interesting essay, "Writers and Madness" (*Partisan Review*, January-February, 1947), William Barrett has taken issue with this point and has insisted that a clear distinction is to be made between the relation that exists between the scientist and his work and the relation that exists between the artist and his work. The difference, as I understand it, is in the claims of the ego. The artist's ego makes a claim upon the world which is personal in a way that the scientist's is not, for the scientist, although he does indeed want prestige and thus "responds to one of the deepest urges of his ego, it is only that his prestige may come to attend his person through the public world of other men; and it is not in the end his own being that is exhibited or his own voice that is heard in the learned report to the Academy." Actually, however, as is suggested by the sense which mathematicians have of the *style* of mathematical thought, the creation of the abstract thinker is as deeply involved as the artist's —see *An Essay on the Psychology of Invention in the Mathematical Field* by Jacques Hadamard, Princeton University Press, 1945—and he quite as much as the artist seeks to impose *himself*, to *express* himself. I am of course not maintaining that the processes of scientific thought are the same as those of artistic thought, or even that the scientist's creation is involved with his total personality *in the same way* that the artist's is—I am maintaining only that the scientist's creation is as *deeply* implicated with his total personality as is the artist's.

This point of view seems to be supported by Freud's monograph on

Further, not only power but also failure or limitation must be accounted for by the theory of neurosis, and not merely failure or limitation in life but even failure or limitation in art. Thus it is often said that the warp of Dostoevsky's mind accounts for the brilliance of his psychological insights. But it is never said that the same warp of Dostoevsky's mind also accounted for his deficiency in insight. Freud, who greatly admired Dostoevsky, although he did not like him, observed that "his insight was entirely restricted to the workings of the abnormal psyche. Consider his astounding helplessness before the phenomenon of love; he really only understands either crude, instinctive desire or masochistic submission or love from pity." [6] This, we must note, is Freud's comment not merely on the extent of the province which Dostoevsky chose for his own, but on his failure to understand what, given the province of his choice, he might be expected to understand.

And since neurosis can account not only for intellectual success and for failure or limitation but also for mediocrity, we have most of society involved in neurosis. To this I have no objection—I think most of society is indeed involved in neurosis. But with neurosis accounting for so much, it cannot be made exclusively to account for one man's literary power.

We have now to consider what is meant by genius when its source is identified as the sacrifice and pain of neurosis.

In the case of Henry James, the reference to the neurosis of his personal life does indeed tell us something about the latent intention of his work and thus about the reason for some large part of its interest for us. But if genius and its source are what we are dealing with, we must observe that the reference to neurosis tells us nothing about James's passion, energy, and devotion, nothing about his architectonic

---

Leonardo. One of the problems that Freud sets himself is to discover why an artist of the highest endowment should have devoted himself more and more to scientific investigation, with the result that he was unable to complete his artistic enterprises. The particular reasons for this that Freud assigns need not be gone into here; all that I wish to suggest is that Freud understands these reasons to be the working out of an inner conflict, the attempt to deal with the difficulties that have their roots in the most primitive situations. Leonardo's scientific investigations were as necessary and "compelled" and they constituted as much of a claim on the whole personality as anything the artist undertakes; and so far from being carried out for the sake of public prestige, they were largely private and personal, and were thought by the public of his time to be something very like insanity.

[6] From a letter quoted in Theodor Reik's *From Thirty Years With Freud*, p. 175.

skill, nothing about the other themes that were important to him which are not connected with his unconscious concern with castration. We cannot, that is, make the writer's inner life exactly equivalent to his power of expressing it. Let us grant for the sake of argument that the literary genius, as distinguished from other men, is the victim of a "mutilation" and that his fantasies are neurotic.[7] It does not then follow as the inevitable next step that his ability to express these fantasies and to impress us with them is neurotic, for that ability is what we mean by his genius. Anyone might be injured as Henry James was, and even respond within himself to the injury as James is said to have done, and yet not have his literary power.

The reference to the artist's neurosis tells us something about the material on which the artist exercises his powers, and even something about his reasons for bringing his powers into play, but it does not tell us anything about the source of his power, it makes no causal connection between them and the neurosis. And if we look into the matter, we see that there is in fact no causal connection between them. For, still granting that the poet is uniquely neurotic, what is surely not neurotic, what indeed suggests nothing but health, is his power of using his neuroticism. He shapes his fantasies, he gives them social form and reference. Charles Lamb's way of putting this cannot be improved. Lamb is denying that genius is allied to insanity; for "insanity" the modern reader may substitute "neurosis." "The ground of the mistake," he says, "is, that men, finding in the raptures of the higher poetry a condition of exaltation, to which they have no parallel in their own experience, besides the spurious resemblance of it in dreams and fevers, impute a state of dreaminess and fever to the poet. But the true poet dreams being awake. He is not possessed by his subject but has dominion over it. . . . Where he seems most to recede from humanity, he will be found the truest to it. From beyond the scope of nature if he summon possible existences, he subjugates them to the law of her consistency. He is beautifully loyal to that sovereign directress, when he appears most to betray and desert her. . . . Herein the great and the little wits are differenced; that if the latter wander ever so little from

---

[7] I am using the word *fantasy*, unless modified, in a neutral sense. A fantasy, in this sense, may be distinguished from the representation of something that actually exists, but it is not opposed to "reality" and not an "escape" from reality. Thus the idea of a rational society, or the image of a good house to be built, as well as the story of something that could never really happen, is a fantasy. There may be neurotic or non-neurotic fantasies.

nature or natural existence, they lose themselves and their readers. . . . They do not create, which implies shaping and consistency. Their imaginations are not active—for to be active is to call something into act and form—but passive as men in sick dreams."

The activity of the artist, we must remember, may be approximated by many who are themselves not artists. Thus, the expressions of many schizophrenic people have the intense appearance of creativity and an inescapable interest and significance. But they are not works of art, and although Van Gogh may have been schizophrenic he was in addition an artist. Again, as I have already suggested, it is not uncommon in our society for certain kinds of neurotic people to imitate the artist in his life and even in his ideals and ambitions. They follow the artist in everything except successful performance. It was, I think, Otto Rank who called such people half-artists and confirmed the diagnosis of their neuroticism at the same time that he differentiated them from true artists.

Nothing is so characteristic of the artist as his power of shaping his work, of subjugating his raw material, however aberrant it be from what we call normality, to the consistency of nature. It would be impossible to deny that whatever disease or mutilation the artist may suffer is an element of his production which has its effect on every part of it, but disease and mutilation are available to us all—life provides them with prodigal generosity. What marks the artist is his power to shape the material of pain we all have.

At this point, with our recognition of life's abundant provision of pain, we are at the very heart of our matter, which is the meaning we may assign to neurosis and the relation we are to suppose it to have with normality. Here Freud himself can be of help, although it must be admitted that what he tells us may at first seem somewhat contradictory and confusing.

Freud's study of Leonardo da Vinci is an attempt to understand why Leonardo was unable to pursue his artistic enterprises, feeling compelled instead to advance his scientific investigations. The cause of this Freud traces back to certain childhood experiences not different in kind from the experiences which Dr. Rosenzweig adduces to account for certain elements in the work of Henry James. And when he has completed his study Freud makes this *caveat:* "Let us expressly emphasize that we have never considered Leonardo as a neurotic. . . . We no longer believe that health and disease, normal and nervous, are sharply distinguished from each other. We know today that neurotic symptoms are substitutive formations for certain repressive acts which must result in the course of our development from the child to the cultural man, that we all produce such substitutive formations, and that only the amount, intensity, and distribution of these substitutive formations justify the practical conception of illness. . . ." The statement becomes the more striking when we remember that in the course of his study Freud has had occasion to observe that Leonardo was both homosexual and sexually inactive. I am not sure that the statement that Leonardo was not a neurotic is one that Freud would have made at every point in the later development of psychoanalysis, yet it is in conformity with his continuing notion of the genesis of culture. And the *practical,* the quantitative or economic, conception of illness he insists on in a passage in the *Introductory Lectures.* "The neurotic symptoms," he says, ". . . are activities which are detrimental, or at least useless, to life as a whole; the person concerned frequently complains of them as obnoxious to him or they involve suffering and distress for him. The principal injury they inflict lies in the expense of energy they entail, and, besides this, in the energy needed to combat them. Where the symptoms are extensively developed, these two kinds of effort may exact such a price that the person suffers a very serious impoverishment in available mental energy which consequently disables him for all the important tasks of life. This result depends principally upon the amount of energy taken up in this way; therefore you will see that 'illness' is essentially a practical conception. But if you look at the matter from a theoretical point of view and ignore this question of degree, you can very well see that we are all ill, i.e., neurotic; for the conditions required for symptom-formation are demonstrable also in normal persons."

We are all ill: the statement is grandiose, and its implications— the implications, that is, of understanding the totality of human nature in the terms of disease—are vast. These implications have never been properly met (although I believe that a few theologians have responded to them), but this is not the place to attempt to meet them. I have brought forward Freud's statement of the essential sickness of the psyche only because it stands as the refutation of what is implied by the literary use of the theory of neurosis to account for genius. For if we are all ill, and if, as I have said, neurosis can account for everything, for failure and mediocrity—"a very serious impoverishment of available mental energy"—as well as for genius, it cannot uniquely account for genius.

This, however, is not to say that there is no connection between neurosis and genius, which would be tantamount, as we see, to saying that there is no connection between human nature and genius. But the connection lies wholly in a particular and special relation which the artist has to neurosis.

In order to understand what this particular and special connection is we must have clearly in mind what neurosis is. The current literary conception of neurosis as a *wound* is quite misleading. It inevitably suggests passivity, whereas, if we follow Freud, we must understand a neurosis to be an *activity,* an activity with a purpose, and a particular kind of activity, a *conflict.* This is not to say that there are no abnormal mental states which are not conflicts. There are; the struggle between elements of the unconscious may never be instituted in the first place, or it may be called off. As Freud says in a passage which follows close upon the one I last quoted, "If regressions do not call forth a prohibition on the part of the ego, no neurosis results; the libido succeeds in obtaining a real, although not a normal, satisfaction. But if the ego . . . is not in agreement with these regressions, conflict ensues." And in his essay on Dostoevsky Freud says that "there are no neurotic complete masochists," by which he means that the ego which gives way completely to masochism (or to any other pathological excess) has passed beyond neurosis; the conflict has ceased, but at the cost of the defeat of the ego, and now some other name than that of neurosis must be given to the condition of the person who thus takes himself beyond the pain of the neurotic conflict. To understand this is to become aware of the curious complacency with which literary men regard mental disease. The psyche of the neurotic is not equally complacent; it regards with the greatest fear the chaotic and destructive forces it contains, and it struggles fiercely to keep them at bay.[8]

[8] In the article to which I refer in the note on page 103, William Barrett says that he prefers the old-fashioned term "madness" to "neurosis." But it is not quite for him to choose—the words do not differ in fashion but in meaning. Most literary people, when they speak of mental illness, refer to neurosis. Perhaps one reason for this is that the neurosis is the most benign of the mental ills. Another reason is surely that psychoanalytical literature deals chiefly with the neurosis, and its symptomatology and therapy have become familiar; psychoanalysis has far less to say about psychosis, for which it can offer far less therapeutic hope. Further, the neurosis is easily put into a causal connection

We come then to a remarkable paradox: we are all ill, but we are ill in the service of health, or ill in the service of life, or, at the very least, ill in the service of life-in-culture. The form of the mind's dynamics is that of the neurosis, which is to be understood as the ego's struggle against being overcome by the forces with which it coexists, and the strategy of this conflict requires that the ego shall incur pain and make sacrifices of itself, at the same time seeing to it that its pain and sacrifice be as small as they may.

But this is characteristic of all minds: no mind is exempt except those which refuse the conflict or withdraw from it; and we ask wherein the mind of the artist is unique. If he is not unique in neurosis, is he then unique in the significance and intensity of his neurosis? I do not believe that we shall go more than a little way toward a definition of artistic genius by answering this question affirmatively. A neurotic conflict cannot ever be either meaningless or merely personal; it must be understood as exemplifying cultural forces of great moment, and this is true of any neurotic conflict at all. To be sure, some neuroses may be more interesting than others, perhaps because they are fiercer or more inclusive; and no doubt the writer who makes a claim upon our interest is a man who by reason of the energy and significance of the forces in struggle within him provides us with the largest representation of the culture in which we, with him, are involved; his neurosis may thus be thought of as having a connection of concomitance with his literary powers. As Freud says in the Dostoevsky essay, "the neurosis . . . comes into being all the more readily the richer the complexity which has to be controlled by his ego." Yet even the rich complexity which his ego is doomed to control is not the definition of the artist's genius, for we can by no means say that the artist is pre-eminent in the rich complexity of elements in conflict within him. The slightest acquaintance with the clinical literature of psychoanalysis will suggest that a rich complexity of struggling elements is no uncommon possession. And that same literature will also make it abundantly clear that the

---

with the social maladjustments of our time. Other forms of mental illness of a more severe and degenerative kind are not so widely recognized by the literary person and are often assimilated to neurosis with a resulting confusion. In the present essay I deal only with the conception of neurosis, but this should not be taken to imply that I believe that other pathological mental conditions, including actual madness, do not have relevance to the general matter of the discussion.

devices of art—the most extreme devices of poetry, for example—are not particular to the mind of the artist but are characteristic of mind itself.

But the artist is indeed unique in one respect, in the respect of his relation to his neurosis. He is what he is by virtue of his successful objectification of his neurosis, by his shaping it and making it available to others in a way which has its effect upon their own egos in struggle. His genius, that is, may be defined in terms of his faculties of perception, representation, and realization, and in these terms alone. It can no more be defined in terms of neurosis than can his power of walking and talking, or his sexuality. The use to which he puts his power, or the manner and style of his power, may be discussed with reference to his particular neurosis, and so may such matters as the untimely diminution or cessation of its exercise. But its essence is irreducible. It is, as we say, a gift.

We are all ill: but even a universal sickness implies an idea of health. Of the artist we must say that whatever elements of neurosis he has in common with his fellow mortals, the one part of him that is healthy, by any conceivable definition of health, is that which gives him the power to conceive, to plan, to work, and to bring his work to a conclusion. And if we are all ill, we are ill by a universal accident, not by a universal necessity, by a fault in the economy of our powers, not by the nature of the powers themselves. The Philoctetes myth, when it is used to imply a causal connection between the fantasy of castration and artistic power, tells us no more about the source of artistic power than we learn about the source of sexuality when the fantasy of castration is adduced, for the fear of castration may explain why a man is moved to extravagant exploits of sexuality, but we do not say that his sexual power itself derives from his fear of castration; and further the same fantasy may also explain impotence or homosexuality. The Philoctetes story, which has so established itself among us as explaining the source of the artist's power, is not really an explanatory myth at all; it is a moral myth having reference to our proper behavior in the circumstances of the universal accident. In its juxtaposition of the wound and the bow, it tells us that we must be aware that weakness does not preclude strength nor strength weakness. It is therefore not irrelevant to the artist, but when we use it we will do well to keep in mind the other myths of the arts, recalling what Pan and Dionysius suggest of

the relation of art to physiology and superabundance, remembering that
to Apollo were attributed the bow and the lyre, two strengths together,
and that he was given the lyre by its inventor, the baby Hermes—that
miraculous infant who, the day he was born, left his cradle to do mis-
chief: and the first thing he met with was a tortoise, which he greeted
politely before scooping it from its shell, and, thought and deed being
one with him, he contrived the instrument to which he sang "the
glorious tale of his own begetting." These were gods, and very early
ones, but their myths tell us something about the nature and source of
art even in our grim, late human present.

Dickens

George Santayana

If Christendom should lose everything that is now in the melting-pot, human life would still remain amiable and quite adequately human. I draw this comforting assurance from the pages of Dickens. Who could not be happy in his world? Yet there is nothing essential to it which the most destructive revolution would be able to destroy. People would still be as different, as absurd, and as charming as are his characters; the springs of kindness and folly in their lives would not be dried up. Indeed, there is much in Dickens which communism, if it came, would only emphasise and render universal. Those schools, those poorhouses, those prisons, with those surviving shreds of family life in them, show us what in the coming age (with some sanitary improvements) would be the nursery and home of everybody. Everybody would be a waif, like Oliver Twist, like Smike, like Pip, and like David Copperfield; and amongst the agents and underlings of social government, to whom all these waifs would be entrusted, there would surely be a goodly sprinkling of Pecksniffs, Squeers', and Fangs; whilst the Fagins would be everywhere commissioners of the people. Nor would there fail to be, in high places and in low, the occasional sparkle of some Pickwick or Cherryble Brothers or Sam Weller or Mark Tapley; and the voluble Flora Finchings would be everywhere in evidence, and the strong-minded Betsey Trotwoods in office. There would also be, among the inefficient, many a Dora and Agnes and Little Emily—with her charm but without her tragedy, since this is one of the things which the promised social reform would happily render impossible; I mean, by removing all the disgrace of it. The only element in the world of Dickens which would become obsolete would be the setting, the atmosphere of material instrumentalities and arrangements, as travelling by coach is obsolete; but travelling by rail, by motor, or by airship will emotionally be much the same thing. It is worth noting how such instrumentalities, which absorb modern life, are admired and enjoyed by Dickens, as they were by Homer. The poets ought not to be afraid of them; they exercise the mind congenially, and can be played with joyfully. Consider the black ships and the chariots of Homer, the coaches and river-boats of Dickens, and the aeroplanes of to-day; to what would an unspoiled young mind turn with more interest? Dickens tells us little of English sports, but he shares the sporting nature of the Englishman, to whom the whole material world is a playing-field, the scene giving ample scope to his love of action, legality, and pleasant achievement. His art is to sport according to the rules of the game, and to do things for the sake of doing them, rather than for any ulterior motive.

It is remarkable, in spite of his ardent simplicity and openness of heart, how insensible Dickens was to the greater themes of the human imagination—religion, science, politics, art. He was a waif himself, and utterly disinherited. For example, the terrible heritage of contentious religions which fills the world seems not to exist for him. In this matter he was like a sensitive child, with a most religious disposition, but no religious ideas. Perhaps, properly speaking, he had no *ideas* on any subject; what he had was a vast sympathetic participation in the daily life of mankind; and what he saw of ancient institutions made him hate them, as needless sources of oppression, misery, selfishness, and rancour. His one political passion was philanthropy, genuine but felt only on its negative, reforming side; of positive utopias, or enthusiasms we hear nothing. The political background of Christendom is only, so to speak, an old faded back-drop for his stage; a castle, a frigate, a gallows, and a large female angel with white wings standing above an orphan by an open grave—a decoration which has to serve for all the melodramas in his theatre, intellectually so provincial and poor. Common life as it is lived was varied and lovable enough for Dickens, if only the pests and cruelties could be removed from it. Suffering wounded him, but not vulgarity; whatever pleased his senses and whatever shocked them filled his mind alike with romantic wonder, with the endless delight of observation. Vulgarity—and what can we relish, if we recoil at vulgarity?—was innocent and amusing; in fact, for the humourist, it was the spice of life. There was more piety in being human than in being pious. In reviving Christmas, Dickens transformed it from the celebration of a metaphysical mystery into a feast of overflowing simple kindness and good cheer; the church bells were still there—in the orchestra; and the angels of Bethlehem were still there—painted on the back-curtain. Churches, in his novels, are vague, desolate places where one has ghastly experiences, and where only the pew-opener is human; and such religious and political conflicts as he depicts in *Barnaby Rudge* and in *A Tale of Two Cities* are street brawls and prison scenes and conspiracies in taverns, without any indication of the contrasts in mind or interests between the opposed parties. Nor had Dickens any lively sense for fine art, classical tradition, science, or even the manners and feelings of the upper classes in his own time and country: in his novels we may almost say there is no army, no navy, no church, no sport, no distant travel, no daring adventure, no feeling for the watery wastes and the motley nations of the planet, and—luckily, with his notion of them—no lords and ladies. Even love of the traditional sort is hardly in Dickens' sphere—I mean the soldierly passion in which a rather rakish gallantry was sobered by devotion, and loyalty rested on pride. In Dickens love is sentimental or benevolent or merry or sneaking or canine; in his last book he was going to describe a love that was passionate and criminal; but love for him was never chivalrous, never poetical. What he paints most tragically is a quasi-paternal devotion in the old to the young, the love of Mr. Peggotty for Little Emily, or of Solomon Gills for Walter Gay. A series of shabby little adventures, such as might absorb the interest of an average youth, were romantic enough for Dickens.

I say he was disinherited, but he inherited the most terrible negations. Religion lay on him like the weight of the atmosphere, sixteen pounds to the square inch, yet never noticed nor mentioned. He lived and wrote in the shadow of the most awful prohibitions. Hearts petrified by legality and falsified by worldliness offered, indeed, a good subject for a novelist, and Dickens availed himself of it to the extent of always contrasting natural goodness and happiness with whatever is morose; but his morose people were wicked, not virtuous in their own way; so that the protest of his temperament against his environment never took a radical form nor went back to first principles. He needed to feel, in his writing, that he was carrying the sympathies of every man with him. In him conscience was single, and he could not conceive how it could ever be divided in other men. He denounced scandals without exposing shams, and conformed willingly and scrupulously to the proprieties. Lady Dedlock's secret, for instance, he treats as if it were the sin of Adam, remote, mysterious, inexpiable. Mrs. Dombey is not allowed to deceive her husband except by pretending to deceive him. The seduction of Little Emily is left out altogether, with the whole character of Steerforth, the development of which would have been so important in the moral experience of David Copperfield himself. But it is not public prejudice alone that plays the censor over Dickens' art; his own kindness and even weakness of heart act sometimes as marplots. The character of Miss Mowcher, for example, so brilliantly introduced, was evidently intended to be shady, and to play a very important part in the story; but its original in real life, which was recognised, had to be conciliated, and the sequel was omitted and patched up with an apology—itself admirable—for the poor dwarf. Such a sacrifice does honour to Dickens' heart; but artists should meditate on their works in time, and it is easy to remove any too great likeness in a portrait by a few touches making it more consistent than real people are apt to be; and in this case, if the little creature had been really guilty, how much more subtle and tragic her apology for herself might have been, like that of the bastard Edmund in *King Lear!* So, too, in *Dombey and Son,* Dickens could not bear to let Walter Gay turn out badly, as he had been meant to do, and to break his uncle's heart as well as the heroine's; he was accordingly transformed into a stage hero miraculously saved from shipwreck, and Florence was not allowed to reward the admirable Toots, as she should have done, with her trembling hand. But Dickens was no free artist; he had more genius than taste, a warm fancy not aided by a thorough understanding of complex characters. He worked under pressure, for money and applause, and often had to cheapen in execution what his inspiration had so vividly conceived.

What, then, is there left, if Dickens has all these limitations? In our romantic disgust we might be tempted to say, Nothing. But in fact almost everything is left, almost everything that counts in the daily life of mankind, or that by its presence or absence can determine whether life shall be worth living or not; because a simple good life is worth living, and an elaborate bad life is not. There remain in the first place eating and drinking; relished not bestially, but humanly, jovially, as the sane and exhilarating basis for everything else. This is a sound English beginning; but the immediate sequel, as the England of that day presented it to Dickens, is no less delightful. There is the ruddy glow of the hearth; the sparkle of glasses and brasses and well-scrubbed pewter; the savoury fumes of the hot punch, after the tingle of the wintry air; the coaching-scenes, the motley figures and absurd incidents of travel; the changing sights and joys of the road. And then, to balance this, the traffic of ports and cities, the hubbub of crowded streets, the luxury of shop-windows and of palaces not to be entered; the procession of the passers-by, shabby or ludicrously genteel; the dingy look and musty smell of their lodgings; the labyrinth of back-alleys, courts, and mews, with their crying children, and scolding old women, and listless, half-drunken loiterers. These sights, like fables, have a sort of moral in them to which Dickens was very sensitive; the important airs of nobodies on great occasions, the sadness and preoccupation of the great as they hasten by in their morning or on their pressing affairs; the sadly comic characters of the tavern; the diligence of shop-keepers, like squirrels turning in their cages; the children peeping out everywhere like grass in an untrodden street; the charm of humble things, the nobleness of humble people, the horror of crime, the ghastliness of vice, the deft hand and shining face of virtue passing through the midst of it all; and finally a fresh wind of indifference and change blowing across our troubles and clearing the most lurid sky.

I do not know whether it was Christian charity or naturalistic insight, or a mixture of both (for they are closely akin), that attracted Dickens particularly to the deformed, the half-witted, the abandoned, or those impeded or misunderstood by virtue of some singular inner consecration. The visible moral of these things, when brutal prejudice does not blind us to it, comes very near to true philosophy; one turn of the screw, one flash of reflection, and we have understood nature and human morality and the relation between them.

In his love of roads and wayfarers, of river-ports and wharves and the idle or sinister figures that lounge about them, Dickens was like Walt Whitman; and I think a second Dickens may any day appear in America, when it is possible in that land of hurry to reach the same degree of saturation, the same unquestioning pleasure in the familiar facts. The spirit of Dickens would be better able to do justice to America, which although it may seem nothing but a noisy nebula to the impressionist, is not a nebula but a concourse of very distinct individual bodies, natural and social, each with its definite interest and story. Walt Whitman had a sort of transcendental philosophy which swallowed the universe whole, supposing there was a universal spirit in things identical with the absolute spirit that observed them; but

Dickens was innocent of any such clap-trap, and remained a true spirit in his own person. Kindly and clear-sighted, but self-identical and unequivocally human, he glided through the slums like one of his own little heroes, uncontaminated by their squalor and confusion, courageous and firm in his clear allegiances amid the flux of things, a pale angel at the Carnival, his heart aflame, his voice always flute-like in its tenderness and warning. This is the true relation of spirit to existence, not the other which confuses them; for this earth (I cannot speak for the universe at large) has no spirit of its own, but brings forth spirits only at certain points, in the hearts and brains of frail living creatures, who like insects flit through it, buzzing and gathering what sweets they can; and it is the spaces they traverse in this career, charged with their own moral burden, that they can report on or describe, not things rolling on to infinity in their vain tides. To be hypnotised by that flood would be a heathen idolatry. Accordingly Walt Whitman, in his comprehensive democratic vistas, could never see the trees for the wood, and remained incapable, for all his diffuse love of the human herd, of ever painting a character or telling a story; the very things in which Dickens was a master. It is this life of the individual, as it may be lived in a given nation, that determines the whole value of that nation to the poet, to the moralist, and to the judicious historian. But for the excellence of the typical single life, no nation deserves to be remembered more than the sands of the sea; and America will not be a success, if every American is a failure.

Dickens entered the theatre of this world by the stage door; the shabby little adventures of the actors in their private capacity replace for him the mock tragedies which they enact before a dreaming public. Mediocrity of circumstances and mediocrity of soul forever return to the centre of his stage; a more wretched or a grander existence is sometimes broached, but the pendulum soon swings back, and we return, with the relief with which we put on our slippers after the most romantic excursion, to a golden mediocrity—to mutton and beer, and to love and babies in a suburban villa with one frowsy maid. Dickens is the poet of those acres of yellow brick streets which the traveller sees from the railway viaducts as he approaches London; they need a poet, and they deserve one, since a complete human life may very well be lived there. Their little excitements and sorrows, their hopes and humours are like those of the Wooden Midshipman in *Dombey and Son;* but the sea is not far off, and the sky—Dickens never forgets it—

is above all those brief troubles. He had a sentiment in the presence of this vast flatness of human fates, in spite of their individual pungency, which I think might well be the dominant sentiment of mankind in the future; a sense of happy freedom in littleness, an open-eyed reverence and religion without words. This universal human anonymity is like a sea, an infinite democratic desert, chock-full and yet the very image of emptiness, with nothing in it for the mind, except, as the Moslems say, the presence of Allah. Awe is the counterpart of humility—and this is perhaps religion enough. The atom in the universal vortex ought to be humble; he ought to see that, materially, he doesn't much matter, and that morally his loves are merely his own, without authority over the universe. He can admit without obloquy that he is what he is; and he can rejoice in his own being, and in that of all other things in so far as he can share it sympathetically. The apportionment of existence and of fortune is in Other Hands; his own portion is contentment, vision, love, and laughter.

Having humility, that most liberating of sentiments, having a true vision of human existence and joy in that vision, Dickens had in a superlative degree the gift of humour, of mimicry, of unrestrained farce. He was the perfect comedian. When people say Dickens exaggerates it seems to me they can have no eyes and no ears. They probably have only *notions* of what things and people are; they accept them conventionally, at their diplomatic value. Their minds run on in the region of discourse, where there are masks only and no faces, ideas and no facts; they have little sense for those living grimaces that play from moment to moment upon the countenance of the world. The world is a perpetual caricature of itself; at every moment it is the mocker and the contradiction of what it is pretending to be. But as it nevertheless intends all the time to be something different and highly dignified at the next moment it corrects and checks and tries to cover up the absurd thing it was; so that a conventional world, a world of masks is superimposed on the reality itself. Humour is the perception of this illusion, the fact allowed to pierce here and there through the convention, whilst the convention continues to be maintained, as if we had not observed its absurdity. Pure comedy is more radical, cruder, in a certain sense less human; because comedy throws the convention over altogether, revels for a moment in the fact, and brutally says to the notions of mankind, as if it slapped them in the face, There, take that! That's what you really are! At this the polite world pretends to laugh not tolerantly as it does at humour, but a little angrily. It does not like to see itself by chance in the glass, without having had time to compose its features for demure self-contemplation. "What a bad mirror," it exclaims; "it must be concave or convex; for surely I never looked like that. Mere caricature, farce, and horse play. Dickens exaggerates; I never was so sentimental as that; I never saw anything so dreadful; I don't believe there were ever any people like Quilp, or Squeers, or Serjeant Buzfuz." But the polite world is lying; there *are* such people; we are such people ourselves in our true moments, in our veritable impulses; but we are careful to stifle and to hide those moments from ourselves and from the world; to purse and pucker ourselves into the mask of our conventional personality; and so simpering, we profess that it is very coarse and inartistic of Dickens to undo our life's work for us in an instant, and remind us of what we are. And as to other people, though we may allow that considered superficially they are often absurd, we do not wish to dwell on their eccentricities, nor to mimic them. On the contrary, it is good manners to look away quickly, to suppress a smile, and to say to ourselves that the ludicrous figure in the street is not at all comic, but a dull ordinary Christian, and that it is foolish to give any importance to the fact that its hat has blown off, that it has slipped on an orange-peel and unintentionally sat on the pavement, that it has a pimple on its nose, that its one tooth projects over its lower lip, that it is angry with things in general, and that it is looking everywhere for the penny which it holds tightly in its hand. That may fairly represent the moral condition of most of us at most times; but we do not want to think of it; we do not want to see; we gloss the fact over; we console ourselves before we are grieved, and reassert our composure before we have laughed. We are afraid, ashamed, anxious to be spared. What displeases us in Dickens is that he does not spare us; he mimics things to the full; he dilates and exhausts and repeats; he wallows. He is too intent on the passing experience to look over his shoulder, and consider whether we have not already understood, and had enough. He is not thinking of us; he is obeying the impulse of the passion, the person, or the story he is enacting. This faculty, which renders him a consummate comedian, is just what alienated from him a later generation in which people of taste were aesthetes and virtuous people were higher snobs; they wanted a mincing art, and he gave them copious improvisation, they wanted analysis and development, and he gave them absolute comedy. I must confess, though the fault is mine and not his, that sometimes his absoluteness is too much for me. When I come to the death of Little Nell, or to What the Waves were always Saying, or even to the incorrigible perversities of the pretty Dora, I skip. I can't take my liquor neat in such draughts, and my inner man says to Dickens, Please don't. But then I am a coward in so many ways! There are so many things in this world that I skip, as I skip the undiluted Dickens! When I reach Dover on a rough day, I wait there until the Channel is smoother; am I not travelling for pleasure? But my prudence does not blind me to the admirable virtue of the sailors that cross in all weathers, nor even to the automatic determination of the seasick ladies, who might so easily have followed my example, if they were not the slaves of their railway tickets and of their labelled luggage. They are loyal to their tour, and I to my philosophy. Yet as wrapped in my great-coat and sure of a good dinner, I pace the windy pier and soliloquise, I feel the superiority of the bluff tar, glad of breeze, stretching a firm arm to the unsteady passenger, and watching with a masterful thrill of emotion the home cliffs receding and the foreign coasts ahead. It is only courage (which Dickens had without knowing it) and universal kindness (which he knew he had) that are requisite to nerve us for a true vision of this world. And as some of us are cowards about crossing the Channel, and others about "crossing the bar," so almost everybody is a coward about his own humanity. We do not consent to be absurd, though absurd we are. We have no fundamental humility. We do not wish the moments of our lives to be caught by a quick eye in their grotesque initiative, and to be pilloried in this way before our own eyes. For that reason we don't like the truth. Dickens could don the comic mask with innocent courage; he could wear it with a grace, ease, and irresistible vivacity seldom given to men. We must go back for anything like it to the very greatest comic poets, to Shakespeare or to Aristophanes. Who else, for instance, could have penned this:

"It was all Mrs. Bumble. She would do it," urged Mr. Bumble; first looking round to ascertain that his partner had left the room.

"That is no excuse," replied Mr. Brownlow. "You were present on the occasion of the destruction of these trinkets, and indeed are the more guilty of the two, in the eye of the law; for the law supposes that your wife acts under your direction."

"If the law supposes that," said Mr. Bumble, squeezing his hat emphatically in both hands, "the law is a ass, a idiot. If that's the eye of the law, the law is a bachelor; and the worse I wish the law is, that his eye may be opened by experience—by experience.''

Laying great stress on the repetition of these two words, Mr. Bumble fixed his hat on very tight, and putting his hands in his pockets, followed his helpmate downstairs.

This is high comedy; the irresistible, absurd, intense dream of the old fool, personifying the law in order to convince and to punish it. I can understand that this sort of thing should not be common in English literature, nor much relished; because pure comedy is scornful, merciless, devastating, holding no door open to anything beyond. Cultivated English feeling winces at this brutality, although the common people love it in clowns and in puppet shows; and I think they are right. Dickens, who surely was tender enough, had so irresistible a comic genius that it carried him beyond the gentle humour which most Englishmen possess to the absolute grotesque reality. Squeers, for instance, when he sips the wretched dilution which he has prepared for his starved and shivering little pupils, smacks his lips and cries: "Here's richness!" It is savage comedy; humour would come in if we understood (what Dickens does not tell us) that the little creatures were duly impressed and thought the thin liquid truly delicious. I suspect that English sensibility prefers the humour and wit of Hamlet to the pure comedy of Falstaff; and that even in Aristophanes it seeks consolation in the lyrical poetry for the flaying of human life in the comedy itself. Tastes are free; but we should not deny that in merciless and rollicking comedy life is caught in the act. The most grotesque creatures of Dickens are not exaggerations or mockeries of something other than themselves; they arise because nature generates them, like toadstools; they exist because they can't help it as we all do. The fact that these perfectly self-justified beings are absurd appears only by comparison, and from outside; circumstances, or the expectations of other people, make them ridiculous and force them to contradict themselves; but in nature it is no crime to be exceptional. Often, but for the savagery of the average man, it would not even be a misfortune. The sleepy fat boy in *Pickwick* looks foolish; but in himself he is no more foolish, nor less solidly self-justified, than a pumpkin lying on the ground. Toots seems ridiculous; and we laugh heartily at his incoherence, his beautiful waistcoats, and his extreme modesty; but when did anybody more obviously grow into what he is because he couldn't grow otherwise? So with Mr. Pickwick, and Sam Weller, and Mrs. Gamp, and Micawber, and all the rest of this wonderful gallery; they are ridiculous only by accident, and in a context in which they never intended to appear. If Oedipus and Lear and Cleopatra do not seem ridiculous, it is only because tragic reflection has taken them out of the context in which, in real life, they would have figured. If we saw them as facts, and not as emanations of a poet's dream, we should laugh at them till doomsday; what grotesque presumption, what silly whims, what mad contradiction of the simplest realities! Yet we should not laugh at them without feeling how real their griefs were; as real and terrible as the griefs of children and of dreams. But facts, however serious inwardly, are always absurd outwardly; and the just critic of life sees both truths at once, as Cervantes did in *Don Quixote*. A pompous idealist who does not see the ridiculous in all things is the dupe of his sympathy and abstraction; and a clown, who does not see that these ridiculous creatures are living quite in earnest, is the dupe of his egotism. Dickens saw the absurdity, and understood the life; I think he was a good philosopher.

It is usual to compare Dickens with Thackeray, which is like comparing the grape with the gooseberry; there are obvious points of resemblance, and the gooseberry has some superior qualities of its own; but you can't make red wine of it. The wine of Dickens is of the richest, the purest, the sweetest, the most fortifying to the blood; there is distilled in it, with the perfection of comedy, the perfection of morals. I do not mean, of course, that Dickens appreciated all the values that human life has or might have; that is beyond any man. Even the greatest philosophers, such as Aristotle, have not always much imagination to conceive forms of happiness or folly other than those which their age or their temperament reveals to them; their insight runs only to discovering the *principle* of happiness, that it is spontaneous life of any sort harmonised with circumstances. The sympathies and imagination of Dickens, vivid in their sphere, were no less limited in range; and of course it was not his business to find philosophic formulas; nevertheless I call his the perfection of morals for two reasons: that he put the distinction between good and evil in the right place, and that he felt this distinction intensely. A moralist might have excellent judgment, he might see what sort of life is spontaneous in a given being and how far it may be harmonised with circumstances, yet his heart might remain cold, he might not suffer nor rejoice with the suffering or joy he fore saw. Humanitarians like Bentham and Mill, who talked about the greatest happiness of the greatest number, might conceivably be moral prigs in their own persons, and they might have been chilled to the bone in their theoretic love of mankind, if they had the wit to imagine in what, as a matter of fact, the majority would place their happiness. Even if their theory had been correct (which I think it was in intention, though not in statement) they would then not have been perfect moralists, because their maxims would not have expressed their hearts. In expressing their hearts, they ought to have embraced one of those forms of "idealism" by which men fortify themselves in their bitter passions or in their helpless commitments: for they do not wish mankind to be happy in its own way, but in theirs. Dickens was not one of those moralists who summon every man to do himself the greatest violence so that he may not offend them, nor defeat their ideals. Love of the good of others is something that shines in every page of Dickens with a truly celestial splendour. How entirely limpid is his sympathy with life—a sympathy uncontaminated by dogma or pedantry or snobbery or bias of any kind! How generous is this keen, light spirit, how pure this open heart! And yet, in spite of this extreme sensibility, not the least wobbling; no deviation from a just severity of judgment, from an uncompromising distinction between white and black. And this happens as it ought to happen; sympathy is not checked by a flatly contrary prejudice or commandment, by some categorical imperative irrelevant to human nature; the check, like the cheer, comes by tracing the course of spontaneous impulse amid circumstances that inexorably lead it to success or to failure. There is a bed to this stream, freely as the water may flow; when it comes to this precipice it must leap, when it runs over these pebbles it must sing, and when it spreads into that marsh it must become livid and malarial. The very sympathy with human impulse quickens in Dickens the sense of danger; his very joy in joy makes him stern to what kills it. How admirably drawn are his surly villains! No rhetorical vilification of them, as in a sermon; no exaggeration of their qualms or fears; rather a sense of how obvious and human all their courses seem from their own point of view; and yet no sentimental apology for them, no romantic worship of rebels in their madness or crime. The pity of it, the waste of it all, are seen not by a second vision but by the same original vision which revealed the lure and the drift of the passion. Vice is a monster here of such sorry mien, that the longer we see it the more we deplore it; that other sort of vice which Pope found so seductive was perhaps only some innocent impulse artificially suppressed, and called a vice because it broke out inconveniently and displeased the company. True vice is human nature strangled by the suicide of attempting the impossible. Those so self-justified villains of Dickens never elude their fates. Bill Sikes is not let off, neither is Nancy; the oddly benevolent Magwitch does not escape from the net, nor does the unfortunate young Richard Carstone, victim of the Circumlocution Office. The horror and ugliness of their fall are rendered with the hand of a master; we see here, as in the world, that in spite of the romanticists it is not virtue to rush enthusiastically along any road. I think Dickens is one of the best friends mankind has ever had. He has held the mirror up to nature, and of its reflected fragments has composed a fresh world, where the men and women differ from real people only in that they live in a literary medium, so that all ages and places may know them. And they are worth knowing, just as one's neighbours are, for their picturesque characters and their pathetic fates. Their names should be in every child's mouth; they ought to be adopted members of every household. Their stories cause the merriest and the sweetest chimes to ring in the fancy, without confusing our moral judgment or alienating our interest from the motley commonplaces of daily life. In every English-speaking home, in the four quarters of the globe, parents and children will do well to read Dickens aloud of a winter's evening; they will love winter, and one another, and God the better for it. What a wreath that will be of ever-fresh holly, thick with bright berries, to hang to this poet's memory—the very crown he would have chosen.

The Irony of Swift

F. R. Leavis

Swift is a great English writer. For opening with this truism I have a reason: I wish to discuss Swift's writings—to examine what they are; and they are (as the extant commentary bears witness) of such a kind that it is peculiarly difficult to discuss them without shifting the focus of discussion to the kind of man that Swift was. What is most interesting in them does not so clearly belong to the realm of things made and detached that literary criticism, which has certainly not the less its duties towards Swift, can easily avoid turning—unawares, and that is, degenerating—into something else. In the attempt to say what makes these writings so remarkable, reference to the man who wrote is indeed necessary; but there are distinctions. For instance, one may (it appears), having offered to discuss the nature and import of Swift's satire, find oneself countering imputations of misanthropy with the argument that Swift earned the love of Pope, Arbuthnot, Gay, several other men and two women: this should not be found necessary by the literary critic. But the irrelevancies of Thackeray and of his castigator, the late Charles Whibley—irrelevancies not merely from the point of view of literary criticism—are too gross to need placarding; more insidious deviations are possible.

The reason for the opening truism is also the reason for the choice of title. To direct the attention upon Swift's irony gives, I think, the best chance of dealing adequately, without deviation or confusion, with what is essential in his work. But it involves also (to anticipate an objection) a slight to the classical status of *Gulliver's Travels,* a book which, though it may represent Swift's most impressive achievement in

From *The Common Pursuit* by F. R. Leavis. Reprinted by permission of Chatto & Windus, Ltd.

the way of complete creation—the thing achieved and detached—does not give the best opportunities for examining his irony. And *Gulliver's Travels,* one readily agrees, hasn't its classical status for nothing. But neither is it for nothing that, suitably abbreviated, it has become a classic for children. What for the adult reader constitutes its peculiar force— what puts it in so different a class from *Robinson Crusoe*—resides for the most part in the fourth book (to less extent in the third). The adult may re-read the first two parts, as he may *Robinson Crusoe,* with great interest, but his interest, apart from being more critically conscious, will not be of a different order from the child's. He will, of course, be aware of an ingenuity of political satire in *Lilliput,* but the political satire is, unless for historians, not very much alive to-day. And even the more general satire characteristic of the second book will not strike him as very subtle. His main satisfaction, a great deal enhanced, no doubt, by the ironic seasoning, will be that which Swift, the student of the *Mariner's Magazine* and of travellers' relations, aimed to supply in the bare precision and the matter-of-fact realness of his narrative.

But what in Swift is most important, the disturbing characteristic of his genius, is a peculiar emotional intensity; that which, in *Gulliver* confronts us in the Struldbrugs and the Yahoos. It is what we find ourselves contemplating when elsewhere we examine his irony. To lay the stress upon an emotional intensity should be matter of common place: actually, in routine usage, the accepted word for Swift is "intel lectual." We are told, for instance, that his is pre-eminently "intellectual satire" (though we are not told what satire is). For this formula the best reason some commentators can allege is the elaboration of analogies —their "exact and elaborate propriety" [1]—in *Gulliver.* But a muddled perception can hardly be expected to give a clear account of itself; the stress on Swift's "intellect" (Mr Herbert Read alludes to his "mighty in telligence")[2] registers, it would appear, a confused sense, not only of the mental exercise involved in his irony, but of the habitually critical atti tude he maintains towards the world, and of the negative emotions he specializes in.

From "critical" to "negative" in this last sentence is, it will be observed, a shift of stress. There are writings of Swift where "critical" is the more obvious word (and where "intellectual" may seem corre spondingly apt)—notably, the pamphlets or pamphleteering essays in

[1] Churton Collins.
[2] *English Prose Style.*

which the irony is instrumental, directed and limited to a given end. The *Argument Against Abolishing Christianity* and the *Modest Proposal,* for instance, are discussible in the terms in which satire is commonly discussed: as the criticism of vice, folly or other aberration, by some kind of reference to positive standards. But even here, even in the *Argument,* where Swift's ironic intensity undeniably directs itself to the defence of something that he is intensely concerned to defend, the effect is essentially negative. The positive itself appears only negatively—a kind of skeletal presence, rigid enough, but without life or body; a necessary pre-condition, as it were, of directed negation. The intensity is purely destructive.

The point may be enforced by the obvious contrast with Gibbon— except that between Swift's irony and Gibbon's the contrast is so complete that any one point is difficult to isolate. Gibbon's irony, in the fifteenth chapter, may be aimed against, instead of for, Christianity, but contrasted with Swift's it is an assertion of faith. The decorously insistent pattern of Gibbonian prose insinuates a solidarity with the reader (the implied solidarity in Swift is itself ironical—a means to betrayal), establishes an understanding and habituates to certain assumptions. The reader, it is implied, is an eighteenth-century gentleman ("rational," "candid," "polite," "elegant," "humane"); eighteen hundred years ago he would have been a pagan gentleman, living by these same standards (those of absolute civilization); by these standards (present everywhere in the stylized prose and adroitly emphasized at key points in such phrases as "the polite Augustus," "the elegant mythology of the Greeks") the Jews and early Christians are seen to have been ignorant fanatics, uncouth and probably dirty. Gibbon as a historian of Christianity had, we know, limitations; but the positive standards by reference to which his irony works represent something impressively realized in eighteenth-century civilization; impressively "there" too in the grandiose, assured and ordered elegance of his history. (When, on the other hand, Lytton Strachey, with a Gibbonian period or phrase or word, a "remarkable," "oddly" or "curious," assures us that he feels an amused superiority to these Victorian puppets, he succeeds only in conveying his personal conviction that he feels amused and superior.)

Gibbon's irony, then, habituates and reassures, ministering to a kind of judicial certitude or complacency. Swift's is essentially a matter of surprise and negation; its function is to defeat habit, to intimidate and to demoralize. What he assumes in the *Argument* is not so much a common acceptance of Christianity as that the reader will be ashamed to have to recognize how fundamentally unchristian his actual assumptions, motives and attitudes are. And in general the implication is that it would shame people if they were made to recognize themselves unequivocally. If one had to justify this irony according to the conventional notion of satire, then its satiric efficacy would be to make comfortable non-recognition, the unconsciousness of habit, impossible.

A method of surprise does not admit of description in an easy formula. Surprise is a perpetually varied accompaniment of the grave, dispassionate, matter-of-fact tone in which Swift delivers his intensities. The dissociation of emotional intensity from its usual accompaniments inhibits the automatic defence-reaction:

> He is a Presbyterian in politics, and an atheist in religion; but he chooses at present to whore with a Papist.

> What bailiff would venture to arrest Mr Steele, now he has the honour to be your representative? and what bailiff ever scrupled it before?

Or inhibits, let us say, the normal response; since "defence" suggests that it is the "victim" whose surprise we should be contemplating, whereas it is our own, whether Swift's butt is Wharton or the atheist or mankind in general. "But satire, being levelled at all, is never resented for an offence by any, since every individual makes bold to understand it of others, and very wisely removes his particular part of the burden upon the shoulders of the World, which are broad enough and able to bear it." [3] There is, of course, no contradiction here; a complete statement would be complex. But, actually, the discussion of satire in terms of offence and castigation, victim and castigator, is unprofitable, though the idea of these has to be taken into account. What we are concerned with (the reminder is especially opportune) is an arrangement of words on the page and their effects—the emotions, attitudes and ideas that they organize.

Our reaction, as Swift says, is not that of the butt or victim; nevertheless, it necessarily entails some measure of sympathetic self-projection. We more often, probably, feel the effect of the words as an intensity in the castigator than as an effect upon a victim: the dissociation of animus from the usual signs defines for our contemplation a peculiarly intense contempt or disgust. When, as sometimes we have to do, we talk in

[3] *A Tale of a Tub*: the Preface.

terms of effect on the victim, then "surprise" becomes an obviously apt word; he is to be betrayed, again and again, into an incipient acquiescence:

Sixthly. This would be a great Inducement to Marriage, which all wise Nations have either encouraged by Rewards, or enforced by Laws and Penalties. It would increase the Care and Tenderness of Mothers towards their Children, when they were sure of a Settlement for Life, to the poor Babes, provided in some Sort by the Publick, to their annual Profit instead of Expence; we should soon see an honest Emulation among the married Women, *which of them could bring the fattest Child to the Market.* Men would become as *fond* of their Wives, during the Time of their Pregnancy, as they are now of their *Mares* in Foal, their *Cows* in Calf, or *Sows* when they are ready to farrow, nor offer to beat or kick them (as is too *frequent* a Practice) for fear of a Miscarriage.

The implication is: "This, as you so obligingly demonstrate, is the only kind of argument that appeals to you; here are your actual faith and morals. How, on consideration, do you like the smell of them?"

But when in reading the *Modest Proposal* we are most engaged, it is an effect directly upon ourselves that we are most disturbingly aware of. The dispassionate, matter-of-fact tone induces a feeling and a motion of assent, while the burden, at the same time, compels the feelings appropriate to rejection, and in the contrast—the tension—a remarkably disturbing energy is generated. A sense of an extraordinary energy is the general effect of Swift's irony. The intensive means just indicated are reinforced extensively in the continuous and unpredictable movement of the attack, which turns this way and that, comes now from one quarter and now from another, inexhaustibly surprising—making again an odd contrast with the sustained and level gravity of the tone. If Swift does for a moment appear to settle down to a formula it is only in order to betray; to induce a trust in the solid ground before opening the pitfall.

"His *Tale of a Tub* has little resemblance to his other pieces. It exhibits a vehemence and rapidity of mind, a copiousness of images, a vivacity of diction, such as he afterwards never possessed, or never exerted. It is of a mode so distinct and peculiar, that it must be considered by itself; what is true of that, is not true of anything else he has written." What Johnson is really testifying to here is the degree in which the *Tale of a Tub* is characteristic and presents the qualities of Swift's genius in concentrated form. "That he has in his works no

metaphors, as has been said, is not true," says Johnson a sentence or
two later, "but his few metaphors seem to be received rather by necessity
than choice." This last judgment may at any rate serve to enforce
Johnson's earlier observation that in the *Tale of a Tub* Swift's powers
function with unusual freedom. For the "copiousness of images" that
Johnson constates is, as the phrase indicates, not a matter of choice but
of essential genius. And, as a matter of fact, in this "copiousness of
images" the characteristics that we noted in discussing Swift's pamphleteering irony have their supreme expression.

It is as if the gift applied in *Gulliver* to a very limiting task—
directed and confined by a scheme uniting a certain consistency in
analogical elaboration with verisimilitude—were here enjoying free play.
For the bent expressing itself in this "copiousness" is clearly fundamental. It shows itself in the spontaneous metaphorical energy of Swift's
prose—in the image, action or blow that, leaping out of the prosaic manner, continually surprises and disconcerts the reader: "such a man, truly
wise, creams off Nature, leaving the sour and the dregs for philosophy
and reason to lap up." It appears with as convincing a spontaneity in
the sardonic vivacity of comic vision that characterizes the narrative,
the presentment of action and actor. If, then, the continual elaborate
play of analogy is a matter of cultivated habit, it is a matter also of
cultivated natural bent, a congenial development. It is a development
that would seem to bear a relation to the Metaphysical fashion in verse
(Swift was born in 1667). The spirit of it is that of a fierce and insolent
game, but a game to which Swift devotes himself with a creative intensity.

And whereas the mind of man, when he gives the spur and
bridle to his thoughts, does never stop, but naturally sallies out into
both extremes of high and low, of good and evil, his first flight of
fancy commonly transports him to ideas of what is most perfect,
finished, and exalted, till, having soared out of his own reach and
sight, not well perceiving how near the frontiers of height and depth
border upon each other, with the same course and wing he falls down
plump into the lowest bottom of things, like one who travels the
east into the west, or like a straight line drawn by its own length
into a circle. Whether a tincture of malice in our natures makes us
fond of furnishing every bright idea with its reverse, or whether
reason, reflecting upon the sum of things, can, like the sun, serve
only to enlighten one half of the globe, leaving the other half by
necessity under shade and darkness, or whether fancy, flying up to
the imagination of what is highest and best, becomes over-short,

and spent, and weary, and suddenly falls, like a dead bird of paradise, to the ground. . . .

One may (without difficulty) resist the temptation to make the point by saying that this is poetry; one is still tempted to say that the use to which so exuberant an energy is put is a poet's. "Exuberant" seems, no doubt, a paradoxical word to apply to an energy used as Swift uses his; but the case is essentially one for paradoxical descriptions.

In his use of negative materials—negative emotions and attitudes—there is something that it is difficult not to call creative, though the aim always is destructive. Not all the materials, of course, are negative; the "bird of paradise" in the passage above is alive as well as dead. Effects of this kind, often much more intense, are characteristic of the *Tale of a Tub,* where surprise and contrast operate in modes that there is some point in calling poetic. "The most heterogeneous ideas are yoked by violence together"—and in the juxtaposition intensity is generated.

"Paracelsus brought a squadron of stink-pot-flingers from the snowy mountains of Rhaetia"—this (which comes actually from the *Battle of the Books*) does not represent what I have in mind; it is at once too simple and too little charged with animus. Swift's intensities are intensities of rejection and negation; his poetic juxtapositions are, characteristically, destructive in intention, and when they most seem creative of energy are most successful in spoiling, reducing and destroying. Sustained "copiousness," continually varying, and concentrating surprise in sudden local loci, cannot be represented in short extracts; it must suffice here to say that this kind of thing may be found at a glance on almost any page:

Meantime it is my earnest request that so useful an undertaking may be entered upon (if their Majesties please) with all convenient speed, because I have a strong inclination before I leave the world to taste a blessing which we mysterious writers can seldom reach till we have got into our graves, whether it is that fame, being a fruit grafted on the body, can hardly grow and much less ripen till the stock is in the earth, or whether she be a bird of prey, and is lured among the rest to pursue after the scent of a carcass, or whether she conceives her trumpet sounds best and farthest when she stands on a tomb, by the advantage of a rising ground and the echo of a hollow vault.

It is, of course, possible, to adduce Swift's authority for finding that his negations carry with them a complementary positive—an implicit assertion. But (*pace* Charles Whibley) the only thing in the nature of a positive that most readers will find convincingly present is self-assertion—*superbia*. Swift's way of demonstrating his superiority is to destroy, but he takes a positive delight in his power. And that the reader's sense of the negativeness of the *Tale of a Tub* is really qualified comes out when we refer to the Yahoos and the Struldbrugs for a test. The ironic detachment is of such a kind as to reassure us that this savage exhibition is mainly a game, played because it is the insolent pleasure of the author: "demonstration of superiority" is as good a formula as any for its prevailing spirit. Nevertheless, about a superiority that asserts itself in this way there is something disturbingly odd, and again and again in the *Tale of a Tub* we come on intensities that shift the stress decisively and remind us how different from Voltaire Swift is, even in his most complacent detachment.

I propose to examine in illustration a passage from the *Digression Concerning the Original, the Use, and Improvement of Madness in a Commonwealth* (i.e., Section IX). It will have, in the nature of the case, to be a long one, but since it exemplifies at the same time all Swift's essential characteristics, its length will perhaps be tolerated. I shall break up the passage for convenience of comment, but, except for the omission of nine or ten lines in the second instalment, quotation will be continuous:

For the brain in its natural position and state of serenity disposeth its owner to pass his life in the common forms, without any thought of subduing multitudes to his own power, his reasons, or his visions, and the more he shapes his understanding by the pattern of human learning, the less he is inclined to form parties after his particular notions, because that instructs him in his private infirmities, as well as in the stubborn ignorance of the people. But when a man's fancy gets astride on his reason, when imagination is at cuffs with the senses, and common understanding as well as common sense is kicked out of doors, the first proselyte he makes is himself; and when that is once compassed, the difficulty is not so great in bringing over others, a strong delusion always operating from without as vigorously as from within. For cant and vision are to the ear and the eye the same that tickling is to the touch. Those entertainments and pleasures we most value in life are such as dupe and play the wag with the senses. For if we take an examination of what is generally understood by happiness, as it has respect either to the understanding or to the senses, we shall find all its properties and adjuncts will herd under this short definition, that it is a perpetual possession of being well deceived.

Swift's ant-like energy—the business-like air, obsessed intentness and unpredictable movement—have already had an effect. We are not, at the end of this instalment, as sure that we know just what his irony is doing as we were at the opening. Satiric criticism of sectarian "enthusiasm" by reference to the "common forms"—the Augustan standards—is something that, in Swift, we can take as very seriously meant. But in the incessant patter of the argument we have (helped by such things as, at the end, the suggestion of animus in that oddly concrete "herd") a sense that direction and tone are changing. Nevertheless, the change of tone for which the next passage is most remarkable comes as a disconcerting surprise:

And first, with relation to the mind or understanding, it is manifest what mighty advantages fiction has over truth, and the reason is just at our elbow; because imagination can build nobler scenes and produce more wonderful revolutions than fortune or Nature will be at the expense to furnish. . . . Again, if we take this definition of happiness and examine it with reference to the senses, it will be acknowledged wonderfully adept. How sad and insipid do all objects accost us that are not conveyed in the vehicle of delusion! How shrunk is everything as it appears in the glass of Nature, so that if it were not for the assistance of artificial mediums, false lights, refracted angles, varnish, and tinsel, there would be a mighty level in the felicity and enjoyments of mortal men. If this were seriously considered by the world, as I have a certain reason to suspect it hardly will, men would no longer reckon among their high points of wisdom the art of exposing weak sides and publishing infirmities—an employment, in my opinion, neither better nor worse than that of unmasking, which, I think, has never been allowed fair usage, either in the world or the playhouse.

The suggestion of changing direction does not, in the first part of this passage, bring with it anything unsettling: from ridicule of "enthusiasm" to ridicule of human capacity for self-deception is an easy transition. The reader, as a matter of fact, begins to settle down to the habit, the steady drift of this irony, and is completely unprepared for the sudden change of tone and reversal of attitude in the two sentences beginning "How sad and insipid do all objects," etc. Exactly what the change means or is, it is difficult to be certain (and that is of the essence of the effect). But the tone has certainly a personal intensity and the ironic detachment seems suddenly to disappear. It is as if one found Swift in the place—at the point of view—where one expected to find his butt. But the ambiguously mocking sentence with which the paragraph ends reinforces the uncertainty.

The next paragraph keeps the reader for some time in uneasy doubt. The irony has clearly shifted its plane, but in which direction is the attack going to develop? Which, to be safe, must one dissociate oneself from, "credulity" or "curiosity"?

In the proportion that credulity is a more peaceful possession of the mind than curiosity, so far preferable is that wisdom which converses about the surface to that pretended philosophy which enters into the depths of things and then comes gravely back with informations and discoveries, that in the inside they are good for nothing. The two senses to which all objects first address themselves are the sight and the touch; these never examine further than the colour, the shape, the size, and whatever other qualities dwell or are drawn by art upon the outward of bodies; and then comes reason officiously, with tools for cutting, and opening, and mangling, and piercing, offering to demonstrate that they are not of the same consistence quite through. Now I take all this to be the last degree of perverting Nature, one of whose eternal laws is to put her best furniture forward. And therefore, in order to save the charges of all such expensive anatomy for the time to come, I do here think fit to inform the reader that in such conclusions as these reason is certainly in the right; and that in most corporeal beings which have fallen under my cognisance the outside hath been infinitely preferable to the in, whereof I have been further convinced from some late experiments. Last week I saw a woman flayed, and you will hardly believe how much it altered her person for the worse.

The peculiar intensity of that last sentence is, in its own way, so decisive that it has for the reader the effect of resolving uncertainty in general. The disturbing force of the sentence is a notable instance of a kind already touched on: repulsion is intensified by the momentary co-presence, induced by the tone, of incipient and incompatible feelings (or motions) of acceptance. And that Swift feels the strongest animus against "curiosity" is now beyond all doubt. The natural corollary would seem to be that "credulity," standing ironically for the "common forms"—the sane, socially sustained, common-sense illusions—is the positive that the reader must associate himself with and rest on for safety. The next half-page steadily and (to all appearances) unequivocally confirms this assumption:

Yesterday I ordered the carcass of a beau to be stripped in my presence, when we were all amazed to find so many unsuspected faults under one suit of clothes. Then I laid open his brain, his heart, and his spleen, but I plainly perceived at every operation that the farther we proceeded, we found the defects increase upon us in number and bulk; from all of which I justly formed this conclusion to myself, that whatever philosopher or projector can find out an art to sodder and patch up the flaws and imperfections of Nature, will deserve much better of mankind and teach us a much more useful science than that, so much in present esteem, of widening and exposing them (like him who held anatomy to be the ultimate end of physic). And he whose fortunes and dispositions have placed him in a convenient station to enjoy the fruits of this noble art, he that can with Epicurus content his ideas with the films and images that fly off upon his senses from the superficies of things, such a man, truly wise, creams off Nature, leaving the sour and the dregs for philosophy and reason to lap up.

Assumption has become habit, and has been so nourished that few readers note anything equivocal to trouble them in that last sentence: the concrete force of "creams off," "sour," "dregs" and "lap up" seems unmistakably to identify Swift with an intense animus against "philosophy and reason" (understood implicitly to stand for "curiosity" the anatomist). The reader's place, of course, is with Swift.

The trap is sprung in the last sentence of the paragraph:

This is the sublime and refined point of felicity called the possession of being well-deceived, the serene peaceful state of being a fool among knaves.

What is left? The next paragraph begins significantly: "But to return to madness." This irony may be critical, but "critical" turns out, in no very long run, to be indistinguishable from "negative." The positives disappear. Even when, as in the Houyhnhnms, they seem to be more substantially present, they disappear under our "curiosity." The Houyhnhnms, of course, stand for Reason, Truth and Nature, the Augustan positives, and it was in deadly earnest that Swift appealed to these; but how little at best they were anything solidly realized, comparison with Pope brings out. Swift did his best for the Houyhnhnms, and they may have all the reason, but the Yahoos have all the life. Gulliver's master "thought Nature and reason were sufficient guides for a reasonable animal," but nature and reason as Gulliver exhibits them are curiously negative, and the reasonable animals appear to have nothing in them to guide. "They have no fondness for their colts or foals, but the care they take in educating them proceeds entirely from the dictates of reason." This freedom from irrational feelings and impulses simplifies other matters too: "their language doth not abound in variety

of words, because their wants and passions are fewer than among us."
And so conversation, in this model society, is simplified: "nothing
passed but what was useful, expressed in the fewest and most significant
words . . ." "Courtship, love, presents, jointures, settlements, have no
place in their thoughts, or terms whereby to express them in their language. The young couple meet and are joined, merely because it is the
determination of their parents and friends: it is what they see done
every day, and they look upon it as one of the necessary actions of a
reasonable being." The injunction of "temperance, industry, exercise,
and cleanliness . . . the lessons enjoined to the young ones of both
sexes," seems unnecessary; except possibly for exercise, the usefulness of
which would not, perhaps, be immediately apparent to the reasonable
young.

The clean skin of the Houyhnhnms, in short, is stretched over a
void; instincts, emotions and life, which complicate the problem of
cleanliness and decency, are left for the Yahoos with the dirt and the
indecorum. Reason, Truth and Nature serve instead; the Houyhnhnms
(who scorn metaphysics) find them adequate. Swift too scorned metaphysics, and never found anything better to contend for than a skin, a
surface, an outward show. An outward show is, explicitly, all he con-
tends for in the quite unironical *Project for the Advancement of Religion,* and the difference between the reality of religion and the show
is, for the author of the *Tale of a Tub,* hardly substantial. Of Jack we
are told, "nor could all the world persuade him, as the common phrase
is, to eat his victuals like a Christian." It is characteristic of Swift that
he should put in these terms, showing a complete incapacity even to
guess what religious feeling might be, a genuine conviction that Jack
should be made to kneel when receiving the Sacrament.

Of the intensity of this conviction there can be no doubt. The
Church of England was the established "common form," and, moreover, was Swift's church: his insane egotism reinforced the savagery
with which he fought to maintain this cover over the void, this decent
surface. But what the savagery of the passage from the *Digression*
shows mainly is Swift's sense of insecurity and of the undisguisable
flimsiness of any surface that offered.

The case, of course, is more complex. In the passage examined
the "surface" becomes, at the most savage moment, a human skin.
Swift's negative horror, at its most disturbing, becomes one with his
disgust-obsession: he cannot bear to be reminded that under the skin

there is blood, mess and entrails; and the skin itself, as we know from *Gulliver*, must not be seen from too close. Hypertrophy of the sense of uncleanness, of the instinct of repulsion, is not uncommon; nor is its association with what accompanies it in Swift. What is uncommon is Swift's genius and the paradoxical vitality with which this self-defeat of life—life turned against itself—is manifested. In the *Tale of a Tub* the defeat is also a triumph; the genius delights in its mastery, in its power to destroy, and negation is felt as self-assertion. It is only when time has confirmed Swift in disappointment and brought him to more intimate contemplation of physical decay that we get the Yahoos and the Struldbrugs.

Here, well on this side of pathology, literary criticism stops. To attempt encroachments would be absurd, and, even if one were qualified, unprofitable. No doubt psychopathology and medicine have an interesting commentary to offer, but their help is not necessary. Swift's genius belongs to literature, and its appreciation to literary criticism.

We have, then, in his writings probably the most remarkable expression of negative feelings and attitudes that literature can offer—the spectacle of creative powers (the paradoxical description seems right) exhibited consistently in negation and rejection. His verse demands an essay to itself, but fits in readily with what has been said. "In poetry," he reports of the Houyhnhnms, "they must be allowed to excel all other mortals; wherein the justness of their similes and the minuteness as well as exactness of their descriptions are, indeed, inimitable. Their verses abound very much in both of these. . . ." The actuality of presentment for which Swift is notable, in prose as well as verse, seems always to owe its convincing "justness" to, at his least actively malicious, a coldly intense scrutiny, a potentially hostile attention. "To his domesticks," says Johnson, "he was naturally rough; and a man of rigorous temper, with that vigilance of minute attention which his works discover, must have been a master that few could bear." *Instructions to Servants* and the *Polite Conversation* enforce obviously the critical bearing and felicity of Johnson's remark.

A great writer—yes; that account still imposes itself as fitting, though his greatness is no matter of moral grandeur or human centrality; our sense of it is merely a sense of great force. And this force, as we feel it, is conditioned by frustration and constriction; the channels of life have been blocked and perverted. That we should be so often invited to regard him as a moralist and an idealist would seem to be mainly a witness to the power of vanity, and the part that vanity can play in literary appreciation: *saeva indignatio* is an indulgence that solicits us all, and the use of literature by readers and critics for the projection of nobly suffering selves is familiar. No doubt, too, it is pleasant to believe that unusual capacity for egotistic animus means unusual distinction of intellect; but, as we have seen, there is no reason to lay stress on intellect in Swift. His work does indeed exhibit an extraordinary play of mind; but it is not great intellectual force that is exhibited in his indifference to the problems raised—in, for instance, the *Voyage to the Houyhnhnms*—by his use of the concept, or the word, "Nature." It is not merely that he had an Augustan contempt for metaphysics; he shared the shallowest complacencies of Augustan common sense: his irony might destroy these, but there is no conscious criticism.

He was, in various ways, curiously unaware—the reverse of clairvoyant. He is distinguished by the intensity of his feelings, not by insight into them, and he certainly does not impress us as a mind in possession of its experience.

We shall not find Swift remarkable for intelligence if we think of Blake.

Clarissa and Emma as Phèdre

Dorothy Van Ghent

The great traditional love-stories present an ironic antagonism between instinct and society, instinct and law. Love is an occult power, an enchantment working automatically. It is obstructed by the most rigorous taboos. By the coupling and multiplication of taboos, all social institutionalism is represented and the terms of the opposition are tragically equalized. The lovers are sacrificed to their passion, which thus equates elliptically with the passion for death. This intricately structured form of the love-myth retains, with varying emphasis, its archaic sacramental significance. Sacramentally, the fertility god or goddess dies to renew life, the movement toward death is uninvolved, and there is no "obstacle." In Racine's *Phèdre,* the image of Venus as a great gluttonous bird, with talons fixed in her prey, reflects the destructiveness and inhumanity of the pure sensual passion; but the formal terms of the action show the passion as destructive, not primarily in its own nature, but because of its selection of a particular kind of barricaded object (Racine multiplies obstacles by giving Hippolyte a lover). Then as Phèdre falls back from one rationalization of her impulse to another—from the enmity of Venus, to Oenone's bad advice, to her own ancestry—the image of the great bird is displaced by one more bestial, that of the sun-bull. Phèdre's original doom, the doom of her priestly family, is used as an additional pressure in the tragic structure of oppositions between instinct and society. That is, the archaic, sacramental significance of the myth gives oblique enforcement to the sense of the automatism of instinct, its uncontrollable independent working, even though, in the more complex mythical structure, the center of significance is no longer renewal of life through death, but

Reprinted by permission of the author.

the relationship between individual and group—with the taboos, rebellion of instinct, outrage of law, and defeat that this relationship implies.

Emma Bovary, too, in the appalling automatism of her passion, is a member of the sun-family. But in her story, instinct and society do not confront each other antagonistically. There are no social "obstacles" to Emma's passion, equalized with it in strength; there is nothing in her circumstances to prevent her from committing adultery to her heart's content—if it were adultery that could content her heart; nor does her love choose a single object for its torment, but three—the Viscount (in fantasy), Rodolphe, and Léon—and three is a number that can stand for any series. Hence what appears to be a peculiar arbitrariness in the structure of the book. Charles, her husband, is the most factitious of "obstacles"; he is simply "there" (*Charles était là*), vegetative and inert; at the end, the child gives him a push with her finger and he falls over dead. Emma's relationship with the other chief character in the book, Homais (*homo,* but particularly sapient man, enlightened man, scientific man, progressive man, representative of an advanced social organization), is perfectly external, without dramatic moment in her career. Her significant relationships are with Lheureux and the blind man, and both of these are symbolic projections of her doom, evoked mysteriously by the scent of love, that is, by the scent of death, and associated ever more closely with her as the scent grows stronger:—Lheureux (the "happy"), vulture, scavenger, death-bird ("he looked at her fixedly, while in his hand he held two long papers that he slid between his nails": the buried metaphor of Lheureux as a bird, strangely like and yet violently unlike the bird-image of Venus, governs his mode of appearance); and the blind man—defects of the flesh, sensual frailty, physical corruption—who, by a forced narrative contrivance is brought to Emma's window when she is dying, with his song of maids in May whose petticoats are blown away. Her fatality is simpler than that of the tragic Phèdre, though related to it under the archaic aspect of the love-myth. Her simple direction is that of flesh back to earth, where presumably she fertilizes Lestiboudois' potato-seedlings. This direction is, of course, motored and made to signify by the fact of her sensuality: hers is the appetitive flesh, consuming itself in its pleasures.

Society, in *Madame Bovary,* is a complex of abstractions, bourgeois routines, clichés of thought and action, impotent skills. One can use the word "dead" to describe this society, thinking in terms of two kinds of death. A person dies only if he has been alive; Emma's is this kind of death—the death of the flesh that has felt and desired and rejoiced. Society is dead in having overpassed sensuality and become abstract—as its advance position is indicated in Homais, and its usual impotence in Binet, Bournisien, Rodolphe, Léon, even down to Lestiboudois with his corpse-planted potatoes. Being dead, this society cannot die. Emma's career has no social articulation because of the lack of points of possible contact between the sensual and the abstract, the living-dying and the dead-living. Her career locates, gives meaning to, and condemns the social death, but it does not do this at the level of a novel of manners. In the book as a novel of manners, Emma is a fool, herself condemned by foolishness. It does it at the level of myth, where she is a love-goddess.

In Richardson's *Clarissa Harlowe,* the death of the love-goddess exalts to admiration and gives supernatural sanction to the social abstractness and impotence. The love-goddess herself is, by a curious inversion of imagination, not the sensual woman but the woman immune to and irrelevant to sense. In the overthought of the book, where Clarissa's will to purity and Lovelace's will to defilement are hypostatized as in universal conflict, Lovelace appears to be an evil divinity and an anti-social principle: this is in the overt "Puritan myth" as such, which Richardson used to teach the "highest and most important doctrines of Christianity" (as he stated his intention). In the appearance of conflict, *Clarissa* affords a parallel with the ancient love-stories, where two equal powers, instinct in the individual as against the social organization, are pitted: here, daemonic sexual desire, and the representative purity of marriageable daughters, the market-bait of the financially consolidating bourgeois clan. But this relationship of conflict between Lovelace and Clarissa is only one center in a several-centered mythical construction; and even in the "Puritan myth" deliberately employed by Richardson, the appearance of a tragic equality of powers is misleading—a dramatic but undigested Manichaean element in the Puritan theology; for the universe is really a Harlowe-universe and is well loaded against Lovelace, as is shown by Clarissa's apotheosis and the minutely accurate distribution of rewards and punishments. The center of mythological significance that is pertinent to our subject lies in the underthought of the book and is read in the constant bombardment of sexual imagery even when the idea of the scene is the resistance of the chaste woman. Here there is no conflict. Inasmuch as Lovelace effects Clarissa's death and her return "to her Father's house" as the divinely sexless daughter—permanently chaste because dead—he is an instrument of the primal Harlowe-economy, the economy of death. He is a kind of moral employee of Mr. Harlowe, the living scourge exercised by the father upon the rebellious daughter who has "gone off with a man." ("Going off with a Man, is the thing I wanted most to make inexcusable," Richardson said. There is perhaps no word with emotional resonance occurring so frequently in *Clarissa* as the word "man.") Love itself is a non-sensual passion; it is an abstract, mechanical, obsessive concentration on murder; Lovelace is Jack the Ripper and Clarissa is Jill the Ripped. Instinct leads to death, not because it is anti-social, but because it acts in collusion with society and is instrumental to the hegemony of death. *Clarissa* is, therefore, not a tragedy, but—in the sense that it has the "happy ending" of death—a comedy, a "divine comedy."

The symbol of "the man" begins to evolve in Clarissa's first private interview with Solmes, the suitor approved by the Harlowes; he has splay feet, he sits "asquat" like a toad, he exhibits an "advancing posture," his "ugly weight" presses against her hoop. But Solmes's symbolic function as suitor is rather quickly over with; all he has to do, in this role, is to be repellent. Actually, he is just one more Harlowe male, sexless economic man—"rich Solmes"—through whom, under the universal governance of abstraction, the female must find her right use. He is approved by the Harlowes not only because he will make them richer, but also (for this is Richardson and not Balzac) because he is sure to duplicate the Harlowe nest in the future Solmes family; and not only to duplicate its form, but to attach the Solmes nest to the Harlowe nest, enlarging the colony but also consolidating it, so that the daughter will not really "go off with a man" but remain in her spiritual home, "her Father's house." More than increased wealth and a bought title for the Harlowes are at issue; the stakes are both societal and metaphysical.

"The man" proper—the man as lover and therefore as outlaw, social threat, and at the same time divine scourge of instinct, the predestined and adorable executioner—is focused in Lovelace. He offers to Clarissa the temptation of the wilderness: miracle (sex), mystery (death), and authority (divinity). And as she says, "Get thee behind me," she takes ravenously all he gives, for her immensely important duty as culture-heroine is to experience the most extreme sexual violence and to remain inviolate, to die for all women through the sexual assault but to die doubly in the traditional punning sense, and to become divine for all fathers of daughters and brothers of sisters as the martyr of a tribal organization in which there must be no love (remember what happened to Clary Harlowe!). She screams when she sees Lovelace in the garden, "A man!" "Ah, this man, my dear!" she exclaims to Miss Howe. "The man, my dear, looked quite ugly!" she tells her friend, after a predatory approach on Lovelace's part, and she complains of his "savage kiss" reddening her hand. Miss Howe confirms her notion of men: they are a "vile race of reptiles." Miss Howe would not be married to "any man breathing whom I at present know." Somewhere Joseph Conrad speaks of "the fascination of the abomination," and the phrase applies nicely to Lovelace. He is a woman's dream, the infantile imago of the male, the appealing figure of the sex-murderer (he complacently enumerates his mistresses who have died in childbirth), and he is all wit, all charm—the aristocrat. Even Miss Howe (whom he schemes, in fantasy, to abduct, along with her mother, by taking them on board ship, there to seduce them both), after being present at a party where Lovelace has fluttered the dovecotes, confesses that she has begun to see him in her dreams. With fairy-tale logic, Richardson has the beef-faced older sister, Arabella, wish on Clarissa that she may be seen a diseased Cressid begging along London streets—destiny envied by all Cinderella's sisters, along with captivity in a brothel—, and the surly brother, over-acting the paternal rapacity, engage Lovelace in a duel and confine his sister on bread and water.

Because the passion which is the subject of the novel is non-sensual, the field of sensibility is restricted to what can be *seen*. This restriction might appear to be an exigency of the letter-vehicle, for Clarissa can see herself only in mirrors, and others have to write of her as they see her. But the optical tactic works through devices especially emphatic of the seen; the image is usually framed, by mirror, key-hole, or door-frame (the most extreme case in point is the episode of the rape itself, when the door of the room is left open and "female figures flit" across it, watching); and by the distancing and framing for the eye, a large number of associations are excluded that might operate in an erotic context —as color-modulations, tactile impressions, nature-sounds, etc. Clarissa's seductiveness is for the narcist, the voyeur, and the sadist; she is the love-goddess of abstractionists and of a society gone abstract. In her perfect exclusion from sense-life, she offers the powerful ideality of the debile woman, thin and ever smart-shop. She "only eat a little bread." She refuses toast and is induced to drink a glass of water. Her diet is prescribed: water-gruel, weak broths, a dish of tea with milk. She is "like a half-broken-stalked lily." She wears white clothes only, whose dirt-resistance is set off by a horrid garret. She is ill "in a white satin night-gown, ever elegant!" After the rape, she gives all her clothes away, except for the suit with the everlasting laundry-guarantee, and Lovelace says, "Some disappointed fair ones would have hanged, some drowned themselves. My beloved only revenges herself upon her clothes." Phèdre finds her ornaments and her veils an encumbrance and a clumsy irrelevance: *"Que ces vains ornements, que ces voiles me pèsent!"* Knowing herself as flesh consumed by sensual passion, she would tear off her clothes because her moral honesty cannot tolerate that she should be disguised to others. Emma Bovary's garments are an aesthetic system for the refinement, elaboration, and enlargement of sense-life. Clarissa's are a part of, and as abstract as, her anatomy; they represent the maidenhead entrusted to her by her father, who invested in six expensive suits of it in anticipation of her marriage to Solmes, who was going to add some jewels; getting rid of the clothes is a ritualistic reenactment of the rape.

The optical image in *Clarissa* does not delay in the field of sense, even in the relatively abstract field of vision, but converts immediately to sexual idea—but to the sexual idea not as sensuality but as opening, tearing, cutting, stabbing, with its complement in the patience of the rent tissue, the flowing liquid (feminine tears), and the limp body. Clarissa temptingly brandishes keys; Lovelace obtains the key, and Clarissa absurdly says, "All my doors are fast, and nothing but the key-hole open, and the key of late put into that . . . ," suggesting the violent Picasso-like simplification of anatomy which is both her own portrait and a symbolic projection of the action of the book as it is endlessly repeated in detail. The dagger sinks constantly into the heart in metaphor before the phallus does, and the love-death is preparatively and afterwards reminiscently imitated in fainting-fits, cutting of laces, and the scenting of linen with hartshorn. In the fire-scene, with "nothing but an under petticoat, her lovely bosom half open," Clarissa picks up a "sharp-pointed scissors" and makes as if to stab herself. Again, having disordered her headdress and torn her neck-ruffles, she takes a penknife; "holding the pointed knife to her heaving bosom," she says, "Approach me, Lovelace . . . I dare die." And again, she implores him to do away with her, "baring, with still more frantic violence, part of her enchanting neck,—Here, here, said the soul-harrowing beauty, let thy pointed mercy enter!" Lovelace, using decent censorship, does it with drugs. After her death, he makes the final ritual necrophiliac gesture: he wants to "open" her, take out her heart.

The scene in the death-room is an astonishing one. The room is crowded with people, all pressing around the dying woman to obtain her blessing and receive some portion of her *mana*. The mourning is as public as possible; every sigh, every groan, every tear is recorded. One is given to understand that nothing could be a greater social good than Clarissa's death, nothing could be more enjoyable than to watch her in her charmingly performed death-throes, nothing a greater privilege than to be present at this festival of death and to sniffle in the common orgy. The *pietà* is purely feminine (Clarissa insists in her will that only members of her own sex touch her body), the appropriate dues of women to that woman who has miraculously managed to eat her cake and keep it. Though absurd, Clarissa has an archetypal greatness and a secret, underhanded, double-dealing association with the seeds of things, for she takes upon herself a social dream: the steriliza-tion of instinct, the supremacy of the "Father," the consolidation of society in abstraction, the cult of death; and while, through her, the systematic inhibitions of a culture are gratefully removed, and the for-bidden allowed mysterious indulgence, at the same time she gives super-natural sanction to those inhibitions, confirming them as the order of the universe, and provides a whipping-post for the indulgence. Her classic significance as love-goddess lies in the fact that she dies to pro-mote not fertility but sterility, and her myth is still vigorous in her two epigones, the ghost-woman of *Vogue*—debile, expensive, a smoke of clothes without skeletal support—and the many-breasted woman of *True Confessions* and *True Detective Stories,* in torn dishabille, with rolling eye-balls, and a dagger pointing at her.

Against the abstractions of *Clarissa,* Emma Bovary's sensual prov-ince is immense, and this is Emma's limitation, as grotesque as that of Clarissa: the limitation to the sensual. In contrast with Clarissa's white-ness, exquisite modulations of color, light and shade, play over Emma, defining her mode of being.

The sunshade, of silk of the colour of pigeons' breasts, through which the sun shone, lighted up with shifting hues the white skin of her face. She smiled under the tender warmth, and drops of water could be heard falling one by one on the stretched silk.

Whereas Clarissa's clothes are an allegorical representation of virginity, whose use is solely that of tearing and rending, Emma's are a complex sense-construct designed to delay and sustain aesthetic experience.

He saw her from behind in the glass between two lights. Her black eyes seemed blacker than ever. Her hair, undulating towards the ears, shone with a blue lustre; a rose in her chignon trembled on its mobile stalk, with artificial dewdrops on the tip of the leaves. She wore a gown of pale saffron trimmed with three bouquets of pompon roses mixed with green.

Toward the end of the final adulterous episode, she rips off her clothes savagely, but this is in the manner of Phèdre. At this point, her clothes are already in the talons of the death-bird Lheureux.

As exclusively as Emma is sensual, so is her world abstract: Charles, a vegetable lump, "serenely heavy," his mind an inorganic patchwork of other people's ideas (like the patchwork of the famous hat, with its successive layers of knobs, lozenges, rabbit-skin, cardboard); Homais with his pills, poultices, pickled foetuses, and clichés of progress; Léon with his Bohemian clichés; Rodolphe with his stud-farm clichés; Bournisien with his clichés of the catechism and the confessional; Lheureux with his receipts; Binet with his napkin-rings. Between Emma, as the sensual-organic, and the world she lives in, as the abstract-inorganic, there is no intercourse. Emma is, then, not the "weak, silky, vulgar little woman" that she would be if she were the romantic woman living under ordinary pedestrian conditions. Her extraordinary limitation gives her the profundity of a vital principle. Her mysterious dimensions, her beauty and her corruption, her uninvolved career toward death, are those of the sense-life under the aspect of Eros, for it is in love that the senses concentrate, toward love that they mature, and failing from love that they decay. Hence her relationship with the blind man—Homais' bitterest foe, whom he finally succeeds in getting locked up, as Emma herself has been locked out of the century of progress, in which the senses and death have no place.

Her mode of being is evoked incantatorily. Images of taste, touch, and temperature, involving teeth, tongue, fingers, skin, are manifold. Drinking curaçao, she "laughed at getting none of it, while with the tip of her tongue passing between her small teeth she licked drop by drop the bottom of her glass." "Emma from time to time cooled her cheeks with the palms of her hands, and cooled these again on the knobs of the huge fire-dogs." Sewing, she pricks her fingers, "which she then put to her mouth to suck them." "With the tips of her fingers she caught her dress at the knee." "Delicately, with her gloved hands, she picked off the coarse grass and the thistledown." At the Vaubyessard ball,

Iced champagne was poured out. Emma shivered all over as she felt it cold in her mouth. . . . She was just eating a maraschino ice that she held with her left hand in a silver-gilt cup, her eyes half-closed, and the spoon between her teeth.

"The musicians were cooling the tips of their fingers on their tongues." "She saw herself again as formerly, skimming with her finger the cream off the milk-pans in the dairy." The nurse, asking for brandy to rub the child's feet with, says, "They're as tender as one's tongue." Emma "bought a plan of Paris, and with the tip of her finger she walked about the capital." "She was as pleased as a child to push with her finger the large tapestried door." "Emma . . . clutching the velvet of the box with her nails." "Madame Bovary was already dipping her finger in the holy water." It is Emma's exclusive limitation to the sensual that gives the scene of the extreme unction, at the end of the book, its structural significance and that raises it above the level of Bournisien's clichés. The priest lays the oil

First, upon the eyes, that had so coveted all worldly pomp; then upon the nostrils, that had been greedy of the warm breeze and odours; then upon the mouth, that had uttered lies, that had curled with pride and cried out in lewdness; then upon the hands that had delighted in sensual touches; and finally upon the soles of the feet, so swift of yore, when she was running to satisfy her desires, and that would now walk no more.

As Albert Thibaudet says, in his book on Flaubert, Emma is not in love with a lover but with lovers, not with men but with love. But as the passion which animates her demands more of her lovers than they can contribute as men, so, also, she is more than herself as a country doctor's wife. She is Aphrodite: on her forest ride with Rodolphe, her face appears under her veil "in a bluish transparency as if she were floating under azure waves." The men inflecting her love-career are all three confused in the odor of the Viscount's hair-pomade. Rodolphe has recently been on a party in the same pleasure-boat where she picnics with Léon; she runs to rendezvous with Léon in the same lane where she had formerly met Rodolphe; she meets the Viscount again as she is hurrying from her last appointment with Léon. In each case, sexuality is given its mythological dimension by the serpent-image. After dancing with the Viscount ("Their legs commingled. . . . A torpor seized her . . . ," etc.) she is taken to the hothouse

where strange plants, bristling with hairs, rose in pyramids under hanging vases, whence, as from overfilled nests of serpents, fell long green cords interlacing.

On her last voluptuous night with Rodolphe, they watch the moon on the river:

The silver sheen seemed to writhe through the very depths like a headless serpent covered with luminous scales.

And in her final desperate throes with Léon, the image appears again:

She undressed brutally, tearing off the thin laces of her corset that nestled around her hips like a gliding snake . . . there was upon that brow covered with cold drops, on those quivering lips, in those wild eyes, in the strain of those arms, something vague and dreary that seemed to Léon to glide between them subtly as if to separate them.

Beginning as an image associated with aroused sexuality, the serpent eventually suggests separation, corruption, and death, concentrating thus, with bold traditionalism, the significance of the serpent as phallus and as inhabitant of the tomb, cult-object of love and death-deity; and evoking the significance of the goddess of beauty and love as Kore, daughter of Chthon, bride of death.

The final adulterous episode begins with Emma in a cab with Léon, departing from the Rouen cathedral. Behind them is the beadle's voice, shouting, "The Resurrection, the last Judgment, Paradise, King David, and the Condemned in Hell-flames," and in counterpoint against this eschatology, Léon from within the cab grunts out street-names to the driver and tells him, "Go on! Go on!" while

The good folk opened large wonder-stricken eyes at this sight, so extraordinary in the provinces, a cab with blinds drawn, and which appeared thus constantly shut more closely than a tomb.

Emma had dreamed of a honeymoon "in post-chaises behind blue silken curtains"; she makes her adulterous visits in the Hirondelle, going between Yonville and Rouen. The good folk of Rouen might well open large wonder-stricken eyes at the sight of the tomb-like cab, for it is drawn by Eros and Thanatos, and it has come from Eleusis and passed through Jerusalem.

From the beginning, Emma's sensual life has opened to her the perspective of the abyss, the abyss of infinite feeling hardly discriminable from the abyss of infinite non-feeling. "Her journey to Vaubyessard had made a hole in her life, like one of those great crevasses that a storm will sometimes make in one night in mountains."

Love, she thought, must come suddenly, with great outbursts and lightnings,—a hurricane of the skies, which falls upon life, revolutionises it, roots up the will like a leaf, and sweeps the whole heart into the abyss.

"She wished at the same time to die and to live in Paris." Her sickness, *amour-maladie,* is of her nature; that is, it is of the senses as such, meaning life and therefore meaning death, and it is not "conditioned" by her special social lot. Even before her first expedition in adultery, "she was lost in the terrible cold that pierced her"; "no help came, no sun rose, there was night on all sides." Charles vaguely feels "something fatal and incomprehensible whirling round him," and Rodolphe does not understand "what was all this worry about so simple an affair as love." Lheureux understands. He is already trailing Rodolphe and Emma at the fair, drawn by the death-smell, and he arrives instantly after the arrangement for the assignations with Léon. Hippolyte, too, close. His cries, "sharp spasms like the far-off howling of some beast being slaughtered," traverse the scene of Emma's illumination, when she sees Charles as irrescuably ineffectual, repents of "her past virtue as of a crime," and revels "in all the evil ironies of triumphant adultery." Against this abyss that smells of sperm and decomposition, and orchestrated with the cries of Hippolyte, there sounds, on Sundays, the monotonous humming of Binet's lathe, turning out napkin-rings: the idiotic concentration of the artisan, sunlit against the cold shadow of the sensual ages. Binet's senseless work is an extreme version of the environing social abstractness, and because it is insane it enters into more profound context with Emma's doom. When she goes up to the attic to read Rodolphe's jilt-letter, she hears Binet's lathe in the street below:

The luminous ray that came straight up from below drew the weight of her body towards the abyss . . . she had but to yield, to let herself be taken; and the humming of the lathe never ceased, like an angry voice calling her.

The insanity of an abstract world is for a moment identified with the insanity of the abyss: the two deaths for a savage moment identified—that of the living-dying and that of the dead-living.

On her return from her last trip to Rouen, she is with Homais in the Hirondelle. "All within her and around her was abandoning her. She felt lost, sinking at random into indefinable abysses." And immediately the counterpointed detail of the bourgeois routine is offered ironically accentuating, like the humming of Binet's lathe, the hysteria and doom of the abyss: Homais has purchased six *cheminots* for his wife—"Madame Homais was very fond of these small, heavy turban shaped loaves, that are eaten in Lent with salt butter . . . ," etc. (Each notation plays insistently on the same incommensurables: Homais and Emma have met at the *"Croix-Rouge"*; he has bought the bread of a baker in the *Rue Massacre;* the bread is a *Lenten* loaf.) They meet the blind man on the road—one of Breughel's blind men, a medieval moral emblem:

The blind man sank down on his haunches, with his head thrown back, whilst he rolled his greenish eyes, lolled out his tongue, and rubbed his stomach with both hands, as he uttered a kind of hollow yell like a famished dog.

And then again almost instantly, beside the blind man's howl, back to Binet and another kind of frenzy, not the frenzy of the death-bound flesh but that of the abstraction-intoxicated mind:

He was alone in his garret, busy imitating in wood one of those indescribable bits of ivory, composed of crescents, of spheres hollowed out one within the other, the whole as straight as an obelisk, and of no use whatever. . . .

When Emma dies, she too lolls out her tongue like the blind man. "The whole of her tongue protruded from her mouth." But she laughs when he sings at the window:

> Pour amasser diligemment
>   Les épis que la faux moissonne,
> Ma Nannette va s'inclinant
>   Vers le sillon qui nous les donne.

For it is of Emma herself that he sings, May-queen, Kore, earth-daughter, who goes bending toward the furrow, who is, like the corn, harvested by the scythe. Her changes in death are gruesome, for the same reason the blind man is gruesome: she is "the horror." Beside the horror, perfectly external to it and complacent, sit the Church and Science, the one degenerated into clichés, the other generating clichés. "We shall end," they say, "by understanding one another." Strangely, it is only Charles who recognizes the horror: Charles, the vegetative "there" and "that," the poor rudimentary potential of organism, who has been fabulously robbed of the vision of life.

Clarissa Harlowe and *Madame Bovary* are each beyond comparison technically, and to juxtapose them for comparison is to concede nothing to differences in time or artistic development. Their comparison as versions of love-myth is illuminating inasmuch as both, the one ingenuously, the other ironically, give a universal voice to modern idealism, giving dramatic form and religious significance to the same given mass of aspirations, attitudes, customs, and passions. The myth of *Clarissa* conforms naïvely to that acquisitive idealism that has been morally rationalized by Puritanism and afforded religious depth by fear, perverted sexuality, and death-worship. It is a paean to death, with the rape-motif central. The myth of *Madame Bovary* conforms deliberately to the archaic mode and is centered in the ancient, tragic, religious intelligence of the value and destructibleness of life. The myth is given precise temporal dimension by its modern setting in a culture which denies both the value of life and, with obstinate irrational logic, its destructibleness. When life is denied, it cannot really be destroyed, for it is already destroyed.

Hawthorne and the
Problem of Allegory

Yvor Winters

*At the moment of execution—with the halter
about his neck and while Colonel Pyncheon sat
on horseback, grimly gazing at the scene—
Maule had addressed him from the scaffold,
and uttered a prophecy, of which history as well
as fireside tradition, has preserved the very
words. "God," said the dying man, pointing
his finger, with a ghastly look, at the undis-
mayed countenance of his enemy, "God will
give him blood to drink!"*
—The House of the Seven Gables

Of Hawthorne's three most important long works—*The Scarlet
Letter, The House of the Seven Gables,* and *The Marble Faun*—the first
is pure allegory, and the other two are impure novels, or novels with
unassimilated allegorical elements. The first is faultless, in scheme and
in detail; it is one of the chief masterpieces of English prose. The second and third are interesting, the third in particular, but both are
failures, and neither would suffice to give the author a very high place
in the history of prose fiction. Hawthorne's sketches and short stories,
at best, are slight performances; either they lack meaning, as in the case
of "Mr. Higginbotham's Catastrophe," or they lack reality of embodi-

ment, as in the case of "The Birthmark," or, having a measure of both, as does "The Minister's Black Veil," they yet seem incapable of justifying the intensity of the method, their very brevity and attendant simplification, perhaps, working against them; the best of them, probably, is "Young Goodman Brown." In his later romances, *Septimius Felton, Dr. Grimshaw's Secret, The Ancestral Footstep,* and *The Dolliver Romance,* and in much of *The Blithedale Romance* as well, Hawthorne struggles unsuccessfully with the problem of allegory, but he is still obsessed with it.

Hawthorne is, then, essentially an allegorist; had he followed the advice of Poe and other well-wishers, contemporary with himself and posthumous, and thrown his allegorizing out the window, it is certain that nothing essential to his genius would have remained. He appears to have had none of the personal qualifications of a novelist, for one thing: the somber youth who lived in solitude and in contemplation in Salem, for a dozen years or more, before succumbing to the charms and propinquity of Miss Sophia Peabody and making the spasmodic and only moderately successful efforts to accustom himself to daylight which were to vex the remainder of his life, was one far more likely to concern himself with the theory of mankind than with the chaos, trivial, brutal, and exhausting, of the actuality. Furthermore, as we shall see more fully, the Puritan view of life was allegorical, and the allegorical vision seems to have been strongly impressed upon the New England literary mind. It is fairly obvious in much of the poetry of Emerson, Emily Dickinson, Byrant, Holmes, and even Very—Whittier, a Quaker and a peasant, alone of the more interesting poets escaping; Melville, relatively an outsider, shows the impact of New England upon his own genius as much through his use of allegory as through his use of New England character; and the only important novelist purely a New Englander, aside from Hawthorne, that is, O. W. Holmes, was primarily concerned with the Puritan tendency to allegory, as its one considerable satirist, yet was himself more or less addicted to it.

These matters are speculative. That New England predisposed Hawthorne to allegory cannot be shown; yet the disposition in both is obvious. And it can easily be shown that New England provided the perfect material for one great allegory, and that, in all likelihood, she was largely to blame for the later failures.

The Puritan theology rested primarily upon the doctrine of predestination and the inefficaciousness of good works; it separated men sharply and certainly into two groups, the saved and the damned, and, technically, at least, was not concerned with any subtler shadings. This in itself represents a long step toward the allegorization of experience, for a very broad abstraction is substituted for the patient study of the minutiae of moral behavior long encouraged by Catholic tradition. Another step was necessary, however, and this step was taken in Massachusetts almost at the beginning of the settlement, and in the expulsion of Anne Hutchinson became the basis of governmental action: whereas the wholly Calvinistic Puritan denied the value of the evidence of character and behavior as signs of salvation, and so precluded the possibility of their becoming allegorical symbols—for the orthodox Calvinist, such as Mrs. Hutchinson would appear to have been, trusted to no witness save that of the Inner Light—it became customary in Massachusetts to regard as evidence of salvation the decision of the individual to enter the Church and lead a moral life.

The Puritans [says Parkes] were plain blunt men with little taste for mysticism and no talent for speculation. A new conception was formulated by English theologians, of whom William Ames was the most influential. The sign of election was not an inner assurance it was a sober decision to trust in Christ and obey God's law. Those who made this sober decision might feel reasonably confident that they had received God's grace; but the surest proof of it was its fruit in conduct; complete assurance was impossible. It was assumed that all was the work of grace; it was God, without human coöperation, who caused the sober decision to be made. But in actual practice this doctrine had the effect of unduly magnifying man's ability to save himself, as much as Calvin's conception had unduly minimized it; conversion was merely a choice to obey a certain code of rules, and did not imply any emotional change, any love for God, or for holiness, or any genuine religious experience religion in other words was reduced to mere morality.[1]

Objective evidence thus took the place of inner assurance, and the behavior of the individual took on symbolic value. That is, any sin was evidence of damnation; or, in other words, any sin represented all sin. When Hester Prynne committed adultery, she committed an act as purely representative of complete corruption as the act of Faustus in signing a contract with Satan. This view of the matter is certainly not Catholic and is little short of appalling; it derives from the fact that

[1] *The Puritan Heresy*, by H. B. Parkes, The Hound and Horn, V-2, Jan.-March, 1932, pp. 173-4. See also *The Pragmatic Test*, by H. B. Parkes, The Colt Press, San Francisco.

although, as Parkes states in the passage just quoted, there occurred an exaggeration of the will in the matter of practical existence, this same will was still denied in the matter of doctrine, for according to doctrine that which man willed had been previously willed by God.

The belief that the judgment of a man is predestined by God, and the corollary that the judgment of a good man, since all men are either good or bad, purely and simply, is the judgment of God, may lead in the natural course of events to extraordinary drama; and this the more readily if the actors in the drama are isolated from the rest of the world and believe that the drama in which they take part is of cosmic importance and central in human destiny. Andrews writes: "The belief that God had selected New England as the chosen land was profoundly held by the Puritans who went there. Winthrop himself in 1640 wrote to Lord Saye and Sele of 'this good land which God hath found and given to his people,' adding that 'God had chosen this country to plant his people in.' Cotton in his sermon, *God's Promise to His Plantation* (London, 1634), devotes much space to the same idea—'This place is appointed me of God.'" [2] And Schneider writes on the same subject: "No one can live long in a Holy Commonwealth without becoming sensitive, irritable, losing his sense of values and ultimately his balance. All acts are acts either of God or of the devil; all issues are matters of religious faith; and all conflicts are holy wars. No matter how trivial an opinion might appear from a secular point of view, it became vital when promulgated as a theological dogma; no matter how harmless a fool might be, he was intolerable if he did not fit into the Covenant of Grace; no matter how slight an offense might be, it was a sin against Almighty God and hence infinite. Differences of opinion became differences of faith. Critics became blasphemers, and innovators, heretics." [3] And again: ". . . the mind of the Puritan was singularly unified and his imagination thoroughly moralized. The clergy were, of course, the professional moral scientists, but the laymen were no less dominated by such mental habits. The common man and illiterate shared with the expert this interest in divining God's purposes in the course of events. No event was merely natural; it was an act of God and was hence charged with that 'numinous' quality which gives birth to both prophetic insight and mystic illumination." [4] And again: "Nature was in-

---

[2] *The Colonial Period of American History*, by Charles M. Andrews, Yale University Press, 1934, Vol. I, p. 386, note 2.
[3] *The Puritan Mind*, by H. W. Schneider, Henry Holt & Co., 1930, pp. 51-2.
[4] *Ibid.*, p. 48.

structive to them only in so far as it suggested the hidden mysterious operations of designing agents. God and devil were both active, scheming, hidden powers, each pursuing his own ends by various ministrations, and natural events were therefore to be understood only in so far as they showed evidence of some divine or diabolical plot." [5]

Now according to the doctrine of predestination, if we interpret it reasonably, Hester merely gave evidence, in committing adultery, that she had always been one of the damned. This point of view, if really understood, could never have led to the chain of events which Hawthorne described in *The Scarlet Letter;* neither could it have led to the events of the actual history of New England. It is at this point that we must consider that fluid element, history, in connection with dogma, for Hester, like the witches who so occupied the Mathers, was treated as if she had willfully abandoned the ways of God for the ways of Satan. This final illogicality introduces the element of drama into the allegory of *The Scarlet Letter* and into the allegorical morality of the Puritans.

The English Puritans who settled Massachusetts were socially the product of centuries of the type of ethical discipline fostered by the Catholic and Anglo-Catholic Churches. They may have denied the freedom of the will and the efficaciousness of good works by lip, but by habit, and without really grasping the fact, they believed in them and acted upon them. Edwards exhorts sinners to repent while preaching the doctrine of the inability to repent; the Mathers wrestled with demons physically and in broad daylight, and quite obviously felt virtuous for having done so; in fact, to such a pass did Puritanism come, that Melville's Ahab, who willfully embarks upon the Sea of Unpredictability in order to overtake and slay the Spirit of Evil—an effort in which he is predestined and at the end of which he is predestined to destruction—appears to us merely the heroic projection of a common Puritan type. The Puritan may be said to have conceived the Manicheistic struggle between Absolute Good and Absolute Evil, which he derived through the processes of simplification and misunderstanding which have already been enumerated, as a kind of preordained or mechanical, yet also holy combat, in which his own part was a part at once intense and holy and yet immutably regulated.

There were at least two motives in the new environment which tended to intensify the effect of habit in this connection: one was the

inevitable impulse given to the will by the exaltation attendant upon a
new religious movement; the other was the impulse given by the su-
premely difficult physical surroundings in which the new colonies
found themselves. Foster writes on these points: "The first Puritans,
sure in their own hearts that they were the elect of God, found the
doctrine necessary to sustain them in the tremendous struggle through
which they passed. . . . Hence the doctrine nerved to greater activity;
and it produced a similar effect during the first period of the promulga-
tion of Calvinism, among every nation which accepted the system." [6]
The force of the will was strengthened at the beginning, then, at the
same time that its existence was denied and that reliance upon its manner of functioning (that is, upon good works) was, from a doctrinal
standpoint, regarded as sin. The will, highly stimulated, but no longer
studied and guided by the flexible and sensitive ethical scholarship of
the Roman tradition, might easily result in dangerous action.

Andrews speaks of this subject as follows:

The dynamic agency . . . the driving force which overrode all
opposition, legal and otherwise, was the profound conviction of the
Puritan leaders that they were doing the Lord's work. They looked
upon themselves as instruments in the divine hand for the carrying
out of a great religious mission, the object of which was the rebuild-
ing of God's church in a land—the undefiled land of America—
divinely set apart as the scene of a holy experiment that should
renovate the church at large, everywhere corrupt and falling into
ruins. This new and purified community was to be the home of a
saving remnant delivered from the wrath to come and was to serve
as an example to the mother church of a regenerated form of faith
and worship. It was also to become a proselyting center for the
conversion of the heathen and the extension of the true gospel
among those who knew it not. In the fulfillment of this mission
the Puritans counted obstacles, moral and physical, of no moment.
Theirs was a religious duty to frustrate their enemies, to eradicate
all inimical opinions, religious and political, and to extend the field
of their influence as widely as possible. Once they had determined
on their rules of polity and conduct, as laid down in the Bible and
interpreted by the clergy, they had no doubts of the justness and
rightness of their course. The means employed might savor of harsh-
ness and inequity, but at all costs and under all circumstances, error,
sin, and idolatry, in whatever form appearing and as determined by
themselves, must be destroyed. In the process, as events were to
prove, a great many very human motives played an important part

[6] *A Genetic History of the New England Theology*, by Frank Hugh Foster,
University of Chicago Press, 1907, p. 29.

in interpreting the law of God, and personal likes and dislikes, hypocrisy, prejudice, and passion got badly mixed with the higher and more spiritual impulses that were actively at work purging the church of its errors.[7]

Over a long period, however, the doctrine of predestination would naturally lead to religious apathy, for it offered no explicit motive to action; and this is precisely that to which it led, for after the Great Awakening of the middle of the eighteenth century, itself a reaction to previous decay in the Church, the Church lost power rapidly, and by the opening of the nineteenth century was succumbing on every hand to Unitarianism, a mildly moralistic creed, in which the element of supernaturalism was minimized, and which, in turn, yielded rapidly among the relatively intellectual classes to Romantic ethical theory, especially as propounded by the Transcendentalists. "It has never been a good way to induce men to repent," says Foster, "to tell them that they cannot."[8] Or at least the method has never been highly successful except when employed by a rhetorician of the power of Edwards, or by an orator of the effectiveness of Whitefield; and the effect can scarcely be expected long to outlive the immediate presence of the speaker. The Unitarians, in depriving the ethical life of the more impressive aspects of its supernatural sanction, and in offering nothing to take the place of that sanction, all but extinguished intensity of moral conviction, although their own conviction—we may see it portrayed, for example in *The Europeans,* by Henry James, and exemplified in the lucid and classical prose of W. E. Channing—was a conviction, at least for a period, of the greatest firmness and dignity. Emerson eliminated the need of moral conviction and of moral understanding alike, by promulgating the allied doctrines of equivalence and of inevitable virtue. In an Emersonian universe there is equally no need and no possibility of judgment; it is a universe of amiable but of perfectly unconscious imbeciles; it is likewise a universe in which the art of the fictionist—or for that matter, any other art—can scarcely be expected to flourish. A fictionist who has been in any considerable measure affected by Emersonian or allied concepts, or even who is the product of the historical sequence which gave rise to Emerson, is likely to find himself gravely confused and may even find himself paralyzed; and we have only to read such a document, to cite a single example, as *The New Adam and*

[7] Charles M. Andrews, *op. cit.*, Vol. I, pp. 430-1.
[8] Frank Hugh Foster, *op. cit.*, p. 29.

Eve, to realize that Hawthorne's own moral ideas, in spite of his intense but conflicting moral sentiments, and in spite of his professed dislike for Emerson's philosophy, were much closer to the ideas of Emerson than to those of Edwards.

Now in examining Hawthorne, we are concerned with two historical centers: that of the first generation of Puritans in New England, in which occurs the action of *The Scarlet Letter;* and that of the post-Unitarian and Romantic intellectuals, in which was passed the life of Hawthorne.

Hawthorne, by nature an allegorist, and a man with a strong moral instinct, regardless of the condition of his ideas, found in the early history of his own people and region the perfect material for a masterpiece. By selecting sexual sin as the type of all sin, he was true alike to the exigencies of drama and of history. In the setting which he chose, allegory was realism, the idea was life itself; and his prose, always remarkable for its polish and flexibility, and stripped, for once, of all superfluity, was reduced to the living idea, it intensified pure exposition to a quality comparable in its way to that of great poetry.

The compactness and complexity of the allegory will escape all save the most watchful readers. Let us consider the following passage as a representative example. Hester has learned that the magistrates and clergy are considering whether or not she ought to be separated from her child, and she waits upon Governor Bellingham in order to plead with him:

On the wall hung a row of portraits, representing the forefathers of the Bellingham lineage, some with armor on their breasts, and others with stately ruffs and robes of peace. All were characterized by the sternness and severity which old portraits so invariably put on; as if they were the ghosts, rather than the pictures, of departed worthies, and were gazing with harsh and intolerant criticism at the pursuits and enjoyments of living men.

At about the center of the oaken panels, that lined the hall, was suspended a suit of mail, not, like the pictures, an ancestral relic, but of the most modern date; for it had been manufactured by a skillful armorer in London, the same year in which Governor Bellingham came over to New England. There was a steel head-piece, a cuirass, a gorget, and greaves, with a pair of gauntlets and a sword hanging beneath; all, especially the helmet and breast-plate, so highly burnished as to glow with white radiance, and scatter an illumination everywhere about the floor. This bright panoply was not meant for mere idle show, but had been worn by the Governor on many a solemn muster and training field, and had glittered, moreover, at the head of a regiment in the Pequot war. For, though bred a lawyer, and accustomed to speak of Bacon, Coke, Noye, and Finch as his professional associates, the exigencies of this new country had transformed Governor Bellingham into a soldier as well as a statesman and ruler.

Little Pearl—who was as greatly pleased with the gleaming armor as she had been with the glittering frontispiece of the house—spent some time looking into the polished mirror of the breast-plate. "Mother," cried she, "I see you here. Look! Look!"

Hester looked, by way of humoring the child; and she saw that, owing to the peculiar effect of the convex mirror, the scarlet letter was represented in gigantic and exaggerated proportions, so as to be greatly the most prominent feature of her appearance. In truth, she seemed absolutely hidden behind it. Pearl pointed upward, also, at a similar picture in the head-piece; smiling at her mother with the elfish intelligence that was so familiar an expression on her small physiognomy. That look of naughty merriment was likewise reflected in the mirror, with so much breadth and intensity of effect, that it made Hester Prynne feel as if it could not be the image of her own child, but of an imp who was seeking to mold itself into Pearl's shape.

The portraits are obviously intended as an apology for the static portraits in the book, as an illustration of the principle of simplification by distance and by generalization; the new armor, on the other hand, is the new faith which brought the Puritans to New England, and which not only shone with piety—"especially the helmet and breast-plate," the covering of the head and heart—but supported them in their practical struggles with physical adversaries, and which in addition altered their view of the life about them to dogmatic essentials, so that Hester was obliterated behind the fact of her sin, and Pearl transformed in view of her origin. Governor Bellingham, in his combination of legal training with military prowess, is representative of his fellow colonists, who displayed in a remarkable degree a capacity to act with great strength and with absolutely simple directness upon principles so generalized as scarcely to be applicable to any particular moral problem, which mastered moral difficulties not by understanding them, but by crushing them out.

Historically and relatively considered, Richard Bellingham might conceivably have been spared this function in the story, for of his group he was one of the two or three most humane and liberal; but the qualities represented were the qualities of the group of which he was a leader, and were extremely evident in most of the actions of the colony. Perhaps the best—or in another sense, the worst—embodiment of these qualities is to be found in John Endecott, of whom Andrews gives the following characterization:

Endecott had few lovable qualities. He was stern, unyielding, and on some subjects a zealot. Johnson apostrophizes him as "strong, valiant John," whom Christ had called to be his soldier, but the Old Planters, most if not all of whom were Anglicans and demanded service according to the Book of Common Prayer, deemed themselves slaves and took in very bad part his determination to suppress the Church of England in the colony. They preferred Roger Conant, who though a less forcible man was one much easier to get along with. Endecott's later career discloses his attitude toward those who differed with him—the heathen Indian, the Quaker, the prisoner before him for judgment, and the Brownes and other up-holders of the Anglican service who were disaffected with the Puritan government. It also shows his dislike of forms and devices that offended him—the Book of Common Prayer, the cross of St. George, and the Maypole. He was hard, intolerant, and at times cruel. Even the Massachusetts government caused him "to be sadly admonished for his offense" in mutilating the flag at Salem in 1635, charging him with "rashness, uncharitableness, indiscretion, and exceeding the limits of his calling"; and again in the same year "committed" him for losing his temper. Endecott once apologized to Winthrop for striking "goodman Dexter," acknowledging that he was rash, but saying that Dexter's conduct "would have pro-voked a very patient man." The best that can be said of him has been said by Chapple ("The Public Service of John Endecott," Historical Collections, Essex Institute), an essay in the best Palfrey manner. It is odd that Endecott should have chosen for his seal a skull and cross-bones.[9]

It is interesting to observe in such a passage, as in many others, that the Puritans cannot be discussed, nor can they discuss each other, with-out the language employed exceeding the limits proper to predestinar-ians and invoking the traditional morality of the older churches; yet the attempt to ignore this traditional morality as far as might be, and, in the matter of formal doctrine, to repudiate it, unquestionably had much to do with the formation of such characters as Professor Andrews here describes and as Hawthorne in the last passage quoted from him sym-bolizes. The imperceptive, unwavering brutality of many of the actions committed in the name of piety in the Massachusetts colonies more than

[9] Charles M. Andrews, *op. cit.*, Vol. I, p. 361, note 3.

justified the curse and prophecy uttered by Matthew Maule, that God would give these Puritans blood to drink; in the name of God, they had violently cut themselves off from human nature; in the end, that is in Hawthorne's generation and in the generation following, more than one of them drank his own heart's blood, as Hawthorne himself must have done in his ultimate and frustrated solitude, and more than one of them shed it.

It is noteworthy that in this passage from *The Scarlet Letter* Hawthorne turns his instrument of allegory, the gift of the Puritans, against the Puritans themselves, in order to indicate the limits of their intelligence; it is noteworthy also that this act of criticism, though both clear and sound, is negative, that he nowhere except in the very general notion of regeneration through repentance establishes the nature of the intelligence which might exceed the intelligence of the Puritans, but rather hints at the ideal existence of a richer and more detailed understanding than the Puritan scheme of life is able to contain. The strength of *The Scarlet Letter* is in part safe-guarded by the refusal to explore this understanding; the man who was able in the same lifetime to write *The New Adam and Eve,* to conceive the art-colony described in *The Marble Faun,* and to be shocked at the nude statues of antiquity, was scarcely the man to cast a clear and steady light upon the finer details of the soul.

The conception of the book in general is as cleanly allegorical as is the conception of the passage quoted. Hester represents the repentant sinner, Dimmesdale the half-repentant sinner, and Chillingworth the unrepentant sinner. The fact that Chillingworth's sin is the passion for revenge is significant only to the extent that this is perhaps the one passion which most completely isolates man from normal human sympathies and which therefore is most properly used to represent an unregenerate condition.

The method of allegorization is that of the Puritans themselves; the substance of the allegory remained in a crude form a part of their practical Christianity in spite of their Calvinism, just as it remained in their non-theological linguistic forms, just as we can see it in the language of the best poems of so purely and mystically Calvinistic a writer as Jones Very, a living language related to a living experience, but overflowing the limits of Calvinistic dogma; Hawthorne's point of view was naturally more enlightened than that of the Puritans themselves, yet it was insufficiently so to enable him to recover the traditional

Christian ethics except in the most general terms and by way of historical sympathy, for had a more complete recovery been possible, he would not have been so narrowly bound to the method of allegory and the frustration of the later romances would scarcely have been so complete.

Once Hawthorne had reduced the problem of sin to terms as general as these, and had brought his allegory to perfect literary form, he had, properly speaking, dealt with sin once and for all; there was nothing further to be said about it. It would not serve to write another allegory with a new set of characters and a different sin as the motive; for the particular sin is not particular in function, but is merely representative of sin in general, as the characters, whatever their names and conditions may be, are merely representative of the major stages of sin —there is no escape from the generality so long as one adheres to the method. There was nothing further, then, to be done in this direction, save the composition of a few footnotes to the subject in the form of sketches.

The only alternative remaining was to move away from the allegorical extreme of narrative toward the specific, that is, toward the art of the novelist. The attempt was made, but fell short of success. In *The House of the Seven Gables* and in *The Marble Faun* alike the moral understanding of the action—and there is a serious attempt at such understanding, at least in *The Marble Faun*—is corrupted by a provincial sentimentalism ethically far inferior to the Manicheism of the Puritans, which was plain and comprehensive, however brutal. And Hawthorne had small gift for the creation of human beings, a defect allied to his other defects and virtues: even the figures in *The Scarlet Letter* are unsatisfactory if one comes to the book expecting to find a novel, for they draw their life not from simple and familiar human characteristics, as do the figures of Henry James, but from the precision and intensity with which they render their respective ideas; the very development of the story is neither narrative nor dramatic, but expository. When, as in *The Marble Faun* or *The House of the Seven Gables,* there is no idea governing the human figure, or when the idea is an incomplete or unsatisfactory equivalent of the figure, the figure is likely to be a disappointing spectacle, for he is seldom if ever a convincing human being and is likely to verge on the ludicrous. Hawthorne had not the rich and profound awareness of immediacy which might have saved a writer such as Melville in a similar predicament.

His effort to master the novelist's procedure, however, was not sustained, for his heart was not in it. In *The Blithedale Romance,* he began as a novelist, but lost himself toward the close in an unsuccessful effort to achieve allegory; the four unfinished romances represent similar efforts throughout.

His procedure in the last works was startlingly simple; so much so, that no one whom I can recollect has run the risk of defining it.

In *The Scarlet Letter* there occurs a formula which one might name the formula of alternative possibilities. In the ninth chapter, for example, there occurs the following passage:

The people, in the case of which we speak, could justify its prejudice against Roger Chillingworth by no fact or argument worthy of serious refutation. There was an aged handicraftsman, it is true, who had been a citizen of London at the period of Sir Thomas Overbury's murder, now some thirty years agone; he testified to having seen the physician, under some other name, which the narrator of the story had now forgotten, in company with Dr. Forman, the famous old conjuror, who was implicated in the affair of Overbury. Two or three individuals hinted, that the man of skill, during his Indian captivity, had enlarged his medical attainments by joining in the incantations of the savage priests; who were universally acknowledged to be powerful enchanters, often performing seemingly miraculous cures by their skill in the black art. A large number—many of them were persons of such sober sense and practical observation that their opinions would have been valuable in other matters—affirmed that Roger Chillingworth's aspect had undergone a remarkable change while he had dwelt in the town, and especially since his abode with Dimmesdale. At first, his expression had been calm, meditative, scholar-like. Now, there was something ugly and evil in his face, which they had not previously noticed, and which grew still more obvious to sight the oftener they looked upon him. According to the vulgar idea, the fire in his laboratory had been brought from the lower regions, and was fed with infernal fuel; and so, as might be expected, his visage was getting sooty with smoke.

In such a passage as this, the idea conveyed is clear enough, but the embodiment of the idea appears far-fetched, and Hawthorne offers it whimsically and apologetically, professing to let you take it or leave it. Another example occurs in the eighteenth chapter; Dimmesdale and Hester are sitting in the forest, planning the flight which ultimately is never to take place, and Pearl, the symbolic offspring of the untamed elements of human nature, and hence akin to the forest, which, in the Puritan mind, was ruled by Satan in person, plays apart: "A fox,

startled from his sleep by her light footstep on the leaves, looked in-
quisitively at Pearl, as doubting whether it were better to steal off or
renew his nap on the same spot. A wolf, it is said—but here the tale
has surely lapsed into the improbable—came up and smelt of Pearl's
robe, and offered his savage head to be patted by her hand. The truth
seems to be, however, that the mother-forest, and these wild things
which it nourished, all recognized a kindred wildness in the human
child." Similarly, in *The Marble Faun,* one never learns whether Dona-
tello had or had not the pointed ears which serve throughout the book
as the physical symbol of his moral nature; the book ends with the question being put to Kenyon, who has had opportunities to observe, and
with his refusing to reply.

This device, though it becomes a minor cause of irritation through
constant recurrence, is relatively harmless, and at times is even used
with good effect. If we reverse the formula, however, so as to make
the physical representation perfectly clear but the meaning uncertain,
we have a very serious situation; and this is precisely what occurs, in
some measure toward the close of *The Blithedale Romance,* and without mitigation throughout the four unfinished romances. We have in
the last all of the machinery and all of the mannerisms of the allegorist,
but we cannot discover the substance of his communication, nor is he
himself aware of it so far as we can judge. We have the symbolic foot-
print, the symbolic spider, the symbolic elixirs and poisons, but we have
not that of which they are symbolic; we have the hushed, the tense and
confidential manner, on the part of the narrator, of one who imparts a
grave secret, but the words are inaudible. Yet we have not, on the
other hand, anything approaching realistic fiction, for the events are
improbable or even impossible, and the characters lack all reality. The
technique neither of the novelist nor of the allegorist was available to
Hawthorne when he approached the conditions of his own experience:
he had looked for signals in nature so long and so intently, and his
ancestors before him had done so for so many generations, that, like a
man hypnotized, or like a man corroded with madness, he saw them;
but he no longer had any way of determining their significance, and he
had small talent for rendering their physical presence with intensity.

Percy Boynton,[10] in quoting the following passages from *Septimius
Felton,* refers to it as a self-portrait: "As for Septimius, let him alone a

[10] *Literature and American Life,* by Percy H. Boynton, Ginn and Co., 1936,
p. 518.

moment or two, and then they would see him, with his head bent down, brooding, brooding, his eyes fixed on some chip, some stone, some common plant, any commonest thing, as if it were the clew and index to some mystery; and when, by chance startled out of these meditations, he lifted his eyes, there would be a kind of perplexity, a dissatisfied, foiled look in them, as if of his speculations he found no end."

It is in this generation and the next that we see most clearly and bitterly the realization of Maule's prophecy. These men were cut off from their heritage, from their source of significance, and were abnormally sensitive to the influence of European Romanticism. In Emerson[11] the terms of New England mysticism and of Romantic amoralism were fused and confused so inextricably that we have not yet worked ourselves free of them. In Poe, a man born without a background, New England or any other, Romantic doctrine was introduced directly, in a form free of theological terminology, but in a form none the less which would tend in the long run to support the influence of Emerson. In Melville, the greatest man of his era and of his nation, we find a writer superior at certain points in his career—in books such as *Moby Dick* and *Benito Cereno,* for example—to the confusion and apparently understanding it; at other points—in books like *Mardi* and *Pierre,*—succumbing to the confusion; at all points in his career made to suffer for the confusion of contemporary literary taste; and at the end, settling himself in silence, a figure more difficult to face than the later Hawthorne—more difficult, because more conscious, more controlled, and more nearly indifferent.

In Henry Adams we see the curse at work most clearly: intellectual but inconsecutive, unable to justify any principle of action, yet with a character of the highest, a character which demanded not only just action but its justification, he was damned to a kind of restless torment; in which, though an historian of great learning and of high academic distinction, he transformed the Middle Ages by a process of subtle falsification, into a symbol of his own latter-day New England longing; in which, though a stylist of great power and precision, he propounded the aesthetic theory that modern art must be confused to express confusion;[12] in which, though a philosopher of a sort, he created one of the most unphilosophical theories of history imaginable, as a poetic symbol of his own despair. In the suicide of Henry Adams' wife it is

[11] This subject is fully discussed by H. B. Parkes, The Hound and Horn, V-4, July-Sept., 1932, pp. 581-601, and *The Pragmatic Test.*
[12] See the last three or four pages of *Mont Saint-Michel and Chartres.*

conceivable that we see the logical outcome of his own dilemma, an outcome in his own case prevented by the inheritance of character, which, like the inheritance of confusion, was bequeathed him by early New England.[13]

In *The Scarlet Letter,* then, Hawthorne composed a great allegory; or, if we look first at the allegorical view of life upon which early Puritan society was based, we might almost say that he composed a great historical novel. History, which by placing him in an anti-intellectual age had cut him off from the ideas which might have enabled him to deal with his own period, in part made up for the injustice by facilitating his entrance, for a brief time, into an age more congenial to his nature. Had he possessed the capacity for criticizing and organizing conceptions as well as for dramatizing them, he might have risen superior to his disadvantages, but like many other men of major genius he lacked this capacity. In turning his back upon the excessively simplified conceptions of his Puritan ancestors, he abandoned the only orderly concepts, whatever their limitations, to which he had access, and in his last work he is restless and dissatisfied. The four last romances are unfinished, and in each successive one he sought to incorporate and perfect elements from those preceding; the last, *The Dolliver Romance,* which he had sought to make the best, had he lived, is a mere fragment, but on the face of it is the most preposterous of all. His dilemma, the choice between abstractions inadequate or irrelevant to experience on the one hand, and experience on the other as far as practicable unilluminated by understanding, is tragically characteristic of the history of this country and of its literature; only a few scattered individuals, at the cost of inordinate labor, and often impermanently, have achieved the permeation of human experience by a consistent moral understanding which results in wisdom and in great art. If art is to be measured by the greatness of the difficulties overcome—and the measure is not wholly unreasonable, for there can scarcely be virtue without a comprehension of sin, and the wider and more careful the comprehension the richer the virtue—then these few writers are very great indeed. Hawthorne, when he reversed his formula of alternative possibilities, and sought to grope his way blindly to significance, made the choice of the later Romantics; and his groping was met wherever he moved by the smooth and impassive surface of the intense inane.

[13] This idea is very ably defended by Katherine Simonds, the *New England Quarterly,* December, 1936.

Phases of Fiction

Virginia Woolf

The following pages attempt to record the impressions made upon the mind by reading a certain number of novels in succession. In deciding which book to begin with and which book to go on with, the mind was not pressed to make a choice. It was allowed to read what it liked. It was not, that is to say, asked to read historically, nor was it asked to read critically. It was asked to read only for interest and pleasure and, at the same time, to comment as it read upon the nature of the interest and the pleasure that it found. It went its way, therefore, independent of time and reputation. It read Trollope before it read Jane Austen and skipped, by chance or negligence, some of the most celebrated books in English fiction. Thus, there is little reference or none to Fielding, Richardson or Thackeray.

Yet, if nobody save the professed historian and critic reads to understand a period or to revise a reputation, nobody reads simply by chance or without a definite scale of values. There is, to speak metaphorically, some design that has been traced upon our minds which reading brings to light. Desires, appetites, however we may come by them, fill it in, scoring now in this direction, now in that. Hence, an ordinary reader can often trace his course through literature with great exactness and can even think himself, from time to time, in possession of a whole world as inhabitable as the real world. Such a world, it may be urged against it, is always in process of creation. Such a world, it may be added, likewise against it, is a personal world, a world limited and unhabitable perhaps by other people, a world created in obedience to tastes that may be peculiar to one temperament and distasteful to

Reprinted by permission of Harcourt, Brace and Company.

another—indeed, any such record of reading, it will be concluded, is bound to be limited, personal, erratic.

In its defense, however, it may be claimed that if the critic and the historian speak a more universal language, a more learned language, they are also likely to miss the centre and to lose their way for the simple reason that they know so many things about a writer that a writer does not know about himself. Writers are heard to complain that influences—education, heredity, theory—are given weight of which they themselves are unconscious in the act of creation. Is the author in question the son of an architect or a bricklayer? Was he educated at home or at the university? Does he come before or after Thomas Hardy? Yet no one of these things is in his mind, perhaps, as he writes and the reader's ignorance, narrowing and limiting as it is, has at least the advantage that it leaves unhampered what the reader has in common with the writer, though much more feebly: the desire to create.

Here, then, very briefly and with inevitable simplifications, an attempt is made to show the mind at work upon a shelf full of novels and to watch it as it chooses and rejects, making itself a dwelling place in accordance with its own appetites. Of these appetites, perhaps, the simplest is the desire to believe wholly and entirely in something which is fictitious. That appetite leads on all the others in turn. There is no saying, for they change so much at different ages, that one appetite is better than another. The common reader is, moreover, suspicious of fixed labels and settled hierarchies. Still, since there must be an original impulse, let us give the lead to this one and start upon the shelf full of novels in order to gratify our wish to believe.

I

The Truth-Tellers

In English fiction there are a number of writers who gratify our sense of belief—Defoe, Swift, Trollope, Borrow, W. E. Norris, for example; among the French, one thinks instantly of Maupassant. Each of them assures us that things are precisely as they say they are. What they describe happens actually before our eyes. We get from their novels the same sort of refreshment and delight that we get from seeing something actually happen in the street below. A dustman, for example, by an awkward movement of his arm knocks over a bottle apparently containing Condy's Fluid which cracks upon the pavement. The dustman gets down; he picks up the jagged fragments of the broken bottle; he turns to a man who is passing in the street. We cannot take our eyes off him until we have feasted our powers of belief to the full. It is as if a channel were cut, into which suddenly and with great relief an emotion hitherto restrained rushes and pours. We forget whatever else we may be doing. This positive experience overpowers all the mixed and ambiguous feelings of which we may be possessed at the moment. The dustman has knocked over a bottle; the red stain is spreading on the pavement. It happens precisely so.

The novels of the great truth-tellers, of whom Defoe is easily the English chief, procure for us a refreshment of this kind. He tells us the story of Moll Flanders, of Robinson Crusoe, of Roxana, and we feel our powers of belief rush into the channel, thus cut, instantly fertilizing and refreshing our entire being. To believe seems the greatest of all pleasures. It is impossible to glut our greed for truth, so rapacious is it. There is not a shadowy or insubstantial word in the whole book to startle our nervous sense of security. Three or four strong, direct strokes of the pen carve out Roxana's character. Her dinner is set indisputably on the table. It consists of veal and turnips. The day is fine or cloudy; the month is April or September. Persistently, naturally, with a curious, almost unconscious iteration, emphasis is laid upon the very facts that most reassure us of stability in real life, upon money, furniture, food, until we seem wedged among solid objects in a solid universe.

One element of our delight comes from the sense that this world, with all its circumstantiality, bright and round and hard as it is, is yet complete, so that in whatever direction we reach out for assurance we receive it. If we press on beyond the confines of each page, as it is our instinct to do, completing what the writer has left unsaid, we shall find that we can trace our way; that there are indications which let us realize them; there is an under side, a dark side to this world. Defoe presided over his universe with the omnipotence of a God, so that his world is perfectly in scale. Nothing is so large that it makes another thing too small; nothing so small that it makes another thing too large.

The name of God is often found on the lips of his people, but they invoke a deity only a little less substantial than they are themselves, a being seated solidly not so very far above them in the tree tops. A divinity more mystical, could Defoe have made us believe in him, would so have discredited the landscape and cast doubt upon the substance of the men and women that our belief in them would have perished at the heart. Or, suppose that he let himself dwell upon the green shades of the forest depths or upon the sliding glass of the summer stream. Again, however much we were delighted by the description, we should have been uneasy because this other reality would have wronged the massive and monumental reality of Crusoe and Moll Flanders. As it is, saturated with the truth of his own universe, no such discrepancy is allowed to intrude. God, man, nature are all real, and they are all real with the same kind of reality—an astonishing feat, since it implies complete and perpetual submission on the writer's part to his conviction, an obdurate deafness to all the voices which seduce and tempt him to gratify other moods. We have only to reflect how seldom a book is carried through on the same impulse of belief, so that its perspective is harmonious throughout, to realize how great a writer Defoe was. One could number on one's fingers half a dozen novels which set out to be masterpieces and yet have failed because the belief flags; the realities are mixed; the perspective shifts and, instead of a final clarity, we get a baffling, if only a momentary confusion.

Having, now, feasted our powers of belief to the full and so enjoyed the relief and rest of this positive world existing so palpably and completely outside of us, there begins to come over us that slackening of attention which means that the nerve in use is sated for the time being. We have absorbed as much of this literal truth as we can and we begin to crave for something to vary it that will yet be in harmony with it. We do not want, except in a flash or a hint, such truth as Roxana offers us when she tells us how her master, the Prince, would sit by their child and "loved to look at it when it was asleep." For that truth is hidden truth; it makes us dive beneath the surface to realize it and so holds up the action. It is, then, action that we want. One desire having run its course, another leaps forward to take up the burden and no sooner have we formulated our desire than Defoe has given it to us. "On with the story"—that cry is forever on his lips. No sooner has he got his facts assembled than the burden is floated. Perpetually springing up, fresh and effortless, action and event, quickly succeeding each other thus, set in motion this dense accumulation of facts and keep the breeze blowing in our faces. It becomes obvious, then, that if his people are sparely equipped and bereft of certain affections, such as love of husband and child, which we expect of people at leisure, it is that they may move quicker. They must travel light since it is for adventure that they are made. They will need quick wits, strong muscles and a rocky common sense on the road they are to travel rather than sentiment, reflection or the power of self-analysis.

Belief, then, is completely gratified by Defoe. Here, the reader can rest himself and enter into possession of a large part of his domain. He tests it; he tries it; he feels nothing give under him or fade before him. Still, belief seeks fresh sustenance as a sleeper seeks a fresh side of the pillow. He may turn, and this is likely, to someone closer to him in time than Defoe in order to gratify his desire for belief (for distance of time in a novel sets up picturesqueness, hence unfamiliarity). If he should take down, for example, some book of a prolific and once esteemed novelist, like W. E. Norris, he will find that the juxtaposition of the two books brings each out more clearly.

W. E. Norris was an industrious writer who is well worth singling out for enquiry if only because he represents that vast body of forgotten novelists by whose labors fiction is kept alive in the absence of the great masters. At first, we seem to be given all that we need: girls and boys, cricket, shooting, dancing, boating, love making, marriage; a park here; a London drawing room there; here, an English gentleman; there, a cad; dinners, tea parties, canters in the Row; and, behind it all, green and gray, domestic and venerable, the fields and manor houses of England. Then, as one scene succeeds another, half-way through the book, we seem to have a great deal more belief on our hands than we know what to do with. We have exhausted the vividness of slang; the modernity, the adroit turn of mood. We loiter on the threshold of the scene, asking to be allowed to press a little further; we take some phrase and look at it as if it ought to yield us more. Then, turning our eyes from the main figures, we try to sketch out something in the background, to pursue these feelings and relations away from the present moment; not, needless to say, with a view to discovering some overarching conception, something which we may call "a reading of life." No, our desire is otherwise: some shadow of depth appropriate to the bulk of the figures; some Providence such as Defoe provides or morality such as he suggests, so that we can go beyond the age itself without falling into inanity.

Then, we discover it is the mark of a second-rate writer that he cannot pause here or suggest there. All his powers are strained in keeping the scene before us, its brightness and its credibility. The surface is all; there is nothing beyond.

Our capacity for belief, however, is not in the least exhausted. It is only a question of finding something that will revive it for us. Not Shakespeare and not Shelley and not Hardy; perhaps, Trollope, Swift, Maupassant. Above all, Maupassant is the most promising at the moment, for Maupassant enjoys the great advantage that he writes in French. Not from any merit of his own, he gives us that little fillip which we get from reading a language whose edges have not been smoothed for us by daily use. The very sentences shape themselves in a way that is definitely charming. The words tingle and sparkle. As for English, alas, it is *our* language—shop-worn, not so desirable, perhaps. Moreover, each of these compact little stories has its pinch of gunpowder, artfully placed so as to explode when we tread on its tail. The last words are always highly charged. Off they go, *bang,* in our faces and there is lit up for us in one uncompromising glare someone with his hand lifted, someone sneering, someone turning his back, someone catching an omnibus, as if this insignificant action, whatever it may be, summed up the whole situation forever.

The reality that Maupassant brings before us is always one of the body, of the senses—the ripe flesh of a servant girl, for example, or the succulence of food. *"Elle restait inerte, ne sentant plus son corps, et l'esprit dispersé, comme si quelqu'un l'eût d'échiqueté avec un de ces instruments dont se servent les cardeurs pour effiloquer la laine des matelas."* Or her tears dried themselves upon her cheeks *"comme des gouttes d'eau sur du fer rouge."* It is all concrete; it is all visualized. It is a world, then, in which one can believe with one's eyes and one's nose and one's senses; nevertheless, it is a world which secretes perpetually a little drop of bitterness. Is this all? And, if this is all, is it enough? Must we, then, believe this? So we ask. Now that we are given truth unadorned, a disagreeable sensation seems attached to it, which we must analyze before we go further.

Suppose that one of the conditions of things as they are is that they are unpleasant, have we strength enough to support that unpleasantness for the sake of the delight of believing in it? Are we not shocked somehow by *Gulliver's Travels* and *Boule de Suif* and *La Maison Tellier?* Shall we not always be trying to get round the obstacle of ugliness by saying that Maupassant and his like are narrow, cynical and unimaginative when, in fact, it is their truthfulness that we resent—the fact that leeches suck the naked legs of servant girls, that there are brothels, that human nature is fundamentally cold, selfish, corrupt? This discomfort at the disagreeableness of truth is one of the first things that shakes very lightly our desire to believe. Our Anglo-Saxon blood, perhaps, has given us an instinct that truth is, if not exactly beautiful, at least pleasant or virtuous to behold. But let us look once more at truth and, this time, through the eyes of Anthony Trollope,[1] "a big, blustering, spectacled, loud voiced hunting man . . . whose language in male society was, I believe, so lurid that I was not admitted to breakfast with him . . . who rode about the country establishing penny posts, and wrote, as the story goes, so many thousand words before breakfast every day of his life."

Certainly the Barchester Novels tell the truth and the English truth, at first sight, is almost as plain of feature as the French truth, though with a difference. Mr. Slope is a hypocrite, with a "pawing, greasy way with him." Mrs. Proudie is a domineering bully. The Archdeacon is well-meaning but coarse grained and thick cut. Thanks to the vigour of the author, the world of which these are the most prominent inhabitants goes through its daily rigmarole of feeding and begetting children and worshipping with a thoroughness, a gusto, which leave us no loophole of escape. We believe in Barchester as we believe in the reality of our own weekly bills. Nor, indeed, do we wish to escape from the consequences of our belief, for the truth of the Slopes and the Proudies, the truth of the evening party where Mrs. Proudie has her dress torn off her back under the light of eleven gas jets, is entirely acceptable.

At the top of his bent Trollope is a big, if not first-rate novelist, and the top of his bent came when he drove his pen hard and fast after the humours of provincial life and scored, without cruelty but with hale and hearty common sense, the portraits of those well-fed, black-coated, unimaginative men and women of the 'fifties. In his manner with them, and his manner is marked, there is an admirable shrewdness, like that of a family doctor or solicitor, too well acquainted with human foibles to judge them other than tolerantly and not above the human weakness of liking one person a great deal better than another for no good reason. Indeed, though he does his best to be severe and is at his best when most so, he could not hold himself aloof, but let us

[1] *Vignettes of Memory* by Lady Violet Greville.

know that he loved the pretty girl and hated the oily humbug so vehe-
mently that it is only by a great pull on his reins that he keeps himself
straight. It is a family party over which he presides and the reader who
becomes, as time goes on, one of Trollope's most intimate cronies has
a seat at his right hand. Their relation becomes confidential.

All this, of course, complicates what was simple enough in Defoe
and Maupassant. There, we were plainly and straightforwardly asked
to believe. Here, we are asked to believe, but to believe through the
medium of Trollope's temperament and, thus, a second relationship is
set up with Trollope himself which, if it diverts us, distracts us also.
The truth is no longer quite so true. The clear, cold truth, which seems
to lie before us unveiled in *Gulliver's Travels* and *Moll Flanders* and
La Maison Tellier, is here garnished with a charming embroidery. But
it is not from this attractive embellishment of Trollope's personality
that the disease comes which in the end proves fatal to the huge, substantial, well buttressed and authenticated truth of the Barchester Novels. Truth itself, however unpleasant, is interesting always. But, unfortunately, the conditions of story telling are harsh; they demand that
scene shall follow scene; that party shall be supported by another party,
one parsonage by another parsonage; that all shall be of the same calibre;
that the same values shall prevail. If we are told here that the palace
was lit by gas, we must be told there that the manor house was faithful to the oil lamp. But what will happen if, in process of solidifying
the entire body of his story, the novelist finds himself out of facts or
flagging in his invention? Must he then go on? Yes, for the story has
to be finished: the intrigue discovered, the guilty punished, the lovers
married in the end. The record, therefore, becomes at times merely a
chronicle. Truth peters out into a thin-blooded catalogue. Better would
it be, we feel, to leave a blank or even to outrage our sense of probabil-
ity than to stuff the crevices with this makeshift substance: the wrong
side of truth is a worn, dull fabric, unsteeped in the waters of imagination and scorched. But the Novel has issued her orders; I consist, she
says, of two and thirty chapters; and who am I, we seem to hear the
sagacious and humble Trollope ask, with his usual good sense, that I
should go disobeying the Novel? And he manfully provides us with
makeshifts.

If, then, we reckon up what we have got from the truth-tellers, we
find that it is a world where our attention is always being drawn to
things which can be seen, touched and tasted, so that we get an acute

sense of the reality of our physical existence. Having thus established our belief, the truth-tellers at once contrive that its solidity shall be broken before it becomes oppressive by action. Events happen; coincidence complicates the plain story. But their actions are all in keeping one with another and they are extremely careful not to discredit them or alter the emphasis in any way by making their characters other than such people as naturally express themselves to the full in active and adventurous careers. Then, again, they hold the three great powers which dominate fiction—God, Nature and Man—in stable relation so that we look at a world in proper perspective; where, moreover, things hold good not only here at the moment in front of us but, there, behind that tree or among those unknown people far away in the shadow behind those hills. At the same time, truth-telling implies disagreeableness. It is part of truth—the sting and edge of it. We cannot deny that Swift, Defoe and Maupassant all convince us that they reach a more profound depth in their ugliness than Trollope in his pleasantness. For this reason, truth-telling easily swerves a little to one side and becomes satiric. It walks beside the fact and apes it, like a shadow which is only a little more humped and angular than the object which casts it. Yet, in its perfect state, when we can believe absolutely, our satisfaction is complete. Then, we can say, though other states may exist which are better or more exalted, there is none that makes this unnecessary, none that supersedes it. But truth-telling carries in its breast a weakness which is apparent in the works of the lesser writers or in the masters themselves when they are exhausted. Truth-telling is liable to degenerate into perfunctory fact-recording, the repetition of the statement that it was on Wednesday that the Vicar held his mothers' meeting which was often attended by Mrs. Brown and Miss Dobson in their pony carriage, a statement which, as the reader is quick to perceive, has nothing of truth in it but the respectable outside.

At length, then, taking into account the perfunctory fact-recording, the lack of metaphor, the plainness of the language and the fact that we believe most when the truth is most painful to us, it is not strange that we should become aware of another desire welling up spontaneously and making its way into those cracks which the great monuments of the truth-tellers wear inevitably upon their solid bases. A desire for distance, for music, for shadow, for space, takes hold of us. The dustman has picked up his broken bottle; he has crossed the road; he begins to lose solidity and detail over there in the evening dusk.

II

The Romantics

It was a November morning, and the cliffs which overlooked the ocean were hung with thick and heavy mist, when the portals of the ancient and half ruinous tower, in which Lord Ravenswood had spent the last and troubled years of his life, opened, that his mortal remains might pass forward to an abode yet more dreary and lonely.

No change could be more complete. The dustman has become a lord; the present has become the past; homely Anglo-Saxon speech has become Latin and many syllabled; instead of pots and pans, gas jets and snug broughams, we have a half ruinous tower and cliffs, the ocean and November, heavy in mist. This past and this ruin, this lord and this autumn, this ocean and this cliff are as delightful to us as the change from a close room and voices to the night and the open air. The curious softness and remoteness of the *Bride of Lammermoor,* the atmosphere of rusty moorland and splashing waves, the dark and the distance actually seem to be adding themselves to that other more truthful scene which we still hold in mind, and to be giving it completeness. After that storm this peace, after that glare this coolness. The truth tellers had very little love, it seems, of nature. They used nature almost entirely as an obstacle to overcome or as a background to complete, not esthetically for contemplation or for any part it might play in the affairs of their characters. The town, after all, was their natural haunt. But let us compare them in more essential qualities: in their treatment of people. There comes towards us a girl tripping lightly and leaning on her father's arm:

. . . Lucy Ashton's exquisitely beautiful, yet somewhat girlish features, were formed to express peace of mind, serenity, and indifference to the tinsel of worldly pleasure. Her locks, which were of shadowy gold, divided on a brow of exquisite whiteness, like a gleam of broken and pallid sunshine upon a hill of snow. The expression of the countenance was in the last degree gentle, soft, timid and feminine, and seemed rather to shrink from the most casual look of a stranger than to court his admiration.

Nobody could less resemble Moll Flanders or Mrs. Proudie. Lucy Ashton is incapable of action or of self-control. The bull runs at her and she sinks to the ground; the thunder peals and she faints. She falters out the strangest little language of ceremony and politeness, "O if you be a man, if you be a gentleman assist me to find my father." One might say that she has no character except the traditional; to her father she is filial; to her lover, modest; to the poor, benevolent. Compared with Moll Flanders, she is a doll with sawdust in her veins and wax in her cheeks. Yet we have read ourselves into the book and grow familiar with its proportions. We come, at length, to see that anything more individual or eccentric or marked would lay emphasis where we want none. This tapering wraith hovers over the landscape and is part of it. She and Edgar Ravenswood are needed to support this romantic world with their bare forms, to clasp it round with that theme of unhappy love which is needed to hold the rest together. But the world that they clasp has its own laws. It leaves out and eliminates no less drastically than the other. On the one hand, we have feelings of the utmost exaltation—love, hate, jealousy, remorse; on the other hand, raciness and simplicity in the extreme. The rhetoric of the Ashtons and the Ravenswoods is completed by the humours of peasants and the cackle of village women. The true romantic can swing us from earth to sky; and the great master of romantic fiction, who is undoubtedly Sir Walter Scott, uses his liberty to the full. At the same time, we retort upon this melancholy which he has called forth, as in the *Bride of Lammermoor*. We laugh at ourselves for having been so moved by machinery so absurd. However, before we impute this defect to romance itself, we must consider whether it is not Scott's fault. This lazy-minded man was quite capable when the cold fit was on him of filling a chapter or two currently, conventionally, from a fountain of empty, journalistic phrases which, for all that they have a charm of their own, let the slackened attention sag still further.

Carelessness has never been laid to the charge of Robert Louis Stevenson. He was careful, careful to a fault—a man who combined most strangely a boy's psychology with the extreme sophistication of an artist. Yet, he obeyed no less implicitly than Walter Scott the laws of romance. He lays his scene in the past; he is always putting his characters to the sword's point with some desperate adventure; he caps his tragedy with homespun humour. Nor can there be any doubt that his conscience and his seriousness as a writer have stood him in good stead. Take any page of *The Master of Ballantrae* and it still stands wear and tear; but the fabric of the *Bride of Lammermoor* is full of holes and patches; it is scamped, botched, hastily flung together. Here, in Stevenson, romance is treated seriously and given all the advantages of the most refined literary art, with the result that we are never left to consider what an absurd situation this is or to reflect that we have no emotion left with which to meet the demand made upon us. We get, on the contrary, a firm, credible story, which never betrays us for a second but is corroborated, substantiated, made good in every detail. With what precision and cunning a scene will be made visible to us as if the pen were a knife which sliced away the covering and left the core bare!

It was as he said: there was no breath stirring; a windless stricture of frost had bound the air; and as we went forth in the shine of the candles, the blackness was like a roof over our heads.

Or, again:

All the 27th that rigorous weather endured: a stifling cold; folk passing about like smoking chimneys; the wide hearth in the hall piled high with fuel; some of the spring birds that had already blundered north into our neighbourhood besieging the windows of the house or trotting on the frozen turf like things distracted.

"A windless stricture of frost . . . the folk passing about like smoking chimneys"—one may search the Waverley Novels in vain for such close writing as this. Separately, these descriptions are lovely and brilliant. The fault lies elsewhere, in the whole of which they are a part. For in those critical minutes which decide a book's fate, when it is finished and the book swims up complete in the mind and lets us look at it, something seems lacking. Perhaps it is that the detail sticks out too prominently. The mind is caught up by this fine passage of description, by that curious exactitude of phrase; but the rhythm and sweep of emotion which the story has started in us are denied satisfaction. We are plucked back when we should be swinging free. Our attention is caught by some knot of ribbon or refinement of tracery when in fact we desire only a bare body against the sky.

Scott repels our taste in a thousand ways. But the crisis, that is the point where the accent falls and shapes the book under it, is right. Slouching, careless as he is, he will at the critical moment pull himself together and strike the one stroke needed, the stroke which gives the book its vividness in memory. Lucy sits gibbering "couched like a hare upon its form." "So, you have ta'en up your bonnie bridegroom?" she says, dropping her fine lady's mincing speech for the vernacular. Ravenswood sinks beneath the quicksands. "One only vestige of his fate appeared. A large sable feather had been detached from his hat, and the rippling waves of the rising tide wafted it to Caleb's feet. The old man took it up, dried it, and placed it in his bosom." At both these points the writer's hand is on the book and it falls from him shaped. But in *The Master of Ballantrae,* though each detail is right and wrought so as separately to move our highest admiration, there is no such final consummation. What should have gone to help it seems, in retrospect, to stand apart from it. We remember the detail, but not the whole. Lord Durisdeer and the Master die together but we scarcely notice it. Our attention has been frittered away elsewhere.

It would seem that the romantic spirit is an exacting one; if it sees a man crossing the road in the lamplight and then lost in the gloom of the evening, it at once dictates what course the writer must pursue. We do not wish, it will say, to know much about him. We desire that he shall express our capacity for being noble and adventurous; that he shall dwell among wild places and suffer the extremes of fortune; that he be endowed with youth and distinction and allied with moors, winds and wild birds. He is, moreover, to be a lover, not in a minute, introspective way, but largely and in outline. His feelings must be part of the landscape; the shallow browns and blues of distant woods and harvest fields are to enter into them; a tower, perhaps, and a castle where the snapdragon flowers. Above all, the romantic spirit demands here a crisis and there a crisis in which the wave that has swollen in the breast shall break. Such feelings Scott gratifies more completely than Stevenson, though with enough qualification to make us pursue the question of romance and its scope and its limitations a little further. Perhaps here it might be interesting to read *The Mysteries of Udolpho.*

The Mysteries of Udolpho have been so much laughed at as the type of Gothic absurdity that it is difficult to come at the book with a fresh eye. We come, expecting to ridicule. Then, when we find beauty, as we do, we go to the other extreme and rhapsodize. But the beauty and the absurdity of romance are both present and the book is a good test of the romantic attitude, since Mrs. Radcliffe pushes the liberties of romance to the extreme. Where Scott will go back a hundred years to get the effect of distance, Mrs. Radcliffe will go back three hundred. With one stroke, she frees herself from a host of disagreeables and enjoys her freedom lavishly.

As a novelist, it is her desire to describe scenery and it is there that her great gift lies. Like every true writer, she shoulders her way past every obstacle to her goal. She brings us into a huge, empty, airy world. A few ladies and gentlemen, who are purely Eighteenth Century in mind, manner and speech, wander about in vast champaigns, listen to nightingales singing amorously in midnight woods; see the sun set over the lagoons of Venice; and watch the distant Alps turn pink and blue from the turrets of an Italian castle.

These people, when they are well born, are of the same blood as Scott's gentry; attenuated and formal silhouettes who have the same curious power of being in themselves negligible and insipid but of merging harmoniously in the design.

Again, we feel the force which the romantic acquires by obliterating facts. With the sinking of the lights, the solidity of the foreground disappears, other shapes become apparent and other senses are roused. We become aware of the danger and darkness of our existence; comfortable reality has proved itself a phantom too. Outside our little shelter we hear the wind raging and the waves breaking. In this mood our senses are strained and apprehensive. Noises are audible which we should not hear normally. Curtains rustle. Something in the semi-darkness seems to move. Is it alive? And what is it? And what is it seeking here? Mrs. Radcliffe succeeds in making us feel all this, largely because she is able to make us aware of the landscape and, thus, induces a detached mood favorable to romance; but in her, more plainly than in Scott or Stevenson, the absurdity is evident, the wheels of the machine are visible and the grinding is heard. She lets us see clearly more than they do what demands the romantic writer makes upon us.

Both Scott and Stevenson, with the true instinct of the imagination, introduced rustic comedy and broad Scots dialect. It is in that direction, as they rightly divined, that the mind will unbend when it relaxes. Mrs. Radcliffe, on the other hand, having climbed to the top of her pinnacle, finds it impossible to come down. She tries to solace us with comic passages, put naturally into the mouths of Annete and Ludovico who are servants. But the break is too steep for her limited and ladylike mind and she pieces out her high moments and her beautiful atmosphere with a pale reflection of romance which is more tedious than any ribaldry. Mysteries abound. Murdered bodies multiply; but she is incapable of creating the emotion to feel them by, with the result that they lie there, unbelieved in; hence, ridiculous. The veil is drawn; there is the concealed figure; there is the decayed face; there are the writhing worms—and we laugh.

Directly the power which lives in a book sinks, the whole fabric of the book, its sentences, the length and shape of them, its inflections, its mannerisms, all that it wore proudly and naturally under the impulse of a true emotion become stale, forced, unappetizing. Mrs. Radcliffe slips limply into the faded Scott manner and reels off page after page in a style illustrated by this example:

Emily, who had always endeavoured to regulate her conduct by the nicest laws, and whose mind was finely sensible, not only of what is just in morals, but of whatever is beautiful in the feminine character, was shocked by these words.

And so it slips along and so we sink and drown in the pale tide. Nevertheless, Udolpho passes this test: it gives us an emotion which is both distinct and unique, however high or low we rate the emotion itself.

If we see now where the danger of romance lies: how difficult the mood is to sustain; how it needs the relief of comedy; how the very distance from common human experience and strangeness of its elements become ridiculous—if we see these things, we see also that these emotions are in themselves priceless jewels. The romantic novel realizes for us an emotion which is deep and genuine. Scott, Stevenson, Mrs. Radcliffe, all in their different ways, unveil another country of the land of fiction; and it is not the least proof of their power that they breed in us a keen desire for something different.

Thackeray: *Vanity Fair*

Arnold Kettle

Thackeray's method in *Vanity Fair* is in all essentials the method of Fielding in *Tom Jones*. To call the method panoramic, as many critics do (and in particular Mr. Percy Lubbock in *The Craft of Fiction*) is true but can be misleading. It is true in the sense that Thackeray's vision shifts about, that he surveys a broad field of territory and that the reader is kept at a certain distance from the scene.

The core of *Vanity Fair* is not a developing emotional situation involving the intense experience of a limited number of characters. We do not get "inside" one particular character and see the action through the imprint upon his consciousness, nor do we become so closely involved in a concrete situation (seeing it, so to speak, backward and forward and from many angles) that we have a sense of encompassing the whole complex of forces that makes such a situation vital. Even at a big dramatic moment, such as the famous scene when Rawdon Crawley returns from the spunging-house and finds Becky and Lord Steyne together, we do not have the effect of a vital clash of conflicting forces.

We wonder what is going to happen, we relish the theatrical quality of the scene; but our emotions are not deeply engaged because we know that nothing truly disturbing or exquisitely comic will be revealed; nothing will be changed, neither Becky nor Rawdon nor Steyne nor us. Even the ambiguity which Thackeray is at pains to achieve—"was Becky innocent?"—does not succeed in making us look at the scene in a fresh way, because the issue is morally a false one. Whether Becky is actually Steyne's mistress or not scarcely matters. And Thackeray knows it scarcely matters; with the result that the raising of the issue gives the impression of a sexual archness rather than

Reprinted by permission of Hutchinson and Company, Ltd.

that of a genuine ambiguity, the effect of which would be, by raising an important doubt in our mind, to make us suddenly see the episode in a new way, with a new flash of insight.

Everything in *Vanity Fair* remains at a distance because between the scene and the reader there always stands, with an insistent solidity, Thackeray himself. Of course it is true that every novelist stands between the scene of his novel and the reader, controlling and directing our attention. But by a Jane Austen or an Emily Brontë or a Dickens the directing is done, not necessarily unobtrusively (we are always aware of Dickens especially), but with an eye primarily on the object or the scene that is being revealed, whereas with Thackeray one has constantly the sense that the scene itself is less important than something else.

Take, for instance, the very first episode of *Vanity Fair*, the great scene of the departure of Amelia and Becky from Miss Pinkerton's academy in Chiswick Mall at the climax of which Becky throws the dictionary out of the coach window into the garden. It is a beautifully and dramatically conceived scene, an episode that is to tell us more about Becky than fifty pages of reminiscence; but notice how Thackeray handles the climax:

> Sambo of the bandy legs slammed the carriage-door on his young weeping mistress. He sprang up behind the carriage. "Stop!" cried Miss Jemima, rushing to the gate with a parcel.
>
> "It's some sandwiches, my dear," said she to Amelia. "You may be hungry, you know; and Becky, Becky Sharp, here's a book for you that my sister—that is, I,—Johnson's Dictionary, you know; you mustn't leave us without that. Good-bye. Drive on, coachman. God bless you!"
>
> And the kind creature retreated into the garden, overcome with emotions.
>
> But, lo! and just as the coach drove off, Miss Sharp put her pale face out of the window, and actually flung the book back into the garden.
>
> This almost caused Jemima to faint with terror.
>
> "Well, I never," said she; "what an audacious—" Emotion prevented her from completing either sentence. The carriage rolled away. . . .

This is excellent, but there is one word in the passage that prevents the scene from being fully dramatic and stops it achieving its potential force—the word "actually" in the sentence describing the flinging of the book. This one word colours the scene, investing it with a sense of scandalized amazement which may well reflect Miss Jemima's feelings but which weakens (not disastrously, of course, but appreciably) the objective force of the episode. After all, we know without that adverb what Miss Jemima's feelings are; its only function in the description is in fact to bring a particular colouring to the scene. It is Thackeray who steps in and in stepping in reduces the whole episode. The tone of that "actually" is the tone that puts almost everything in *Vanity Fair* at a distance.

Does it necessarily matter, this distancing of a novel by its author? I do not think it matters at all if it is a successful part of a consistent plan. Fielding achieves it very successfully in *Tom Jones,* so does Samuel Butler in the greater part of *The Way of All Flesh.* But the method, it must be recognized, puts an enormous strain on the author. If we are to be constantly seeing a novel through a kind of haze of reflectiveness spread around it by the author, then the comments, the reflections, the qualities of mind of the writer have got to be distinguished by quite remarkable understanding and control. We have seen how, in *Oliver Twist,* the conscious attitudes of Dickens are very frequently inadequate to what he is portraying. With Dickens this does not matter very much because his dramatic method concentrates the whole attention on the developing scene and makes the comment unimportant (one can mentally skip it without doing violence to the novel).

But with Thackeray's method the opposite holds. Everything depends on the capacity of the novelist to encompass in his own personality an adequate attitude to what he is describing. If he succeeds he will indeed cast around his puppets that understanding and humanity which (in Henry James's words about Fielding) do "somehow really enlarge, make everyone and everything important." But if his attitudes are less than adequate, then by driving his characters into the distance he will be weakening his whole effect.

The description "panoramic" may become misleading when applied to *Vanity Fair* if the word suggests that the individual characters in Thackeray's novel are not important, that the book has anything of the nature of the documentary. Mr. Lubbock (whose pages on Thackeray are consistently stimulating) seems to me on rather dangerous ground when he writes:

Not in any single complication of incident, therefore, nor in any single strife of will, is the subject of Vanity Fair to be discerned. It is nowhere but in the impression of a world, a society, a time—

certain manners of life within a few square miles of London, a hundred years ago. Thackeray flings together a crowd of the people he knows so well, and it matters not at all if the tie that holds them to each other is of the slightest; it may easily chance that his good young girl and his young adventuress set out together on their journey, their paths may even cross from time to time later on. The light link is enough for the unity of his tale, for that unity does not depend on an intricately woven intrigue. It depends in truth upon one fact only, the fact that all his throng of men and women are strongly, picturesquely typical of the world from which they are taken, that all in their different ways can add to the force of its effect. The book is not the story of any one of them, it is the story that they unite to tell, a chapter in the notorious career of well-to-do London.

There is so much that is true here that it may seem a little pedantic and ungenerous to insist that it is not altogether helpful. It is indeed true that the subject of *Vanity Fair* is a society—the world of well-to-do Britain (not merely London) at the beginning of the last century. But it is also true that this subject is seen in terms not of a general impression but of specific human relationships. "An impression of manners" is not an accurate description. As we look back on Thackeray's novel we recall a whole world, a bustling, lively, crowded world; but we recall it in terms of individual people and their relationships. These people are presented to us, by and large, in the tradition of the comedy of humours. That is to say each has particular characteristics, somewhat exaggerated and simplified, by which they are easily comprehensible.

These characters are almost always static [Mr. Edwin Muir has said]. They are like a familiar landscape, which now and then surprises us when a particular effect of light or shadow alters it, or we see it from a new prospect. Amelia Sedley, George Osborne, Becky Sharp, Rawdon Crawley—these do not change as Eustacia Vye and Catherine Earnshaw do; the alteration they undergo is less a temporal one than an unfolding in a continuously widening present. Their weaknesses, their vanities, their foibles, they possess from the beginning and never lose to the end; and what actually does change is not these, but our knowledge of them.

This is, broadly speaking, true, but not quite fair. Some of the characters in *Vanity Fair* do change; Pitt Crawley, for instance, who begins as a simple unworldly prig, blossoms out with a fortune into an ambitious worldly idiot, and yet remains the same person, and particularly Amelia, who, in her infuriating way, develops a good deal in the course

of the novel.[1] The important point, however, is that Thackeray's puppets (it is a pity he used the word, for it has encouraged an under-
estimation of his subtlety) are all involved in human relationships
which, though not presented with much intimacy or delicacy of analysis,
are for the most part true and convincing relationships.

We know, for instance, quite precisely enough the quality of
George Osborne's feeling for Amelia or of Rawdon's for Becky. The
latter relationship could scarcely be better illustrated than by the letter Rawdon writes from the spunging-house:

"Dear Becky" (Rawdon wrote),—"*I hope you slept well.* Don't
be *frightened* if I don't bring you in your *coffy*. Last night as I was
coming home smoaking, I met with an *accadent*. I was *nabbed* by
Moss of Cursitor Street—from whose *gilt and splendid parler* I write
this—the same that had me this time two years. Miss Moss brought
in my tea—she is grown very *fat*, and as usual, had *her stockens down
at heal.*

"It's Nathan's business—a hundred and fifty—with costs, hundred and seventy. Please send me my desk and some *cloths*—I'm in
pumps and a white tye (something like Miss M's stockings)—I've
seventy in it. And as soon as you get this, Drive to Nathan's—
offer him seventy-five down, and ask *him to renew*—say I'll take wine
—we may as well have some dinner sherry; but not *picturs*, they're
too dear.

"If he won't stand it. Take my ticker and such of your things as
you can *spare*, and send them to *Balls*—we must, of coarse, have the
sum to-night. It won't do to let it stand over, as to-morrow's
Sunday; the beds here are not very *clean*, and there may be other
things out against me—I'm glad it an't Rawdon's Saturday for coming home. God bless you.

"Yours in haste,
"R.C.

"*P.S.*—Make haste and come."

Every sentence of this is masterly. Thackeray is marvellously good at
depicting typical upper-class young men—the sketch of James Crawley
with his "dawgs" is a delightful minor example—the kind of people
of whom Matthew Arnold wrote: "One has often wondered whether
upon the whole earth there is anything so unintelligent, so unapt to

---

[1] One or two characters change quite unconvincingly, not because they
develop organically but because Thackeray seems to change his plans for them
half-way through. Lady Jane Sheepshanks (who marries Pitt Crawley) is
one of these. Some critics consider that Amelia changes in this way only, but
I think the evidence is against them.

perceive how the world is really going, as an ordinary young Englishman of our upper class." Now it is true that we do not enter intimately into the feelings of any of these characters, but it would be wrong to suppose they are any the less human. When we say we know the quality of their feelings what we mean is that we know all *about* those feelings, not that we share them in the way we share Emma's responses. But it is not, even in the very broadest sense, their manners that are the subject of the book.

The central relationship with which Thackeray, like Fielding and Richardson and Jane Austen, is concerned is marriage. *Vanity Fair* is about the difficulties of personal relationships, particularly marriage relationships, in nineteenth-century, upper-class English society. It is a well-organized novel despite its discursiveness and some lapses in construction (the most clumsy being the return to England of Dobbin and Joseph Sedley; the chronology and therefore what has been well called the choreography is very confused here). The planning of the double story of Becky and Amelia is by no means as casual as Mr. Lubbock would seem to suggest. Not only do the two girls stand in a complementary relation to each other—the one active and "bad," the other passive and "good"—but their careers are juxtaposed in contrasting curves of development, Becky's curve rising in the centre of the book, Amelia's declining. The fact that from the death of George at Waterloo to the reunion at Pumpernickel the two women scarcely meet does not weaken the pattern of the book nor blur the underlying contrast between them, for each is playing her necessary part.

Lord David Cecil in his essay on Thackeray notices the strong pattern of the book but seems curiously imperceptive as to its significance.

The characters of the two girls are designed to illustrate the laws controlling Vanity Fair as forcibly as possible. And in order to reveal how universally these laws work, they are of strongly-contrasted types.

Amelia is an amiable character, simple, modest and unselfish. But, says Thackeray, in Vanity Fair such virtue always involves as a corollary a certain weakness. Amelia is foolish, feeble and self-deceived. She spends a large part of her youth in a devotion, genuine enough to begin with, later merely a sentimental indulgence in her emotions, to a man unworthy of her. For him she rejects a true lover; and though she is ultimately persuaded to marry this lover it is only, ironically enough, through the chance caprice of the woman for whom her first love had rejected her. Nor is she wholly saved from the punishment of her error. By the time he marries her, her true lover has learnt to see her as she is.

Becky, the second "heroine" is not weak and self-deceived; she is a "bad" character, a wolf not a lamb, artful, bold and unscrupulous. But she, no more than Amelia, can escape the laws governing the city of her nativity. By nature a Bohemian, she is beguiled, by the false glitter surrounding the conventional rank and fashion which are the vulgar and predominant idols of Vanity Fair, to spend time and energy in trying to attain them. She succeeds, but she is not satisfied. Nor is she able to maintain her success. She is too selfish to treat the husband, who is necessary to her position, with the minimum of consideration necessary to keep him. She sinks to the underworld of society. But her eyes are not opened; and the rest of her life is spent in trying to retrieve herself, so far successfully that we see her last as a charitable dowager, a pattern of respectability, a final flamboyant example of the deceptiveness of outward appearances in Vanity Fair.

This parallel structure extends to the men who enter Amelia's and Becky's lives; they are similarly contrasted, similarly self-deceived. . . .

This appears to me a remarkable example of criticism gone wrong, missing the essential point of the novel under consideration. To write of Becky as "beguiled by the false glitter surrounding the conventional rank and fashion, etc." is surely to miss the vital question: what else could Becky do? And once we ask that question it becomes irrelevant to talk of self-deception. Lord David Cecil, having insisted that the book is about a society, Vanity Fair, then proceeds to abstract the characters morally from that society and discuss them as though they had any existence outside it. Because he sees the individual and society as separate entities and social "laws" as something abstract and distinct from personal moral standards he misses the vital motive-force of the novel.

The trouble with Becky is not that "she is too selfish, etc." (It is not selfishness of that type that leads to the intrigue with Lord Steyne, nor is the keeping of a husband in that sense Becky's greatest necessity.) Becky's dilemma—and Amelia's for that matter—is the dilemma of Jane Fairfax in *Emma* and of almost all the heroines of English fiction from Moll Flanders onwards. What is a young woman of spirit and intelligence to do in the polite but barbarous world of bourgeois society? Only two courses are open to her, the passive one of acquiescence to subjugation or the active one of independent rebellion.[2] The only hope of a compromise solution is the lucky chance of finding an understanding man like Mr. Darcy or Mr. Knightley, rich enough to buy certain civilized values and kind enough to desire them; but the snag is that the Mr. Knightleys require something Becky by her very fate (she has had a harder fight than Jane Fairfax) can never have— "true elegance of mind." You cannot pick that up in Soho or slaving for Miss Pinkerton.

Becky, like Moll and Clarissa and Sophia (each after her own fashion) before her, rebels. She will not submit to perpetual slavery and humiliation within the governess trade. And so she uses consciously and systematically all the men's weapons plus her one natural material asset, her sex, to storm the men's world. And the consequence is of course morally degrading and she is a bad woman all right. But she gains our sympathy nevertheless—not our approving admiration but our human fellow-feeling—just as Heathcliff does, and she too gains it not in spite but because of her rebellion. She gains it from the moment she flings kind Miss Jemima's dictionary out of the window and thereby rejects the road that would have led her to become a Miss Jemima herself. It is this act that sets in motion the vital vibrations of the book, and it is interesting to compare it with that other act of rebellion that sets off so vastly different a book as *Wuthering Heights*.

There is no mystery about the vitality and fascination of Becky Sharp. It is not a sentimental sympathy that she generates. Thackeray, the Victorian gentleman, may tone down her rebellion by ambiguous adverbs and a scandalized titter, but the energy he has put into her is more profound than his morals or his philosophy and she sweeps him

---

[2] It is interesting to notice how in *Vanity Fair* as in the eighteenth-century novels the one thing that none of the important characters (however hard pressed) ever contemplates doing is physical work. For a woman the job of governess or companion is degradation enough, below that is unthinkable, however critical one's situation, and as a last resort prostitution is a greatly preferable alternative to labour. As for men, the typical solution—credit and the generosity of relatives breaking down—is a commission in the Army. This failing, Newgate or the spunging-house is the next step, with the extreme possibility of a life of crime. But no one ever becomes a worker and the reason is obvious. Once one had passed from the owning to the labouring class one was lost. One never got back and life, to one who had once known the standards of the civilized world, was simply not worth living. George Osborne found he could not possibly live on two thousand a year; but it is left to Amelia to discover that "women are working hard, and better than she can, for twopence a day." (Chap. L.)

along. Of course Becky is unadmirable (though for the moment when she tells Amelia the truth about George Osborne, "that selfish humbug, that low-bred cockney-dandy, that padded booby, etc.," one can forgive her much), but what else could she have been?

"It isn't difficult to be a country gentleman's wife," Rebecca thought. "I think I could be a good woman if I had five thousand a year. I could dawdle about in the nursery, and count the apricots on the wall. I could water plants in a green-house, and pick off dead leaves from the geraniums. I could ask old women about their rheumatisms, and order half-a-crown's worth of soup for the poor. I shouldn't miss it much, out of five thousand a year. I could even drive out ten miles to dine at a neighbour's, and dress in the fashions of the year before last. I could go to church and keep awake in the great family pew; or go to sleep behind the curtains and with my veil down, if I only had practice. I could pay everybody, if I had but the money . . ."

In other words she could have been, with luck, someone not unlike Mrs. Elton in *Emma,* though she would have played her cards a good deal better. She could alternatively, of course, have had a shot at being Amelia. Amelia also could be a very good woman (by Victorian standards) on five thousand a year and at the conclusion of the book is in this happy condition. But not before the consequences of being Amelia have been pretty thoroughly shown up, even to the wooden old war-horse, Dobbin.

Amelia is often regarded as one of Thackeray's failures, the weak link in *Vanity Fair.* I think this is because too many readers want her to be something she cannot be within the pattern of the book—a heroine. Certainly as a heroine she cuts a very feeble figure. Certainly, too, there is a recurring ambiguity in Thackeray's attitude to her. If we tend to think of her as a heroine *manquée* it is largely his fault, for in the first part of the novel it is hard to believe that his comments on poor, tender, abused little Amelia are in any deep sense ironical. And yet if we expect too much of Amelia we cannot put all the blame on Thackeray. We are warned in the first chapter by the tone of: "She had twelve intimate and bosom friends out of the twenty-four young ladies . . ." And by Chapter XII we should realize that Amelia is not being produced for our uncritical approval:

. . . in the course of a year [love] turned a good young girl into a good young woman—to be a good wife presently when the happy time should come. This young person (perhaps it was very imprudent in her parents to encourage her, and abet her in such idolatry and silly, romantic ideas), loved, with all her heart, the young officer in his Majesty's service with whom we have made a brief acquaintance. She thought about him the very first moment on waking; and his was the very last name mentioned in her prayers. She never had seen a man so beautiful or so clever; such a figure on horseback: such a dancer: such a hero in general. Talk of the Prince's bow! what was it to George's? She had seen Mr. Brummell, whom everybody praised so. Compare such a person as that to her George! . . . He was only good enough to be a fairy prince; and oh, what magnanimity to stoop to such a humble Cinderella! . . .

(Here again Thackeray does not play quite fair. It is pretty clear that the "goods" of the first sentence are not to be taken quite at their face-value, but the tone of "silly, romantic ideas" is highly ambiguous. Against whom is the irony directed?) Certainly after fifteen years of self-deception as widow no one can go on taking Amelia as deserving our unqualified sympathy. And indeed the whole section dealing with the Sedleys' life at Fulham is done with a realism that precludes un-critical attitudes. Had Thackeray been by this time wallowing in the kind of sentimentality which many readers feel is implicit in his atti-tude to Amelia, he would scarcely have permitted himself the realism of allowing young George to leave his mother with barely a regret. Nor would he have risked the final description of his heroine as a "tender little parasite."

No, Amelia is no more the heroine of *Vanity Fair* than Becky. She is, rather, the opposite possibility, the image that Becky might have chosen to become. And it is Thackeray's merit that he shows us Amelia as she is, a parasite, gaining life through a submission that is not even an honest submission, exploiting her weakness, deceiving even herself.

The weakness in the pattern of *Vanity Fair* lies not in Amelia (despite the ambiguities I have referred to) but in Dobbin. It is he who lets down the novel, not merely because he is in the psychological sense unconvincing, but because he fails to bear the weight of the positive values implicit in the pattern of the book, values which, had they been successfully embodied, would have made of this novel a greater *Tom Jones,* a real comic epic in prose.

Dobbin begins as a sheepish but sensitive schoolboy fighting the snobs, but as the novel proceeds he becomes a sort of clothes-horse of the respectable middle-class virtues. He is shrewd and cultured (young

George Osborne finds him a mine of information during their trip through Europe) but simple and steadfast. How any man of such sense and character could remain utterly in love, in quite an adolescent way, with Amelia all those years Thackeray can neither explain nor convince us. Perhaps his is a case of arrested development in the emotional sphere? But no, there is no such suggestion to be found. We are to take Dobbin seriously. He is not a hero but he is a rock, or rather an oak, the rugged old oak around which the tender parasite clings.

The effect of Dobbin is to keep, obscurely but nevertheless quite definitely, in the background of the novel a wooden sort of norm, an average but good man, certainly not a rebel yet just as certainly untainted by the values of Vanity Fair. It is because he is thus untainted that Dobbin is psychologically unconvincing as a character and useless to the pattern of the book. For Thackeray's great strength, by and large, is his ability to see his characters as parts of a concrete social situation. His concern, for instance, with financial details in his novel is an example not of a trivial naturalism but of his power of setting his people so firmly in the world that we believe in them completely even though we know comparatively little about them.

We do not know very much, when all is said, about Becky herself. We can only guess how happy she is, what qualms she may have, precisely what emotions drive her to act as she does. We do not know how much she likes Rawdon and her unkindness to her child is not quite convincing. She is, as we have noticed, always at a distance. And yet she is emphatically there, alive beyond a doubt, one of the great characters in all fiction. How does Thackeray do it? Fundamentally, I suggest, by this precise and firm placing of a character in a concrete social situation. We may not be told very much about what Becky *feels* but we know exactly what her situation is. We know her relationship, financial and social (in the broadest sense), with every other character in the book and we know the guiding principle of her conduct, that she wants to be mistress of her own life.

And so the psychological gaps, the gaps in analysis, the ambiguities surrounding her do not matter much. Indeed there is a sense in which their absence is a positive strength, for most such analysis in novels involves unreal abstraction, presents problems of character in a static way and diverts attention from the reality of the character's actions by an exclusive concentration on his motives. In a very important sense we know more about Becky than about, say, Proust's hero. Like Oliver Twist and Jeanie Deans she has a typical, symbolic quality which makes her an individual and yet more than an individual.

This sort of typicality is regarded by some critics as a weakness in art. To say of a character that he is a type is supposed to show a deficiency, a failure to individualize on the part of the author. But in fact characters in literature who are in no sense typical cannot well be artistically interesting. If Hamlet were an isolated creature, a being whose individuality made him essentially and utterly different from other individuals, a neurotic who had lost touch with the typical contours of human existence and relationships, he would not be a great artistic character. He is in fact no less an individual for being a type, a fact which Shakespeare recognized well enough when he presented him in the convention of the melancholic man, a class of character easily recognizable by and significant to the Elizabethan audience.

The artistic type (and here we see the value of the old theory of "humours" despite its psychological crudity) is not an average, not a lowest common multiple of human characteristics, but rather the embodiment of certain forces which come together in a particular social situation to create a peculiar kind of vital energy. Molière's miser is not a typical man in the sense of being an average man, but he is a type, a more-than-individual as well as a very definite, unique individual. Charlie Chaplin on the screen is not an average man (no one has ever seen anybody quite like him) and yet he is unmistakably typical, not just an oddity for all his uniqueness, but somehow more typical of the "little man," the individual worker in our industrial society, than any little man we actually know; and in this lies his greatness.

Thackeray's best characters seem to me types in just this sense, and it is this quality that gives them their vitality despite their distance from the reader, the limits to our knowledge about them and the crippling inadequacy of Thackeray's comments. Becky is an unmistakable individual, yet she is every woman of spirit rebelling against the humiliations forced on her by certain social assumptions. Old Osborne, similarly, is every successful nineteenth-century business man, encased in a gloomy, luxurious ugliness in that big house in Russell Square. How solid he is! How all respectable England trembles at the horror of his anger when he hears his son has married a bankrupt's daughter! How a whole world and its values comes crowding up as he leans over and speaks to his grandson when he hears of old John Sedley's death:

"You see," said old Osborne to George, "what comes of merit and industry, and judicious speculations, and that. Look at me and my banker's account. Look at your poor grandfather, Sedley, and his failure. And yet he was a better man than I was, this day twenty years—a better man, I should say, by ten thousand pound."

Thackeray himself does his best to destroy his picture of the ruling-class world. Only at certain moments will he remove himself from the position of chorus and allow the scene to make its full effect. Then his talent for the extreme and the bizarre is given full scope. Old Osborne reacting to George's death; the wicked old Sir Pitt Crawley, helpless, dumb and half-insane, sobbing pitifully when left in the charge of a servant-girl; Lady Bareacres sitting in her horseless carriage in Brussels; the description of Lord Steyne's house and family: such episodes are extraordinarily successful. But constantly, throughout the whole novel, the effect produced by what the characters do is weakened or dissipated by the author's comments.

It is not so much the sense of these comments as their tone that is disastrous. It is an ambiguous tone. In the worst of senses it is vulgar. Thackeray's attitude to nearly all his main characters—and especially Amelia and Becky—is ambiguous. And the ambiguity does not arise from subtlety, a sense that the whole truth can never be told, that there is always a complicating factor in every judgment; it comes from pusilanimity, from a desire to expose illusions and yet keep them.

The artistic motive-force of *Vanity Fair* is Thackeray's vision of bourgeois society and of the personal relationships engendered by that society. That is what his novel is about. And the sweep and vividness of it, the vitality of Becky, the rich and teeming comic life of the panorama, all derive from the insight and honesty of Thackeray's vision. He pierces the hypocrisies of Vanity Fair, reveals the disgusting, brutal, degrading sordidness behind and below its elegant glitter. It is the heyday of bourgeois society that he paints, the days when an expanding economy could for a while carry along the hangers-on through the credit it generated (this is how Becky and Rawdon manage to live well on nothing a year) despite its pitiless rejection of its failures like old John Sedley. And the human feeling of Thackeray rebels at this society. And yet . . . and yet . . . doesn't he rather like it? To put the doubt in literary terms: is *Vanity Fair* a novel of utter integrity, as *Wuthering Heights* is?

The human indignation is constantly diluted by the clubman's bogus mellowness, not the mellowness of Fielding which is based on the real (though limited) security of the English revolution, but the mellowness of the successful novelist who has looked the world in the face and doesn't care to go on looking. He turns to a loose and general cynicism:

Ah! *Vanitas Vanitatum!* Which of us is happy in this world? Which of us has his desire? or, having it, is satisfied?—Come, children, let us shut up the box and the puppets, for our play is played out.

It is the feeblest of endings, the flattest of statements of faith. And one doesn't even feel that Thackeray means it.

Kafka and the Dream

Selma Fraiberg

I

For most of his life, it appears, Kafka lived on terms of dangerous intimacy with the world of the dream. He possessed a kind of sensory knowledge of the dream and the dimensions of consciousness which could only be achieved by a man who had an extraordinary relationship to his own inner life. This knowledge did not come from a clinical study of his own states of consciousness, and I feel certain that it did not come from psychoanalytic texts. Kafka was not an academic student of the mind. He was however a meticulous observer of his own mental activity.

There is evidence that he experienced mental states in which dream-like images and fantasies emerged, then were caught and held in consciousness, naked specimens of unconscious productions. Often he preserved these things in his notebooks, recorded along with the texts of nocturnal dreams, obsessional thoughts, fragments of memories, and hundreds of other bits and pieces of the disordered contents of his inner world. Here and there in the Kafka stories a piece from this attic debris makes its ghostly reappearance. In many instances a dream, a fantasy, or a piece of imagery recorded in the notebooks becomes the starting point for a sketch or a story. There is evidence, then, that he not only made exhaustive investigations of his own mental processes but also made use of his discoveries in his writing.

Introspection for Kafka was not a reflective process but a disease, the compulsion of his morbid guilt, which drew him deeper and deeper into psychic depths in hopeless pursuit of the crime and the judgment. It was an obsessional occupation which became a torment for him and

Reprinted by permission of the author.

slowly widened the gap between himself and the real world. In 1922 this estrangement reached a critical point and Kafka viewed his mental state with alarm. On January 16 he writes: "This past week I suffered something very like a breakdown . . ." ". . . impossible to sleep, impossible to endure life, or, more exactly, the course of life. The clocks are not in unison; the inner one runs crazily on at a devilish or demoniac or in any case inhuman pace, the outer one limps along at its usual speed. What else can happen but that the two worlds split apart, and they do split apart, or at least clash in a fearful manner. There are doubtless several reasons for the wild tempo of the inner process; the most obvious one is introspection, which will suffer no idea to sink tranquilly to rest but must pursue each one into consciousness, only itself to become an idea, in turn to be pursued by renewed introspection." And later in the same entry: "The solitude that for the most part has been forced on me, in part voluntarily sought by me—but what was this if not compulsion too?—is now losing all its ambiguity and approaches its dénouement. Where is it leading? The strongest likelihood is, that it may lead to madness. . . ." Later that month the panic gives way to melancholy resignation. On January 28 he writes: ". . . for I am now a citizen of this other world, whose relationship to the ordinary one is the relationship of the wilderness to cultivated land. . . ." And on the following day he writes: ". . . it is only that the attraction of the human world is so immense, in an instant it can make one forget everything. Yet the attraction of my world too is strong. . . ."

The mental crisis did not end as he feared in madness, but in disease. This was the year of the onset of Kafka's tuberculosis. He understood his illness and wrote to Brod, "My head has made an appointment with my lungs behind my back."

Of the two worlds, Kafka's and "the human world," it was the first that he knew best. Kafka wrote about himself, his inner experience, and the struggle with nameless tyrants, the lustful couples who copulate within the sight of the law, the endless tribunal, the comic-tragic bureaucrats and corrupt officials—all of these were not conceived as allegories for his time but were events of inner life. (His own comments and interpretations of his works repeatedly bear this out.) If his writings achieve the effect of satire and broad social caricature, it is because the dream is in itself a caricature of life; the dream is in one sense an allegory. Moreover Kafka knew this and understood it very well. In a conversation Janouch says to Kafka: "The *Metamorphosis* is a terrible dream, a terrible conception." Kafka replies: "The dream reveals the reality, which conception lags behind. That is the horror of life—the terror of art. . . ."

I think it is also a mistake to look upon his writings, as Charles Neider proposes, as "freudian allegories" or to speak of Kafka's deliberate use of "freudian symbols." If Kafka was acquainted with psychoanalytic ideas (and there is some evidence for this), he did not pluck his symbols from clinical texts like an amateur with a drugstore dream book. The use of the term "freudian symbols" is, in itself, an embarrassment in considering this view, for Freud was not the inventor of dream symbols but their investigator, and he repeatedly acknowledged his debt to the creative writers who were the discoverers of symbolism, including that of the dream.

No formula for dream interpretation exists in psychoanalysis. A dream, a symbol, can be properly interpreted only through the personal associations of the dreamer. While Freud brought attention to a number of "universal" symbols, he repeatedly stressed the multideterminants in symbol choice, and hence the futility of assigning a single meaning to a symbol. Neider's extrapolation of symbols, his mechanical interpretations, and codification of the symbol types result in a piece of analysis which is psychoanalytically unsound and which debases the work studied. It is worth mentioning, too, that many of the symbols which he has dealt with are interpreted arbitrarily by him and without the authority of clinical investigation. So far as I know no clinical investigator has found that a court stands for "the unconscious" or a boarding house for "the preconscious," and I think it very unlikely that this will ever be demonstrated.

Moreover, we must admit that even those symbols which are properly speaking "universal" are not in themselves the material for creative work. Symbols are sterile things in themselves; it is only when the symbol is animated through personal experience, when it acquires dimensions of meaning and ambiguity, that it can evoke emotional reactions.

Kafka may have profited from the psychoanalytic investigation of dreams and dream symbolism, but he wrote out of inner experience. An investigation of Kafka symbolism will demonstrate repeatedly how little he was influenced by the arbitrary dream symbol. It seems to me to be as unprofitable to try to understand Kafka and his writing in terms of "freudian symbols" as it is to understand a dream apart from the dreamer's own associations.

If Kafka knew the world of the dream better than the rest of us, he was not indebted to Freud but to his personal suffering. He called himself, at last, "a citizen of this other world." He was not like the rest of us, the nocturnal visitors, who are favored on return with a merciful amnesia or dim recall. He had taken up his ghostly residence there, and habituation had given his eyes a special kind of night vision so that the forms and events of the dream which ordinary dreamers call uncertain and indistinct were tangible and real, capable of description in fine detail. Even the texts of his own dreams, recorded in his note-books, are remarkable for the recall of detail and the visual preciseness.

The danger in such intimacy with the dream world is that the connections to the other world may be lost, and this danger was real and known to Kafka. His writing was the bridge, the connection between the two worlds; it was the strongest of the bonds which united him with the real world. And the writings themselves told the same story of the danger, or the failure, or the impossibility of human connections.

He wrote his biography in his symbolism of lost connections—the intercepted letters, the interrupted coitus, the telephones with the connections to nowhere. There is the indescribable loneliness and sadness of the little train in "The Railroad of Kalda" which makes its way into the frozen interior of Russia and regularly comes to its end in the middle of the wilderness, never to reach its destination. It is a train without mission, bearing a tiny freight and a few passengers in the course of the year, running its course between nowhere and nowhere. At the train stop the company's agent dwells in solitude in an abandoned wooden shed, in despair of life and afraid of death. The Kalda story, too, is unfinished. No man can write the end of his autobiography.

These symbols of lost connections, like all powerful symbols (and unlike those symbols which are plucked cheaply from dream books), are highly stratified and rich in latent meaning. They speak of the failures in human connections and communication which are recurrent motifs in Kafka's writing and his life. The wretched railroad of Kalda, once conceived by its owners in a surge of capitalist daring and hope, has come to nothing, a toy train chugging its way through vast space to its absurd and melancholy end in the wastes. This is the parable of

Kafka's failure in the eyes of his father. And the ridiculous railroad, this mockery of men's extravagant hopes and ambitions, is Kafka's symbol for the failure of his own ambitions, and for the failure of his lifelong struggle with an unconquerable opponent, here represented as the vastness of a wilderness which cannot be spanned by the tiny train, in real life by the figure of a giant, the father, before whom Kafka remained an insignificant dwarf as boy and grown man. It is the symbol for the unfinished work, the uncompleted writings. It is the comment on Kafka's religious views, the failure to reach anything "beyond." And it is the symbol of biological failure. The little train which is never to reach its destination speaks eloquently and touchingly of Kafka's sexual impotence. The little train comes to its end in the middle of the wilderness, a full day's journey from Kalda, discharges its few passengers, its small freight, and returns. And the ground of this tiny settlement was frozen solid, we are told. "I was too weak to conquer the soil," said the company's agent. "A stubborn soil that was frozen solid until spring and that even resisted the sharp edge of my new axe. Whatever seed one sowed in it was lost."

It is a striking fact that Kafka, the "citizen of this other world," should have established his human fellowship in his writings through the fraternity of the dream. He had only the frailest connections with what he called "the human world," and his life was a tragedy of lost and broken communications with that world. Yet his literary genius was most pronounced in his ability to communicate elemental emotion and primal experience. It is a communication which is direct and powerful and owes its effect to a profound insight; it is the creation through the device of the private dream of a world of collective memory where each man can know his fellow.

II

It is probable that when the current enthusiasm for Kafka has run its course Kafka will emerge with less stature as a writer but with undiminished prestige as an innovator in the technique of the psychological novel. For Kafka has brought a thoroughly original and revolutionary approach to the problem of the representation of psychic dimensions in literature.

We must consider that the discoveries of psychoanalysis have made demands upon the writer which are entirely unlike those of other systems of ideas. A theory of biology, of society, of politics, or of history can be given suitable expression within the framework of a narrative without straining the conventional means of communication. But a scientific theory of psychic dimensions and the primary processes of thought and imagery make unique demands upon the writer's equipment and his technique when he attempts to represent these ideas in his work.

Language, itself, as an instrument of the reasoning ego, seems opposed to working for unreason in the service of the unconscious. The higher order of thinking which is implicit in language is incompatible with the archaic mental system which governs the primary thought processes. The dream, for example, doesn't "speak" a language. It can only represent words and ideas through pictures. The spoken word or phrase, if it comes into the dream at all, is torn from the context of waking life and played back like a dusty record. Similarly, the writer's conventional devices of narration oppose the representation of unconscious thought processes. The story-teller gives order to his materials; the dreamer gives disorder to his. The story reveals, makes explicit, intends to communicate its meaning; the manifest dream conceals, disguises, has no intention of communicating.

It is understandable, then, that the writers who have attempted to bring this dimension of mind into the scope of their work have usually found it necessary to experiment upon the language itself and the techniques of narration. In one way or another these writers tried to recreate the world of the unconscious by borrowing the method of unconscious thought processes, the so-called "primary process." The dream's method of plastic representation, ellipsis, condensation, and symbol formation, provided models for a new writing. The writer's problem of narration of unconscious mental processes also found solutions in the model of the dream. The dream dispenses with logical connections. Its contents are brought together only because of their associative links and without regard for order or coherence. Its meaning can be established only through translation. The transposition of unconscious thought processes in writing led to various types of "stream of consciousness" writing which, like the dream, could be understood only through interpretation.

Kafka did not trouble himself at all with the mechanical problems of entering the dream world. He found an easy solution to the problem of the language barrier. He simply walked through it. His prose style, which Mann described as "a conscientious, curiously explicit, objective, clean, and correct style," undergoes no distortions, employs no language tricks, and is perfectly consistent and reasonable in the reporting of events, real or delusional.

No one has succeeded with this device as Kafka has. No one else can evoke the world of the dream with such chilling authenticity. Kafka's so-called "dream technique" springs from a conception of the dream as a work of art. Kafka explored the aesthetic properties of the dream. He understood the primary relationship between unconscious mental processes and the form and composition of the dream. By taking the dream as his model in his own compositions, he achieved the perfect formal conditions for the representation of unconscious experience. Now this, in itself, is not an innovation; experimental writers of this century have turned to this method of composition repeatedly in the attempt to evoke the qualities of the dream. But when Kafka unites the structural aspects of the dream with his narrative technique, his compositions achieve the most extraordinary effects of the dream itself. This is all the more impressive when we regard the seeming artlessness, the unambitious character of his narrative technique. It is simply the narration of a dream by a dreamer.

One evening I returned home to my room from the office somewhat later than usual—an acquaintance had detained me below at the house entrance for a long time—opened the door (my thoughts were still engrossed by our conversation, which had consisted chiefly of gossip about people's social standing), hung my overcoat on the hook and was about to cross over to the washstand when I heard a strange, spasmodic breathing. I looked up and, on top of the stove that stood deep in the gloom of the corner, saw something alive. Yellowish glittering eyes stared at me; large round woman's breasts rested on the shelf of the stove, on either side beneath the unrecognizable face; the creature seemed to consist entirely of a mass of soft white flesh; a thick yellowish tail hung down beside the stove, its tip ceaselessly passing back and forth over the cracks of the tiles. The first thing I did was to cross over with long strides and sunken head—nonsense! nonsense! I kept repeating like a prayer. . . .

The effect of this passage, the immediate sense of the nightmare, is achieved not by its contents alone, not by the stove monster, but by the prose treatment. It is the conventional narration, the factual, ordinary rendering of this event which produces the effect of the uncanny. This is entirely in accord with the psychological mechanism in the experience of the uncanny by which unreal events are perceived as real, the inanimate is animated, and the delusion or dream obtains conviction. Kafka demonstrates by this technique that the quality of uncanniness which we attribute to the dream and the delusion is not a property of the dream itself or of unconscious experience; it belongs to the ego, the representative of consciousness and reality, and is produced when a repressed idea is given illusory confirmation by an event in consciousness with the effect of momentarily breaking off the ego's contact with reality.

Now since the uncanny is not a quality of the dream itself, but derives from an impairment of an ego faculty, that of reality testing, a narrative which attempts to simulate the experience of dreaming or to evoke the "uncanniness" of the dream must deceive the critical and judging faculties of the ego through a prose which apparently sustains logic and belief at the same time that it affirms the delusion. The ideal prose for this treatment is everyday speech, a factual narration in simple declarative sentences. The narration of events and visions from a night-world in the ordinary, accustomed prose of waking life produces exactly that sense of dissolving reason which makes reality a dream and the dream a reality, in essence the quality of uncanniness.

Let us consider whether the same effect could be achieved through an experiment upon the language itself and the mode of narration. Now a prose which attempts to evoke the experience of dreaming by borrowing the method of the dream work must break up the structure of speech in order to bring it into a primitive system of thought. Syntax has no place in primary mental processes, and such a narrative needs to free itself from the order and restriction of language, yet cannot abandon it completely for functional reasons. Meaning will suffer through this treatment, of course, but this is a dimension of mind which is cut off from the higher mental faculties, has no reason of its own, no order or coherence, and for many purposes of the writer the obscurity and ambiguity of this liberated prose will strengthen the analogy to dreaming. Similarly, by abandoning the patterns of everyday speech, the writer can introduce phrasing and rhythms which recall the fluidity and merging forms of unconscious thought processes. Such a radical departure from the spoken language can include words themselves. The dream can be taken as a model for bold invention and license in language. For although it "speaks no language," it represents the word in visual forms and symbols which both mask and unmask the language of waking life and reveal the infinitely ramified structure of meaning. The writer who takes this license of the dream for himself can achieve dimensions of meaning and a richness of allusion unparalleled in everyday speech. It is unnecessary to add that these experiments upon the language demand such powerful gifts of imagination in a writer that they have only rarely produced important results.

This writing which bends the language, changes its order, its accustomed phrasing and usage, can achieve many effects of its own in the representation of unconscious mental processes, but it cannot achieve the effect of the uncanny or cause the reader to experience the dream-like narrative as a dream. We stand outside of the dream in reacting to this writing; certain sensory effects of the dream are induced in us, but we are not deluded. Our knowledge that this is unreal or that this is a dream is not even momentarily destroyed. This is because the distortions of language have already stamped the experience as unreal. It is analogous to a situation described by Freud in his essay on "The Uncanny." He demonstrates that the feeling which we describe as uncanny is always dependent in fiction or in life upon the appearance of unreal events as real, but when, as in fairy tales, the setting and the frankly animistic character of the events depart from the world of reality from the start, the feeling of uncanniness cannot be obtained. In the fairy tale or any fictional form that by its setting or form of presentation states its unreal character, the reader *willingly* participates in the delusion. In producing the experience of the uncanny in fiction, the writer must take care to exclude his reader's judgment and criticism and cause him to participate in the fictional delusion without a moment's reflection or the exercise of consciousness.[1]

The authentic dream quality, which Kafka achieves, owes a large part of its effect to narrative devices which temporarily dissolve the reader's sensory contact with reality and cause him to fall back upon archaic forms of thinking. Kafka erases the boundaries between reality and the dream; his transition from one world to another is as imperceptible as the moment between waking and sleeping. In much of Kafka's writing there is this ghostly treading between two worlds, made all the more sinister by the insubstantial and muted forms of reality and the electrifying clarity of the delusion and the dream. The passage from the ordinary event of coming home from the office and hanging up a coat to the extraordinary vision of a monster occurs with-

[1] For another treatment of the "uncanny" in Kafka's writing, see M. B. Hecht, "Uncanniness, Yearning and Franz Kafka's Works," *Imago*, April, 1952.

out an interval. In analogy with the dream the interval does not exist; it is not remarked upon for the same reason that no man knows the moment he falls asleep, loses this self for the other self in the dream, or leaves his bed to flee through hollow corridors. In recreating through the narrative the psychic transition from waking to dreaming, Kafka brings the reader directly into the dream. He causes the reader to suspend reason and criticism, to submit to the delusion, through the simple device of juxtaposing reality and the dream in agreement with the psychic experience of the emerging dream.

The effect is strengthened when the narrative, as in the stove-monster sequence, proceeds to treat fantastic events as real in the same way that events of the dream are experienced as real by the dreamer. The narrator did not imagine that he saw a monster; he *saw* it; and the description of the monster in fine detail supports the delusional effect in much the same way that the eye-witnesses of flying saucers support their delusions through minute descriptions of the little men, their clothing, and the size and appearance of the craft.

Kafka's use of metaphor must also be considered in a study of his "dream technique." In the dream a metaphor is represented in its literal aspect. In the metaphor, for example, it is "as if" Kafka were a species of vermin; in the story "Metamorphosis," as in a dream representation, he *is* a noxious bug. In many places in Kafka's diaries we can trace the evolution of a story or details of a story from a metaphor. In the "Letter to My Father," for example, Kafka has the father answer his reproaches in an imaginary speech in which the father says, "And there is the fight of the vermin, which not only bite, but at the same time suck the blood on which they live. . . ." In the diaries he speaks of the broken engagement with F. B. as "the tribunal in the hotel," and employs other metaphors to represent his engagement as "an arrest," himself as "a criminal." Later, in *The Trial,* we see the concrete representation of these metaphors (though I do not wish to imply that the meaning of the work is contained in these metaphors alone). Similarly we can find the genesis for the story "The Burrow" in these remarks in his diary, October 6, 1915: "Various types of nervousness. I think noises can no longer disturb me, though to be sure I am not doing any work now. Of course, the deeper one digs one's pit, the quieter it becomes, the less fearful one becomes, the quieter it becomes." In "The Burrow" he represents his illness, his fear of life, in a literal treatment of the metaphorical allusion. The small, frightened animal has dug deep into the ground, and with cunning and ingenuity he has created a labyrinth in which he is snug and safe and which assures him escape in case of danger. "But the most beautiful thing about my burrow is the stillness."

III

In any circumstances, the relationship between art and the dream is difficult to analyze. The psychoanalytic investigator needs to bear in mind Trilling's insistence that the dream-art analogy must be corrected to allow for the artist's conscious command of his fantasy. He quotes Lamb: "The . . . poet dreams being awake. He is not possessed by his subject but he has dominion over it."

Kafka provides a special case for the study of the relationship between the dream and creative work. He has given us evidence that he employed his dreams and the productions of dream-like states in his writing. In his diaries Kafka records a large number of his own dreams. Many of these are terror dreams, dreams of torture, mutilation, flight from attackers, of lepers and whores and disease, filth, excrement, and monotonously, regularly, dreams of the father, the formidable opponent who cannot be conquered and who cannot be escaped. A number of these dreams become the starting point for a story or a sketch in the diaries, so that we can if we wish examine the relationship between the two.

Like all victims of recurrent terror dreams, Kafka suffered from insomnia. He feared sleep; he feared his dreams, and the struggle against sleep and the yearning for sleep were in themselves a repetition of a lifelong struggle, as if sleep had become the formidable opponent who could not be conquered and to whom it was dangerous to submit. In a conversation with Janouch he says, "Perhaps my insomnia only conceals a great fear of death. Perhaps I am afraid that the soul—which in sleep leaves me—will never return. Perhaps insomnia is only an all too vivid sense of sin, which is afraid of the possibility of a sudden judgment. Perhaps insomnia is itself a sin. Perhaps it is a rejection of the natural."

He wrote at night. *"Wenn es nicht diese grauenvollen, schlaflosen Nächte gäbe, so würde ich überhaupt nicht schreiben. So wird mir aber immer meine dunkle Einzelhaft bewusst."* But the apparitions of the dream which he fended off through sleeplessness forced their way into the fantasies and obsessive thoughts which occupied him at these times. These fantasies were themselves very close to dream productions and were the sources of a number of stories and sketches. On one occasion Janouch attempts to pin down Kafka on the meaning of *The Verdict*. Kafka, after some embarrassment, says, "*The Verdict* is the spectre of a night." "What do you mean?" "It is a spectre." "And yet you wrote it," Janouch says. And Kafka replies, "That is merely the verification, and so the complete exorcism of the spectre." So that writing for Kafka was also the rite and the magic act for the subduing of his disturbing visions. In another conversation with Janouch he allies writing and conjuration: *"Das Schreiben ist eben eine Art von Geister-beschwörung."*

Kafka has left us an extraordinary record for the study of the relationships between his dreams and dream-like fantasies and his writings. I am particularly interested in the dream-story sequences in his diaries which show us how he worked with the materials of his own dreams. In each of these we see how the problem of the dream is taken up in the waking state, and how the elements of the dream are recomposed in the story.

In the example which follows, I employ a method of analysis which requires some justification to begin with. I am committed, of course, to the psychoanalytic principle that a dream or an imaginative work cannot be fully analyzed without the associations of the dreamer or the artist. In these studies of the dream-story sequences, it can be demonstrated that the elements of the story which are related to the dream can be regarded as associations to the dream, that is, that the story takes up the dream thoughts, the latent content of the dream, and develops these thoughts in a new composition. (This does not mean of course that the latent *meaning* of the dream is made conscious to the writer, or that the story is an explication of the dream by the writer.) In analyzing the dream-story sequences, I also make use of any other source materials, circumstantial or historical, which have a demonstrable relationship to the content of the dream or the story. When Kafka tells us the circumstances under which the dream is dreamed or the story is written, we can assume a relationship between these circumstances and the production of a dream or a story that can be safely employed in an analytic investigation. We are justified in making the same use of a biographical fact (like the relationship of Kafka to his father) when this information is required for analytic study. Similarly, when Kafka shows preference for a certain type of imagery, we can regard this imagery as over-determined in the psychoanalytic sense and can draw inferences from its use in other writings which we are permitted to employ in the present investigation. So far as possible I have avoided any arbitrary interpretations of symbols.

The Dream of the Letter and the Merchant Messner Sketch

In the diary entry for November 24, 1913 (also during the period of struggle against marriage with F. B.), Kafka records a dream which is followed by a story in which certain elements of the dream are employed. *The dream:*

I am sitting in the garden of a sanatorium at a long table, at the very head, and in the dream I actually see my back. It is a gloomy day, I must have gone on a trip and am in an automobile that arrived a short time ago, driving up in a curve to the front of the platform. They are just about to bring in the food when I see one of the waitresses, a young delicate girl wearing a dress the color of autumn leaves, approaching with a very light or unsteady step through the pillared hall that served as the porch of the sanatorium, and going down into the garden. I don't yet know what she wants but nevertheless point questioningly at myself to learn whether she wants me. And in fact she brings me a letter. But I open it and a great number of thin sheets covered with writing come out, all of them in the strange handwriting. I think, this can't be the letter I'm expecting, it is a very thin letter and a strange, thin, unsure handwriting. I begin to read, leaf through the pages and recognize that it must be a very important letter and apparently from F.'s youngest sister. I eagerly begin to read, then my neighbor on the right, I don't know whether man or woman, probably a child, looks down over my arm at the letter. I scream, "No!" The round table of nervous people begins to tremble. I have probably caused a disaster. I attempt to apologize with a few hasty words in order to go on with the reading. I bend over my letter again, only to wake up without resistance, as if awakened by my own scream. With complete awareness I force myself to fall asleep again, the scene reappears, in fact I quickly read two or three more misty lines of the letter, nothing of which I remember, and lose the dream in further sleep.

The story: In the story which follows the dream entry in the diary, the dream details of "a message" and "an interruption" are brought together again. Following is a summary of the sketch:

The old merchant Messner, laboriously ascending the stairs to his room, is confronted by a young man who has stationed himself in a dark corner. The merchant "still groaning from the exertion of his climb" demands to know who this is and what he wants. The young man introduces himself as a student named Kette. He has come to deliver a message to the merchant. The student wishes to discuss the message in Messner's room. Messner obstinately refuses. "I do not receive guests at night." If the student wishes to give him the message, he can give it now, in the hall. The student protests. The merchant dismisses him curtly. He is not interested in the message. "Every message that I am spared is a gain. I am not curious." He enters his room, locks the door upon the protesting Kette. A moment later there is a persistent knocking on the door. "The knocking came the way children at play scatter their knocks over the whole door, now down low, dull against the wood, now up high, clear against the glass." The merchant approaches the door a stick in hand. "Is anyone still out there?" "Yes. Please open the door for me." Messner opens the door and advances toward the student with his stick. "Don't hit me," the student warns him. "Then go!" The merchant points his finger at the stair. "But I can't," said the student and ran up to Messner so surprisingly. . . .

The story breaks off here, just as the dream breaks off at the point, "I have probably caused a disaster" and with the dreamer's hasty apology.

Certain elements of the dream reappear in the story. In the dream someone, "probably a child," interrupts the reading of the important message, invades the privacy of the dreamer through spying upon the letter. In the story a young student interrupts the old man, creates a disturbance late at night, disturbs the privacy of the merchant. The connection between the child in the dream and the student is further suggested by the knocking on the door in the story which is likened to the knocking of children at play. The antagonists in the dream, the dreamer and a child, become the merchant Messner and the student Kette. The "merchant" is a familiar character in Kafka's writings. He is Kafka's merchant father. *Kette,* chain, might signify the bond which tied Kafka to his father. (See also Kafka's own analysis of the name Georg Bendeman in *The Verdict* in which he identifies *Bende* with bonds, the bonds between father and son. *Diaries,* I, p. 278.) The symbolism becomes clear. The chain, the bonds which tie father and son cannot be severed. Here the link to F. B. in the dream is seen, for Kafka himself understood and explicitly stated in his diaries and his own analysis of *The Verdict* that it was the tie between himself and his father which made marriage with F. B. impossible.

The message in the dream is contained in the letter, but it is a message which is not received, so to speak, because of the interruption. When the dreamer returns to it after waking, he can read a few more "misty lines," none of which he remembers, then loses the dream in further sleep. In the story, too, the message is never delivered. The merchant does not want to hear it. (In both instances the nature of the message is not known.) The letter, the message, seem to belong to the group of "lost communication" symbols in Kafka's writing which were mentioned earlier and are analogous, particularly, to the telephones in *The Castle*. They are failures in human connections, of course, here represented in the dream by the symbol of a letter from a woman and in the story by the message for the man. His life conflict is delineated in these terms. He cannot receive a woman's love (he cannot read the letter in the dream), and he cannot give his love to a man (the thwarted message for Messner in the story).

In examining the connections between the dream and the story, we should give our attention to those details which are most highly charged with feeling. In the dream it is the interruption, the invasion of privacy, and the "no" which create anxiety in the dreamer. These details must be highly over-determined in the dream with threads leading to the dream day and current experience and other threads leading back to infantile experience. It is possible that those details represent (among many other things) the conflict over marriage which was uppermost in Kafka's thoughts during this period. For Kafka saw marriage as an invasion of his privacy, "then I'll never be alone again," and an interference with his writing, "But then would it not be at the expense of my writing? Not that, not that!" (Both quotations are from his "Summary of all the arguments for and against my marriage," July 21, 1913.) But also he desired this marriage and in his list of arguments there is one in favor of marriage, "Inability to bear life alone." I think, then, that these thoughts made their way into the dream details. He is "eager" to read the letter which has a connection with F., but "someone" interferes, invades his privacy, and his cry of "no!" is the vehement protest against marriage, the invasion of his privacy, the interference with his work.

But these interpretations would account only for those motives in the dream that are provided by a current conflict. These details must also have threads which lead back into infantile experience. In an early draft of this paper, I attempted to reconstruct a childhood memory from these details which I could not support on any basis except clinical experience in dream interpretation. While such tentative constructions are allowable in psychoanalytic investigation, the test of validation is provided by the live patient or subject of the investigation, i.e., the patient will confirm or not confirm the analyst's construction. In this case, it seemed, the subject of my investigation could never offer the necessary confirmation. His diaries and recollections provided me with nothing more specific for my purposes, and while I thought I found evidence in certain of his writings, the use of imaginative works for "evidence" could bring forth the same criticism as the use of dream details for "evidence." We still don't know if it really happened. So, in this earlier draft I wrote in a tentative construction based on these dream details which read as follows: "The details in the dream suggest a crisis in childhood, an interruption by a child, an invasion of privacy, and a severe prohibition represented by the 'no!,' an early disaster which caused a small child to tremble in fear. (In the dream reversal 'the round table of nervous people began to tremble.')" I could not pursue this further and I was also bothered by the fact that the connecting links between the dream details, my reconstruction, and the Messner-Kette story could not be clearly established.

Last year the text of Kafka's "Letter to My Father" was published in full for the first time. In a long outpouring of old griefs and reproaches, there is one memory to which Kafka himself attached the greatest importance and which provided unexpected confirmation of my construction and the connecting links between the dream and the Messner-Kette story.

There is only one episode in the early years of which I have a direct memory. You may remember it, too. Once in the night I kept on whimpering for water, not, I am certain, because I was thirsty, but probably partly to be annoying, partly to amuse myself. After several vigorous threats had failed to have any effect, you took me out of bed, carried me out onto the *pavlatche* (a balcony) and left me there alone for a while in my nightshirt, outside the shut door. I am not going to say this was wrong—perhaps at the time there was really no other way of getting peace and quiet that night—but I mention it as typical of your methods of bringing up a child and their effect on me. I dare say I was quite obedient afterwards at that period, but it did me inner harm. What was for me a matter of course, that senseless asking for water, and the extraordinary terror of being carried outside were two things that I, my nature being what it was, could never properly connect with each other. Even years afterwards I suffered from the tormenting fancy that the huge man, my father, the ultimate authority, would come almost for no reason at all and take me out of bed in the night and carry me out onto the *pavlatche*, and that therefore I was such a mere nothing for him.

This memory has made its way into the dream and the story. I would like to propose from the evidence of Kafka's recorded dreams and his stories that this experience was not the only one in which he disturbed his father at night with disastrous consequences, for the theme of sexual observation occurs repeatedly in Kafka's dreams and his writings. But he is probably truthful in saying that this episode is the only one of his early years of which he has a direct memory, for such infantile sexual scenes as I have inferred from the material ordinarily undergo repression. It is even probable that Kafka's memory of the disturbance at night which he describes obtained its dreadful proportions in his child's eyes from an earlier interruption the memory of which was repressed. We would then regard the memory which was retained in consciousness as a screen memory, that is, certain qualities of the repressed experience are displaced onto the later, more innocent interruption at night, the one that survives in memory.

But for our purposes here we can work best with the memory which Kafka has given us, the crisis at night which led to the forceful eviction of a small boy and the punishment of being locked out on a balcony. For it is clear that Kafka has written into the Messner-Kette story the scene of this childhood calamity, the disturbance at night which provoked his father's anger. The details are there: the interruption at night, the student's plea to be heard, to deliver the message, the merchant's angry refusal, the locking out of the intruder, the persistent demands of the student, the menacing reappearance of the merchant, with the command to leave, and the student's last protest. With very few changes, the story of the childhood crisis is retold. The conflict between a small boy and his father becomes a conflict between two strangers, an older man and a student, aptly named Messner and Kette. It is a compact statement of the idea that the conflict between father and son persists unchanged in the adult years of the son. The story is unfinished. It breaks off when the merchant commands the student to leave. " 'But I can't,' said the student and ran up to Messner so surprisingly. . . ." We are reminded of the dream now which ends abruptly at the point, "I have probably caused a disaster," and with the dreamer's hasty apology.

Now I think we can understand the relationship between the dream of the letter and the story. It is as if the dreamer takes up the problem of the dream in the waking state, searches for its meaning, and comes up with a memory, an association to one of the dream elements. It is probable that the dream details of the interruption by the child, the cry "No!" and the observation "I have probably caused a disaster," those details which are highly charged with feeling, lead the dreamer's waking associations back to the event in childhood. The story then makes use of the memory, recasts and resets it as the encounter between the merchant Messner and the student Kette.

But then we need to ask, "What is the motive in *writing* the story, or, more exactly, in putting this memory into the form of a story?" By doing this Kafka attempts to get rid of the painful effects of this memory through repetition, through experiencing it once again in order to overcome it. He gives the childhood event a second existence in the story. The original conflict led to disaster because the antagonists were a small boy and his powerful father. In the new edition he tries out the event once again with the antagonists a young man and an old and wheezing merchant, as if this time there might be hope for a different outcome. But the young man is defeated by the old man once again as if the problem can find no solution in the imagination either.

We have seen the connection between details in the dream, a memory, and a story, but in reading the story of Messner-Kette we feel that in the process of re-working these details into a story something got lost. There is an emptiness in this story which we cannot immediately account for when we consider its source in a dream and a memory which were highly charged with emotion. Now the effect of this story is certainly intended by Kafka; it is satirical, absurd, and its author is saying, "Here is a spectacle for you! A young man and an aging man are like a small boy and his father, but the old man still has his power and the young man is still a weakling, a child who whimpers at night outside his father's room." But even the irony is weakened in this story by the absence of any emotional quality.

It seems that in the process of utilizing a dream detail and a memory in a story the ideational content was preserved but the emotional content was lost. We have already mentioned as one of the advantages of a conscious fantasy over a dream that the conscious ego can control the quantities of affect and can admit into consciousness only those quantities which can be tolerated. It is even possible for the ego to permit a fantasy or a memory to emerge into consciousness while its accompanying affects are held back by the repressive mechanisms. In this way once painful memories appear in consciousness as empty or disembodied images, ghosts of themselves which hold no real terror because they are not alive, are not animated by the original full charge of energy. Similarly, the grossest, the most naked sensual fantasies can be admitted to conscious expression if they are deprived of their accompanying affects. The quality of the mental production is then altered accordingly so that the fantasy seems dead, unreal.

Now this is a quality which appears very strongly in Kafka's writings. Think of the torture in "In the Penal Colony," the scene, "The Whippers," in *The Trial*. The detachment which accompanies these descriptions is the mental quality of the writer who admitted these awful visions into consciousness by making them silent, by anesthetizing the vital parts. Only in this way could he confront his specters without dread. Kafka's people, the people of his stories, are the product of this emotional isolation. They do not live; they imitate the living. They are human abstractions and abstractions of human qualities exactly as dream people are. We could never believe in Kafka's people if we did not take them as dream people and accept Kafka's world as a dream world.

From these ideas on the defenses against affect which Kafka employed in his writing, I think I can also deduce the reason why so many of his stories are unfinished. Frequently Kafka's stories and sketches break off at the critical moment as a dream breaks off when a signal of danger occurs. It seems probable to me that at those points in Kafka's stories where a strong emotion threatens to break through the defenses, the story breaks off. We never find out what it was that the student Kette was about to do or say at the critical point in the Messner-Kette story. The story breaks off just as the dream breaks off and this may be for the same reasons.

IV

In this example we see how the story takes up the problem of the dream, how the latent dream thoughts are transformed in the waking state and worked into a new composition. The story stands in the same relationship to the dream as a dreamer's waking associations to his dream and its elements can be regarded as associations to the dream.

There is this difference, of course: ordinarily when a man pursues his thoughts in relationship to a dream, these thoughts, if they are free associations, will emerge in a formless, chaotic stream. Now Kafka does bind these disordered elements together in a narrative, but the narrative is as indifferent to the conventions of story telling as is the manifest dream. The comparison between these two should be closely examined. The latent dream thoughts are themselves disordered fragments and what we call the manifest dream, the "story" of the dream, is the attempt on the part of the dream work to give a semblance of order and coherence to materials which have no logical connections and are governed by primitive thought processes. Freud called this aspect of the dream work "secondary elaboration." The resulting "story" in the dream when considered as a composition is loosely and often indifferently strung together in a narrative which combines its elements without regard for compatibility, temporal sequence, or the boundaries of space. (While many dreams do present an intelligible façade, when we say "like a dream" we usually mean the disordered dream, the absurd dream.)

Kafka's stories, as in the example studied, are associations to the dream and are also composed like the dream. The so-called "dream technique" is like the dream's own method of composition, the process of secondary elaboration. There is no doubt that Kafka deliberately employed this device of the dream for reproducing the effect of the dream in his stories. But I think it is also true, as I mentioned earlier, that his gift in recreating the dream world in his stories derived from illness. I want to emphasize that I do not think Kafka was psychotic, but the danger of psychosis was very real, probably as real as he feared. He never actually lost touch with reality, never lost his citizenship in the real world even when he pronounced himself "a citizen of this other world." His writing must be considered as his strongest bond to the real world and may even be responsible for maintaining his contact with reality.

I think I can support this last statement from certain remarks of Kafka regarding the conditions under which he wrote. If it were not for the sleepless nights he would not write at all, he says. (This should not be taken literally, of course, but it is a fact that most of his writing was the work of these sleepless nights, and we have seen the close connection between these nocturnal fantasies and the anxiety dreams which he warded off through insomnia.) He himself connects his fear of sleep and his fear of death. "Perhaps I am afraid that the soul—which in sleep leaves me—will never return." In psychological terms, he is afraid of sleep because in sleep he loses the self, or awareness of self, and there is the danger that he may not recover it. This is a common fear in severe neuroses, when the danger of losing the self and the ties to reality is real. This extreme peril to the ego gives rise in many serious neuroses (and psychoses as well) to creative spells in which the ego attempts to counteract the loosening of its bonds to reality by energetically recreating aspects of the objective world. (Ernst Kris develops this psychoanalytic idea in a group of brilliant essays dealing with the phenomenon of restitution in art.) But the restitutive function of art is not confined to morbid states, and I feel that I am doing this psychoanalytic theory an injustice by introducing it in this context. In Kafka's case, however, we need the clinical observations on restitution in order to explain the function of writing in his neurosis. Only one who is in great danger of losing the self and the real world will fear sleep as Kafka did. This explains why Kafka wrote only of himself. He needed to affirm and reaffirm his uncertain existence in the real world through creating images of himself, through giving himself an existence on paper. In this way his writing preserved his ties to reality.

The problem of art and neurosis is often brought in irrelevantly to the study of a work. In Kafka's writing the problem not only is relevant but intrudes itself into the study of his works. We cannot understand his writing without understanding him, and this must be counted as a failure in the work. The ambiguity of his writing has given rise to a Kafka criticism in which the works have stimulated impressions and fantasies like the ink blots on the Rorschach test. With the publication in recent years of the Kafka notebooks, letters, conversations, and miscellaneous pieces, Kafka as Mystic, Kafka as Cabalist, Kafka as Prophet, Kafka as Social Critic, and a large number of other Kafkas have receded, and we are left to read Kafka as Joseph K. and as Gregor Samsa, a man who has less to say about the world he lived in than about the world that lived in him.

Kafka offers himself and his disease as a symbol which exercises an extraordinary attraction in our time. For mental illness is the romantic disease of this age just as tuberculosis was in the past century. His writing is expiation, atonement, an extreme mortification before his human judges, and the bond he creates between himself and his reader is in part the bond of guilt, of unconscious sin. But this does not account for his vogue during the past twenty years. The awe and mysticism which surround the figure of Kafka and his writings bring to mind those feelings which are aroused in us by a premonitory dream. When the events of the dream or of inner life are reproduced in the world of reality, we are inclined to endow both the dream and the dreamer with magical and divine qualities. The events of our recent history have appeared to us like the full-scale performance of Kafka's tormented dreams. The peril to our reason has given a significance to Kafka's writings which, we must grant, was not altogether his intention.

Kafka appears, finally, as a crippled writer, a man in whom the disease and the art were united in a kind of morbid love so that neither could set the other free. *"Die Kunst ist für den Künstler ein Leid, durch das er sich füer ein neues Leid befreit,"* he said. His writing represented, among other things, an attempt to free himself from neurotic suffering, to repeat and to relive it in order to conquer it. But behind each door with Kafka there was another door, as in the imagery of the legend "Before the Law." An unending chain of events led backward into earliest times, and the conquest of danger and of suffering was a succession of battles in which a new enemy grew in the spot of the last one vanquished, and the new enemy was only a replica of the one who came before.

The disease which produced extraordinary dreams exerted its morbid influence on the creative process as well. The striving for synthesis, for integration and harmony which are the marks of a healthy ego and a healthy art are lacking in Kafka's life and in his writings. The conflict is weak in Kafka's stories because the ego is submissive; the unequal forces within the Kafka psyche create no tension within the reader, only a fraternal sadness, an identification between a writer and reader which takes place in the most solitary regions of the ego.

Crime and Punishment

A STUDY OF DOSTOEVSKY'S NOVEL

R. P. Blackmur

Crime and Punishment has upon most readers an impact as immediate and obvious and full as the news of murder next door; one *almost* participates in the crime, and the trivial details become obsessively important. It has besides a secondary impact, by which, as one feels it, one discovers that one has been permanently involved in the nature of the crime: one has somehow contributed to the clarification of the true residual nature of crime in general through having contributed to the enactment of this crime in particular. It is the feeling of this impact that leads us to say our powers of attention have been exhausted. But there is a third and gradual impact, which comes not only at the end but almost from the beginning to the end, creating in us new and inexhaustible powers of attention. This is the impact of what Dostoevsky meant by punishment. The three impacts are united by the art of the novelist, and they are felt simultaneously. It is only that we are not aware at the time of the triple significance, and must, when it does transpire, rebuild it analytically. Thus we may come to estimate what it is that we know —what it is that has been clarified in the history of Raskolnikov which we had known all along in ourselves without being aware of it: we estimate our own guilt.

A crime is above all an act against the institutions of human law, custom, or religion; and there is a sense in which any act may be understood as criminal, for if the institution cannot be found against which it is committed, then it may be called an anarchic act—against

Reprinted by permission of the author.

some institution that has not yet come to exist, but which will exist because of the crime. This notion comes from putting Rousseau's dusty vision in reverse. If, as Rousseau thought for one inspired moment, the evils of living come mostly from human institutions, it is as likely true, though not as inspired, that our institutions arise out of the evil that we do. It is LaForgue who has said it best, and without any but poetic logic to blister his cry:

Allez, stérile ritournelles!
La Vie est vraie et criminelle! .

This cry of LaForgue represents the lyric sense that must inhabit every criminal who truly imagines his crime, if only for a flash, *before* he commits it to act. What the criminal imagines afterwards is another thing and we shall come to it. Here it is the crime only that has been imagined, and the promise of liberation in the cry within.

So it is with Raskolnikov. If we feel his case in terms of the LaForgue lines we can understand both the motivation of his crime and the external logic of most of his conduct afterwards. It is the story of *Crime and Punishment* at the level of its immediate impact. We are very near it; it is the murder that only by some saving accident we did not ourselves commit—as we did not make a million, win a race, or conquer Europe, all the things it is still not impossible to do, and which, because we have not done them, may yet tempt us to murder. Between temptation and deed there is no distance at all in symbolic meaning. With that symbolic strength in mind, the story of Raskolnikov becomes not only possible but probable, and, as we attend it, not only probable but proved. Let us look and see.

How easy it is to believe that this young, handsome, proud, and sensitive boy might be drawn *first of all* to the possibility of murder as the way out of an intolerable situation. It is the situation of poverty, debt, starvation, shabbiness, sickness, loneliness; for Raskolnikov has reached such a stage of privation that even thought has become a luxury —a kind of luxurious hallucinated hysteria; an extremity in which only the rashest dream seems a normal activity. It is the situation of the sponge, too, for Raskolnikov has come to depend on his mother and sister for help they cannot afford to give, for help they can give only by prostituting themselves in marriage and servile relationships. The sponge who is aware that he is a sponge is in an awkward situation; the pride of his awareness deprives him of the use of the exactions he makes; and that is how it is with Raskolnikov, as he lies in his attic committing symbolic murder. He deceives himself, proudly, that he has conceived murder to symbolise his mother's and sister's freedom as well as his own. He lends his dark motive the external colour of a good deed, and then identifies the colour with the motive, and forgets what the murder, dark within him, really is. But to starve and be a sponge, that is not all Raskolnikov has to put up with in his pride; he is in the situation, too, of the proud man of intellect who has as yet done nothing and who is afraid that there will be nothing for him to do unless he invents it. Not only can he do nothing for his poverty or for his family, he is in the terrible position of being unable to do any-thing for himself. Such is his pride, that none of the ordinary things men do will be enough; and such is his pride, too, that none of the things ordinary people—his mother, his sister, his forgotten friends—can do for him are tolerable to him; he is the man for whom no one can do anything. Deeper still, he is that part of all men which cannot be touched, but which must create an image of itself in some extraordi-nary deed, some act against ordinary people and against the ordinary part of himself. The extraordinary wells within him and inundates the ordinary self with its fever. And in that fever, which never leaves him while we know him, the possibility of murder becomes the necessity of murder.

What is fully imagined as necessary has goodness and freedom at the very heart of its horror, a sentiment which may be interpreted in different ways, having to do either with the tearing down of order or with the envelopment of disorder, or, finally, with the balancing of several disorders so as to form an order. At the level of immediate impact, Raskolnikov's story is concerned with the tearing down of order; that is the melodrama which carries us along and exhausts our attention. What Dostoevsky does to that story, the immense clarification of secret life and intimate impulse which he brings to it, composes the secondary impact of the story, and brings us to the second stage where the disorder brought about in the first stage is enveloped by the created personality of Raskolnikov. Actually, the two processes go on at once, in the sense that no matter how far into the second stage Dostoevsky leads us, the first stage is never left behind, but is rather always present, a frame of action and image, to carry the significance of the second stage. This is to say that Dostoevsky never fails of the primary task of the novelist; if his story seems for the moment to have been left behind, it is only that in reality it has got ahead of us, and when we catch up we see how much has been done without our noticing it. The story of the Crime is blended with the clarification of the Punishment; the actor creates the role which expresses the nature and significance of his deed; Raskolnikov, in the end, becomes the product of his crime, but still depends on it to command our attention.

That is how Dostoevsky envelops the disorder consequent upon Raskolnikov's attempt at the destruction of order. With the third possibility, whereby the imagination not only envelops disorder—our substantial chaos—in a created personality, but proceeds to balance the sense of several disorders—the tensions of chaos—against each other so as to form a new order; with this possibility Dostoevsky has little to do. It is not that he was necessarily unequal to the task, but that the nature, source, and direction of his insights did not lead him to undertake it. His view of necessity was simpler, and his sense of possibility more simplified, than the task would require; his vision was that of the primitive Christian, and that vision was so powerful within him that it blinded him to everything else. To him the edge of the abyss of sin was the horizon of salvation by faith, and suffering was the condition of vision. Sin was the Crime, and the suffering created by faith was the Punishment.

If we push the operation of this insight one step further, it becomes evident that the act of life itself is the Crime, and that to submit, by faith, to the suffering of life at the expense of the act is to achieve salvation—or, if you like a less theological phrase, it is to achieve integration or wholeness of personality. It is only dramatically true that the greater the sin the greater the salvation, and it is only arbitrarily true that any one act is sinful more than another act or than all acts. The crime of Raskolnikov, and its punishment in created suffering, could have been as great if he had never stirred from his room, if only the novelist's imagination could have conceived them. But the imagination requires images, as vision requires fables and thought requires formulas, before conceptions can be realised; which is to say that the faculties of men are not equal to their needs except by the intervention of symbols which they discover rather than create, and which they discover best of all in stories of violence, or of the sense of violence, or of the promise of violence.

So we watch, with the immediate attention which discovers meaning, the process of Raskolnikov trying to make a hero—a complete man

—of himself by committing a foul and frivolous murder. Any animal might strike another down without need when the odour of blood is thick, and it means nothing. But we are shown how much this murder of an old and malevolent pawnbroker, ripe for death, as Raskolnikov says, ripe as a louse, is not meaningless but huge with meaning. The meaning begins with the stench of Petersburg, the stench of the detailed plans, the stench of pothouses, the pervading sense of the filthy possibilities of the human heart, and the glittering eyes of the victim peering through the slit of the door. The meaning grows more meaningful, irretrievably meaningful, when in the second chapter we are exposed to Marmeladov in the stinking tavern and hear his confession of drunken humiliation and of what it has brought upon Katerina his wife in the way of sickness and shame and anger and hairpulling, and brought upon his daughter too, in her glad submissive acceptance of the humiliation of prostitution. It is impossible to *say* how this adds to the richness of Raskolnikov's motive, but like the general images of stench and violence and drunkenness, it is impossible not to *know,* and very precisely, how much it does add. Let us say that it exposes Raskolnikov, and through him the reader, to a kind of dead-level human degradation in terms of images which revolt him as he assents to them.

At any rate they fit him—for the purposes of the story—they fit him to see as further degradation the events which his mother's letter reports to him. Before he opens the letter we see his cluttered mind in his sleazy room trying to work around the idea of a "fortune all at once"; and in the letter he reads how indeed that is precisely what Douania his sister is about to get by selling herself to Luzhin. Douania has permitted herself or has been driven to do just the practical, ordinary thing which Raskolnikov, the extraordinary man, is unable to do, and which—as it is being done for *him*—is the more intolerably humiliating to him. Her marriage is like the prostitution of Sonia. Thinking of it, Hamlet-like, the idea of the murder rediscovers itself most naturally in his mind, and he finds that he had *felt beforehand* that it would come back; it has begun to acquire a kind of reality quite independent of him except that it requires to be completed.

Your ordinary novelist might well have now proceeded to the completion of the deed, but Dostoevsky saw deeper into the nature of the deed and knew that it required further preparation, so that it might be as ripe as the victim. Raskolnikov goes out for a breath of air and to escape the pressure of his dilemma. But there is no escape, except from one level of intensity to a deeper level. Walking on the boulevard the double pressure of Sonia and of Douania springs upon him in the shape of the drunken young girl, with the torn dress, and indecorous posture, evidently just seduced and then discarded, who is being pursued by the plump gentleman. In his shabby and dishevelled pride, and with his uprooted and irresolute mind he first attempts to save the girl and then gives it up as a bad job; he revolts against his revulsion, reminding himself of the percentage theory of vice whereby "a certain number" are bound to go that way, and resolves forthwith to go see Razumihin, that simpleton of a man who takes things as they are. But again he changes his mind; he cannot see Razumihin till after "It." The image of the debauched girl has set the murder to pursuing him still more closely. He contrives for himself, as he thinks, an escape in the green islands of the Neva, where there is no stench, no drunkenness, no human filth. The human filth is stronger. He first buys himself a glass of vodka, and then walks out exhausted, turning aside on the way home and falls asleep in the bushes, where a dream assaults him with a fresh image of the little sorrel horse beaten to death because it cannot pull all humanity. In the dream he rushes to kiss the bleeding face of the horse as it dies, and at that moment wakes. The moment of waking is the nearest he comes to renouncing his crime before committing it, and it is the nearest, too, that he comes to realising its nature before the event. "It was as though an abscess that had been forming for a month past in his heart had suddenly broken. Freedom, freedom! He was free from that spell, that sorcery, that obsession!" He had reached the point which Shakespeare, in his own play of Crime and Punishment, *Measure for Measure,* calls the point where the two prayers cross, where, in the human heart, good and evil are created in the one gesture.

It was coincidence, you will remember, that decided the event. Raskolnikov happened to hear, on his way home, that the old pawnbroker would be left alone at seven the following evening, and he heard it at precisely the moment that he had given up the idea of the murder, when he had, in fact, begun again to use his reason and will. But the other thing had grown in him like a disease, and feeding on the coincidence, was able to destroy his will and reason, that is to say his sense of propriety in the social order. It may be observed, for those who carp at the use of coincidence as belittling the probabilities, that on the contrary the use of coincidence in art, like the sense of it in life, heightens the sense of inevitability; for coincidence is the artist's way of representing those forces in us not ourselves. Coincidence, properly dealt with, creates our sense of that other self within us whom we neither can ever quite escape nor quite meet up with.

In this case it is the perfected chain of coincidence, upon which Dostoevsky lavishes so many pages, that builds up the murder so that it is a kind of separate being existing between Raskolnikov and his victim. As he climbs the stairs, he feels that Alyona Ivanovna ought to be ready for him, ready to be murdered, for he feels that the murder is somewhere between them, other than either, but equally accessible to both. It was in the nature of Dostoevsky's insight to see always that the actor and the patient are both implicated in the deed, and that they are joined by it. The actor, in this case, has more consciousness than the patient of the implication; in *The Idiot* it is the other way round, and Myshkin, the patient, is shown as more conscious, or more representative, of the deeds that are done to him than the doers of the deeds can possibly be. In *Crime and Punishment,* it is Sonia who is perhaps the counterpart of Myshkin, for to her all deeds happen whether the doers realise it or not, and they happen, moreover, completely. It is perhaps because Raskolnikov is the other sort, the sort who requires of a deed that before it is credible or fully significant he must do it himself. He does not believe in the murder until he has done it, and not altogether even then. Constantly it slips away, a thing he realises that he has forgotten, or a thing he has to re-enact, to emphasise, and so a thing that tends to lose its meaning except as he identifies himself with it; whereas to Sonia, once she has learned of it, once she has submitted herself to the idea of it in him, she has no doubts about it and it is entirely meaningful. Nothing herself, Sonia is able to contain everything; while Raskolnikov, who must be everything himself, can contain nothing for long. Dante would have known how to punish him, looking for a mirror through an eternal hell; but Dostoevsky has rather to transform him in order to save him, or more accurately to show him as about to be saved in Sonia's eyes.

But he is not transformed for a long time, never permanently in the book; never can he leave the murder which fixed him, nor the images of which it was made: the images of stench, poverty, drunkenness, vanity, sick-hunger, lechery, and intellectual debauchery, through which the murder comes to be a deed in being, with the double power of invocation and growth. At first, indeed, he forgets it for the images and the sickness which went with it, and when he wakes to it he finds

that instead of feeling it behind him it has somehow got ahead of him
and he is driven to catch up to it. Instead of freedom, power, completeness, he is more at loss than ever, and more incoherent, there are only
"scraps and shreds of thought," suspicions, excitements, alarms, and
fresh temptations to extraordinary declarations of himself. This is, of
course, the first phase of the Punishment for the Crime, that having
striven by the crime to reach a complete solution of his incomplete life,
he should find himself not only less complete than ever and more way-
ward but actually perilously incoherent, with a personality on the verge
of dissipation. He lives in a haunted vertigo, into which for the time
he can invoke only the shrieking phantoms of rage and dread. He is
in the position, so humiliating to his continuing pride, where he is
completely powerless as the perfectly good man, as powerless as Sonia.
There is nothing he can yet see to do for himself, and nothing any
longer that he can do for others. When the police send for him about
his IOU which his landlady had sold, he feels himself possessed by "a
gloomy sensation of agonising, everlasting solitude and remoteness," and
knows that it will never be possible for him to appeal to anyone in any
circumstance of life. There is a sense in which Dostoevsky might have
stopped at this point, for he had put Raskolnikov on the path at the
end of which lay the meaning of his Crime as Punishment. For as in
the Christian psychology no man may complete himself in deed, so the
meaning of a deed can never be completed within the history of the man
who enacts it. Only the judgment completes either the man, or his
deed, or his meaning.

But both the deed and the meaning can continue in their course of
meaningfulness. The growth of meaning is infinite. At the moment he
feels his agonising solitude form consciously within him he hears the
police discuss the murder; that is, it is given to him from outside for
the first time, and as not his murder, but as an object in no one's possession; at once he is driven to confess, to seize it for his own, but a
combination of the fumes of paint and the pang of creation cause him
to faint. When he comes to, he goes out leaving a strange impression
and a potent silence behind him.

Out of that strangeness and silence grows the pursuit-game which
occupies the rest of the book, for Raskolnikov, having decided that
suspicions may have been roused about him from his peculiar conduct,
begins playing a complicated and eccentric game, or rather a set of
games. He pursues the police, eggs the police on to pursue him, and

himself both pursues the murder, the acknowledgment of it, and denies it whenever he comes face to face with it. The result of all this rash, tortuous, and vain activity is that he creates such an image of the murder that at last it overwhelms him. He plays his hands so that others play to him. In the event, there is nothing for anyone to believe about him except the extraordinary reality of the murder. He could not have made more certain of his arrest and imprisonment had that been his entire object. Only he delayed it, played with it, encouraged it to develop, in order to get the full savour of it and of himself.

First he rouses unconscious suspicions in Razumihin, then in Zossim—of the doctor in whom the suspicions may have been quite conscious, for he looked at Raskolnikov "curiously" whenever there was opportunity, and especially after that scene where Raskolnikov himself first realises the murder in a parallel and arbitrary image which brims and trembles as you look at it. It is that image which comes when Raskolnikov lies abed listening to the doctor and Razumihin talk of the murder, and how a house-painter has been mixed up in it. Nastasya, who is present, bursts out that Lizaveta was murdered, too.

"Lizaveta," murmured Raskolnikov hardly audibly.

"Lizaveta, who sold old clothes. Didn't you know her? She used to come here. She mended a shirt for you, too."

Raskolnikov turned to the wall where in the dirty, yellow paper he picked out one clumsy, white flower with brown lines on it and began examining how many petals there were in it, how many scallops in the petals and how many lines on them. He felt his arms and legs as lifeless as though they had been cut off. He did not attempt to move, but stared obstinately at the flower.

It is so that the murder is brought home by the housemaid's first mention of the other and incidental murder of Lizaveta. We feel what passed in Raskolnikov's mind, and feel it as if it passed in his face, and in his hands, too: quite as if he had plucked the scalloped petals of the clumsy white flower off the wallpaper. Razumihin, who was simple, may have seen nothing, but the doctor, looking at this dissenting soul, surely saw what Raskolnikov saw in the flower even if he could not then have named it. The blankest or the most conventional image is, as Dostoevsky knew, the best to hold the deepest symbol if only there is enough tension present when it is named. It is only another instance of this device that when Raskolnikov is about to go into the bar where he meets and gives himself away to Zametov, he first sees a good many drunken women, some of forty and some of seventeen, almost all of whom "had blackened eyes." Raskolnikov, who had gone out to end *this,* as he put it to himself, reflects upon this bevy with blackened eyes and pocked cheeks, that even the worst life is precious.

"Only to live, to live and live! Life, whatever it may be! . . . How true it is! Good God, how true! Man is a vile creature! . . . And vile is he who calls him vile for that," he added a moment later.

Whereupon he proceeds to risk his life, to make it precious, by playing like Hamlet on Rosencrantz and Guildenstern, upon the suspicious nerves of Zametov the police clerk as he drank tea in a restaurant. This scene, like the two great scenes with Porfiry, and like the last scene with Svidrigailov, shows Raskolnikov clinging with a kind of ultimate shuddering tenacity to his original proud role of the extraordinary man, the role of Napoleon within the little man, and clinging the more desperately because in the act of playing it he sees the role is false, the role of the condemned man whose life is thereby sweet.

What else happens at the same time, the history of the growth of the Punishment along with the realisation of the Crime, is of course present in these scenes, but it has been instigated in other scenes— those with his mother and sister and Luzhin and Razumihin and the Marmeladovs; and it is perfected in other scenes still, those with Sonia especially, though these scenes might well be lifeless and pointless without their counterparts with Porfiry and Svidrigailov. There is a synergy—a working together and back and forth—between these counterparts much as there is a synergy between the two parts, the proud, self-willed part and the meek, submissive part of Raskolnikov's character. This working together takes place, and the resultant unity is seen, not because there is any logical or organic connection between the parts, but because, quite to the contrary, the conflicting elements are dramatised in association, in parallels that, as they say, never actually meet except as opposites. The more nearly they seem to be forced into meeting, the more disparate they actually show themselves to be. The fusion, if it can be called a fusion, is in the dramatic *product* of the conflicting elements, not of the elements themselves.

It is something along these lines, I think, that the theory of the "doubles" in Dostoevsky must be approached, and this whether we think of single characters or of whole books and the doubleness of the conflicts within either. Let us look at Raskolnikov, who is usually thought of as a typical Dostoevsky Double. He is self-willed and will-less, he is proud and he becomes humiliated, he loves Sonia and hates her at the same moment, he is fond of Razumihin and cannot tolerate him, he is on the edge both of confession and of anathema all along, he is good to the point of giving all that he has and evil to the point of taking life; and in short there is neither certainty nor limit to any of his moods or acts; any role is dominant for the moment to another role that may at once take its place because it has been really dominant underneath. But he is not these roles in turn, he is the product of all their playing taken together. In any pair, the one may be taken as the idea of the other, and the other the reality of the idea, and the only alternation is as to which, at a given moment, is idea and which reality. The relation is rather like that between the idea of murder and the image of the white flower on the wallpaper, where we can reverse it and say it is the relation between the idea of the flower and the image of the murder. What we get is a kind of steady state precariously maintained between the conflicting elements. The balance tips, but it recovers in the act of tipping. We should feel it as we feel similar physiological states in the body—only as the disturbance and forward drive of life— were it not that the language itself and Dostoevsky's taste for seeing the opposite to every presented element have together a tendency to formularise pure types, and then to ignore for the moment what does not exemplify the type. What happens is, by language and its dialectic mode, that Dostoevsky's imagination arrests, for the maximum possible amount of attention, the moments when the balance does tip from love to hate, from pride to humiliation, from idea to deed, from image to tension, and by the arrest, by the attention which is bent upon the moment of arrest, we see how the one in each case fecundates the other. We seem to see deeply what they make together by seeing wilfully what they are apart.

By a little progress of this notion, we can say that Raskolnikov is balanced in turn against the other characters in this novel, and that the other characters and their stories make something with Raskolnikov which is quite different from anything found in them as types, though there would be no product of their whole conflict if there was not a great deal that was living within each type, from Razumihin to Porfiry to Svidrigailov to Sonia, and all the rest. As illustration, let us take first the Marmeladov family, and consider by what astonishing luck it was that Dostoevsky thought of putting them into the history of Raskolnikov and the punishment of his crime. They were to have been, the whole little crowd of them, a novel all to themselves called "The Drunkards," a novel showing, no doubt, all the ills and humiliations that can come from the head of a poor family who has given over to heavy drinking. The luck is that Dostoevsky had them all going, with past and present and future, when Raskolnikov happened to meet old Marmeladov in the tavern and heard his humiliating confession with such apparently inexplicable sympathy. The truth is that he has something deeply in common with him, and again that Marmeladov has something which he has not yet but which he must have. What they have in common comes out when Marmeladov says that he has *nowhere to turn* except to his sick and somewhat crazy wife. Raskolnikov sees that it is not Marmeladov the good-natured drunk that turns, but Marmeladov humiliated, on hands and knees, with his hair pulled, Marmeladov in the mud which he Raskolnikov has not yet reached, but will reach in good time. Man grows used to everything, the scoundrel, says Raskolnikov, and adds: But what if he is not a scoundrel?

The scene is something like the great scenes in Dickens, caricature by direct observation, with the differences that Dostoevsky—and this is perhaps the way Dostoevsky himself read Dickens—replaces zest of observation for its own sake with the severity of attention that is based upon zeal, and replaces the anguish of social consciousness with the dignity of religion. Marmeladov, like Micawber, is able to represent much beyond himself because he is something of a buffoon; he can talk and act for talking and acting's sake; and he can be honest, and let himself go, just to see what will happen; he can see himself at his worst in order to be at his best. And so he does; he produces, to show himself at his utmost, and for the sake of Raskolnikov, for the sake of this new strange novel in which he unconsciously finds himself, the character and personality of Sonia, whom Raskolnikov needs as complement and salvation, and whom the novel needs for mechanics and plot. And not Sonia only, he also produces, by just the agency of his being, scenes in which all manner of things which bear on the novel can take place. His death, his funeral, the lyric insanity of Katerina his wife and her death-dance in the streets, all these are provided with new and enrichened context by the accidental meeting in the tavern of the *distrait* Raskolnikov and the drunken buffoon Marmeladov. And not only Marmeladov himself, but each of his family, as he precipitates their fates through his drunkenness and buffoonery, add to the context of Raskolnikov's growing fate.

Together they furnish him with his own opposite. As he is the person who above all must act, they are the persons who must be acted upon. He is the criminal, and they are the victims, victims generally and all the way through in much the same way that the old pawnbroker was in Raskolnikov's eyes "ripe" to be murdered. No degradation is too great for the old drunkard who has nowhere to turn; you have only to put fresh degradation in his way and he will take it up with gusto. Katerina, too, eager to find insult in everyone's speech, in his absence or in his presence, imagines insult and injury upon herself at every opportunity. The children, even, with their illness and their rags cannot be treated except with brutality. And as for Sonia, she is not only eager and willing, she fairly demands further humiliation. By prostituting herself, this thin, bird-like creature, almost without a body, shows herself as inviting at best further depravity; for surely no one not depraved, no one not desiring to sack the *last* citadel of integrity, would have any use for her. Sonia had to come from such a family, for only out of the experience of such utter humiliation could her own perfect humility grow. As they are damned so she is blessed, by the enormous shift in significance caused by the shift of a single syllable. It is Gide, who knew Dostoevsky well, who observed that where humility opened the gates of heaven, humiliation opened those of hell. Sonia's blessedness is built upon the bottomlessness of their hell. She accepts, and makes into inner strength, a worse stage of the experience which tore them apart.

Thus, as Raskolnikov comes into contact with Marmeladov and his wife, as he probes them with his intellect, they absorb his sense of himself into a kind of private hell, an abyss beyond soundings, quite off the continental shelf of consciousness which his intellect, however demoniac, can reach. But Sonia, and this is the secret of her personality, can no more be penetrated by Raskolnikov's intellect than her soul can be ravished through the degradation of her body. That is her attraction as a prostitute: that she cannot be prostituted in anything that she has to offer; and that is her power over Raskolnikov, the power of perfect submissiveness which in another place Dostoevsky calls the greatest power in the world: it is the power that he cannot attain by any deed, but that can be attained by imitation, by suffering what she has suffered. It is the power of her suffering, the happiness of it, that not so much overcomes him as it infects or fecundates him. For he is not overcome, though it is promised that he will be; he fights back, the very feeling of her goodness, his very sense of the stigma of her faith, aggravates his pride and the intellectual structure upon which his pride is built, so that when he goes to her for comfort and strength he finds that he has to torture her, and to repel her at every level. The love he feels for her is also and simultaneously hate, and there is no difference between the emotions as he feels them, only as he intellectually knows what they are. And this is an example of the profound psychological rightness of Dostoevsky's judgment, for surely it takes only a pause for judgment to see that as hate or pride is the burden Raskolnikov carries so love or humility is the *burden* of Sonia's life. If she feels his burden as love and accepts it as of nature, he must feel the burden of her love as intolerable. He is indeed a kind of Prodigal Son who finds the love with which he is welcomed the very burden from which he ran away in the first place. It was not of Sonia that he made the following remark but thinking of her and just before seeing her, so it fits all the more: "Oh, if only I were alone and no one loved me and I too had never loved anyone! *Nothing of all this would have happened.*"

It will be remembered that earlier in the book Razumihin has explained to Douania that her brother is perhaps a person incapable of love. Razumihin may have meant only that Raskolnikov is a lonely fellow, but he was literally right as well; no one can be said to love who does not feel as acceptable the burden of love in return, and who does not feel, too, that in loving someone positively, he is imposing the most difficult of human burdens. Sonia knows this in herself, by intuition directed inwards as well as outwards, as a condition of her being, and it is to that double burden that she submits.

Like the crime which existed *between* the old pawnbroker, so between Sonia and Raskolnikov there exists her intuition of love, which she feels so strongly that he *must* know, that gradually by a contagion from her understanding he does know it. It is a love, this unassailable love of the unsmirchable prostitute, that has nothing to do with sex. Not that it might not have been sexual, and even might have taken the means of a kind of ultimate lechery of the spirit, and still have been within the Christian insight, but that Dostoevsky was unable ever to create a character or a mood which showed more than the most superficial aspects of sexual awareness. His people were not eunuchs or in any way deprived of sex but they were born without it. It is love *manqué* that Dostoevsky deals with, love *malgré-lui;* and it is for this reason perhaps that Dostoevsky is able to show love as pure spiritual renunciation. That is why, too, in what was to others the romantic fancy of purity in a prostitute, he sees a kind of exorbitant and omnivorous reality: a true dramatic enactment of the idea of purity. That is why, again, he so often concerns his characters with the idea of debauching young girls, girls before puberty, in whom sex as anyone else would have understood it would not have ripened, so that the debauchery would be of the actor alone.

If these remarks help explain the character and power of Sonia who is of the character of the saint, they help with the others as well, most particularly with the riddle of Svidrigailov, to whom we shall come in a moment for his own sake, but whom now we shall consider in his relation with the character of Douania, Raskolnikov's sister. This young lady is painted as all abloom with normality; she and her mother belong in Dostoevsky's long gallery of simple, intelligent, sincere, generous, impulsive, and dependably decent women, young and old, of whom there are samples in almost every one of his novels—as, to give but one example, Mme. Epanchin and her daughter Aglaia in *The Idiot*. Always they serve the same purpose, to act as foils or background for the extraordinary actions of distorted or driven individuals, such as Raskolnikov and Myshkin. They preserve their identity and their normal responsiveness through every form of violence and disorder; it is their normality which, by contrast, promotes the meaningfulness of the good and bad angels, the light and the dark angels, whose actions make the stories. Nothing in themselves but attractive types, they come to life in terms of the protagonists.

In *Crime and Punishment* they represent the normal conduct from which Raskolnikov departs; they represent the order of society which he tears down and envelops; it is them, their lives, to whom he gives meaning. In the same way Luzhin, the bourgeois on the make, and Lebetziatnikov the nihilist reformer, are caricatures, the one malicious and the other kindly, of normal types of eccentricity within the ordered society which produces at its extremes the super-egotist Raskolnikov and the super-reformer Sonia. But these figures gather part of their meaning from the driven, demoniac, "secret" character of Svidrigailov, the lecher of women and debaucher of souls: the mysterious figure whose evil is concentrated in what is asserted to be, but never shown, his intense and overweening sexuality. As an example of sexual behaviour, Svidrigailov is incredible. Sex is Dostoevsky's symbol for a diabolic, destructive power, which he can sense but cannot measure, and which he cannot otherwise name. This aspect of the Svidrigailov type of figure is Dostoevsky's attempt to explain, to dramatise and invoke a force which he does not seem ever to have understood but which he knows must exist. It is a lonely, awkward, proud sort of power, hovering always on the brink of suicide; it is haunted and haunting; it is the power of the "Other" thing, the other self, the dark side of the self, the substance and drive of that secret world in us which the devil creates, the power which in conventional life—the life which we mostly live—we successfully ignore, so that we tend to estimate its presence in others rather than in ourselves—as if others were our othermost selves. Thus Douania's soul had been imperilled by Svidrigailov's attempt to seduce her, and imperilled precisely by Svidrigailov's technique, which he outlines to Raskolnikov, of assaulting her through purity. He has caused her purity, not her baser emotions but her purity, somehow to desire him, and she had been rescued, in the first instance, in the nick of time: by the confusion, in Marfa Petrovna's eyes, of her purity with her lust. Raskolnikov understands well enough what the risk is—that his sister may be contaminated, that her decency may somehow come to absorb the temptation which Svidrigailov affords her in the new terms of his generosity. What he does not understand is the means by which the contamination, the trespass, will take place, which is by the frustration of violence on Douania's part when in the lonely room with the locked door, she tries so hard to shoot him. She is left by the desperate effort—by the fruitless tumescence of her spirit—in a very ambiguous state, which the story of Raskolnikov's Crime and Punishment did not have time to develop. One is not sure whether in that scene Douania has absorbed something from Svidrigailov, or whether Svidrigailov has absorbed what he wanted from Douania. Something has passed between them, at any rate, which leaves Svidrigailov either done for or contented, either vastated or fully occupied. In either case his remaining hours are justified—his visit to his little girl fiancée and his farewell present, the adventure in the hotel-room, the mouse in the bed, the five-year-old girl whose smile turns in his dream to a harlot's grin, the dream of the flood, which is to say the coming of judgment, and the suicide at dawn. We feel that the enigma of Svidrigailov has either been solved beyond our understanding or that it did not really exist—quite the problem of the devil. At any rate, his function has been fulfilled for everyone but Raskolnikov.

His relations to Raskolnikov have gone beyond those with the others, in both scope and intent, however much they may depend for their actuality upon the others. For Svidrigailov is a foil for the whole story. He comes before the crime, in a way induces the crime to come into being, is the first to perceive the crime, and in a way *finishes* the crime without (since he does not have Raskolnikov's luck in finding Sonia) reaching the punishment. He *is* Raskolnikov in simpler perspective, he is Raskolnikov's other self, a mirror of being into which Raskolnikov never quite dares to look. He is the mystery of Raskolnikov's other self. The sense of him is symbolic, as it always is with mystery. Because he is a mystery beforehand, and exhibits himself mysteriously and providentially, he gathers meaning as he goes along, but not too clearly. He has the advantage of being not well understood, the figure grasped at but not caught, whom we are always about to understand. In fact we have frequently the sense of understanding him perfectly until we stop to query what it is we understand, when we find only that he represents precisely that secret life within us which drives us into incomprehensible actions. Like the character of Stavrogin in *The Possessed,* of whom Dostoevsky says in his notes that he was not *meant* to be understood, but was meant rather to be a reservoir of the portentous, the possible, the mysterious, he is the symbolic clarification of that which cannot be expressed other than symbolically. He is the promise upon which we lean, knowing that it cannot be kept. He recedes like the horizon that follows us, only when we look.

Perhaps we may say that Svidrigailov envelops the disorder brought about by Raskolnikov's crime by imaging a kind of order which we cannot reach but which is always about to overwhelm us. He is a symbol of the mystery of the abyss, and it is a great witness to the depth of Dostoevsky's imagination that he is able to create in the flesh, with eyes too blue and flesh too youthful, such figures at will.

It is no less a test of Dostoevsky's skill—not his depth but his skill —that he is able to employ the one remaining major character in the book without, as it were, creating him at all. I mean, of course, that thirty-five-year-old roly-poly of the disengaged intellect called Porfiry, that man whose life, as he insists to Raskolnikov, is already finished, who has no other life to live, and nothing to do with what remains to him but probe and prance intellectually. Porfiry is so much a victim of moral fatigue that he is beneath every level of being but that of intellectual buffoonery. He represents order; he understands desire, ambition, all forms of conduct, but he knows nothing of the sources and ends of conduct, except that he can catch at them, in the midst of the game of the drowning man which he plays so long and so skilfully, like so many straws that only just elude his dancing fingers. But he is unreal, except as an agency of the plot, something to make the wheels go round; he is a fancy of the pursuing intellect whom Raskolnikov must have invented had he not turned up of his own accord. As Svidrigailov and Sonia between them represent the under-part, and the conflict in the under-part, of Raskolnikov's secret self, so Porfiry represents the maximum possible perfection of the artificial, intellectual self under whose ministrations Raskolnikov *reasons* himself into committing his crime, and who therefore is the appropriate instrument for driving him to the point of confessing it. It is Porfiry, who has no morals and no faith, who is all the proud game of intellect, who whenever he comes to sack Raskolnikov leaves him in a state of collapse, just as it is either Svidrigailov or Sonia who gives him strength. Porfiry knows what he must do, and can point it out to him in the example of the peasant who came forward to take the suffering of the crime upon his guiltless shoulders, he knows all the intellect can know, and perhaps knows that it must collapse, but he cannot push Raskolnikov over the brink, because he knows it only conventionally, by rote. He understands the Crime, because he represents that against which it was committed, and knows with what it was committed, but he cannot touch the Punishment, the completion of the Crime, because it must take place in a region of the soul beyond his grasp, the region which reason, argument, all the armament of order only clutter up and from which they must be swept, the region where the assumption of guilt by all that is innocent within the self takes place through the submission of the sinful, acting self to the faithful, waiting self, which waits, in Dostoevsky's primitive Christian insight, only to be created.

I think we have touched both upon the elements that go to make up the obvious and immediate impact of Raskolnikov's crime and its consequences in action, and upon the elements which as we understand them as exhibited in the various characters leave us all—not Russians, not fanatics of humiliation, not the distorted shadowy figures of Dostoevsky's novel alone, but all of us without exception—deeply implicated in the nature of the Crime. A word remains with which to fasten upon the nature of the Crime an indication of the nature of the Punishment. I do not know that there is a word ready to hand, for we have fallen quite out of the way of thinking in insights and images with the simple, direct intensity which was Dostoevsky's second nature. We lack the anterior conviction, the conviction before we begin to think, with which Dostoevsky mastered the relationship of man to God. But at least in saying that, we state Dostoevsky's major and abiding theme. To punish Raskolnikov, to bring him to retribution, to atonement, Dostoevsky had only to create his relationship to God, and to show at the same time how that relationship sprang from the nature of man as a creature of God quite apart from the structure of human society as an institution of men's minds. Dostoevsky believed that as Christ the innocent one took upon himself the suffering of all the innocent ones in the world, and so redeemed them along with the guilty, so the individual man has in him an innocent part which must take on the suffering caused by the guilty part. As he saw it, in our crime we create our guilt. Perhaps the commonplace example of false arrest will begin to make an analogue for what he meant. Which of us, falsely arrested, would not at once begin to assess his guilt, even for the crime which brought about the false arrest? And you would assess this guilt the more clearly because you were aware of the haphazard, the hazarded, character of your innocence. Similarly, the depth of your guilt would be measured by the depth of your faith, which would then, if you had imagination enough, transform you.

It should be emphasised that it was transformation, not reformation, that Dostoevsky envisaged. Reformation would have dealt with the mere guilty act against society. Transformation, through suffering, is alone able to purge the guilt of being.

Finally, we may draw some comparisons, in this search for means of clarifying the nature of Dostoevsky's notion of punishment, from recent history in our own country. When Mooney was released from his generation of false imprisonment, it soon turned out that he had no symbolic dignity, but represented rather a mere miscarriage of institutional justice; and so with the Scottsboro boys; so, too, with Dreyfus in the last century, for Dreyfus had no dignity. But if we think of Sacco and Vanzetti, does there not arise within us at once a sense that their great and terrifying symbolic dignity is due to Vanzetti, having assumed, with profound humility, the whole devastating guilt of the industrial society which killed him? Whether Vanzetti was innocent or guilty in law has become an irrelevant question. But the guilt which his last words and letters, his last conduct, somehow expiated, which was our guilt, remains permanently in question; for Vanzetti, like Raskolnikov, showed himself in the humiliation of his punishment, in humble relation to God.

Regulated Hatred

AN ASPECT OF THE WORK OF
JANE AUSTEN

D. W. Harding

I

The impression of Jane Austen which has filtered through to the reading public, down from the first-hand critics, through histories of literature, university courses, literary journalism and polite allusion, deters many who might be her best readers from bothering with her at all. How can this popular impression be described? In my experience the first idea to be absorbed from the atmosphere surrounding her work was that she offered exceptionally favourable openings to the exponents of urbanity. Gentlemen of an older generation than mine spoke of their intention of re-reading her on their deathbeds; Eric Linklater's cultured Prime Minister in *The Impregnable Women* passes from surreptitious to abandoned reading of her novels as a national crisis deepens. With this there also came the impression that she provided a refuge for the sensitive when the contemporary world grew too much for them. So Beatrice Kean Seymour writes (*Jane Austen*): "In a society which has enthroned the machine-gun and carried it aloft even into the quiet heavens, there will always be men and women—Escapist or not, as you please—who will turn to her novels with an unending sense of relief and thankfulness."

I was given to understand that her scope was of course extremely

Reprinted by permission of the author.

restricted, but that within her limits she succeeded admirably in expressing the gentler virtues of a civilised social order. She could do this because she lived at a time when, as a sensitive person of culture, she could still feel that she had a place in society and could address the reading public as sympathetic equals; she might introduce unpleasant people into her stories but she could confidently expose them to a public opinion that condemned them. Chiefly, so I gathered, she was a delicate satirist, revealing with inimitable lightness of touch the comic foibles and amiable weaknesses of the people whom she lived amongst and liked.

All this was enough to make me quite certain I didn't want to read her. And it is, I believe, a seriously misleading impression. Fragments of the truth have been incorporated in it but they are fitted into a pattern whose total effect is false. And yet the wide currency of this false impression is an indication of Jane Austen's success in an essential part of her complex intention as a writer: her books are, as she meant them to be, read and enjoyed by precisely the sort of people whom she disliked; she is a literary classic of the society which attitudes like hers, held widely enough, would undermine.

In order to enjoy her books without disturbance those who retain the conventional notion of her work must always have had slightly to misread what she wrote at a number of scattered points, points where she took good care (not wittingly perhaps) that the misreading should be the easiest thing in the world. Unexpected astringencies occur which the comfortable reader probably overlooks, or else passes by as slight imperfections, trifling errors of tone brought about by a faulty choice of words. Look at the passage in *Northanger Abbey* where Henry Tilney offers a solemn reprimand of Catherine's fantastic suspicions about his father:

> Dear Miss Morland, consider the dreadful nature of these suspicions you have entertained. What have you been judging from? Remember the country and the age in which we live. Remember that we are English, that we are Christians. Consult your own understanding, your own sense of the probable, your own observation of what is passing around you. Does our education prepare us for such atrocities? Do our laws connive at them? Could they be perpetrated without being known, in a country like this, where social and literary intercourse is on such a footing, and where roads and newspapers lay everything open?

Had the passage really been as I quote it nothing would have been out of tone. But I omitted a clause. The last sentence actually runs: "Could they be perpetrated without being known, in a country like this, where social and literary intercourse is on such a footing, where every man is surrounded by a neighbourhood of voluntary spies, and where roads and newspapers lay everything open?" "Where every man is surrounded by a neighbourhood of voluntary spies"—with its touch of paranoia that surprising remark is badly out of tune both with "Henry's astonishing generosity and nobleness of conduct" and with the accepted idea of Jane Austen.

Yet it comes quite understandably from someone of Jane Austen's sensitive intelligence, living in her world of news and gossip interchanged amongst and around a large family. She writes to Cassandra (September 14th, 1804), "My mother is at this moment reading a letter from my aunt. Yours to Miss Irvine of which she had had the perusal (which by the bye in your place I should not like) has thrown them into a quandary about Charles and his prospects. The case is that my mother had previously told my aunt, without restriction, that . . . whereas you had replied to Miss Irvine's inquiries on the subject with less explicitness and more caution. Never mind, let them puzzle on together." And when Fanny Knight (her niece) writes confidentially about her love affair, Jane Austen describes ruses she adopted to avoid having to read the letter to the family, and later implores Fanny to "write *something* that may do to be read or told" (November 30th, 1814).

Why is it that, holding the view she did of people's spying, Jane Austen should slip it in amongst Henry Tilney's eulogies of the age? By doing so she achieves two ends, ends which she may not have consciously aimed at. In such a speech from such a character the remark is unexpected and unbelievable, with the result that it is quite unlikely to be taken in at all by many readers; it slips through their minds without creating a disturbance. It gets said, but with the minimum risk of setting people's backs up. The second end achieved by giving the remark such a context is that of off-setting it at once by more appreciative views of society and so refraining from indulging an exaggerated bitterness. The eulogy of the age is not nullified by the bitter clause, but neither can it wipe out the impression the clause makes on those who attend to it.

One cannot say that here the two attitudes modify one another. The technique is too weak. Jane Austen can bring both attitudes into the picture but she has not at this point made one picture of them. In *Persuasion* she does something of the same kind more delicately. Miss Elliot's chagrin at having failed to marry her cousin is being described in the terms of ordinary satire which invites the reading public to feel superior to Miss Elliot:

> There was not a baronet from A to Z whom her feelings could have so willingly acknowledged as an equal. Yet so miserably had he conducted himself, that though she was at this present time (the summer of 1814) wearing black ribbons for his wife, she could not admit him to be worth thinking of again. The disgrace of his first marriage might, perhaps, as there was no reason to suppose it perpetuated by offspring, have been got over, had he not done worse;

—and then at this point the satire suddenly directs itself against the public instead of Miss Elliot—

but he had, as by the accustomary intervention of kind friends they had been informed, spoken most disrespectfully of them all . . .

In *Emma* the same thing is done still more effectively. Again Jane Austen seems to be on perfectly good terms with the public she is addressing and to have no reserve in offering the funniness and virtues of Mr. Woodhouse and Miss Bates to be judged by the accepted standards of the public. She invites her readers to be just their natural patronising selves. But this public that Jane Austen seems on such good terms with has some curious things said about it, not criticisms, but small notes of fact that are usually not made. They almost certainly go unnoticed by many readers, for they involve only the faintest change of tone from something much more usual and acceptable.

When she says that Miss Bates "enjoyed a most uncommon degree of popularity for a woman neither young, handsome, rich, nor married," this is fairly conventional satire that any reading public would cheerfully admit in its satirist and chuckle over. But the next sentence must have to be mentally re-written by the greater number of Jane Austen's readers. For them it probably runs, "Miss Bates stood in the very worst predicament in the world for having much of the public favour; and she had no intellectual superiority to make atonement to herself, or compel an outward respect from those who might despise her."

This, I suggest, is how most readers, lulled and disarmed by the amiable context, will soften what in fact reads, ". . . and she had no intellectual superiority to make atonement to herself, or frighten those who might hate her into outward respect." Jane Austen was herself at this time "neither young, handsome, rich, nor married," and the passage perhaps hints at the functions which her unquestioned intellectual superiority may have had for her.

This eruption of fear and hatred into the relationships of everyday social life is something that the urbane admirer of Jane Austen finds distasteful; it is not the satire of one who writes securely for the entertainment of her civilised acquaintances. And it has the effect, for the attentive reader, of changing the flavour of the more ordinary satire amongst which it is embedded.

Emma is especially interesting from this point of view. What is sometimes called its greater "mellowness" largely consists in saying quietly and undisguisedly things which in the earlier books were put more loudly but in the innocuous form of caricature. Take conversation for instance. Its importance and its high (though by no means supreme) social value are of course implicit in Jane Austen's writings. But one should beware of supposing that a mind like hers therefore found the ordinary social intercourse of the period congenial and satisfying. In *Pride and Prejudice* she offers an entertaining caricature of card-table conversation at Lady Catherine de Bourgh's house.

Their table was superlatively stupid. Scarcely a syllable was uttered that did not relate to the game, except when Mrs. Jenkinson expressed her fears of Miss de Bourgh's being too hot or too cold, or having too much or too little light. A great deal more passed at the other table. Lady Catherine was generally speaking—stating the mistakes of the three others, or relating some anecdote of herself. Mr. Collins was employed in agreeing to everything her ladyship said, thanking her for every fish he won, and apologising if he thought he won too many. Sir William did not say much. He was storing his memory with anecdotes and noble names.

This invites the carefree enjoyment of all her readers. They can all feel superior to Lady Catherine and Mr. Collins. But in *Emma* the style changes: the talk at the Cole's dinner party, a pleasant dinner party which the heroine enjoyed, is described as ". . . the usual rate of conversation; a few clever things said, a few downright silly, but by much the larger proportion neither the one nor the other—nothing worse than everyday remarks, dull repetitions, old news, and heavy jokes." "Nothing worse"!—that phrase is typical. It is not mere sarcasm by any means. Jane Austen genuinely valued the achievements of the civilisation she lived within and never lost sight of the fact that there might be something vastly worse than the conversation she referred to. "Nothing worse" is a positive tribute to the decency, the superficial friendliness, the absence of the grosser forms of insolence and self-display at the dinner party. At least Mrs. Elton wasn't there. And yet the effect of the comment, if her readers took it seriously, would be that of a disintegrating attack upon the sort of social intercourse they have established for themselves. It is not the comment of one who would have helped to make her society what it was, or ours what it is.

To speak of this aspect of her work as "satire" is perhaps misleading. She has none of the underlying didactic intention ordinarily attributed to the satirist. Her object is not missionary; it is the more desperate one of merely finding some mode of existence for her critical attitudes. To her the first necessity was to keep on reasonably good terms with the associates of her everyday life; she had a deep need of their affection and a genuine respect for the ordered, decent civilisation that they upheld. And yet she was sensitive to their crudenesses and complacencies and knew that her real existence depended on resisting many of the values they implied. The novels gave her a way out of this dilemma. This, rather than the ambition of entertaining a posterity of urbane gentlemen, was her motive force in writing.

As a novelist, therefore, part of her aim was to find the means for unobtrusive spiritual survival, without open conflict with the friendly people around her whose standards in simpler things she could accept and whose affection she greatly needed. She found, of course, that one of the most useful peculiarities of her society was its willingness to remain blind to the implications of a caricature. She found people eager to laugh at faults they tolerated in themselves and their friends, so long as the faults were exaggerated and the laughter "good-natured" —so long, that is, as the assault on society could be regarded as a mock assault and not genuinely disruptive. Satire such as this is obviously a means not of admonition but of self-preservation.

Hence one of Jane Austen's most successful methods is to offer her readers every excuse for regarding as rather exaggerated figures of fun people whom she herself detests and fears. Mrs. Bennet, according to the Austen tradition, is one of "our" richly comic characters about whom we can feel superior, condescending, perhaps a trifle sympathetic, and above all heartily amused and free from care. Everything conspires to make this the natural interpretation once you are willing to overlook Jane Austen's bald and brief statement of her own attitude to her: "She was a woman of mean understanding, little information, and uncertain temper." How many women amongst Jane Austen's acquaintance and amongst her most complacent readers to the present day that phrase must describe! How gladly they enjoy the funny side of the situations Mrs. Bennet's unpleasant nature creates, and how easy it is made for them to forget or never observe that Jane Austen, none the less for seeing how funny she is, goes on detesting her. The thesis that the ruling standards of our social group leave a perfectly comfortable niche for detestable people and give them sufficient sanction to persist, would, if it were argued seriously, arouse the most violent opposition, the most determined apologetics for things as they are, and the most reproachful pleas for a sense of proportion.

Caricature served Jane Austen's purpose perfectly. Under her treatment one can never say where caricature leaves off and the claim to serious portraiture begins. Mr. Collins is only given a trifle more comic exaggeration than Lady Catherine de Bourgh, and by her standards is a possible human being. Lady Catherine in turn seems acceptable as a portrait if the criterion of verisimilitude is her nephew Mr. Darcy. And he, finally, although to some extent a caricature, is near enough natural portraiture to stand beside Elizabeth Bennet, who, like all the heroines, is presented as an undistorted portrait. The simplest comic effects are gained by bringing the caricatures into direct contact with the real people, as in Mr. Collins' visit to the Bennets and his proposal to Elizabeth. But at the same time one knows that, though from some points of view caricature, in other directions he does, by easy stages, fit into the real world. He is real enough to Mrs. Bennet; and she is real enough to Elizabeth to create a situation of real misery for her when she refuses. Consequently the proposal scene is not only comic fantasy, but it is also, for Elizabeth, a taste of the fantastic nightmare in which economic and social institutions have such power over the values of personal relationships that the comic monster is nearly able to get her.

The implications of her caricatures as criticism of real people in real society are brought out in the way they dovetail into their social setting. The decent, stodgy Charlotte puts up cheerfully with Mr. Collins as a husband; and Elizabeth can never quite become reconciled to the idea that her friend is the wife of her comic monster. And that, of course, is precisely the sort of idea that Jane Austen herself could never grow reconciled to. The people she hated were tolerated, accepted, comfortably ensconced in the only human society she knew; they were, for her, society's embarrassing unconscious comment on itself. A recent writer on Jane Austen, Elizabeth Jenkins, puts forward the polite and more comfortable interpretation in supposing Charlotte's marriage to be explained solely by the impossibility of young women's earning their own living at that period. But Charlotte's complaisance goes deeper than that: it is shown as a considered indifference to personal relationships when they conflict with cruder advantages in the wider social world:

> She had always felt that Charlotte's opinion of matrimony was not exactly like her own, but she could not have supposed it possible that, when called into action, she would have sacrificed every better feeling to worldly advantage.

We know too, at the biographical level, that Jane Austen herself, in a precisely similar situation to Charlotte's, spent a night of psychological crisis in deciding to revoke her acceptance of an "advantageous" proposal made the previous evening. And her letters to Fanny Knight show how deep her convictions went at this point.

It is important to notice that Elizabeth makes no break with her friend on account of the marriage. This was the sort of friend—"a friend disgracing herself and sunk in her esteem"—that went to make up the available social world which one could neither escape materially nor be independent of psychologically. The impossibility of being cut off from objectionable people is suggested more subtly in *Emma,* where Mrs. Elton is the high light of the pervasive neglect of spiritual values in social life. One can hardly doubt that Jane Austen's own dealings with society are reflected in the passage where Mr. Weston makes the error of inviting Mrs. Elton to join the picnic party which he and Emma have planned:

> . . . Emma could not but feel some surprise, and a little displeasure, on hearing from Mr. Weston that he had been proposing to Mrs. Elton, as her brother and sister had failed her, that the two parties should unite, and go together, and that as Mrs. Elton had very readily acceded to it, so it was to be, if she had no objection. Now, as her objection was nothing but her very great dislike of Mrs. Elton, of which Mr. Weston must already be perfectly aware, it was

not worth bringing forward: it could not be done without a reproof to him, which would be giving pain to his wife; and she found herself, therefore, obliged to consent to an arrangement which she would have done a great deal to avoid; an arrangement which would, probably, expose her even to the degradation of being said to be of Mrs. Elton's party! Every feeling was offended; and the forbearance of her outward submission left a heavy arrear due of secret severity in her reflections, on the unmanageable good-will of Mr. Weston's temper.

"I am glad you approve of what I have done," said he, very comfortably. "But I thought you would. Such schemes as these are nothing without numbers. One cannot have too large a party. A large party secures its own amusement. And she is a good-natured woman after all. One could not leave her out."

Emma denied none of it aloud, and agreed to none of it in private.

This well illustrates Jane Austen's typical dilemma: of being intensely critical of people to whom she also has strong emotional attachments.

II

The social group having such ambivalence for her, it is not surprising if her conflict should find some outlets not fully within her conscious control. To draw attention to these, however, is not to suggest that they lessen the value of her conscious intention and its achievements.

The chief instance is the fascination she found in the Cinderella theme, the Cinderella theme with the fairy godmother omitted. For in Jane Austen's treatment the natural order of things manages to reassert the heroine's proper pre-eminence without the intervention of any human or quasi-human helper. In this respect she allies the Cinderella theme to another fairy-tale theme which is often introduced—that of the princess brought up by unworthy parents but never losing the delicate sensibilities which are an inborn part of her. This latter theme appears most explicitly in *Mansfield Park*, the unfinished story of *The Watsons*, and, with some softening, in *Pride and Prejudice*. The contrast between Fanny Price's true nature and her squalid home at Portsmouth is the clearest statement of the idea, but in the first four of the finished novels the heroine's final position is, even in the worldly sense, always above her reasonable social expectations by conventional standards, but corresponding to her natural worth.

To leave it at this, however, would be highly misleading. It is the development which occurs in her treatment of the Cinderella theme that most rewards attention. In *Northanger Abbey, Sense and Sensibility* and *Pride and Prejudice* it is handled simply; the heroine is in some degree isolated from those around her by being more sensitive or of finer moral insight or sounder judgment, and her marriage to the handsome prince at the end is in the nature of a reward for being different from the rest and a consolation for the distresses entailed by being different. This is true even of *Northanger Abbey* in spite of the grotesque error of judgment that Catherine Morland is guilty of and has to renounce. For here Jane Austen was interested not so much in the defect in her heroine's judgment as in the absurdly wide currency of the "gothick" tradition that entrapped her. Catherine throws off her delusion almost as something external to herself. And this is so glaring that Jane Austen seems to have been uncomfortable about it: in describing it she resorts to a rather factitious semi-detachment from her heroine.

Her mind made up on these several points, and her resolution formed, of always judging and acting in future with the greatest good sense, she had nothing to do but to forgive herself and be happier than ever; and the lenient hand of time did much for her by insensible gradations in the course of another day.

In *Sense and Sensibility* and *Pride and Prejudice* the heroines are still nearer perfection and even the handsome princes have faults to overcome before all is well. Immediately after her final reconciliation with Mr. Darcy, Elizabeth Bennet is tempted to laugh at his over-confident direction of his friend Bingley's love affair, ". . . but she checked herself. She remembered that he had yet to learn to be laughed at, and it was rather too early to begin."

To put the point in general terms, the heroine of these early novels is herself the criterion of sound judgment and good feeling. She may claim that her values are sanctioned by good breeding and a religious civilisation, but in fact none of the people she meets represents those values so effectively as she does herself. She is never in submissive alliance with the representatives of virtue and good feeling in her social world—there is only a selective alliance with certain aspects of their characters. The social world may have material power over her, enough to make her unhappy, but it hasn't the power that comes from having created or moulded her, and it can claim no credit for her being what she is. In this sense the heroine is independent of those about her and isolated from them. She has only to be herself.

The successful handling of this kind of theme and this heroine brought Jane Austen to the point where a development became psychologically possible. The hint of irrationality underlying the earlier themes could be brought nearer the light. She could begin to admit that even a heroine must owe a great deal of her character and values to the social world in which she had been moulded, and, that being so, could hardly be quite so solitary in her excellence as the earlier heroines are. The emphasis hitherto had been almost entirely on the difference between the heroine and the people about her. But this was to slight the reality of her bond with the ordinary "good" people; there was more to be said for the fundamentals of virtue and seemliness than she had been implying. And so, after the appearance of *Pride and Prejudice,* she wrote to Cassandra, "Now I will try and write of something else, and it shall be a complete change of subject—ordination . . ." (January 29th, 1813).

This sets the tone of *Mansfield Park,* the new novel. Here her emphasis is on the deep importance of the conventional virtues, of civilised seemliness, decorum, and sound religious feeling. These become the worthy objects of the heroine's loyalties; and they so nearly comprise the whole range of her values that Fanny Price is the least interesting of all the heroines. For the first time, Jane Austen sets the heroine in submissive alliance with the conventionally virtuous people of the story, Sir Thomas and Edmund. Mistaken though these pillars of society may in some respects be, the heroine's proper place is at their side; their standards are worthy of a sensitive person's support and complete allegiance.

It is a novel in which Jane Austen pays tribute to the virtuous fundamentals of her upbringing, ranging herself with those whom she considers right on the simpler and more obvious moral issues, and withdrawing her attention—relatively at least—from the finer details of living in which they may disturb her. She allies herself with virtues that are easy to appreciate and reasonably often met with. The result, as one would expect, is a distinct tendency to priggishness. And, of course, the book was greatly liked. "Mr. H[aden] is reading *Mansfield Park* for the first time and prefers it to *P. and P.*" (November 26th, 1815). "Mr. Cook [himself a clergyman] says 'it is the most sensible novel he ever read,' and the manner in which I treat the clergy delights them very much." (June 14th, 1814). Compared with *Mansfield Park*, Jane Austen is afraid that *Emma* will appear "inferior in good sense." (December 11th, 1815). It was after reading *Mansfield Park*, moreover, that the pompously self-satisfied Librarian to the Prince Regent offered her, almost avowedly, his own life story as the basis for a novel about an English clergyman. He must have been one of the first of the admirer-victims who have continued to enjoy her work to this day. And her tactful and respectful reply ("The comic part of the character I might be equal to, but not the good, the enthusiastic, the literary") illustrates admirably her capacity for keeping on good terms with people without too great treachery to herself.

The priggishness of *Mansfield Park* is the inevitable result of the curiously abortive attempt at humility that the novel represents. Although it involves the recognition that heroines are not spontaneously generated but owe much of their personality to the established standards of their society, the perfection of the heroine is still not doubted. And so the effort towards humility becomes in effect the exclamation, "Why, some of the very good people are nearly as good as I am and really do deserve my loyalty!"

There is no external evidence that Jane Austen was other than highly satisfied with *Mansfield Park*, which is, after all, in many ways interesting and successful. But its *reductio ad absurdum* of the Cinderella theme and the foundling princess theme could hardly have been without effect. This, I think, is already visible in the last chapter, which, with its suggestion of a fairy-tale winding up of the various threads of the story, is ironically perfunctory. For instance:

I purposely abstain from dates on this occasion, that every one may be at liberty to fix their own, aware that the cure of unconquerable passions, and the transfer of unchanging attachments, must vary much as to time in different people. I only entreat everybody to believe that exactly at the time when it was quite natural that it should be so, and not a week earlier, Edmund did cease to care about Miss Crawford, and became as anxious to marry Fanny as Fanny herself could desire.

And Sir Thomas's "high sense of having realised a great acquisition in the promise of Fanny for a daughter, formed just such a contrast with his early opinion on the subject when the poor little girl's coming had first been agitated, as time is for ever producing between the plans and decisions of mortals, for their own instruction and their neighbours' entertainment."

Whether or not Jane Austen realised what she had been doing, at all events the production of *Mansfield Park* enabled her to go on next to the extraordinary achievement of *Emma,* in which a much more complete humility is combined with the earlier unblinking attention to people as they are. The underlying argument has a different trend. She continues to see that the heroine has derived from the people and conditions around her, but she now keeps clearly in mind the objectionable features of those people; and she faces the far bolder conclusion that even a heroine is likely to have assimilated many of the more unpleasant possibilities of the human being in society. And it is not that society has spoilt an originally perfect girl who now has to recover her pristine good sense, as it was with Catherine Morland, but that the heroine has not yet achieved anything like perfection and is actually going to learn a number of serious lessons from some of the people she lives with.

Consider in the first place the treatment here of the two favourite themes of the earlier novels. The Cinderella theme is now relegated to the sub-heroine, Jane Fairfax. Its working out involves the discomfiture of the heroine, who in this respect is put into the position of one of the ugly sisters. Moreover the Cinderella procedure is shown in the light of a social anomaly, rather a nuisance and requiring the excuse of unusual circumstances.

The associated theme of the child brought up in humble circumstances whose inborn nature fits her for better things is frankly parodied and deflated in the story of Harriet Smith, the illegitimate child whom Emma tries to turn into a snob. In the end, with the insignificant girl cheerfully married to a deserving farmer, "Harriet's parentage became known. She proved to be the daughter of a tradesman, rich enough to afford her the comfortable maintenance which had ever been hers, and decent enough to have always wished for concealment. Such was the blood of gentility which Emma had formerly been so ready to vouch for!"

Thus the structure of the narrative expresses a complete change in Jane Austen's outlook on the heroine in relation to others. And the story no longer progresses towards her vindication or consolation; it consists in her gradual, humbling self-enlightenment. Emma's personality includes some of the tendencies and qualities that Jane Austen most disliked—self-complacency, for instance, malicious enjoyment in prying into embarrassing private affairs, snobbery, and a weakness for meddling in other people's lives. But now, instead of being attributed in exaggerated form to a character distanced into caricature, they occur in the subtle form given them by someone who in many ways has admirably fine standards.

We cannot say that in *Emma* Jane Austen abandons the Cinderella story. She so deliberately inverts it that we ought to regard *Emma* as a bold variant of the theme and a further exploration of its underlying significance for her. In *Persuasion* she goes back to the Cinderella situation in its most direct and simple form, but develops a vitally important aspect of it that she had previously avoided. This is the significance for Cinderella of her idealised dead mother.

Most children are likely to have some conflict of attitude towards their mother, finding her in some respects an ideal object of love and in others an obstacle to their wishes and a bitter disappointment. For a child such as Jane Austen who actually was in many ways more sensitive and able than her mother, one can understand that this conflict may persist in some form for a very long time. Now one of the obvious appeals of the Cinderella story, as of all stories of wicked stepmothers, is that it resolves the ambivalence of the mother by the simple plan of splitting her in two: the ideal mother is dead and can be adored without risk of disturbance; the living mother is completely detestable and can be hated whole-heartedly without self-reproach.[1]

In her early novels Jane Austen consistently avoided dealing with a mother who could be a genuinely intimate friend of her daughter. Lady Susan, of the unfinished novel, is her daughter's enemy. In *Northanger Abbey* the mother is busy with the household and the younger children. In *Sense and Sensibility* she herself has to be guided and kept in hand by her daughter's sounder judgment. In *Pride and Prejudice* she is Mrs. Bennet. In *Mansfield Park* she is a slattern whom the heroine only visits once in the course of the novel. In *Emma* the mother is dead and Miss Taylor, her substitute, always remains to some extent the promoted governess. This avoidance may seem strange, but

---

[1] This is, needless to say, only a very small part of the unconscious significance which such stories may have for a reader. Most obviously it neglects the relationships of the stepmother and the heroine to the father.

it can be understood as the precaution of a mind which, although in the Cinderella situation, is still too sensitive and honest to offer as a complete portrait the half-truth of the idealised dead mother.

But in *Persuasion* she does approach the problem which is latent here. She puts her heroine in the Cinderella setting, and so heightens her need for affection. And then in Lady Russell she provides a god-mother, not fairy but human, with whom Anne Elliot can have much the relationship of a daughter with a greatly loved, but humanly possible, mother. Jane Austen then goes on to face the implications of such a relationship—and there runs through the whole story a lament for seven years' loss of happiness owing to Anne's having yielded to her godmother's persuasion.

The novel opens with her being completely convinced of the wrongness of the advice she received, and yet strongly attached to Lady Russell still and unable to blame her. Her attitude is, and throughout the book remains, curiously unresolved. "She did not blame Lady Russell, she did not blame herself, for having been guided by her; but she felt that were any young person in similar circumstances to apply to her for counsel, they would never receive any of such certain immediate wretchedness, such uncertain future good." But for all that, the rest of the book shows Anne repeatedly resisting fresh advice from her godmother and being completely vindicated in the upshot.

This might mean that Anne was a repetition of the earlier heroines, detached by her good sense and sound principles from the inferior standards of those about her. That would be true of her relations with her father and eldest sister. But she had no such easy detachment from her godmother. Lady Russell was near enough to the ideal mother to secure Anne's affection, to make her long for the comfort of yielding to her judgment. This satisfaction—the secure submission to a parent who seems completely adequate—was denied Anne by her superior judgment. She was strong enough to retain the insight that separated her from Lady Russell—they never mentioned the episode in the years that followed and neither knew what the other felt about it—but she never came to feel her partial detachment from her as anything but a loss. Nor could she ever regret having yielded to Lady Russell's advice, even though she regretted that the advice had been so mistaken. At the end of the story, reverting to the old dilemma, she tells the lover whom she has now regained:

I have been thinking over the past, and trying to judge of the right and wrong—I mean with regard to myself; and I must believe that I was right, much as I suffered from it—that I was perfectly right in being guided by the friend whom you will love better than you do now. To me, she was in the place of a parent. Do not mistake me, however. I am not saying that she did not err in her service. It was, perhaps, one of those cases in which advice is good or bad only as the event decides and for myself, I certainly never should, in any circumstances of tolerable similarity, give such advice. But I mean that I was right in submitting to her, and that if I had done otherwise, I should have suffered more in continuing the engagement than I did even in giving it up, because I should have suffered in my conscience.

It is in *Persuasion* that Jane Austen fingers what is probably the tenderest spot for those who identify themselves with Cinderella: she brings the idealised mother back to life and admits that she is no nearer to perfection than the mothers of acute and sensitive children generally are.

This attempt to suggest a slightly different emphasis in the reading of Jane Austen is not offered as a balanced appraisal of her work. It is deliberately lop-sided, neglecting the many points at which the established view seems adequate. I have tried to underline one or two features of her work that claim the sort of readers who sometimes miss her—those who would turn to her not for relief and escape but as a formidable ally against things and people which were to her, and still are, hateful.

Our Cousin, Mr. Poe

Allen Tate

When I was about fourteen there were in our house, along with the novels of John Esten Cooke, E. P. Roe, and Augusta Evans, three small volumes of Edgar Allan Poe. That, by my reckoning, was a long time ago. Even then the books were old and worn, whether from use (I suppose not) or from neglect, it did not occur to me to inquire. I remember the binding, which was blue, and the size, which was small, and the paper, which was yellow and very thin. One volume contained the Poems, prefaced by Lowell's famous "biography." In this volume I am sure, for I read it more than the others, was the well-known asymmetrical photograph, which I gazed at by the hour and which I hoped that I should some day resemble. Another volume contained most, or at least the most famous of the Tales: "Ligeia," which I liked best (I learned in due time that Poe had, too); "Morella" and "William Wilson," which I now like best; and "The Fall of the House of Usher," which was a little spoiled for me even at fourteen by the interjection of the "Mad Tryst of Sir Launcelot Canning." Perhaps it was in this volume that I admired "Marginalia," the first "criticism" I remember reading; but I did not discern either the bogus erudition or the sense of high literature which Poe was the first American to distinguish from entertainment and self-improvement through books; the merits as well as the defects went over my head. "Marginalia" could not at any rate have been in the third volume, which was given to a single long work: *Eureka—A Prose Poem*. This astrophilosophical discourse, which the late Paul Valéry took more seriously than any

Reprinted by permission of the publisher, Alan Swallow.

English or American critic ever did, fell in with my readings in popular astronomical books. In the backyard I arranged in a straight line peas, cherries, and oranges, in the proportionate sizes and distances of the sun and planets, and some hundreds of feet away (an inch perhaps to a thousand light-years) an old volley ball of my elder brothers' to represent Alpha Lyrae.

Later, on another occasion, I expect to examine *Eureka* at length, as I read it now, not as I read it at fourteen; yet before I leave it I must mention two other circumstances of my boyhood reading and the feeling that accompanied it. It lives for me as no later experience of ideas lives, because it was the first I had. The "proposition" that Poe undertook to demonstrate has come back to me at intervals in the past thirty-six years with such unpredictable force that now I face it with mingled resignation and dismay. I can say it without looking it up:

In the original unity of the first thing lies the secondary cause of all things, with the germ of their inevitable annihilation.

This is not the place to try to say what Poe meant by it. I could not, at fourteen, have guessed what it meant even after I had read the book; yet it is a fact of my boyhood (which I cannot suppose unique) that this grandiose formula for cosmic cataclysm became a part of my consciousness through no effort of my own but seemed to come to me like a dream, and came back later, like a nursery rhyme, or a tag from a popular song, unbidden.

The other circumstance I am surer of because it was a visible fact, a signature in faded brown ink on the fly-leaf of *Eureka*: it told me years later that the three volumes had been printed earlier than 1870, the year the man who had owned them died. He was my great-grandfather. My mother had said, often enough, or on some occasion that fixed it in memory, that her grandfather had "known Mr. Poe." (She was of the era when all eminent men, living or recently dead, were "Mr.") I knew as a boy that my great-grandfather had been a "poet," and in 1930 I found some of his poems, which I forbear to discuss. He had for a while been editor of the *Alexandria Gazette* at about the time of Mr. Poe's death. Both were "Virginians," though Virginians of somewhat different schools and points of view. I can see my great-grandfather in Poe's description of a preacher who called upon him in the summer of 1848: "He stood smiling and bowing at the madman Poe."

I have brought together these scattered memories of my first reading of a serious writer because in discussing any writer, or in coming
to terms with him, we must avoid the trap of mere abstract evaluation,
and try to reproduce the actual conditions of our relation to him. It
would be difficult for me to take Poe up, "study" him, and proceed to a
critical judgment. One may give these affairs the look of method, and
thus deceive almost everybody but oneself. In reading Poe we are not
brought up against a large, articulate scheme of experience, such as we
see adumbrated in Hawthorne or Melville, which we may partly sever
from personal association, both in the writer and in ourselves. Poe
surrounds us with Eliot's "wilderness of mirrors," in which we see a
subliminal self endlessly repeated or, turning, a new posture of the
same figure. It is not too harsh, I think, to say that it is stupid to suppose that by "evaluating" this forlorn demon in the glass, we dispose
of him. For Americans, perhaps for most modern men, he is with us
like a dejected cousin: we may "place" him but we may not exclude
him from our board. This is the recognition of a relationship, almost
of the blood, which we must in honor acknowledge: what destroyed him
is potentially destructive of us. Not only this; we must acknowledge
another obligation, if, like most men of my generation, we were brought
up in houses where the works of Poe took their easy place on the
shelf with the family Shakespeare and the early novels of Ellen Glasgow.
This is the obligation of loyalty to one's experience: he was in our
lives and we cannot pretend that he was not. Not even Poe's great
power in Europe is quite so indicative of his peculiar "place" as his
unquestioned, if unexamined, acceptance among ordinary gentle people
whose literary culture was not highly developed. The horrors of Poe
created not a tremor in the bosoms of young ladies or a moment's
anxiety in the eyes of vigilant mothers. I suppose the gentlemen of the
South did not read him much after his time; in his time, they could
scarcely have got the full sweep and depth of the horror. Nothing that
Mr. Poe wrote, it was said soon after his death, could bring a blush
to the cheek of the purest maiden.

But I doubt that maidens read very far in the Tales. If they had
they would have found nothing to disconcert the image that Miss
Susan Ingram recorded from a visit of Poe to her family a few weeks
before his death:

Although I was only a slip of a girl and he what seemed to me then
quite an old man, and a great literary one at that, we got on together

beautifully. He was one of the most courteous gentlemen I have ever seen, and that gave great charm to his manner. None of his pictures that I have ever seen look like the picture of Poe that I keep in my memory . . . there was something in his face that is in none of them. Perhaps it was in the eyes.

If he was a madman he was also a gentleman. Whether or not we accept Mr. Krutch's theory, we know, as this sensible young lady knew, that she was quite safe with him. A gentleman? Well, his manners were exemplary (when he was not drinking) and to the casual eye at any rate his exalted idealization of Woman (even of some very foolish women) was only a little more humorless, because more intense, than the standard cult of Female Purity in the Old South.

What Mr. Poe on his own had done with the cult it was not possible then to know. A gentleman and a Southerner, he was not quite, perhaps, a Southern gentleman. The lofty intellect of Ligeia, of Madeline, of Berenice, or of Eleanora, had little utility in the social and economic structure of Virginia, which had to be perpetuated through the issue of the female body, while the intellect, which was public and political, remained under the supervision of the gentlemen. Although Morella had a child (Poe's only heroine, I believe, to be so compromised), she was scarcely better equipped than Virginia Clemm herself to sustain more than the immaculate half of the vocation of the Southern lady. "But the fires," writes Morella's narrator-husband, "were not of Eros." And we know, at the end of the story, that the daughter is no real daughter but, as Morella's empty "tomb" reveals, Morella herself come back as a vampire to wreak upon her "lover" the vengeance due him. Why is it due him? Because, quite plainly, the lover lacked, as he always lacked with his other heroines, the "fires of Eros." The soul of Morella's husband "burns with fires it had never before known . . . and bitter and tormenting to my spirit was the gradual conviction that I could in no manner define their unusual meaning, or regulate their vague intensity." Perhaps in the soul of John Randolph alone of Virginia gentlemen strange fires burned. The fires that were not of Eros were generally for the land and oratory, and the two fires were predictably regulated.

Poe's strange fire is his leading symbol, but there is not space in an essay to list all its appearances. You will see it in the eye of the Raven; in "an eye large, liquid, and luminous beyond comparison," of Roderick Usher; in the burning eye of the old man in "The Tell-Tale Heart"; in

"Those eyes! those large, those shining, those divine orbs," of the Lady
Ligeia. Poe's heroes and heroines are always burning with a hard, gem-
like flame—a bodyless exaltation of spirit that Poe himself seems to
have carried into the drawing-room, where its limited visibility was sufficient guarantee of gentlemanly behavior. But privately, and thus, for
him, publicly, in his stories, he could not "regulate its vague intensity."

I cannot go into this mystery here as fully as I should like; yet I
may, I think, ask a question: Why did not Poe use explicitly the universal legend of the vampire? Perhaps some instinct for aesthetic distance
made him recoil from it; perhaps the literal, business-like way the
vampire went about making its living revolted the "ideality" of Poe.
At any rate D. H. Lawrence was no doubt right in describing as vampires his women characters; the men, soon to join them as "undead,"
have, by some defect of the moral will, made them so.

The mysterious exaltation of spirit which is invariably the unique
distinction of his heroes and heroines is not quite, as I have represented
it, bodyless. *It inhabits a human body but that body is dead. The
spirits prey upon one another with destructive fire which is at once
pure of lust and infernal.* All Poe's characters represent one degree
or another in a movement toward an archetypal condition: the survival
of the soul in a dead body; but only in "The Facts in the Case of
Monsieur Valdemar" is the obsessive subject explicit.

In none of the nineteenth-century comment on "The Fall of the
House of Usher" that I have read, and in none of our own period, is
there a feeling of shock, or even of surprise, that Roderick Usher is
in love with his sister: the relation not being physical, it is "pure." R. H.
Stoddard, the least sympathetic of the serious early biographers, disliked
Poe's morbidity, but admitted his purity. The American case against
Poe, until the first World War, rested upon his moral indifference, or
his limited moral range. The range is limited, but there is no indifference; there is rather a compulsive, even a profound, interest in a moral
problem of universal concern. His contemporaries could see in the love
stories neither the incestuous theme nor what it meant, because it was
not represented literally. The theme and its meaning as I see them are
unmistakable: the symbolic compulsion that drives through, and beyond,
physical incest moves toward the extinction of the beloved's will in
complete possession, not of her body, but of her being; there is the
reciprocal force, returning upon the lover, of self-destruction. Lawrence
shrewdly perceived the significance of Poe's obsession with incestuous

love. Two persons of the least dissimilarity offer the least physical resistance to mutual participation in the *fire* of a common being. Poe's most casual reader perceives that his lovers never do anything but contemplate each other, or pore upon the rigmarole of preposterously erudite, ancient books, most of which never existed. They are living in each other's insides, in the hollows of which burns the fire of will and intellect.

The fire is a double symbol; it lights and it burns. It is overtly the "light" of reason but as action it becomes the consuming fire of the abstract intellect, without moral significance, which invades the being of the beloved. It is the fire that, having illuminated, next destroys. Lawrence is again right in singling out for the burden of his insight the epigraph to "Ligeia," which Poe had quoted from Glanvill: "Man does not yield himself to the angels, nor unto death utterly, save through the weakness of his own feeble will." Why do these women of monstrous will and intellect turn into vampires? Because, according to Lawrence, the lovers have not subdued them through the body to the biological level, at which sanity alone is possible, and they retaliate by devouring their men. This view is perhaps only partly right. I suspect that the destruction works both ways, that the typical situation in Poe is more complex than Lawrence's version of it.

If we glance at "The Fall of the House of Usher" we shall be struck by a singular feature of the catastrophe. Bear in mind that Roderick and Madeline are brother and sister, and that the standard hyperaesthesia of the Poe hero acquires in Roderick a sharper reality than in any of the others, except perhaps William Wilson. His naked sensitivity to sound and light is not "regulated" to the forms of the human situation; it is a mechanism operating apart from the moral consciousness. We have here something like a capacity for mere sensation, as distinguished from sensibility, which in Usher is atrophied. In terms of the small distinction that I am offering here, sensibility keeps us in the world; sensation locks us into the self, feeding upon the disintegration of its objects and absorbing them into the void of the ego. The lover, circumventing the body into the secret being of the beloved, tries to convert the spiritual object into an object of sensation: the intellect which knows and the will which possesses are unnaturally turned upon that part of the beloved which should remain inviolate.

As the story of Usher opens, the Lady Madeline is suffering from a strange illness. She dies. Her brother has, of course, possessed her inner being, and killed her; or thinks he has, or at any rate wishes to think that she is dead. This is all a little vague: perhaps he has deliberately entombed her alive, so that she will die by suffocation—a symbolic action for extinction of being. Why has he committed this monstrous crime? Sister though she is, she is nevertheless not entirely identical with him: she has her own otherness, of however slight degree, resisting his hypertrophied will. He puts her alive, though "cataleptic," into the "tomb." (Poe never uses graves, only tombs, except in "Premature Burial." His corpses, being half dead, are thus only half buried; they rise and walk again.) After some days Madeline breaks out of the tomb and confronts her brother in her bloody cerements. This is the way Poe presents the scene:

". . . Is she not hurrying to upbraid me for my haste? Have I not heard her footsteps on the stair? Do I not distinguish the heavy and horrible beating of her heart? Madman!"—here he sprang furiously to his feet, and shrieked out his syllables, as if in his effort he were giving up his soul—"*Madman! I tell you that she now stands without the door!*"

As if in the superhuman energy of his utterance there had been found the potency of a spell, the huge antique panels to which the speaker pointed threw slowly back, upon the instant, their ponderous and ebony jaws. It was the work of the rushing gust—but then without those doors there *did* stand the lofty and enshrouded figure of the Lady Madeline of Usher. There was blood upon her white robes, and the evidence of some bitter struggle upon every portion of her emaciated frame. For a moment she remained trembling to and fro upon the threshold—then, with a low moaning cry, fell heavily inward upon the person of her brother, and in her violent and now final death-agonies, bore him to the floor a corpse, and a victim to the terrors he had anticipated.

Madeline, back from the tomb, neither dead nor alive, is in the middle state of the unquiet spirit of the vampire, whose heart-beats are "heavy and horrible." There is no evidence that Poe knew any anthropology; yet in some legends of vampirism the undead has a sluggish pulse, or none at all. In falling prone upon her brother she takes the position of the vampire suffocating its victim in a sexual embrace. By these observations I do not suggest that Poe was conscious of what he was doing; had he been, he might have done it even worse. I am not saying, in other words, that Poe is offering us, in the Lady Madeline, a vampire according to Bram Stoker's specifications. An imagination of any power at all will often project its deepest assumptions about life in symbols that duplicate, without the artist's knowledge, certain meanings, the origins of which are sometimes as old as the race. If a writer ambiguously exalts the "spirit" over the "body," and the spirit must live wholly upon another spirit, some version of the vampire legend is likely to issue as the symbolic situation.

Although the action is reported by a narrator, the fictional point of view is that of Usher: it is all seen through his eyes. But has Madeline herself not also been moving toward the cataclysmic end in the enveloping action outside the frame of the story? Has not her *will to know* done its reciprocal work upon the inner being of her brother? Their very birth had violated their unity of being. They must achieve spiritual identity in mutual destruction. The physical symbolism of the fissured house, of the miasmic air, and of the special order of nature surrounding the House of Usher and conforming to the laws of the spirits inhabiting it—all this supports the central dramatic situation, which moves toward spiritual unity through disintegration.

In the original unity of the first thing lies the secondary cause of all things, with the germ of their inevitable annihilation.

Repeated here, in the context of the recurrent subject of the Tales, the thesis of *Eureka* has a sufficient meaning and acquires something of the dignity that Valéry attributed to it. Professor Quinn adduces quotations from mathematical physicists to prove that Poe, in *Eureka,* was a prophet of science. It is a subject on which I am not entitled to an opinion. But even if Professor Quinn is right, the claim is irrelevant, and is only another version of the attempt today to make religion and the arts respectable by showing that they are semi-scientific. Another sort of conjecture seems to me more profitable: that in the history of the moral imagination in the nineteenth century Poe occupies a special place. No other writer in England or the United States, or, so far as I know, in France, went so far as Poe in his vision of dehumanized man.

His characters are, in the words of William Wilson's double, "dead to the world"; they are machines of sensation and will, with correspondences, in the physical universe, of particles and energy. Poe's engrossing obsession in *Eureka* with the cosmic destiny of man issued in a quasi-cosmology, a more suitable extension of his vision than any mythology, home-made or traditional, could have offered him. The great mythologies are populous worlds, but a cosmology need have nobody in it. In Poe's, the hyperaesthetic egoist has put all other men into his void: he is alone in the world, and thus dead to it. If we place Poe against the complete Christian imagination of Dante, whom he resembles in his insistence upon a cosmic extension of the moral predicament, the limits of his range are apparent, and the extent of his insight within those limits. The quality of Poe's imagination can be located, as I see it, in only two places in Dante's entire scheme of the after-life: Cantos XIII and XXXII of the *Inferno*. In Canto XIII, the Harpies feed upon the living trees enclosing the shades of suicides—those "violent against themselves," who will not resume their bodies at the Resurrection, for "man may not have what he takes from himself." In XXXII, we are in Caïna, the ninth circle, where traitors to their kin lie half buried in ice, up to the pubic shadow—"where the doleful shades were . . . sounding with their teeth like storks." Unmotivated treachery, for the mere intent of injury, and self-violence are Poe's obsessive subjects. He has neither Purgatory nor Heaven; and only two stations in Hell.

Let us turn briefly to the question of Poe's style. He has several styles, and it is not possible to damn them all at once. The critical style, which I shall not be able to examine here, is on occasion the best; he is a lucid and dispassionate expositor, he is capable of clear and rigorous logic (even from mistaken premises, as in "The Rationale of Verse"), when he is not warped by envy or the desire to flatter. He is most judicial with his peers, least with his inferiors, whom he either overestimates or wipes out. As for the fictional style, it too, varies; it is perhaps at its sustained best, in point of sobriety and restraint, in the tales of deduction. Exceptions to this observation are "Descent into the Maelström," "The Narrative of Arthur Gordon Pym," and perhaps one or two others in a *genre* which stems from the eighteenth-century "voyage." These fictions demanded a Defoe-like verisimilitude which was apparently beyond his reach when he dealt with his obsessive theme. Again I must make an exception: "William Wilson," one of the serious stories (by serious, I mean an ample treatment of the obsession), is perspicuous in diction and on the whole credible in realistic detail. I quote a paragraph:

The extensive enclosure was irregular in form, having many capacious recesses. Of these, three or four of the largest constituted the play-ground. It was level, and covered with a hard fine gravel. I well remember it had no trees, nor benches, nor anything similar within it. Of course it was in the rear of the house. In front lay a small parterre, planted with box and other shrubs, but through this sacred division we passed only upon rare occasions indeed—such as a first advent to school or a final departure hence, or perhaps, when a parent or a friend having called upon us, we joyfully took our way home for the Christmas or midsummer holidays.

It is scarcely great prose, but it has an eighteenth-century directness, and even elegance, of which Poe was seldom capable in his stories. I surmise that the playground at Dr. Bransby's school at Stoke-Newington, where, as a child, he was enrolled for five years, recalled one of the few periods of his life which he could detach from the disasters of manhood and face with equanimity. Now a part of the description of the Lady Ligeia:

. . . I examined the contour of the lofty and pale forehead—it was faultless—how cold indeed that word when applied to a majesty so divine!—the skin rivalling the purest ivory, the commanding extent and repose, the gentle prominence of the regions above the temples; and the raven-black, the glossy, the luxuriant, the naturally curling tresses, setting forth the full force of the Homeric epithet, "hyacinthine." I looked at the delicate outline of the nose. . . .

But I refrain. It is easy enough to agree with Aldous Huxley and Yvor Winters, and dismiss this sort of ungrammatical rubbish as too cheap, or even too idiotic, to reward the time it takes to point it out. But if Poe is worth understanding at all (I assume that he is), we might begin by asking why the writer of the lucid if not very distinguished passage from "William Wilson" repeatedly fell into the bathos of "Ligeia." I confess that Poe's serious style at its typical worst makes the reading of more than one story at a sitting an almost insuperable task. The Gothic glooms, the Venetian interiors, the ancient wine-cellars (from which nobody ever enjoys a vintage but always drinks "deep") —all this, done up in a glutinous prose, so fatigues one's attention that with the best will in the world one gives up, unless one gets a clue to the power underlying the flummery.

I have tried in the course of these remarks to point in the direction in which the clue, as I see it, is to be found. I do not see it in the influence of the Gothic novel. This was no doubt there; but no man is going to use so much neo-Gothic, over and over again, unless he means business with it; I think that Poe meant business. If the Gothic influence had not been to hand, he would have invented it, or something equally "unreal" to serve his purpose. His purpose in laying on the thick décor was to simulate sensation. Poe's sensibility, for reasons that

I cannot surmise here, was almost completely impoverished. He could feel little but the pressure of his predicament, and his perceptual powers remained undeveloped. Very rarely he gives us a real perception because he is not interested in anything that is alive. Everything in Poe is dead: the houses, the rooms, the furniture, to say nothing of nature and of human beings. He is like a child—all appetite without sensibility; but to be in manhood all appetite, all will, without sensibility, is to be a monster: to feed spiritually upon men without sharing with them a real world is spiritual vampirism. The description of Ligeia's head is that of a dead woman.

Does it explain anything to say that this is necrophilism? I think not. Poe's prose style, as well as certain qualities of his verse,[1] expresses the kind of "reality" to which he had access: I believe I have indicated that it is a reality sufficiently terrible. In spite of an early classical education and a Christian upbringing, he wrote as if the experience of these traditions had been lost: he was well ahead of his time. He could not relate his special reality to a wider context of insights—a discipline that might have disciplined his prose. From the literary point of view he combined the primitive and the decadent: primitive, because he had neither history nor the historical sense; decadent, because he was the conscious artist of an intensity which lacked moral perspective.

But writers tend to be what they are; I know of no way to make one kind into another. It may have been a condition of Poe's genius that his ignorance should have been what it was. If we read him as formal critics we shall be ready to see that it was another condition of his genius that he should never produce a poem or a story without blemishes, or a critical essay that, despite its acuteness in detail, does not evince provincialism of judgment and lack of knowledge. We must bear in mind Mr. Eliot's remark that Poe must be viewed as a whole. Even the fiction and the literary journalism that seem without value add to his massive impact upon the reader.

What that impact is today upon other readers I cannot pretend

---

[1] I expect to examine Poe's verse on another occasion. It may be remarked that his verse rhythms are for the metronome, not the human ear. Its real defects are so great that it is not necessary to invent others, as Mr. T. S. Eliot seems to do in "From Poe to Valéry" (*The Hudson Review*, Autumn, 1949). Thus Mr. Eliot (and I cite only one of his observations that seem to me wrong) complains that "the saintly days of yore" could not be an appropriate time for the Raven to have lived. Elijah was fed by Ravens, a bird which was almost extinct in America in the 1840's. Ravens frequently fed hermits and saints and were in fact a fairly standard feature of saintly equipment.

to know. It has been my limited task to set forth here a little of what one reader finds in him, and to acknowledge in his works the presence of an incentive (again, for one man) to self-knowledge. I do not hesitate to say that had Poe not written *Eureka,* I should have been able, a man of this age, myself to formulate a proposition of "inevitable annihilation." I can only invite others to a similar confession. Back of the preceding remarks lies an ambitious assumption, about the period in which we live, which I shall not make explicit. It is enough to say that, if the trappings of Poe's nightmare strike us as tawdry, we had better look to our own. That particular vision in its purity (Poe was very pure) is perhaps not capable of anything better than Mr. Poe's ludicrous décor. Nor have persons eating one another up and calling it spiritual love often achieved a distinguished style either in doing it or in writing about it. It was not Ugolino, it was Dante who wrote about Ugolino with more knowledge than Ugolino had. Mr. Poe tells us in one of his good poems that from boyhood he had "a demon in my view." Nobody then—my great-grandfather, my mother, three generations—believed him. It is time we did. I confess that his voice is so near that I recoil a little, lest he, Montressor, lead me into the cellar, address me as Fortunato, and wall me up alive. I should join his melancholy troupe of the undead, whose voices are surely as low and harsh as the grating teeth of storks. He is so close to me that I am sometimes tempted to enter the mists of pre-American genealogy to find out whether he may not actually be my cousin.

Dostoevsky in *The Possessed*

Philip Rahv

The tendency of every age is to bury as many classics as it revives. If unable to discover our own urgent meanings in a creation of the past, we hope to find ample redress in its competitive neighbors. A masterpiece cannot be produced once and for all; it must be constantly reproduced. Its first author is a man. Its later ones—time, social time, history.

To be means to recur. In the struggle for survival among works of art those prove themselves the fittest that recur most often. In order to impress itself on our imagination, a work of art must be capable of bending its wondrous, its immortal head to the yoke of the mortal and finite—that is, the contemporary, which is never more than an emphasis, a one-sided projection of the real. The past retains its vitality in so far as it impersonates the present, either in its aversions or ideals; in the same way a classic work renews itself by impersonating a modern one.

If of all the novels of Dostoevsky it is *The Possessed* which now seems closest to us, arousing a curiosity and expectation that belong peculiarly to the age we live in, it is because it deals with problems of radical ideology and behavior that have become familiar to us through our own experience. It is a work at once unique and typically Dostoevskyan. Shaken by the Karamazov fury and full of Dostoevsky's moral and religious obsessions, it is at the same time the one novel in which he explicitly concerned himself with political ideas and with the revolutionary movement.

267

The fact is that it really contains two novels. It was begun as an openly "tendencious" study of the evolution of ideas from fathers to sons, of the development of the liberal idealism of the thirties and forties of the past century into the nihilism and socialism of the sixties and seventies; but Dostoevsky encountered such difficulties in its writing that he finally incorporated into it many conceptions from *The Life of a Great Sinner*, a projected novel in several volumes which was to be his major effort on the subject of atheism. For that reason *The Possessed* might be said to have two sets of characters, one sacred and one profane, one metaphysical and one empirical—the group around Stavrogin, the great sinner, and the group around the Verhovenskys, father and son, who are defined socially and politically. While one set commits sins, the other commits crimes. Externally, in his melodramatic, sinister attractiveness and in the Byronic stress given to his personal relation, Stavrogin derives from early European Romanticism, but in his moral sensuality, in his craving for remorse and martyrdom, he is an authentic member of the Karamazov family. He is doubled within himself as well as through Shatov and Kirillov, his satellites in the story. Shatov represents his Russian, national-messianic side, and Kirillov his "religious atheism"—his experiments with God and eventual destruction of Him to make room for the man-god who kills himself to assert his divinity and prove it.

There can be no doubt that the introduction of Stavrogin into *The Possessed*, which in its first draft relied exclusively on the Verhovenskys for its interest, gives the novel a psychological depth and moral propulsion that bring it up to the level of Dostoevsky's best work in his later period, the period that opens with the appearance of *Notes from Underground* in 1864. For with the introduction of Stavrogin Dostoevsky was able to double the theme of his novel, thus allowing sin and crime, religion and politics, to engage in a mutual criticism of each other. It should be added, however, that the two themes are not fused with entire success. Stavrogin is at times somewhat gratuitously implicated in the younger Verhovensky's political maneuvers; the link between them is often artificial, giving rise to superfluous intricacies of structure and episode. The plot, in part improvised, is insufficiently unified. But this defect is more than made up for—and precisely from the standpoint of plot, always so crucially important in Dostoevsky's creative scheme—by the opportunity provided in Stavrogin's accession to the role of principal hero for the employment of that technique of mystification and suspense, of narrative progression by means of a series of tumultuous scenes and revelations of an agonizing nature, on which the Dostoevskyan novel depends for its essential effects, its atmosphere of scandal and monstrous rumor, its tensions of thought no less than of act and circumstance resolved only when the ultimate catastrophe overwhelms the characters and rolls up the plot. Now Stavrogin, whose character is an enigma toward the solution of which everything in the novel converges, is the kind of central figure perfectly suited to this imaginative scheme.

If in the past social critics dismissed *The Possessed* as a vicious caricature of the socialist movement, today the emergence of Stalinism compels a revision of that judgment. Its peculiar "timeliness" flows from the fact that the motives, actions, and ideas of the revolutionaries in it are so ambiguous, so imbedded in equivocation, as to suggest those astonishing negations of the socialist ideal which have come into existence in Soviet Russia. Emptied of principle, the Communist movement of our time has converted politics into an art of illusion. Stalin's "socialism" is devoid of all norms; never acting in its own name, it can permit itself every crime and every duplicity. Its first rule is to deny its own identity and to keep itself solvent by drawing on the ideological credit of those revolutionary traditions and heroic struggles for freedom which its brutal totalitarianism repudiates in their very essence. In public the rapacious bureaucrat appears masked as the spokesman of the oppressed and exploited. Marxism, and not the savage doctrine of preserving and extending at all costs the power of the usurpers, is his official philosophy. It is a similar element of counterfeit, of a vertiginous interplay of reality and appearance, which makes Dostoevsky's story so prophetic in the light of what we know of the fate of the Russian revolution.

Thus in its Verhovensky parts the novel reminds us of the most recent political phenomena; and it is not by chance that on the occasion of the Moscow trials the world press unanimously recalled to its readers the name of Dostoevsky, the great nay-sayer to the revolution. This occurred twenty years after Dostoevsky's Russia—that realm of wood and dark furious souls—had been ostensibly demolished and a new harmonious society erected on its ruins. The principles of science and reason had triumphed, we were told. But now the creations of a novelist who considered these same principles to be the spawn of Satan were invoked to explain events which science and reason had apparently found inexplicable. It is not worthwhile, however, to examine *The Possessed* in order to appeal to the "Slav soul" for the divulgence of racial or national secrets. The "Slav soul" never explained anything. That swollen concept is the product of the historical romanticism of the Slavophil movement, which substituted brooding about history for making it. Dostoevsky, too, "brooded" in the Slavophil fashion, but that by no means exhausts his contribution to letters. As a suprahistorical essence the "Slav soul" is impartial in its testimony, drawing no distinctions between accusers and accused, or between oppressors and oppressed. If you make the unfathomable perversity of the Slav nature your premise, then logically your conclusion cannot exclude any explanation, no matter how wild and incredible. Hence it is futile to look to the author of *The Possessed* for revelations about specific historical events, such as the Moscow trials; but much can be learned from a study of the interrelationships between his work and the contending forces that he combined into such extraordinary patterns. Although this analyst of contradictions, who was ever vibrating between faith and heresy, made the revolutionary the object of his venom, there is a real affinity between them.

"In everything and everywhere," he wrote to his friend Maikov in 1867, "I go to the very last limit; all my life long I have gone beyond the limit." Whatever his conscious convictions about orthodoxy, monarchy, and the Russian folk, his temperament and the profoundly dissident if not daemonic force of his imaginative dialectic transformed him into a revolutionary influence in Russian life and culture. And it is precisely this "going beyond the limit" that explains why in spite of himself he became, in his very resistance to the revolution, its herald and prophet. Into his Christianity, too, he injected, as Lunacharsky noted, "the maximum of his revolutionism." Thus Russian orthodoxy found in him a dangerous advocate and protector, for his championship of it took the form of ideas so apocalyptic as to disintegrate its traditional and institutional sanctions. There is no stasis in Dostoevsky's religiosity but rather a dynamism destructive of dogma and seeking fulfillment in the triumph of Christian love and truth in the human world. To be sure, this did not escape the notice of the more subtle partisans of orthodoxy, such as Konstantin Leontiev, an original thinker and religious philosopher who valued in religion its dogma more than its ethics. Leontiev accused Dostoevsky of deviating from Christianity in the spirit of Western humanism and of promoting an "earthly eudaemonism with Christian nuances." He wrote that "in the eyes of a Christian these hopes (of brotherhood and love) contradict the direct and very clear prophecy of the Gospels concerning the worsening of human relations right to the very end of the world. Brotherhood and humanitarianism are of course recommended by the New Testament for the saving of the individual soul; but in the New Testament it nowhere says that through these humanitarian efforts man will ultimately come to peace and love—*Christ did not promise us that . . . that is not true!* . . . Christ told or advised us to love our neighbor *in the name of God;* but on the other hand he prophesied that many will not obey Him. It is in this sense exactly that the new European humanism and the humanism of Christianity are clearly antithetical, and very difficult to reconcile." From the standpoint of orthodoxy Leontiev was doubtless right in his strictures. The truth is that Dostoevsky, despite the commitment of his will to reactionary principles, was at bottom so deeply involved in the spiritual and social radicalism of the Russian intelligentsia that he could not help attempting to break through the inner rigidity of the orthodox tradition toward a dynamic idea of salvation; and in a certain sense what this idea came to is little more than an anarcho-Christian version of that "religion of humanity" which continued to inspire the intelligentsia throughout the nineteenth century and by which Dostoevsky himself was inspired in his youth, when together with Belinsky, Petrashevsky, and other social enthusiasts of the 1840's, he took for his guides and mentors such heretical lovers of mankind as Rousseau, Fourier, Saint-Simon, and George Sand.

For if analyzed in terms of his social milieu and affiliations, it becomes clear at once that Dostoevsky was the spokesman not of the *narod*—that is the mass of the Russian people, the peasantry—with which he fancied himself to stand in a relation of congenial intimacy, largely of his own imagining, but of the intelligentsia, a class so precariously situated in Russian society, so tightly squeezed between the feudal-aristocratic power above it and the elemental power of the peasant multitude below it, that it had virtually no social space in which to move and grow. It is this stiflingly narrow basis of the Russian intelligentsia which in some ways accounts for its extremes of thought and behavior—the deadly seriousness of its approach to theoretical and ideological issues, its moods of slackness, dreaminess, and passivity alternating with moods of political intransigence and boundless enthusiasm, its fanaticism and tendencies to schism and heresy-hunting combined with tendencies to self-depreciation and self-hatred. In Dostoevsky these characteristics of the Russian intellectuals are summed up to perfection, and that despite his continual quarrels with them, his nagging criticism of them for their alleged estrangement from the people. By his nagging criticism and contempt, which is really self-contempt, he is all the more identified as one of them. In common with many Russian intellectuals he regarded the mysterious power of the *narod* with a fascination that is precisely the negative of their self-contempt and awareness of their own helplessness. Dostoevsky, by idealizing submission, suffering, and the necessity of bowing down before the people, turned this very negativity inside out, endeavoring to convert it into a positive value. But his ambivalent nature did not permit his losing himself in the contemplation of this false though gratifying luster of the positive.

The fact is that it is not in the construction of harmonies but in the uncovering of antinomies that his genius found its deeper expression. His children of light, like Sonia Marmeladov, Myshkin, Alyosha, and Zossima, are passionally and intellectually inferior to his children of darkness, such as Svidrigailov, Raskolnikov, Stavrogin, Kirillov, and Ivan Karamazov. (Myshkin, in whom his author aspired to create the image of a "positively good man," is no doubt the most alive of the children of light, though in saying this one must consider the telling fact that it is primarily from his malaise rather than from his goodness that he gains his vitality as a character.) Ivan Karamazov, transcending his novelistic framework, is a world-historical creation that overshadows all the saints and pseudo-saints in the Dostoevskyan canon; and one cannot but agree with D. S. Mirsky, who, in discriminating between the lesser and the greater Dostoevsky, notes that his tragedies are "irreducible tragedies that cannot be solved or pacified. . . . His harmonies and solutions are on a shallower level than his conflicts and tragedies. . . . His Christianity . . . did not reach the ultimate depths of his soul." The distinction drawn by Mirsky, and indirectly supported from a theological standpoint by Leontiev, is essential to an accurate understanding of Dostoevsky's relationship to historical Christianity, though nowadays, of course, critics friendly to the new religiosity and aware of the uses to which the example of Dostoevsky may be put in the struggle against secular ideas, tend to ignore an insight so damaging to the cause of tradition and dogma.

Excluded from the sphere of practical life and confronted by the need of thinking their way out from the historical impasse into which backward and calamitous conditions had driven their nation, the Russian intellectuals lived in and through ideas. This almost predacious feeling for ideas and relatedness to them is actualized in Dostoevsky as in no other Russian novelist. To his characters ideas are a source of suffering. Such people are unknown in countries like America, where social tension is at a relatively low point and where, in consequence, the idea counts for very little and is usually dismissed as "theory." Only in a society whose contradictions are unbridled in temper do ideas become a matter of life and death. Such is the historical secret of that Russian intensity which Western critics find so admirable. Alyosha Karamazov, for example, was convinced "as soon as he reflected seriously, of the existence of God and immortality, and at once he said to himself: 'I want to exist for God, and I will accept no compromise.'" In the same way, adds Dostoevsky, "if he had decided that God and immortality did not exist he would at once have become an atheist and a socialist." As simply as that. And in *The Possessed,* Kirillov decides that God "is necessary and must exist," but at the same time he knows that "He doesn't and He can't." "Surely," he says, "you must understand that a man with two such ideas can't go on living." Kirillov shoots himself.

In *The Possessed* it is necessary above all to distinguish between its manifest and latent meaning. A counter-revolutionary novel in its manifest intention and content, what it actually depicts in terms of felt experience is the total disintegration of the traditional order and the inevitability of its downfall. The disintegration is of the soul no less than of the social order; and if Stavrogin, with his stupefaction of ennui and loss of the sense of good and evil, represents the decomposed soul, the decomposed society is represented mainly in Verhovensky together with his followers and easy victims. Disintegration is the real theme of the novel, as it is the real theme of *A Raw Youth, The Brothers Karamazov,* and other major works of Dostoevsky's later period. Thus in *The Possessed,* while setting out to report on the moral depravity of the revolution, Dostoevsky was nevertheless objective enough to demonstrate that Russia could not escape it. The hidden ideologue of radicalism and social prophet in him would not be submerged. If it is true, as it has been repeatedly charged, that there was a good slice of the flunkey in his personal psychology, then he was the kind of flunkey, or rather super-flunkey, who even while bowing and scraping says the most outrageous things to your face. This novel, which so delighted the autocratic regime, in reality generalized its breakdown in the political sphere as well as in the sphere of values and moral experience.

In reading this novel one is never quite certain that Pyotr Verhovensky, its chief revolutionary character, is not an agent of the Czar's secret police. Even as he is engaged in preparing an insurrection, this "authorized representative" of an invisible Central Committee, which is located somewhere abroad and turns out to be a myth, describes himself as "a scoundrel of course and not a socialist." He methodically uses blackmail, slander, drunkenness, and spying to achieve his ends. But what in reality are his ends? Give him state power and you get the kind of social type who makes his way to the top in the Soviet secret police. Verhovensky's plan is to organize a network of human knots whose task is to proselytize and ramify endlessly, and "by systematic denunciation to injure the prestige of local authority, to reduce villages to confusion, to spread cynicism and scandals, together with complete disbelief in everything and an eagerness for something better, and finally, by means of fire, a pre-eminently national method, to reduce the country at a given moment, if need be, to desperation." Verhovensky actually carries out this ingenious plan in the town where the scene of the novel is laid—an unnamed town which stands for the whole of Russia. His associate Shigalov—a character who fits Lenin's definition of the petty-bourgeois "gone mad" but who at the same time, in view of the monstrous consistency of his revolutionary-utopian logic, reminds us if not of Lenin personally then surely of Leninism as an historical phenomenon—busies himself with constructing, on paper, a new form of social organization to guarantee complete equality. Starting with the idea of attaining "unlimited freedom" in his Utopia, he soon arrives at the conclusion that what it will actually produce is "unlimited despotism." This throws him into despair, yet he insists that there can be no other solution to the problems of society. Yulia Mihailovna, a well-born and well-to-do lady, wife of the governor of the province, dreams of reconciling the irreconcilable in her own person, of uniting in the adoration of herself "the correct tone of the aristocratic salons and the free-and-easy, almost pothouse manners" of the youthful nihilists, the system of big landed property with free-thinking socialist notions. (In the unsurpassable portrait of this vain woman Dostoevsky created the model of what has since evolved into a ubiquitous social type—the wealthy and thoroughly bourgeois "friend" or "sympathizer" of the Russian revolution who in his befuddlement tries to reconcile his existing status in society with the self-conceit of playing a progressive role and being "in" on the secrets of history.) And what shall one say of Yulia Mihailovna's husband, the governor, who in his snobbish desire to associate himself with the cause of progress can think of no other objection to the manifestoes urging the people to rebellion except that the ideas expressed in them are "premature." Verhovensky quickly and cruelly turns this objection aside by saying to him: "And how can you be an official of the government after that, when you agree to demolishing churches, and marching on Petersburg with staves, making it all simply a question of date?" Such people are the natural prey of a character like Liputin, an unwashed intriguer, at once a despot and a dreamer, who propounds the theory that there are people on whom clean linen is unseemly. Practicing petty usury, he at the same time holds forth in the language of "the universal republic and harmony of mankind." But the odd thing about him is that he is sincere.

It is exactly through such complex and conflicting motivation that the inevitability of the social breakdown is impressed on the reader's mind. Here the impulse to be rid of a rotting order and to break loose has reached such intensity that it has become objective; penetrating into the innermost, the most differentiated cells of human psychology, it has ceased to be incompatible with degenerate habits and desires. In one scene the writer Karmazinov, a figure through whom the author mercilessly derided Turgenev, describes Russia in terms that approximate the Marxist formula of a revolutionary situation. One must bear in mind that since the intent of the novel is counter-revolutionary, the perception that "Russia as she is has no future" and that "everything here is doomed and awaiting its end" is necessarily put into the mouth of a character, presented as a pompous and conceited coward, at whom we are supposed to laugh. Yet the author makes it plain, even if through indirect means, that Karmazinov is a man of acute intelligence. And Karmazinov so truly predicts what has since come to pass that he is well worth quoting at some length in order to demonstrate how powerfully his author's observation of Russian society was engaged with reality at the very time when he was ostensibly defending this society by writing a novel exposing and satirizing its liberal and socialist enemies. Karmazinov is addressing himself to Verhovensky:

"If the Babylon there [meaning Europe] really does fall, and great will be the fall thereof . . . there's nothing to fall here in Russia, comparatively speaking. There won't be stones to fall, everything will crumble into dirt. Holy Russia has less power of resistance than anything in the world. The Russian peasantry is still held together somehow by the Russian God; but according to the latest accounts the Russian God is not to be relied upon . . . And now, what with railways, what with you . . . I've no faith in the Russian God."

"And how about the European one?"

"I don't believe in any. . . . I was shown the manifestoes here. Every one looks at them with perplexity because they are frightened at the way things are put in them, but every one is convinced of their power even if they don't admit it to themselves. Everything has been rolling downhill, and every one has known for ages that they have nothing to clutch at. I am persuaded of the success of this mysterious propaganda, if only because Russia is now pre-eminently the place in the world where anything you like may happen without any opposition. . . . Holy Russia is a country of wood, of poverty . . . and of danger, the country of ambitious beggars in the upper classes, while the immense majority live in poky little huts. She will be glad of any way to escape; you have only to present it to her. It's only the government that still means to resist, but it brandishes its cudgel in the dark and hits its own men. Everything here is doomed and awaiting the end. Russia as she is has no future. I have become a German and am proud of it."

"But you began about the manifestoes. Tell me everything. How do you look at them?"

"Every one is afraid of them, so they must be influential. They openly unmask what is false and prove that there is nothing to lay hold of among us, and nothing to lean upon. They speak aloud while all is silent. What is most effective about them . . . is the incredible boldness with which they look the truth straight in the face. To look facts straight in the face is only possible to Russians of this generation. No, in Europe they are not yet so bold; it is a realm of stone, there there is still something to lean upon. So far as I see and am able to judge, the whole essence of the Russian revolutionary idea lies in the negation of honor. I like its being so boldly and fearlessly expressed. No, in Europe they wouldn't understand it yet, but that's just what we shall clutch at. For a Russian a sense of honor is only a superfluous burden, and it always has been a burden through all his history. The open 'right to dishonor' will attract him more than anything. . . .'

If any character in *The Possessed* personifies the negation of honor, it is of course Pyotr Verhovensky. But can it be said that he is truly representative of the Russian revolutionary movement? Has it not been pointed out time and again that he is a monster and not a radical? Anyone who has studied Russian history cannot fail to agree that in presenting Verhovensky as typical of radicalism Dostoevsky was oblivious to the innumerable examples of idealistic self-sacrifice which the class struggle in Russia had to show. There can be no doubt of Dostoevsky's spiteful tendenciousness in this respect. Professor Ernest J. Simmons is entirely in the right when he observes, in his book on Dostoevsky, that Verhovensky is no socialist because his ideology is "the criminal creed of the absolutely self-willed man." But where Professor Simmons is wrong, to my mind, is in contenting himself with this observation, as if that disposed of the matter once and for all.

For if it is true that in a factual sense Verhovensky is altogether untypical of the revolutionary movement of Dostoevsky's time, is it not also true, on the other hand, that this same Verhovensky has since become all too typical—typical, that is, of the men whom the Bolshevik revolution has raised to power and established as Russia's ruling elite. There is an uncanny likeness, after all, between "the criminal creed of the absolutely self-willed man" and the creed, prevailing in practice though for obvious reasons unacknowledged in theory, which is the real motive-force of Russia's self-styled socialist masters. And because this likeness has become an historical fact it is no longer possible to dismiss Verhovensky as a monster and not a radical, as Professor Simmons dismisses him in his book. The revolutionary process as it has taken shape in the new order of Stalinism has indisputably confirmed Dostoevsky's insight that the monstrous in human nature is no more incommensurable with the social revolution than it is incommensurable with institutional Christianity. In point of fact, the totalitarian potential of both is incorporated in the principal symbol of the legend of the Grand Inquisitor—the symbol of the tower of Babel that replaces the temple of Christ.

Thus it can now be seen that as a character-image Verhovensky is symbolically representative of the revolution in its results, if not in its original motives. Of course, Dostoevsky was entirely tendencious when he ignored, in *The Possessed,* the role played in the socialist movement by such humanistic and libertarian personalities as Herzen, Cherni-chevsky, and Mikhailovsky; but here again, unfortunately, his bias is vindicated when it is brought home to us that the revolution, not as it is presented in the Marxist textbooks but as it actually developed, fol-lowed the path not of the socialist humanists but of socialist Machiavel-lians like Tkachev and Nechayev. To be sure, if examined in the light of the struggle for freedom in Czarist Russia, the right to dishonor of which Karmazinov speaks (and you may be sure that in this instance he speaks for his author) seems like a vile imputation. Yet the fact is that it is this right, in essence, that the triumphant revolutionaries arrogated to themselves—and precisely in the fashion of the Dostoevskyan man-gods—when they proclaimed moral standards to be a bourgeois prejudice, proceeding on the assumption that to them all is permitted. It is the tragedy of the Russian people that history has proven Dostoevsky to be a truer prophet than Lenin. Only in speaking out of the depths of negation, however, was Dostoevsky a true prophet. Of his positive prophecies none have been fulfilled. The national-Christian ideology of which Shatov is the mouthpiece in *The Possessed* has turned out to be no more than wishful thinking. In the novel Verhovensky murders Shatov, and in real life this crime, endlessly multiplied, has become the foundation of the new Russian state. In this sense Leontiev was again shown to be right against Dostoevsky when he declared that "Russia has only one religious mission, and that is to give birth to anti-Christ." Actually, the anguish of disintegration in Dostoevsky is the creative counterpart of this very idea, an idea strenuously denied in the consolatory and visionary parts of his writings.

But let us look further into Verhovensky's origins in the Russian revolutionary movement of the past century. The biographers of Dostoevsky tell us that the activity of Verhovensky's circle in the novel is an imaginative rendering of the Nechayev episode in the history of Russian radicalism. Now in Nechayevism the revolution suffered its first formidable inroads of Machiavellian deception and double-dealing. Nechayev invented the slogan: "Everything for the revolution—the end justifies the means." He systematically cultivated criminal methods (which are in no way identical with the methods of underground struggle) in the pursuit of his radical ends. Verhovensky's murder of Shatov is patterned on Nechayev's murder of the student Ivanov; and if we know that one section of the *Catechism of a Revolutionary*, composed by Bakunin and Nechayev, calls for "acquaintance with city gossips, prostitutes, and other private sources" for gathering and disseminating information and false rumors, we realize to what an extent, even to the repetition of comic details, the archetype of Nechayev is reproduced in the portrait of Verhovensky.[1] The *Catechism*, moreover,

---

[1] In his political traits, that is. As a psychological type Verhovensky has Nechayev's ruthlessness and immoralism but none of his revolutionary asceticism. As a matter of fact, in his psychological aspects Verhovensky reminds us

contains something more than formulas of conspiracy and provocation. In that document it is written that "everything which promotes the success of the revolution is moral, everything which hinders it is immoral"—a dictum, at once savage and naïve, that Lenin took over in toto, applying it with all the rigor of his political nature and never ceasing to defend it as the only possible ethic consistent with Marxist aims. Lenin's self-will was so inordinate that he always assumed perfect knowledge on his part as to what made for the ultimate success or failure of the revolution. Thus what appeared to him like an objective test of morality rested on nothing whatever except his subjective assumption of perfect knowledge, judgment, and disinterestedness. We can grant him the disinterestedness, but not the knowledge or the judgment. Because of the absolutism of his revolutionary character he failed to look beyond the abstractions of historical materialism to the real interests that lurk behind the ideologies of individuals as well as social groups. He overlooked the inescapable fact that behind every doctrine or program, including his own, there are living men, with immediate and concrete desires, needs, and ambitions, and that this could only mean that Nechayev's dictum would eventually be altered to read that everything is moral which promotes the success, not of the revolution, but of the men who choose to speak in its name, and that everything which hinders them is immoral. Lenin's disregard of the ethics of humanism was implicit in his self-will. The enormity and arrogance of that will is the peculiar sin of Bolshevism, the *hubris* for which Lenin has been paid out by the utter ruin of his revolutionary achievements.

The connection between Nechayevism and the revolution is close indeed. When Bakunin finally repudiated his fanatical disciple he exposed him as one who believed that "in order to create a workable and strong organization one must use as a basis the philosophy of

---

more of such famous *agents provocateurs* as Azev and Malinovsky, both of whom, long after Dostoevsky's time, rose to high positions in the revolutionary movement while in the pay of the *Okhrana*, the Czar's secret police. Azev became head of the powerful terrorist section of the Social Revolutionary Party; Malinovsky, who had Lenin's confidence, became the chief spokesman of the Bolsheviks in the Duma. Of both Azev and Malinovsky it may be said that they were truly Dostoevskyan in their doubleness of character, for they were not police-spies pure and simple but men of ambiguous motivation and dual loyalties who did not know from one day to the other what they really believed in or whether their principal allegiance was to the revolution or to their Czarist paymasters.

Machiavelli and adopt the motto of the Jesuits: 'Violence for the body; lies for the soul.' " It was not until the Grand Inquisitor himself, the dictator Stalin, gained supreme power that Nechayev's central thought was translated into the terms of real life. Still, the totalitarian virus is no doubt present in Lenin's moral opportunism, an opportunism exalted into a principle of socialist organization and propaganda and thus far more pernicious in its consequences than the casual, unthinking pragmatism and the recourse to expediency that as a rule prevail in political affairs. The revolution is a means and not an end; and the outcome of Lenin's absolutizing of the revolution was that the means so completely usurped the end that it was soon transformed into its exact opposite—into a system reminiscent of Shigalov's thesis rather than of the forecasts of Marx and Engels. What is Shigalov's thesis? That the only way to secure unlimited freedom is through unlimited despotism, or rather that the two concepts are ultimately identical. Therefore he proposes that nine-tenths of mankind be deprived of all freedom and individuality while one-tenth enjoys the unbounded power required for the compulsory organization of happiness. Shigalov's "earthly paradise" is nothing if not a remarkable prevision of Stalin's "workers' paradise." And when one comes to appreciate the fact that Dostoevsky's prognosis of the course of the revolution, however crude in detail, is essentially correct in its main outlines, one cannot but admire his astonishing clairvoyance; and that despite his malicious tendenciousness, which we can now put in the proper perspective without in any way justifying it.

This malice, inherent in Dostoevsky's character, was strengthened by his polemical exertions as a writer. Still, there is no denying that he decided against socialism on a principled metaphysical basis. His antipathy to it had nothing in common with the habitual objections of conservative property-holders, office-holders, and ideologues. He understood that "socialism is founded on the principles of science and reason . . . that it is not merely the labor question, it is before all else the atheistic question, the question of the form taken by atheism today"; and in a variant passage of *The Possessed* we find the statement, attributed to Liputin, that "socialism is a substitute for Christianity, it is a new Christianity, which wants to renew the whole world. It is positively the same as Christianity, but without God." Nevertheless he was drawn to it, for he was as much fascinated as repelled by the demonstrations of reason. Like Stavrogin, he never really attained the peace of religious faith, and when he believed he could not actually believe that he believed. He hated socialism because it objectified his lack of belief and both his fear and heretical love of the boundless expansion and change of which the human mind is capable. In his compulsion to test theory by practice he came close to the methods of extreme rationality; and when he subjected Christianity to this rigorous test he found that only a special kind of "idiot" and genius of neuroticism could possibly undertake to lead a Christian life.

His plebeianism was another element that tended to subvert his support of the autocracy and the church. On his subjective-psychological side he remained a democrat, regardless of the shifts that took place in his political convictions; and for this reason he could not restrain himself from berating the older generation of Slavophils for their "aristocratic satiety." Like the critic Belinsky and the poet Nekrasov he belonged to the school of commoners, whose inner affinity was with the psychic distortions and the moral agitation and resentment of Gogol rather than with the objective art of Pushkin. In Dostoevsky's work we do not experience that sense of social hierarchies which affects us so strongly in the novels that Tolstoy wrote before his conversion. In modern times the plebeian world-feeling is one of the intrinsic conditions of heresy, and the spiritual equality which reigns in Dostoevsky's world seems like a kind of inverted socialism, a commune of the spirit.

In *The Possessed* liberal idealism receives the broadest and most perspicacious criticism in the history of political fiction. The comic strokes with which the portrait of the intellectual Stepan Trofimovitch, the elder Verhovensky, is executed, in no way divert us from its enduring reality and social truth. This characterization has enormous contemporary meanings. It is only now, after fascism and communism have severely penalized Western culture for subjecting itself to the timorous and accommodating counsels of the liberals, that we can fully appreciate Stepan Trofimovitch.

A gentleman scholar and aesthete, he simultaneously abuses and adores the revolution. His standing protest he makes by lying down; he is subtle in his feelings, a self-indulgent humanitarian and a parasite. He is superior to Thomas Mann's Settembrini, whose distant relative he is, for he is understood not argumentatively but through a tangible social milieu. And what a hazardous yet just simplification it was to place him in the position of being the charge of a rich and aristocratic lady, of making an assertive dramatic image out of Varvara Petrovna's support of him. This exchange of cash and culture, however, is not conceived as a simple transaction; on the contrary, it entails mutual distrust, bitterness, and emotional tempests—at one and at the same time it involves very real sentiments, even love, and "a mutual exchange of sloppiness."

Stepan Trofimovitch is a typical modern figure, the liberal intellectual with a tender social conscience and a taste for fine feelings and ideas, who, while pluming himself on his advanced position as a champion of the oppressed, is at once thrown into a state of collapse when forced to face the consequences of his own commitments and the cruel exigencies of the historical process. This dilettante of revolution is bound to end up among its first victims. He is unable to cope with his revolutionary son, Pyotr, or with the nihilists whom the latter trains in his base methods. In *Fathers and Sons,* Turgenev's Bazarov, the prototype of the nihilists in the Russian novel, holds the view that a good chemist is worth twenty poets. But Bazarov's nihilism is only a form of moral empiricism; he is an individualist as yet unaware of the potency of political action. A few decades later, in the 1870's, the nihilistic adversaries of Stepan Trofimovitch had already translated Bazarov's moral empiricism into the formulas of political terror and demagoguery. During the Fête—the description of which includes some of the novel's superb scenes—Stepan Trofimovitch defies the political mob by shouting at them: "What is more beautiful, Shakespeare or boots, Raphael or petroleum?" *"Agent provocateur!"* they growl in reply. It is a crushing reply and one that is all too indicative of the manner in which the revolutionaries in power will eventually dispose of the tender-minded intelligentsia. If in his generalizations Dostoevsky recognizes no difference between liberals, nihilists, and socialists, within the living organism of the novel he takes care to distinguish clearly between the elder and younger Verhovensky; paternity in this case is symbolic of a relation of ideas at once positive and negative. The revolutionary doctrine negates liberalism even as it grows out of it. In the historical sense what Pyotr represents is his father's ideas thought out to an outrageously logical conclusion, and for that very reason he becomes his father's worst enemy.

But the vitality of Stepan Trofimovitch's character is by no means confined to the political dimension. He is also a splendidly comical creation, richly illustrating Dostoevsky's gifts as a humorous writer that

have been obscured by his accomplishments as psychologist and dialec-
tician. In Stepan Trofimovitch, this "most innocent of fifty-year old
infants" who is capable of the most surprising and subtle insights,
Dostoevsky reached the apogee of his comic art—an art that produced
such figures as Foma Fromitch of *The Friend of the Family* and that
entire incredible collection of buffoons, like Lebedev of *The Idiot* and
Captain Lebyadkin of *The Possessed,* of whom at least one specimen
is invariably to be found in any Dostoevskyan cast of characters. Stepan
Trofimovitch does not belong to this species. For all his poltroonery,
tormenting vanity, nervous outbreaks, and fondness for French phrases,
he is yet invested with a redeeming generosity and openness of feeling
that converts him into a figure of heroico-comical proportions. We believe in him as we can never believe in his son Pyotr, in whom there is
something cold and amorphous, and whom we can imagine only as a
kind of abstract demon all the more terrible in his fury for being
doomed to beat his wings in a void. He has no ability to transcend his
situation, while his father has this ability above all; and that so endears
him to us that in our sympathy we are persuaded that even if he is a
bundle of human failings in him the human image is still the goad of
love.

There are few scenes in Dostoevsky as marvelous as the scenes
of Stepan Trofimovitch's stormy interviews with his capricious patron-
ess, or of his appearance and declamations at the Fête, or of his engagement to Darya Shatova, and, in particular, of his flight and wanderings
in the countryside, where he meets the Bible-selling woman, wooing her
in his delirium and panic—the flight that ends with his breakdown and
the self-confrontation of those last great reconciling speeches in which,
as if summing up the rhetoric of a lifetime, he salutes "the Eternal and
Infinite Idea" at the same time that he confesses to the lies he has told
through all the years, summoning all to forgiveness, for all are guilty,
all have wronged one another, in the hope that he too will be forgiven.
In those last tremendous pages of the novel we are made to feel as
though Stepan Trofimovitch, lying on his deathbed, has departed from
his character in order to voice, in unison with his author, a great cry of
grief for Holy Russia, a prayer that her sick men be freed of the demons
that possess them so that, whole again and much afraid, they may come
and sit at the feet of Jesus.

It is significant that the passage from the Gospels, which forms
the epigraph to the novel, telling about the sick man cured of his devils

and sitting at the feet of Jesus, is made to resound through Stepan Trofimovitch's last speeches, as if to indicate that the author, despite the vindictive spirit of his initial approach to him, is so taken with his creature that he cannot help lending him a modicum of his own faith and outlook. It is a case of sympathy between the creative artist and the created being, in the sense of Keats' notion of "the poetical Character," which forfeits its own identity in taking unto itself the identities formed by the imagination. ("What shocks the virtuous philosopher delights the chameleon poet," said Keats.) Now in Stepan Trofimovitch, modeled on a handsome Moscow professor by the name of Granovsky, a friend of Herzen and Belinsky, the "virtuous philosopher" in Dostoevsky wanted to score off the generation of the 1840's, whose rational humanism he regarded as a source of infection; but Stepan Trofimovitch turned out differently than is anticipated in the original design. Though his function in the novel is to stand as a reproach to the Westernizing intellectuals, he is creatively assimilated to such a degree that in surpassing himself he assumes other roles, not the least of which is to act as a foil to Dostoevsky in his farewell to the Schilleresque period of his own youth, the period of *Schwärmerei* and idealistic grandiloquence, when at one with his contemporaries he shared the exalted feelings inspired by the rational religion of humanity.

In Stavrogin and his alter egos, Kirillov and Shatov, Dostoevsky was reproducing the obsessions of his ultimate phase. As against radicals like Verhovensky and Karmazinov, they personify the "pure" Russians. Shatov, for instance, becomes the spokesman of the national destiny. What are the Russians like and what is their mission?—that is the problem tormenting him.

Three times, in *Fathers and Sons,* Turgenev essayed to define the "typical Russian," and each time he betrayed his sense of inferiority to the West and the complacent, moderate cast of his sensibility. (The three definitions occur in subordinate verbal constructions: *a.* ". . . a coarse, half-educated, but not ill-natured man, a typical Russian"; *b.* "the only good point in a Russian is his having the lowest possible opinion of himself"; *c.* ". . . a young man at once progressive and a despot, as often happens with Russians.") Dostoevsky was outraged by Turgenev's common sense and persistent depreciation of Russia. Into his own conception of Russia and Russians he injected his characteristic emotion of extremity. The Russians are to him a kingdom of priests and a chosen people; even God is appropriated to its uses. In Shatov's scheme of things God is merely "the synthetic personality of the whole people, taken from its beginning to its end." These national visions anticipate much that Europe was to experience later; and the same holds true of Stavrogin's "life, so to speak, of mockery," of his psychic conundrums that are precursive of many tendencies in twentieth-century European literature.

It is significant that Shatov, who patently speaks for the author in his affirmation of the Russians as a god-bearing people destined to regenerate the world, is unable to attain in his faith the completeness that Kirillov attains in his atheism. For Shatov, though believing in Russian orthodoxy, in the body of Christ, and in the new advent that will take place in Russia, is nevertheless thrown for a loss when asked pointblank whether he actually believes in God. All he can say in reply is "I . . . I will believe in God." Thus he lays himself open to Stavrogin's gibe that he is preparing to cook an uncaught hare—"to cook your hare you must first catch it, to believe in God you must first have a god." Kirillov, on the other hand, is completely certain of his idea that God is dead, and in his obsession with this idea he challenges the universe, setting himself up as its master in the place of God.

Kirillov's atheism is of a desperate intensity without parallel in world literature. It is the atheism of a man so profoundly religious that once he is convinced of the impossibility of God's existence he must refuse at all costs to go on inventing Him; His absence is so agonizing a negation of meaning that he cannot help reacting to it by attempting to blow up the world, and since the world is not his to destroy he can only destroy himself. That seems to me to be the real motive of his suicide. To be sure, the commentators on Dostoevsky have mostly explained it as the consequence of Kirillov's logic of self-will, and it is indeed true that he makes of his suicide the climactic act of his self-willed accession to the role of the man-god. One must distinguish, however, between the logical and existential aspects of this act. Logically it is an assertion of the absolute freedom of his self-will; existentially it expresses the passionate indignation of his atheism, an atheism whose inescapable logic is beyond his endurance. His suicide is thus to be conceived as an explosion of subjectivity protesting the objective godlessness of the world. *Allein zu sein und ohne Götter, das ist er, ist der Tod,* said Hölderlin. To be alone and without gods—that is death; and it is this thought, literally, that compels Kirillov to kill himself. In reading the overpowering description of his suicide and the dialogue that precedes it one becomes aware that here Dostoevsky is picturing nothing less than the self-crucifixion of an atheistic Christ. Consider that shortly before firing his shot Kirillov recalls the crucifixion of old in words of ecstatic pain:

"Listen to a great idea: there was a day on earth, and in the midst of the earth there stood three crosses. One on the Cross had such faith that he said to another, 'Today thou shalt be with me in Paradise.' The day ended; both died and passed away and found neither Paradise nor resurrection. His words did not come true. Listen: that man was the loftiest of all on earth. He was that which gave meaning to life. . . . For that is the miracle, that there never was and never will be another like Him. And if that is so, if the laws of nature did not spare even Him, have not spared even their miracle and made even Him live in a lie and die for a lie, then all the planet is a lie and rests on a lie and on mockery. So then, the very laws of the planet are a lie and the vaudeville of devils. What is there to live for? Answer, if you are a man."

Kirillov's suicide is a parody of the crucifixion of Christ—a parody because in a universe whose laws are "a lie and the vaudeville of devils" there can be no meaningful acts, only parodies.

The atheism of Kirillov is not to be equated with that of some of the modern existentialists. Sartre, for example, defines existentialism as "nothing less than an attempt to draw all the consequences of a coherent atheistic position"; and the chief consequence of the atheistic position is that it forces man to confront his freedom in a world emptied of all values and commands not derived from himself. This idea of man alone in his freedom is of course not alien to Kirillov, but in his dialectic it is so hugely exaggerated that it is transformed into a notion of human omnipotence and made into the basis of the man-god's mad rationale. On this side of it his atheism is a sick phantasy of his soul suffering the ordeal of God's absence. At bottom, however, his atheism is really a form of negative religiosity. It is real nevertheless, and in considering its implications there is no way of absolving the author of complicity in it. If Shatov speaks for him, so does Kirillov; and if the latter manifests more spiritual vitality than the former it is no doubt because Dostoevsky imbued him with a deeper and more personal significance. V. V. Rozanov, a writer who brought exceptional gifts to the interpretation of Dostoevsky, was moved to say, in citing the passage from *The Possessed* quoted above, that "when Dostoevsky wrote those words you feel that through his soul, a single human soul, there passed such a terrifying atheism as has never been experienced before, or, if experienced, has not yet been uttered in words."

The curious thing about the ideas of both Shatov and Kirillov is that they are represented in the novel as emanations of Stavrogin's irony. To them his ideas have become altogether real, whereas he has forgotten them. Stavrogin experiments with life, only incidentally with ideas, and every experiment strengthens the demon of irony that possesses him. There are elements of Christian feeling in him, but only in the sense that at times he is inclined to believe in the devil, never in God. Everyone expects of him something unheard-of, something not expected from other people, for in truth he is a hero of charismatic authority, a leader-type who is bored, however, by his own charisma. That is what is really "new" in the character of Stavrogin, this refusal to make use of his own powers—a refusal caused by the recoil of his consciousness upon itself in the dreadful apprehension of its own limitless freedom. He is free of the sense of good and evil, being convinced that "good and evil do not exist . . . and are but a prejudice." Yet he knows that it is precisely in the attainment of this freedom that he will perish. He says of himself that he ought to commit suicide; but at the same time he rejects suicide for fear of showing greatness of soul, for such greatness could hardly be anything more than "another sham, the last deception in an endless series of deceptions." Dostoevsky, in creating the character-image of Stavrogin, reached the last frontier of the modern imagination, and it is perhaps for this reason, since life did not as yet contain him, that he could not make him "true to life" but was forced to rely almost entirely on his mastery of the devices of melodrama and mystification.

Nearly all the female characters in the novel are in love with Stavrogin, a love which he is incapable of reciprocating. Hence his desires are nothing less than crimes—the crime of murder above all. Thus it is through their love of him that both the imperious Liza and the crippled, half-witted Marya are done in; and Matryosha, the little girl whom he has violated, kills herself. Stavrogin, like Svidrigailov in *Crime and Punishment,* is a sexual marauder, but in his case too it is the *idea* of sex rather than the reality of it that absorbs the imagination. This Dostoevskyan idea of sex is not an abstraction; on the contrary, it is enormously creative in that it at once suggests and exceeds the reality behind it. But it is typical of Dostoevsky that he should have let nothing escape his ideological net, not even the cravings of the flesh and the aberrations of desire.

Of course, Dostoevsky paid for his ideological power by strictly limiting his incursions into the sensuous-material world. He gives us sensations of time, and only seldom of space. He has a prodigious appetite for people, but he is insensitive to textures and objects; his characters act sexually only when aroused by their own moral and spiritual sensuality. This overproduction of the spiritual makes for a constant inner crisis, for an analyzing attitude which shuts him off from nature. It is this quality which permits his narratives their breakneck pace—there is no need to stop when there is nothing to look at. The excessive sociability of his people has the same source. It has often been observed how perpetually dependent they are on externalization through talk and debate. Even in committing suicide they are not alone, and a love scene seldom takes place without the presence of a third person. Dostoevsky stages his climaxes only after he has assembled as many of his characters as possible into one room; and the action, in which the philosophical dialogue is inextricably involved with a story of mystery and crime, moves in a whirlwind manner toward a *denouement* that consumes heroes and victims alike in a conflagration of hatred, pity, resentment, remorse, and love.

If the religious-minded critics of Dostoevsky have emphasized almost exclusively the Christian element in his work, the Marxist critics have permitted political considerations to influence them in disparaging and ignoring his achievements. Gorky spoke of Dostoevsky as "our evil genius," strictly limiting himself to his negative features. Even D. S. Mirsky, who before going over to a Marxist position wrote with fine insight and precision about Dostoevsky, later committed himself to views contradicting his previous evaluations. Thus, in his preface to Edward Hallett Carr's biography of Dostoevsky, he expresses his gratification with Carr for showing up, as it were, his subject. Carr had laid great stress on the literary and Romantic antecedents of Dostoevsky, and Mirsky concludes that he is "modern only in so far as the term modern can be extended to Rousseau, Byron, and Benjamin Constant." He was produced by Russia precisely because she was backward and because "he was a belated parallel in his country to what the Romantics had been in the West." To Mirsky it seems that by labeling Dostoevsky the belated Romantic of a backward country he has effectively removed him from the terrain of the modern; what he has further in mind, of course, is to connect him with the reactionary tendencies of the Romantic movement in Germany and to a lesser extent in France.

In relating Dostoevsky to Romanticism in the way he does, Mirsky suggests the use of the Marxist "law of combined development." But to invoke this law is to disprove Mirsky's approach. The "law of combined development" explains why a bourgeois revolution, when it occurs in a backward country, tends to go beyond itself and to be transformed into a socialist one. A backward country is thus enabled to make up for lost time and outstrip its advanced neighbors, at least politically. There is no reason, however, to confine this phenomenon of accelerated mutation to politics. It also operates on the spiritual plane. To say, then, in this sense, that Dostoevsky was a belated Romantic does not at all mean that the Romantic world was his world or that he restored the Romantic state of mind.

Why is the Russian novel of the nineteenth century so great in its achievements? If the "law of combined development" has any application here, it would point to the need of the Russian novelist to break out ideologically and imaginatively from the blind alley in which his country found itself. This same need impelled him to augment his equipment by taking over as rapidly as he could whatever acquisitions of Western culture were open to him. Even when he rejected this culture, as Dostoevsky did, he was strongly affected by it. Before condemning it he still had to acquire some essential part of it.

To recognize the achievement of the Russian novel of the nineteenth century is to recognize Dostoevsky's supremacy as a modern writer. His one rival is Tolstoy. Only dogmatists of progress, who conceive of it as an even and harmonious development, could presume to commit Dostoevsky to a museum of Romantic antiquities. It is true that he labored to give his genius a religious sanctification, but it must be kept in mind that in the sphere of imaginative creation progress does not simply consist of knowing what is true and what is false from the standpoint of progressive or scientific thought. Dostoevsky not only renovated the traditional properties of Romanticism but also discovered inversions and dissociations in human feeling and consciousness which literature has to this day only imperfectly assimilated. Reactionary in its abstract content, in its aspect as a system of ideas, his art is radical in sensibility and subversive in performance.

Moreover, Romanticism is far from being as dreadful as Mirsky makes out. Its impulse is partly reactionary, of course, but in approaching the old values through the self-consciousness of the new epoch, it responded to new emotions and invented new themes. There are numberless examples of this dual function of Romanticism. Chateaubriand, for instance, was faithful to throne and altar; he set out to defend tradition and belabor Rousseau. "I am not like Rousseau," he wrote in the introduction to *Atala,* "an enthusiast over savages. . . . I do not think that pure nature is . . . beautiful. . . . I have always found it ugly. Let us paint nature, but selected nature (*la belle nature*). Art should not concern itself with the imitation of monsters." This declaration, however, as Sainte-Beuve noted, was belied by the actual content of *Atala,* in which one encounters a crocodile on nearly every page.

Dostoevsky's "crocodiles" are thinking men.

Caldwell: Maker
of Grotesques

Kenneth Burke

Erskine Caldwell's most revealing work is a "sport." I refer to the last story in *American Earth,* "The Sacrilege of Alan Kent." It is divided into three sections, with wholly non-Caldwellian titles, "Tracing Life with a Finger," "Inspiration for Greatness," and "Hours Before Eternity." In these words we catch a tonality of brooding which, though so much a part of America as to have been pronounced by Poe, is more generally associated with the pious satanists who developed the ways of Poe in Europe: Baudelaire, Rimbaud, Lautréamont, and the early Gide. This work is as unique to Caldwell in manner as it is in mood. Whereas his other stories, long or short, are written with the continuity of the undulations along a moving caterpillar's back, "The Sacrilege" is a chain of brief numbered paragraphs, each bluntly set off from the rest. Done with the solemnity of a farewell or a testament, they contain a kind of aphoristic rhetoric, except that the aphorisms are less ideas than tiny plots. We note here a formal resonance, a stentorian quality, obtained by a swift recital of plagues, monstrosities, horrors, obsessions, disasters, and gigantesque imaginings, set against a tender counter-theme: "I never heard a girl whose face and body and eyes were lovely say anything but lovely words." Here we have the symbol of the wanderer, driven by unnamed sins and called by vague visions of a homecoming in female sweetness. The swift segments shunt us back and forth between brutality and wistfulness. Perhaps the grandiose, the violent, and the gentle qualities of the piece are all fused in this bit of purest poetry: "Once the sun was so hot a bird came

Reprinted by permission of the author.

down and walked beside me in my shadow." A section in *Pagany* containing this item was the first thing by Caldwell I ever saw. For days I was noisy in my enthusiasm—but I could not understand how it went with some of his other work.

Now that we have five books to examine, the connections are more easily discernible. It seems to me that Caldwell has elsewhere retained the same balked religiosity as distinguishes "The Sacrilege," but has merely poured it into less formidable molds. We may detect it, transformed, as the incentive leading him to blaspheme and profane for our enjoyment. We may glimpse this balked religiosity in the symbolic transgressions and death penalties that give shape to the plots of *Tobacco Road* and *God's Little Acre*. It is the explicit subject matter of much conversation in all his novels. It is revealed by an almost primitive concern with sexual taboos, and with fertility rites rising in opposition to the theme of castration. In its temperate, more social aspects, it shows as a tendency to deny humans their humaneness, as though the author, secretly abased, wanted to "drag others down" with him. Entertainingly, it appears in still more attenuated form as caricature and humor, the mental state of "refusal" here inducing extravagant incongruities that sometimes can be received with laughter, but are frequently so closely connected with degradation and acute suffering that the effect is wholly grim. Toward the end of his longer works, the goad of balked religiosity provokes grandiloquent moralistic passages wherein his subnormal mannikins, strangely elated by the story's symbolism, transcend themselves and speak of vital purpose with almost evangelical fervor (plus a slight suggestion that they had read D. H. Lawrence). And in an unexpected episode of *Journeyman,* his latest book, Caldwell has even gone so far as to introduce a quality of other-worldliness into the very midst of his human rabbit hutch—for in no other way can I interpret the section (which Horace Gregory has selected for approval) where three men take turns at peering out through a crack in the wall of the barn, while one sermonizes: "It's sitting there and looking through the crack at the trees all day long that sort of gets me. I don't know what it is, and it might not be nothing at all when you figure it out. But it's not the knowing about it, anyway—it's just sitting there and looking through it that sort of makes me feel like heaven can't be so doggone far away."

In taking balked religiosity as the underlying theme upon which his successive works are the variations, I do not want to imply that

Caldwell, like Hemingway, is preparing himself for a return to Rome. His powerful story "Kneel to the Rising Sun" indicates that he can make the change from negativism to affirmation by choices usually called secular. In so far as he is moved by the need of salvation, he seems minded to find it in the alignments of political exhortation, by striving mainly to see that we and he take the right side on matters of social justice. But as partial vindication of my proposal that his cult of incongruity seems to stem from the same source as his social propaganda, I should note that, precisely in this story of a lynching, his emphasis upon the playful scrambling of the old proprieties abates: instead of the humorist's refusal, as shown in his earlier zest to garble the conventions, we get a sober assertion of positive values. He does not merely act to outrage an old perspective by throwing its orders of right and wrong into disarray: he subscribes to an alternative perspective, with positive rights and wrongs of its own, and with definite indications as to what form he wants our sympathies and antagonisms to take. Incidentally, this development suggests the ways in which a motivation essentially nonpolitical or noneconomic can be harnessed in the service of political or economic criticism.

Whether one so apt at entertaining us by *muddling* our judgments will be equally fertile in *stabilizing* judgments remains to be seen. My guess would be that he won't, since he would have to master a whole new technique of expression. His very abilities tend to work against him. Recently I heard one man complain that Caldwell "has yet to learn that the revolution begins above the belt." And I incline to suspect that, in the learning, he may begin to find himself psychologically unemployed. A literary method is tyrannical—it is a writer's leopard-spots—it molds what a writer can say by determining what he can see; hence I should imagine that Caldwell would have to develop by satirizing more complex people rather than by pleading unmistakably for simple ones. But that is a guess about tomorrow's weather.

When I say that Caldwell's particular aptitude has been in scrambling or garbling proprieties, I refer to his deft way of putting the wrong things together. An unendowed writer, for instance, might strain to engross us by lurid description of the sexual act—and the result would be negligible. But such an uninventive writer would probably be quite "proper" in the sense that he accepted the usual conventions as to the privacy of this act. Caldwell can be much more stimulating by merely so altering the customary situation that people are looking on and commenting in the blandest fashion, as in the comically inappropriate episode of this nature in *God's Little Acre*. Or he may have Ty Ty say, without confusion, such things to his daughters and daughter-in-law as would "properly" be said only under the greatest of morbid intensity. By an astounding trick of oversimplification, Caldwell puts people into complex social situations while making them act with the scant, crude tropisms of an insect—and the result is cunning, where Lawrence, by a variant of the same pattern, is as unwieldy as an elephant in his use of vulgar words for romantic love-making. Probably only in the orgy at the end of *Journeyman* does Caldwell become so undiplomatic in his treatment. Here, with almost the literalness of an inventory, he has us observe in each member of the congregation that phenomenon which so mortified Saint John of the Cross, the fact that, since the body has less channels of expression than the mind, acute religious ecstasy may be paralleled neurologically by sexual orgasm.

In the psychology textbooks, we read accounts of experiments whereby the higher centers of an animal's brain are removed, with the result that the animal's responses to stimuli are greatly simplified. A frog, so decerebrated, may jump when prodded, eat when fed, and croak when caressed—but it is evident that with the operation the poor fellow's personality has vanished. He has become less like a living organism, and more like a doorbell, which rings when you press the button. He has lost the part of himself that is sometimes called free will and which Bergson names the "center of indetermination." And his ways, as compared with the ways of a whole frog, are distinctly grotesque. Caldwell often seems to have performed such an operation upon the minds of his characters. As Ty Ty Walden complains in *God's Little Acre,* "There was a mean trick played on us somewhere. God put us in the body of animals and tried to make us act like people." It is a just complaint of Ty Ty's, as the creature of his own private creator. What the decerebrated frog is to the whole frog, Caldwell's characters are to real people. In view of which, it is positively incredible that his extravaganzas, imagined in a world essentially as fantastic as Swift's, should ever have passed for realism.

Pearl, the image of better things in *Tobacco Road,* does not even *speak.* Anderson's gropers stuttered, but in this book the golden-haired child wife who is charged with the novelistic duty of upholding a little corner of glory in the midst of degradation, is totally inarticulate. For her there is no such verbal key as that with which the great sonneteer unlocked his heart. Though married, she sleeps alone; she will not look at her uncouth husband; she refuses to discuss his appetites with him (she cries when he beats her, but "Lov did not consider that as conversation"); and in the end, still wordless, she vanishes, doubtless to become a prostitute in Augusta. Silk stockings in the city, we feel, is her noblest conceivable utopian negation of the physical and spiritual impoverishment all about her; but to her understanding of this little, she will bring a deep, innate delicacy, invisible to all but the novelist and his readers.

In this discussion of Pearl, I may seem to have involved myself in a contradiction. For I speak of Caldwell's subhuman characters, yet I credit them with great delicacy. Here we come to the subtlest feature of Caldwell's method. Where the author leaves out so much, the reader begins making up the difference for himself. Precisely by omitting humaneness where humaneness is most called for, he may stimulate the reader to supply it. When the starved grandmother in *Tobacco Road* lies dying, with her face ground into the soil, and no one shows even an onlooker's interest in her wretchedness, we are prodded to anguish. When these automata show some bare inkling of sociality, it may seem like a flash of ultimate wisdom. I suspect that, in putting the responsibility upon his readers, he is taking more out of the community pile than he puts in. Perhaps he is using up what we already had, rather than adding to our store. He has evoked in us a quality, but he has not materialized it with sufficient quantity. In any event, the silence of Pearl in *Tobacco Road* and the sober burlesque of the men peering through the crack in *Journeyman* are of a piece with the strange albino of *God's Little Acre,* the "conjur" who makes the simple, lyrical declaration to Darling Jill (herself graced with one of the loveliest names in all fiction):

"I wish I had married you," he said, his hands trembling beside her. "I didn't know there was a girl so beautiful anywhere in the country. You're the prettiest girl I've ever seen. You're so soft, and you talk like birdsong, and you smell so good. . . ."

I have denied that Caldwell is a realist. In his tomfoolery he comes closer to the Dadaists; when his grotesqueness is serious, he is a Superrealist. We might compromise by calling him over all a Symbolist (if by a Symbolist we mean a writer whose work serves most readily as case history for the psychologist and whose plots are more intelligible when interpreted as dreams). In *The Saturday Review of Literature* some time ago, Dr. Lawrence S. Kubie took as particularly significant the absence of the motherly woman in Caldwell's fictions, with attendant cult of sterility. And his article gave many relevant clues as to the *nonrational* linkages involved in the imagery of *God's Little Acre*.

In books of complex realistic texture, such as the great social novels of the nineteenth century, we may feel justified in considering the psychologist's comments as an intrusion when he would have us find there merely a sublimation of a few rudimentary impulses. The important thing is not the base, but the superstructure. With fantastic simplifications of the Caldwell sort, however, the symbolic approach has more relevance. Thus, the selection of extreme starvation as a theme for *Tobacco Road* is found to take on a significance besides that of realistic justification when we link it with passages in *God's Little Acre* where Ty Ty, admiring Griselda, declares that the sight of her "rising beauties" makes him feel inspired to "get down and lick something." How possibly explain as mere reporting the episode in *God's Little Acre* about the girls who have replaced the men in the factory, and of whom we read the dreamlike statement, "When they reached the street, they ran back to the ivy-colored wall and pressed their bodies against it and touched it with their lips. The men who had been standing idly before it all day long came and dragged them home and beat them unmercifully for their infidelity"? A factory that could induce such surprising antics must have peculiar connotations not realistically there. And perhaps we come closer to them when recalling how, in this same factory, where the rebellion of the workers takes very unreal forms, Will finally fulfills his determination to "turn on the power," but only after his perverted rape of Griselda. When the old grandmother dies, the sight of her face in the dirt simply reminds her son Jeeter that the soil is right for planting. Immediately after, he is destroyed by fire.

The symbolic relations submerged here begin to suggest themselves when we recall the following facts: In both *Tobacco Road* and *God's Little Acre* we are told that there are two types of people, those who stay on the farm and those who go to the factory. Both Jeeter of *Tobacco Road* and Ty Ty of *God's Little Acre* are the kind that stay on the farm, the first hoping to plant again (a frustrated hope) and the second digging in the bowels of the earth for gold (an exceptional ob-

session to motivate an entire book about contemporary Georgia, though
we may legitimately remember here the golden-haired Pearl of *Tobacco
Road*). In one of the short stories, "Crown Fire," we learn from the
course of the plot that the fire symbol is linked with partial female
acquiescence; and in "The Sacrilege," where the "offense" is unnamed,
we are told, "My mother saw from her bed the reflection in the sky of
red wind-fanned flames. She carried me out into the street and we sat
in the red mud shivering and crying"—sitting in this same soil with
which Jeeter is so impotently preoccupied (since he cannot buy the
seed for planting) and which Ty Ty turns into sterility by digging there
for gold. After Will carries out in actuality the perverse inclination
Ty Ty speaks of, Will can "turn on the power" in the factory. But
though Will here seems to deputize for Ty Ty, Ty Ty's son commits
a murder and must run away. Ty Ty moans that blood has been spilled
upon his land, whereupon he is freed of his obsession to dig gold; and
as the son is leaving, Ty Ty wills that God's little acre be always under
him. Both books are thus permeated with symbolic sins, symbolic
punishments, followed by symbolic purification. At the end of each,
and following the orgy in *Journeyman,* there is the feeling that a cleans-
ing had taken place, that the character who, at the last transformation,
is the bearer of the author's identity, is free to "start anew." All this is
magic, not reason; and I think that we are entitled to inspect it for
the processes of magic. The balked religiosity of which we spoke is
evidently linked with the devious manifestations of "incest-awe"; the
plots are subtly guided by the logic of dreams.

I am not by any means satisfied by the psychoanalytic readings of
such processes to date, though I do believe that in moralistic fantasies
of the Caldwell type, where the dull characters become so strangely
inspired at crucial moments, we are present at a poetic law court where
judgments are passed upon kinds of transgression inaccessible to
jurists, with such odd penalties as no Code Napoléon could ever
schematize.

The short stories (republished in *American Earth* and *We Are the
Living*) as a whole seem too frail. They are hardly more than jottings
in a diary, mere *situations* that Caldwell, with his exceptional turn for
narrative and his liquid style, manages to palm off as plots. I call them
diary jottings because they often give the impression of having suggested themselves to him in this wise: If you were sitting alone in a
strange room, you might think, "What if someone knocked at the

door?" If Caldwell were similarly placed, such a thought might occur to him, and there he would have his story.

He has a sharper sense of beginnings than most writers, as witness in the long story, *Journeyman,* Semon Dye's formal entrance in the lavishly balky and noisy car. Here is a mock announcement of the hero's approach, done with such a blare and fanfare of brasses as Wagner summons to herald the approach of Siegfried. Thus, the author tends to begin with some oddity of situation, which as likely as not suggested itself without a resolution, so that the story merely fades away rather than closes. He shows a surprisingly naïve delight in all the possible ramifications of the thought that girls may be without panties, and he seems to have searched the length and breadth of the country for new situations whereby some significant part or parts can be exposed for us. The basic formula seems to be the use of two unrelated orders of events until they are felt to be related. He gets very appealing pictures of adolescent love—but his most successful venture in the shorter form is probably "Country Full of Swedes," where a family returns to their house across the road after a couple of years' absence, and their sudden prevalence in the locality is amusingly magnified until, for all their obvious peacefulness, they take on the qualities of a vast invasion.

Caldwell's greatest vice is unquestionably repetitiousness. He seems as contented as a savage to say the same thing again and again. Repetition in his prose is so extreme as almost to perform the function of rhyme in verse. In analyzing the first four chapters of *Tobacco Road,* I found that it was simply a continual rearrangement of the same subjects in different sequences: Jeeter wants Lov's turnips, Lov wants Jeeter to make Pearl sleep with him, Jeeter's own turnips all have "damn-blasted green-gutted turnip-worms," hair-lipped Ellie May is sidling up to Lov, Dude won't stop "chunking" a ball against the loose clapboards, Jeeter hopes to sell a load of wood in Augusta—about ten more such details, regiven in changing order, make the content of forty pages. Sometimes when reading Caldwell I feel as though I were playing with my toes.

On a Criticism
of Thomas Hardy

Katherine Anne Porter

The Bishop of Wakefield, after reading Thomas Hardy's latest (and as it proved, his last) novel, *Jude the Obscure,* threw it in the fire, or said he did. It was a warm midsummer, and Hardy suggested that the bishop may have been speaking figuratively, heresy and bonfires being traditionally associated in his mind, or that he may have gone to the kitchen stove. The bishop wrote to the papers that he had burned the book, in any case, and he wrote also to a local M.P. who caused the horrid work to be withdrawn from the public library, promising besides to examine any other novels of Mr. Hardy carefully before allowing them to circulate among the bishop's flock. It was a good day's work, added to the protests of the reviewers for the press, and twenty-five years of snubbing and nagging from the professional moralists of his time; Thomas Hardy resigned as novelist for good. As in the case of the criticism presently to be noted, the attack on his book included also an attack on his personal character, and the bishop's action wounded Thomas Hardy. He seems to have remarked in effect "that if the bishop could have known him as he was, he would have found a man whose personal conduct, views of morality, and of vital facts of religion, hardly differed from his own."

This is an indirect quotation by his second wife, devoted apologist and biographer, and it exposes almost to the point of pathos the basic, unteachable charity of Hardy's mind. Of all evil emotions generated in the snake-pit of human nature, theological hatred is perhaps the most savage, being based on intellectual concepts and disguised in the highest spiritual motives. And what could rouse this hatred in a theologian like the sight of a moral, virtuous, well-conducted man who presumed to agree with him in the "vital facts of religion," at the same time refusing to sign the articles of faith? It was long ago agreed among the Inquisitors that these are the dangerous men.

The bishop threw the book in the fire in 1896. In 1928, Mrs. Hardy was happy to record that another "eminent clergyman of the church" had advised any priest preparing to become a village rector to make first a good retreat and then a careful study of Thomas Hardy's novels. "From Thomas Hardy," concluded this amiable man, "he would learn the essential dignity of country people and what deep and passionate interest belongs to every individual life. You cannot treat them in the mass: each single soul is to be the object of your special and peculiar prayer."

Aside from the marginal note on the social point of view which made it necessary thus to warn prospective rectors that country people were also human entities, each possessed of a soul important, however rural, to God, and the extraordinary fact that an agnostic novelist could teach them what the church and their own hearts could not, it is worth noting again that churchmen differ even as the laymen on questions of morality, and can preach opposing doctrine from the same text. The history of these differences, indeed, is largely the calamitous history of institutional religion. In 1934, a layman turned preacher, almost like a character in a Hardy novel, runs true to his later form by siding with the bishop. Since his spectacular conversion to the theology and politics of the Church of England, Mr. T. S. Eliot's great gifts as a critic have been deflected into channels where they do not flow with their old splendor and depth. More and more his literary judgments have assumed the tone of lay sermons by a parochial visitor, and his newer style is perhaps at its most typical in his criticism of Thomas Hardy:

The work of the late Thomas Hardy represents an interesting example of a powerful personality uncurbed by any institutional attachment or by submission to any objective beliefs; unhampered by any ideas, or even by what sometimes acts as a partial restraint upon inferior writers, the desire to please a large public. He seems to me to have written as nearly for the sake of " self-expression" as a man well can, and the self which he had to express does not strike me as a particularly wholesome or edifying matter of communication. He was indifferent even to the prescripts of good writing: he wrote sometimes overpoweringly well, but always very carelessly; at times his style touches sublimity without ever having passed through the stage of being good. In consequence of his self-absorption, he makes a great deal of landscape; for landscape is a passive creature which lends itself to an author's mood. Landscape is fitted, too, for the purpose of an author who is interested not at all in men's minds, but only in their emotions, and perhaps only in men as vehicles for emotions.

After some useful general reflections on the moral undesirability of extreme emotionalism, meant as a rebuke to Hardy and to which we shall return briefly later, Mr. Eliot proceeds:

I was [in a previous lecture] . . . concerned with illustrating the limiting and crippling effect of a separation from tradition and orthodoxy upon certain writers whom I nevertheless hold up for admiration for what they have attempted against great obstacles. Here I am concerned with the intrusion of the *diabolic* into modern literature in consequence of the same lamentable state of affairs; . . . I am afraid that even if you can entertain the notion of a positive power for evil working through human agency, you may still have a very inaccurate notion of what Evil is, and will find it difficult to believe that it may operate through men of genius of the most excellent character. I doubt whether what I am saying can convey very much to anyone for whom the doctrine of Original Sin is not a very real and tremendous thing.

Granting the premises with extreme reservations, Thomas Hardy was a visible proof of the validity of this disturbing doctrine. He had received early religious training in the Established Church, and by precept and example in a household of the most sincere piety, and of the most aggressive respectability. He remarked once, that of all the names he had been called, such as agnostic (which tag he adopted later, ruefully), atheist, immoralist, pessimist, and so on, a properly fitting one had been overlooked altogether: "churchy." He had once meant to be a parson. His relations with the church of his childhood had been of the homely, intimate, almost filial sort. His grandfather, his father, his uncle, all apt in music, had been for forty years the mainstay of the village choir. He felt at home in the place, as to its customs, feasts, services. He had a great love for the ancient churches, and as a young architect his aesthetic sense was outraged by the fashionable and silly "restorations" amounting to systematic destruction which overtook some of the loveliest examples of medieval church architecture in England during the nineteenth century. His devotion to the past, and to the history and character of his native Wessex became at times a kind of antiquarian fustiness. His personal morals were irreproachable, he had an almost queasy sense of the awful and permanent effects of wrongdoing on the human soul and destiny. Most of his novels deal with these consequences; his most stupendous tragedies are the result of one false step on the part of his hero or heroine. Genius aside, he had all the makings of a good, honest, church-going country squire; but the worm of original sin was settled in his mind, of all fatal places; and his mind led him out of the tradition of orthodoxy into another tradition of equal antiquity, equal importance, equal seriousness, a body of opinion running parallel throughout history to the body of law in church and state: the great tradition of dissent. He went, perhaps not so much by choice as by compulsion of *belief*, with the Inquirers rather than the Believers. His mind, not the greatest, certainly not the most flexible, but a good, candid, strong mind, asked simply the oldest, most terrifying questions, and the traditional, orthodox answers of the church did not satisfy it. It is easy to see how this, from the churchly point of view, is diabolic. But the yawning abyss between question and answer remains the same, and until this abyss is closed, the dissent will remain, persistent, obdurate, a kind of church itself, with its leaders, teachers, saints, martyrs, heroes; a thorn in the flesh of orthodoxy but I think not necessarily of the Devil on that account, unless the intellect and all its questions are really from the Devil, as the Eden myth states explicitly, as the church seems to teach, and Mr. Eliot tends to confirm.

There is a great deal to examine in the paragraphs quoted above, but two words in their context illustrate perfectly the unbridgeable abyss between Hardy's question and Mr. Eliot's answer. One is, of course, the word *diabolic*. The other is *edifying*. That struck and held my eye in a maze, for a moment. With no disrespect I hope to conventional piety, may I venture that in the regions of art, as of religion, edification is not the highest form of intellectual or spiritual experience. It is a happy truth that Hardy's novels are really not edifying. The mental and emotional states roused and maintained in the reader of *The Mayor of Casterbridge* or *The Return of the Native* are considerably richer, invoked out of deeper sources in the whole human consciousness, more substantially nourishing, than this lukewarm word can express. A novel by Thomas Hardy can be a chastening experience, an appalling one, there is great and sober pleasure to be got out of those novels, the mind can be disturbed and the heart made extremely uneasy, but the complacency of edification is absent, as it is apt to be from any true tragedy.

Mr. Eliot includes Lawrence and Joyce in his list of literary men of "diabolic" tendencies. Deploring Lawrence's "untrained" mind, he adds: "A trained mind like that of Mr. Joyce is always aware of what master it is serving . . ."

Untrained minds have always been a nuisance to the military police of orthodoxy. God-intoxicated mystics and untidy saints with only a white blaze of divine love where their minds should have been, are perpetually creating almost as much disorder within the law as outside it. To have a trained mind is no guarantee at all that the possessor is going to walk infallibly in the path of virtue, though he hardly fails in the letter of the law. St. Joan of Arc and St. Francis in their own ways have had something to say about that. The combination of a trained mind and incorruptible virtue is ideal, and therefore rare: St. Thomas More is the first name that occurs to me as example. Hardy's mind, which had rejected the conclusions though not the ethical discipline of organized religion (and he knew that its ethical system in essentials is older than Christianity), was not altogether an untrained one, and like all true Dissenters, he knew the master he was serving: his conscience. He had the mathematical certainties of music and architecture, and the daily, hourly training of a serious artist laboring at his problems over a period of more than half a century. That he was unhampered by ideas is therefore highly improbable. He wrote a few fine poems among a large number of poor ones. He wrote fifteen novels, of which a round half-dozen are well the equal of any novel in the English language; even if this is not to say he is the equal of Flaubert or of Dostoievsky. His notebooks testify to a constant preoccupation with ideas, not all of them his own, naturally, for he inherited them from a very respectable race of thinkers, sound in heterodoxy.

He had got out of the very air of the nineteenth century something from Lucian, something from Leonardo, something from Erasmus, from Montaigne, from Voltaire, from the Encyclopaedists, and there were some powerful nineteenth-century Inquirers, too, of whom we need only mention Darwin, perhaps. Scientific experiment leads first to skepticism; but we have seen in our time, how, pursued to the verge of the infinite, it sometimes leads back again to a form of mysticism. There is at the heart of the universe a riddle no man can solve, and in the end, God may be the answer. But this is fetching up at a great distance still from orthodoxy, and still must be suspect in that quarter. Grant that the idea of God is the most splendid single act of the creative human imagination, and that all his multiple faces and attributes correspond to some need and satisfy some deep desire in mankind; still, for the Inquirers, it is impossible not to conclude that this mystical concept has been harnessed rudely to machinery of the most mundane sort, and has been made to serve the ends of an organization which, ruling under divine guidance, has ruled very little better, and in some respects, worse, than certain rather mediocre but frankly man-made systems of government. And it has often lent its support to the worst evils in secular government, fighting consistently on the side of the heavy artillery. And it has seemed at times not to know the difference between Good and Evil, but to get them hopelessly confused with legalistic right and wrong; justifying the most cynical expedients of worldly government by a high morality; and committing the most savage crimes against human life for the love of God. When you consider the political career of the church in the light of its professed origins and purposes, perhaps Original Sin *is* the answer. But Hardy preferred to remove the argument simply to another ground. As to himself, in his personal life, he had a Franciscan tenderness in regard to children, animals, laborers, the poor, the mad, the insulted and injured. He suffered horror and indignation at human injustice, more especially at the kind committed by entrenched authority and power upon the helpless. In middle age he remembered and recorded an early shock he received on hearing that, in his neighborhood, a young boy, a farm laborer, was found dead of sheer starvation in the fruitful field he had worked to cultivate. When he was planning *The Dynasts,* he wrote in his notebook: "The human race is to be shown as one great net-work or tissue which quivers in every part when one point is shaken, like a spider's web if touched." For Hardy, the death of that boy was a blow that set the whole great web trembling; and all mankind received a lasting wound. Here was a human fate for which human acts were responsible, and it would not serve Hardy at all to put the blame on Original Sin, or the inscrutable decrees of Divine Providence, or any other of the manifold devices for not letting oneself be too uncomfortable at the spectacle of merely human suffering. He was painfully uncomfortable all his life, and his discomfort was not for himself—he was an extraordinarily selfless sort of man—but the pervasiveness of what he considered senseless and unnecessary human misery. Out of the strange simplicity of his own unworldliness he could write at the age of 78: "As to pessimism. My motto is, first correctly diagnose the complaint—in this case human ills—and ascertain the cause: then set about finding a remedy if one exists. The motto or practise of the optimists is: Blind the eyes to the real malady, and use empirical panaceas to suppress the symptoms." Reasonableness: the use of the human intelligence directed toward the best human solution of human ills; such, if you please, was the unedifying proposal of this diabolic soul.

He himself, in his few remarks on public and practical affairs, had always been very reasonable. War, he believed, was an abomination, but it recurred again and again, apparently an incurable ill. He had no theories to advance, but wished merely that those who made wars would admit the real motives; aside from the waste and destruction, which he viewed with purely humane feelings, he objected to the immoralities of statecraft and religion in the matter. He was opposed to capital punishment on the simple grounds that no man has the right to take away the life of another. But he believed it acted as a material deterrent to crime, and if the judges would admit that it was social expediency, with no foundation in true morality, that was another matter. On the Irish question he was acute and explicit in expressing his view in this direction. "Though he did not enter it here [in his notebook] Hardy . . . said of Home Rule that it was a staring dilemma, of which good policy and good philanthropy were the huge horns. Policy for England required that it should not be granted; humanity to Ireland that it should. Neither Liberals nor Conservatives would honestly own up to this opposition between two moralities, but speciously insisted that humanity and policy were both on one side—of course their own." At another time he complained that most of the philosophers began on the theory that the earth had been designed as a comfortable place for man. He could no more accept this theory than he could the theological notion that the world was a testing ground for the soul of man in preparation for eternity, and that his sufferings were part of a "divine" plan, or indeed, so far as the personal fate of mankind was concerned, of any plan at all. He did believe with a great deal of common sense that man could make the earth a more endurable place for himself if he would, but he also realized that human nature is not grounded in common sense, that there is a deep place in it where the mind does not go, where the blind monsters sleep and wake, war among themselves, and feed upon death.

He did believe that there is "a power that rules the world" though he did not name it, nor could he accept the names that had been given it, or any explanation of its motives. He could only watch its operations, and to me it seems he concluded that both malevolence and benevolence originated in the mind of man, and the warring forces were within him alone; such plan as existed in regard to him he had created for himself, his Good and his Evil were alike the mysterious inventions of his own mind; and why this was so, Hardy could not pretend to say. He knew there was an element in human nature not subject to mathematical equation or the water-tight theories of dogma, and this intransigent, measureless force, divided against itself, in conflict alike with its own system of laws and the unknown laws of the universe, was the real theme of Hardy's novels; a genuinely tragic theme in the grand manner, of sufficient weight and shapelessness to try the powers of any artist. Generally so reluctant to admit any influence, Hardy admits to a study of the Greek dramatists, and with his curious sense of proportion, he decided that the Wessex countryside was also the dwelling place of the spirit of tragedy; that the histories of certain obscure persons in that limited locality bore a strong family resemblance to those of the great, the ancient, and the legendary. Mr. Eliot finds Hardy's beloved Wessex a "stage setting," such as the Anglo-Saxon heart loves; and Hardy's Wessex farmers "period peasants pleasing to the metropolitan imagination." Hardy was Anglo-Saxon and Norman; that landscape was in his blood. Those period peasants were people he had known all his life, and I think that in this passage Mr. Eliot simply speaks as a man of the town, like those young rectors who need to be reminded of the individual dignity and importance of the country people. Further, taking all the Hardy characters in a lump, he finds in them only blind animal emotionalism, and remarks: ". . . strong passion is only interesting or significant in strong men; those who abandon themselves without resistance to excitements which tend to deprive them of reason become merely instruments of feeling and lose their humanity; and unless there is moral resistance and conflict there is no meaning." True in part: and to disagree in detail would lead to an endless discussion of *what* exactly constitutes interest in the work of a writer; *what* gives importance to his characters, their intrinsic value as human beings, or the value their creator is able to give them by his own imaginative view of them.

Hardy seems almost to agree with Mr. Eliot for once: "The best tragedy—highest tragedy in short—is that of the WORTHY encompassed by the INEVITABLE. The tragedies of immoral and worthless people are not of the best." My own judgment is that Hardy's characters are in every way superior to those of Mr. Eliot, and for precisely the reason the two writers are agreed upon. Hardy's people suffer the tragedy of being, Mr. Eliot's of not-being. The strange creatures inhabiting the wasteland of Mr. Eliot's particular scene are for the most part immoral and worthless, the apeneck Sweeneys, the Grishkins, and all. . . . They have for us precisely the fascination the poet has endowed them with, and they also have great significance: they are the sinister chorus of the poet's own tragedy, they represent the sum of the poet's vision of human beings without God and without faith, a world of horror surrounding this soul thirsting for faith in God. E. M. Forster has remarked that *The Waste Land* is a poem of real horror, the tragedy of the rains that came too late—or perhaps, never came at all. For how else can one explain the self-absorbed despair of Eliot's point of view, even in religion? That uncontrolled emotion of loathing for his fellow pilgrims in this mortal life? Was there not one soul worth tender treatment, not one good man interesting enough to the poet to inhabit his tragic scene? It is a curious paradox. Hardy feels no contempt for his characters at all; he writes of them as objectively as if they existed by themselves, they are never the background, the chorus, for the drama of his own experience. Beside Eliot's wasteland, with its inhuman beings, Hardy's Wessex seems an airy, familiar place, his characters at least have living blood in them, and though Mr. Eliot complains that Hardy was not interested in the minds of men, still their headpieces are not deliberately stuffed with straw by their creator.

Hardy's characters are full of moral conflicts and of decisions arrived at by mental processes, certainly. Jude, Gabriel Oak, Clym Yeobright, above all, Henchard, are men who have decisions to make, and if they do not make them entirely on the plane of reason, it is because Hardy was interested most in that hairline dividing the rational from the instinctive, the opposition, we might call it, between nature and second nature; that is, between instinct and the habits of thought fixed upon the individual by his education and his environment. Such characters of his as are led by their emotions come to tragedy; he seems to say that following the emotions blindly leads to disaster. Romantic miscalculation of the possibilities of life, of love, of the situation; of refusing to reason their way out of their predicament; these are the causes of disaster in Hardy's novels. Angel Clare is a man of the highest principles, trained in belief, religion, observance of moral law. His failure to understand the real nature of Christianity makes a monster of him at the great crisis of his life. The Mayor of Casterbridge spends the balance of his life in atonement and reparation for a brutal wrong committed in drunkenness and anger; his past overtakes and destroys him. Hardy had an observing eye, a remembering mind; he did not need the Greeks to teach him that the Furies do arrive punctually, and that neither act, nor will, nor intention will serve to deflect a man's destiny from him, once he has taken the step which decides it.

A word about that style which Mr. Eliot condemns as touching "sublimity without ever having passed through the stage of being good." Hardy has often been called by critics who love him, the good simple man of no ideas, the careless workman of genius who never learned to write, who cared nothing for the way of saying a thing.

His own testimony is that he cared a great deal for *what* he said: "My art is to intensify the expression of things, as is done by Crivelli, Bellini, etc., so that the heart and inner meaning is made vividly visible." Again: "The Realities to be the true realities of life, hitherto called abstractions. The old material realities to be placed behind the former, as shadowy accessories." His notebooks are dry, reluctant, unmethodical; he seems to have spent his time and energies in actual labor at his task rather than theorizing about it, but he remarks once: "Looking around on a well-selected shelf of fiction, how few stories of any length does one recognize as well told from beginning to end! The first half of this story, the last half of that, the middle of another . . . the modern art of narration is yet in its infancy." He made few notes on technical procedure, but one or two are valuable as a clue to his directions: "A story must be exceptional enough to justify its telling. We tale tellers are all Ancient Mariners, and none of us is warranted in stopping Wedding Guests . . . unless he has something more unusual to relate than the ordinary experiences of every average man and woman." Again: "The whole secret of fiction and drama—in the constructional part—lies in the adjustment of things unusual to things eternal and universal. The writer who knows exactly how exceptional, and how non-exceptional, his events should be made, possesses the key to the art."

So much for theory. Not much about the importance of style, the care for the word, the just and perfect construction of a paragraph. But Hardy was not a careless writer. The difference between his first and last editions proves this, in matters of style aside from his painful reconstruction of his manuscripts mutilated for serial publication. He wrote and wrote again, and he never found it easy. He lacked elegance, he never learned the trick of the whip-lash phrase, the complicated lariat twirling of the professed stylists. His prose lumbers along, it jogs, it creaks, it hesitates, it is as dull as certain long passages in the Tolstoy of *War and Peace,* for example. That celebrated first scene on Egdon Heath, in *The Return of the Native.* Who does not remember it? And in actual re-reading, what could be duller? What could be more labored than his introduction of the widow Yeobright at the heath fire among the dancers, or more unconvincing than the fears of the timid boy that the assembly are literally raising the Devil? Except for this; in my memory of that episode, as in dozens of others in many of Hardy's novels, I have seen it, I was there. When I read it, it almost disappears from view, and afterward comes back, phraseless, living in its somber clearness, as Hardy meant it to do, I feel certain. This to my view is the chief quality of good prose as distinguished from poetry. By his own testimony, he limited his territory by choice, set boundaries to his material, focused his point of view like a burning glass down on a definite aspect of things. He practiced a stringent discipline, severely excised and eliminated all that seemed to him not useful or appropriate to his plan. In the end his work was the sum of his experience, he arrived at his particular true testimony; along the way, sometimes, many times, he wrote sublimely.

Baudelaire

T. S. Eliot

I

Anything like a just appreciation of Baudelaire has been slow to arrive in England, and still is defective or partial even in France. There are, I think, special reasons for the difficulty in estimating his worth and finding his place. For one thing, Baudelaire was in some ways far in advance of the point of view of his own time, and yet was very much of it, very largely partook of its limited merits, faults, and fashions. For one thing, he had a great part in forming a generation of poets after him; and in England he had what is in a way the misfortune to be first and extravagantly advertised by Swinburne, and taken up by the followers of Swinburne. He was universal, and at the same time confined by a fashion which he himself did most to create. To dissociate the permanent from the temporary, to distinguish the man from his influence, and finally to detach him from the associations of those English poets who first admired him, is no small task. His comprehensiveness itself makes difficulty, for it tempts the partisan critic, even now, to adopt Baudelaire as the patron of his own beliefs.

It is the purpose of this essay to affirm the importance of Baudelaire's prose works, a purpose justified by the translation of one of those works which is indispensable for any student of his poetry.[1] This is to see Baudelaire as something more than the author of the *Fleurs du Mal,* and consequently to revise somewhat our estimate of that book. Baudelaire came into vogue at a time when "Art for Art's

From *Selected Essays* 1917-1932 by T. S. Eliot. Copyright 1932 by Harcourt, Brace and Company. Reprinted by permission of the publisher.

[1] *Journaux Intimes,* translated by Christopher Isherwood, and published by the Blackamore Press and the Beacon Press.

sake" was a dogma. The care which he took over his poems, and the fact that contrary to the fluency of his time, both in France and England he restricted himself to this one volume, encouraged the opinion that Baudelaire was an artist exclusively for art's sake. The doctrine does not, of course, really apply to anybody; no one applied it less than Pater, who spent many years, not so much in illustrating it, as in expounding it as a *theory of life,* which is not the same thing at all. But it was a doctrine which did affect criticism and appreciation, and which did obstruct a proper judgment of Baudelaire. He is in fact a greater man than was imagined, though perhaps not such a perfect poet.

Baudelaire has, I believe, been called a fragmentary Dante, for what that description is worth. It is true that many people who enjoy Dante enjoy Baudelaire; but the differences are as important as the similarities. Baudelaire's inferno is very different in quality and significance from that of Dante. Truer, I think, would be the description of Baudelaire as a later and more limited Goethe. As we begin to see him now, he represents his own age in somewhat the same way as that in which Goethe represents an earlier age. As a critic of the present generation, Mr. Peter Quennell has recently said in his book, *Baudelaire and the Symbolists:*

He had enjoyed a *sense of his own age,* had recognized its pattern while the pattern was yet incomplete, and—because it is only our misapprehension of the present which prevents our looking into the immediate future, our ignorance of today and of its real as apart from its spurious tendencies and requirements—had anticipated many problems, both on the aesthetic and on the moral plane, in which the fate of modern poetry is still concerned.

Now the man who has this sense of his age is hard to analyse. He is exposed to its follies as well as sensitive to its inventions; and in Baudelaire, as well as in Goethe, is some of the outmoded nonsense of his time. The parallel between the German poet who has always been the symbol of perfect "health" in every sense, as well as of universal curiosity, and the French poet who has been the symbol of morbidity in mind and concentrated interests in work, may seem paradoxical. But after this lapse of time the difference between "health" and "morbidity" in the two men becomes more negligible; there is something artificial and even priggish about Goethe's healthiness, as there is about Baudelaire's unhealthiness; we have passed beyond men with restless, critical, curious minds and the "sense of the age"; both men who un-derstood and foresaw a great deal. Goethe, it is true, was interested in many subjects which Baudelaire left alone; but by Baudelaire's time it was no longer necessary for a man to embrace such varied interests in order to have the sense of the age; and in retrospect some of Goethe's studies seem to us (not altogether justly) to have been merely dilettante hobbies. The most of Baudelaire's prose writings (with the exception of the translations from Poe, which are of less interest to an English reader) are as important as the most of Goethe. They throw light on the *Fleurs du Mal* certainly, but they also expand immensely our appre-ciation of their author.

It was once the mode to take Baudelaire's Satanism seriously, as it is now the tendency to present Baudelaire as a serious and Catholic Christian. Especially as a prelude to the *Journaux Intimes* this diversity of opinion needs some discussion. I think that the latter view—that Baudelaire is essentially Christian—is nearer the truth than the former, but it needs considerable reservation. When Baudelaire's Satanism is dissociated from its less creditable paraphernalia, it amounts to a dim intuition of a part, but a very important part, of Christianity. Satanism itself, so far as not merely an affectation, was an attempt to get into Christianity by the back door. Genuine blasphemy, genuine in spirit and not purely verbal, is the product of partial belief, and is as impossi-ble to the complete atheist as to the perfect Christian. It is a way of affirming belief. This state of partial belief is manifest throughout the *Journaux Intimes*. What is significant about Baudelaire is his theological innocence. He is discovering Christianity for himself; he is not assum-ing it as a fashion or weighing social or political reasons, or any other accidents. He is beginning, in a way, at the beginning; and being a discoverer, is not altogether certain what he is exploring and to what it leads; he might almost be said to be making again, as one man, the effort of scores of generations. His Christianity is rudimentary or embryonic; at best, he has the excesses of a Tertullian (and even Tertullian is not considered wholly orthodox and well balanced). His business was not to practise Christianity, but—what was much more important for his time—to assert its *necessity*.

Baudelaire's morbidity of temperament cannot, of course, be ig-nored: and no one who has looked at the work of Crépet or the recent small biographical study of François Porché can forget it. We should be misguided if we treated it as an unfortunate ailment which can be discounted or attempted to detach the sound from the unsound in his work. Without the morbidity none of his work would be possible or significant; his weaknesses can be composed into a larger whole of strength, and this is implied in my assertion that neither the health of Goethe nor the malady of Baudelaire matters in itself: it is what both men made of their endowments that matters. To the eye of the world, and quite properly for all questions of private life, Baudelaire was thoroughly perverse and insufferable: a man with a talent for ingratitude and unsociability, intolerably irritable, and with a mulish determination to make the worst of everything; if he had money, to squander it; if he had friends, to alienate them; if he had any good fortune, to disdain it. He had the pride of the man who feels in himself great weakness and great strength. Having great genius, he had neither the patience nor the inclination, had he had the power, to overcome his weakness; on the contrary, he exploited it for theoretical purposes. The morality of such a course may be a matter for endless dispute; for Baudelaire, it was the way to liberate his mind and give us the legacy and lesson that he has left.

He was one of those who have great strength, but strength merely to *suffer*. He could not escape suffering and could not transcend it, so he *attracted* pain to himself. But what he could do, with that immense passive strength and sensibilities which no pain could impair, was to study his suffering. And in this limitation he is wholly unlike Dante, not even like any character in Dante's Hell. But, on the other hand, such suffering as Baudelaire's implies the possibility of a positive state of beatitude. Indeed, in his way of suffering is already a kind of presence of the supernatural and of the superhuman. He rejects always the purely natural and the purely human; in other words, he is neither "naturalist" nor "humanist." Either because he cannot adjust himself to the actual world he has to reject it in favour of Heaven and Hell, or because he has the perception of Heaven and Hell he rejects the present world: both ways of putting it are tenable. There is in his statements a good deal of romantic detritus; *ses ailes de géant l'empêchent de marcher,* he says of the Poet and of the Albatross, but not convincingly; but there is also truth about himself and about the world. His *ennui* may of course be explained, as everything can be explained in psychological or pathological terms; but it is also, from the opposite point of view, a true form of *acedia,* arising from the unsuccessful struggle towards the spiritual life.

II

From the poems alone, I venture to think, we are not likely to grasp what seems to me the true sense and significance of Baudelaire's mind. Their excellence of form, their perfection of phrasing, and their superficial coherence, may give them the appearance of presenting a definite and final state of mind. In reality, they seem to me to have the external but not the internal form of classic art. One might even hazard the conjecture that the care for perfection of form, among some of the romantic poets of the nineteenth century, was an effort to support, or to conceal from view, an inner disorder. Now the true claim of Baudelaire as an artist is not that he found a superficial form, but that he was searching for a form of life. In minor form he never indeed equalled Théophile Gautier, to whom he significantly dedicated his poems: in the best of the slight verse of Gautier there is a satisfaction, a balance of inwards and form, which we do not find in Baudelaire. He had a greater technical ability than Gautier, and yet the content of feeling is constantly bursting the receptacle. His apparatus, by which I do not mean his command of words and rhythms, but his stock of imagery (and every poet's stock of imagery is circumscribed somewhere), is not wholly perdurable or adequate. His prostitutes, mulattoes, Jewesses, serpents, cats, corpses, form a machinery which has not worn very well; his Poet, or his Don Juan, has a romantic ancestry which is too clearly traceable. Compare with the costumery of Baudelaire the stock of imagery of the *Vita Nuova,* or of Cavalcanti, and you find Baudelaire's does not everywhere wear as well as that of several centuries earlier; compare him with Dante or Shakespeare, for what such a comparison is worth, and he is found not only a much smaller poet, but one in whose work much more that is perishable has entered.

To say this is only to say that Baudelaire belongs to a definite place in time. Inevitably the offspring of romanticism, and by his nature the first counter-romantic in poetry, he could, like any one else, only work with the materials which were there. It must not be forgotten that a poet in a romantic age cannot be a "classical" poet except in tendency. If he is sincere, he must express with individual differences the general state of mind—not as a *duty,* but simply because he cannot help participating in it. For such poets, we may expect often to get much help from reading their prose works and even notes and diaries;

help in deciphering the discrepancies between head and heart, means and end, material and ideals.

What preserves Baudelaire's poetry from the fate of most French poetry of the nineteenth century up to his time, and has made him, as M. Valéry has said in a recent introduction to the *Fleurs du Mal*, the one modern French poet to be widely read abroad, is not quite easy to conclude. It is partly that technical mastery which can hardly be overpraised, and which has made his verse an inexhaustible study for later poets, not only in his own language. When we read

> *Maint joyau dort enseveli*
> *Dans les ténèbres et l'oubli,*
> *Bien loin des pioches et des sondes;*
> *Mainte fleur épanche à regret*
> *Son parfum doux comme un secret*
> *Dans les solitudes profondes,*

we might for a moment think it a more lucid bit of Mallarmé; and so original is the arrangement of words that we might easily overlook its borrowing from Gray's *Elegy*. When we read

> *Valse mélancolique et langoureux vertige!*

we are already in the Paris of Laforgue. Baudelaire gave to French poets as generously as he borrowed from English and American poets. The renovation of the versification of Racine has been mentioned often enough; quite genuine, but might be overemphasized, as it sometimes comes near to being a trick. But even without this, Baudelaire's variety and resourcefulness would still be immense.

Furthermore, besides the stock of images which he used that seems already second-hand, he gave new possibilities to poetry in a new stock of imagery of contemporary life.

> *. . . Au cœur d'un vieux faubourg, labyrinthe fangeux*
> *Ou l'humanité grouille en ferments orageux,*
>
> *On voit un vieux chiffonnier qui vient, hochant le tête*
> *Buttant, et se cognant aux murs comme un poète.*

This introduces something new, and something universal in modern life. (The last line quoted, which in ironic terseness anticipates Corbière, might be contrasted with the whole poem *Bénédiction* which begins the volume.) It is not merely in the use of imagery of common life, not merely in the use of imagery of the sordid life of a great metropolis, but in the elevation of such imagery to the *first intensity*—presenting it as it is, and yet making it represent something much more than itself—that Baudelaire has created a mode of release and expression for other men.

This invention of language, at a moment when French poetry in particular was famishing for such invention, is enough to make of Baudelaire a great poet, a great landmark in poetry. Baudelaire is indeed the greatest exemplar in *modern* poetry in any language, for his verse and language is the nearest thing to a complete renovation that we have experienced. But his renovation of an attitude towards life is no less radical and no less important. In his verse, he is now less a model to be imitated or a source to be drained than a reminder of the duty, the consecrated task, of sincerity. From a fundamental sincerity he could not deviate. The superficies of sincerity (as I think has not always been remarked) is not always there. As I have suggested, many of his poems are insufficiently removed from their romantic origins, from Byronic paternity and Satanic fraternity. The "satanism" of the Black Mass was very much in the air; in exhibiting it Baudelaire is the voice of his time; but I would observe that in Baudelaire, as in no one else, it is redeemed by *meaning something else*. He uses the same paraphernalia, but cannot limit its symbolism even to all that of which he is conscious. Compare him with Huysmans in *A rebours, En route,* and *Là-bas*. Huysmans, who is a first-rate realist of his time, only succeeds in making his diabolism interesting when he treats it externally, when he is merely describing a manifestation of his period (if such it was). His own interest in such matters is, like his interest in Christianity, a petty affair. Huysmans merely provides a document. Baudelaire would not even provide that, if he had been really absorbed in that ridiculous hocus-pocus. But actually Baudelaire is concerned, not with demons, black masses, and romantic blasphemy, but with the real problem of good and evil. It is hardly more than an accident of time that he uses the current imagery and vocabulary of blasphemy. In the middle nineteenth century, the age which (at its best) Goethe had prefigured, an age of bustle, programmes, platforms, scientific progress, humanitarianism, and revolutions which improved nothing, an age of progressive degradation, Baudelaire perceived that what really matters is Sin and Redemption. It is a proof of his honesty that he went as far as he could honestly go and no further. To a mind observant of the post-Voltaire France (*Voltaire . . . le prédicateur des concierges*), a

mind which saw the world of *Napoléon le petit* more lucidly than did
that of Victor Hugo, a mind which at the same time had no affinity
for the *Saint-Sulpicerie* of the day, the recognition of the reality of Sin
is a New Life; and the possibility of damnation is so immense a relief
in a world of electoral reform, plebiscites, sex reform, and dress reform,
that damnation itself is an immediate form of salvation—of salvation
from the ennui of modern life, because it at last gives some significance
to living. It is this, I believe, that Baudelaire is trying to express; and it
is this which separates him from the modernist Protestantism of Byron
and Shelley. It is apparently Sin in the Swinburnian sense, but really
Sin in the permanent Christian sense, that occupies the mind of Baudelaire.

Yet, as I said, the sense of Evil implies the sense of good. Here
too, as Baudelaire apparently confuses, and perhaps did confuse, Evil
with its theatrical representations, Baudelaire is not always certain in
his notion of the Good. The romantic idea of Love is never quite
exorcised, but never quite surrendered to. In *Le Balcon,* which M.
Valéry considers, and I think rightly, one of Baudelaire's most beautiful
poems, there is all the romantic idea, but something more: the reaching
out towards something which cannot be had *in,* but which may be had
partly *through,* personal relations. Indeed, in much romantic poetry the
sadness is due to the exploitation of the fact that no human relations are
adequate to human desires, but also to the disbelief in any further object
for human desires than that which, being human, fails to satisfy them.
One of the unhappy necessities of human existence is that we have to
"find things out for ourselves." If it were not so, the statement of Dante
would have, at least for poets, done once for all. Baudelaire has all the
romantic sorrow, but invents a new kind of romantic nostalgia, a derivative of his nostalgia being the *poésie des départs,* the *poésie des salles
d'attente.* In a beautiful paragraph of the volume in question, *Mon
cœur mis à nu,* he imagines the vessels lying in harbour as saying:
Quand partons-nous vers le bonheur? and his minor successor Laforgue
exclaims: *Comme ils sont beaux, les trins manqués.* The poetry of
flight—which, in contemporary France, owes a great debt to the poems
of the A. O. Barnabooth of Valery Larbaud—is, in its origin in this
paragraph of Baudelaire, a dim recognition of the direction of beatitude.

But in the adjustment of the natural to the spiritual, of the bestial
to the human and the human to the supernatural, Baudelaire is a
bungler compared with Dante; the best that can be said, and that is a

very great deal, is that what he knew he found out for himself. In his book, the *Journaux Intimes,* and especially in *Mon cœur mis à nu,* he has a great deal to say of the love of man and woman. One aphorism which has been especially noticed is the following: *la volupté unique et suprême de l'amour gît dans la certitude de faire le mal.* This means, I think, that Baudelaire has perceived that what distinguishes the relations of man and woman from the copulation of beasts is the knowledge of Good and Evil (of *moral* Good and Evil which are not natural Good and Bad or puritan Right and Wrong). Having an imperfect, vague romantic conception of Good, he was at least able to understand that the sexual act as evil is more dignified, less boring, than as the natural, "life-giving," cheery automatism of the modern world. For Baudelaire, sexual operation is at least something not analogous to Kruschen Salts.

So far as we are human, what we do must be either evil or good;[2] so far as we do evil or good, we are human; and it is better, in a paradoxical way, to do evil than to do nothing: at least, we exist. It is true to say that the glory of man is his capacity for salvation; it is also true to say that his glory is his capacity for damnation. The worst that can be said of most of our malefactors, from statesmen to thieves, is that they are not men enough to be damned. Baudelaire was man enough for damnation: whether he *is* damned is, of course, another question, and we are not prevented from praying for his repose. In all his humiliating traffic with other beings, he walked secure in this high vocation, that he was capable of a damnation denied to the politicians and the newspaper editors of Paris.

III

Baudelaire's notion of beatitude certainly tended to the wishy-washy; and even in one of the most beautiful of his poems, *L'Invitation au voyage,* he hardly exceeds the *poésie des départs.* And because his vision is here so restricted, there is for him a gap between human love and divine love. His human love is definite and positive, his divine love vague and uncertain: hence his insistence upon the evil of love, hence his constant vituperations of the female. In this there is no need to pry for psychopathological causes, which would be irrelevant at best; for his attitude towards women is consistent with the point of view

---

[2] "Know ye not, that to whom ye yield yourselves servants to obey, his servants ye are to whom ye obey: whether of sin unto death, or of obedience unto righteousness?"—Romans vi. 16.

which he had reached. Had he been a woman he would, no doubt, have held the same views about men. He has arrived at the perception that a woman must be to some extent a symbol; he did not arrive at the point of harmonising his experience with his ideal needs. The complement, and the correction to the *Journaux Intimes,* so far as they deal with the relations of man and woman, is the *Vita Nuova,* and the *Divine Comedy.* But—I cannot assert it too strongly—Baudelaire's view of life, such as it is, is objectively apprehensible, that is to say, his idiosyncrasies can partly explain his view of life, but they cannot explain it away. And this view of life is one which has grandeur and which exhibits heroism; it was an evangel to his time and to ours. *La vraie civilisation,* he wrote, *n'est pas dans le gaz, ni dans la vapeur, ni dans les tables tournantes. Elle est dans la diminution des traces du péché originel.* It is not quite clear exactly what *diminution* here implies, but the tendency of his thought is clear, and the message is still accepted by but few. More than half a century later T. E. Hulme left behind him a paragraph which Baudelaire would have approved:

In the light of these absolute values, man himself is judged to be essentially limited and imperfect. He is endowed with Original Sin. While he can occasionally accomplish acts which partake of perfection, he can never himself *be* perfect. Certain secondary results in regard to ordinary human action in society follow from this. A man is essentially bad, he can only accomplish anything of value by discipline—ethical and political. Order is thus not merely negative, but creative and liberating. Institutions are necessary.

Paul Valéry and the
Poetic Universe

William Troy

Distinctions between poetry and prose have usually been of two kinds—those based on conventional form and those based on content. To Aristotle must be credited the belief, inherited in our day by both the Poetry Society of America and the man on the street, that the essential characteristic of poetry is its use of formal meter. As a definition it has indeed the supreme virtue of tangibility. But it is needless to describe the snarls involved in any effort to take proper care of such things as poetic prose or prosaic poetry (verse). This has been an especially trying problem today with the pretty general abandonment or at least relaxation of formal meter and the increasing tendency toward lyricism in the novel. And there is the closely related question of what is poetic diction. The profound faith in the existence in every language of a limited body of words which are hopelessly and inviolably poetic undoubtedly reached its peak in the Victorian period, although it has not entirely disappeared. Identification of poetry with a type of diction mutually agreed upon to be "beautiful," however, is less common in an age which is more and more uncertain of what it means by beauty or anything else. Likewise is this the case with the exponents of the content-theory of poetry; those who believe that as between the beautiful and ugly subjects which exist in the world poetry always chooses the former. Again one is confronted not only with the usual embarrassments of definition but with the historical fact that much of the best contemporary poetry is marked by a more intensified depiction of the

Reprinted by permission of the author.

ugliness of life—in its choice of subject, imagery, and even diction—than is the prose.

Paul Valéry was not the first to endeavor to base the great distinction on less superficial grounds. Long before, Coleridge had foundered heroically in the attempt; and Poe, although he did end up with talking about the science of verse and of the death of a beautiful woman as the most perfect subject for a poem, struggled for a while. In our time a number of enterprising critics—Eliot, Richards, Empson, Ransom, to mention only a few of them—have made serious and invaluable efforts at clarification. But no one has quite equaled Valéry in the philosophical *éclat* with which he went about the matter. Quite apart from the accident that he happened to know rather intimately what he was talking about, he possessed just the right kind of metaphysical agility requisite for the task. Moreover, responsive as he was to the intellectual malaise of the modern world, he sought to relieve it somewhat by pointing to a mode of knowledge and existence which might offer some consolation—the poetic.

If Valéry left no cohesive system of aesthetics, there are enough hints in both his verse and prose to suggest to us what it would have been like. The purpose of these notes is no more than to lay the foundations for what might be a more complete glossary of certain remarks which he made in his preface to Gustave Cohen's admirable exegesis of *Le Cimetière Marin*.[1]

I

The poet, according to my view, gets to know himself through his idols and his privileges, which are not those of the majority. Poetry is distinguished from prose in having neither the same obstacles nor the same licences. The essence of prose is to perish—that is to say, to be "understood," which is to say to be dissolved, destroyed without hope of return, entirely replaced by the image or the impulse which it signifies in linguistic terms. For prose always presupposes the universe of experience and action, a universe in which (or thanks to which) our perceptions and our actions or emotions must finally correspond or respond to each other in a single fashion—uniformly. The practical universe is reducible to an ensemble of ends. Such and such an end attained, the word expires. This universe excludes ambiguity, eliminates it; it demands that one move forward by the shortest routes, and it smothers as soon as pos-

---

[1] All the extended passages in large type are translated by the writer from Paul Valéry's preface to *Explication du Cimetière Marin*, by Gustave Cohen.

sible the harmonics of every event which is made to occur in the mind.

Quite clearly Valéry intends to phrase the whole question in terms of *function*. What are the ends of poetry and prose? (The bludgeoning statement about the moribundity of prose is simply an exhibition of critical shock-tactics.) Poetry is as yet undefined except by elimination. But prose is defined—teleologically. The inner purpose of prose is to enable us to make an adequate adjustment to the world of concrete action and experience. To be adequate such an adjustment must be instantaneous, rapid, and represent a consistent parallel between what we think that we see and how we feel and act. (This will recall of course St. Thomas' much more elaborate treatment of the "adequation" of the subject and the object in the *Summa*.) Moreover, Valéry seems to imply slily that what we call the physical world is really only a kind of projection of ourselves—an objectified ensemble of ends which pre-exist in us as our own needs and desires. In this manner he somewhat dizzily identifies the teleology of the individual, taken as a willing and active being, with cosmology. The world is no more than an image of our minds—the idea which is, of course, the dominating theme of his own verse from *Le Jeune Parque* to the *Narcisse*. What we receive here is the metaphysical statement of the idea. For Valéry is close enough to Bergson to insinuate that our so-called physical universe is an abstract fabrication compounded of will and desire. Later he speaks of the *extreme* difference existing between the "constructive moments of prose and the creative moments of poetry."

What then are some of the logical attributes of prose? In the first place, the words point always to things outside themselves; they are a means to an end; in philosophical terms, they have no ontological value. And as a result their behavior follows a definitely negative pattern. Prose cannot allow itself to indulge in the rich ambiguities of a language not determined by the ideal of economy: it must take the shortest cut to its goal. It must "eliminate" instantly everything that stands in its way. Not for prose are those "harmonics," as Valéry unmistakably infers, which do actually occur when an event, in all its fullness, is produced in the mind.

To return now to the bold declaration with which the passage opens, a declaration which has the impact of a value judgment, we see why it is that prose is doomed by its essence to become extinct. It dies the moment that it is "comprehended"—in the original Latin sense of being absorbed or swallowed up by the conscious mind. For the reader of prose no longer has any use for this language after it has done its appropriate work. Paragraph by paragraph, sentence by sentence, it gives up the ghost. Its being is dissolved into whatever it is *about,* destroyed beyond recall, replaced by the image or action in whose service it is employed.[2]

Needless to say, this analysis is capable of starting up metaphysical fireworks of every sort. There is, for example, the time-element. When we read a novel, a logical discourse, or a scientific description, we are counting off moments of time, each of which cancels out, in value and interest, the previous one. (In its original meaning, the Latin *narrare* is to count; in German, the word is *zahlen.*) Prose of any kind is unfolding history, the present always yielding to the past, and, therefore, moribund. And how does it stand in relation to space? Probably Valéry, following Bergson, would reply that the practical universe, since it refers ultimately to the realm of space, is subject to the limitations which belong to all things that exist in space. It is finite. And every action performed in it is finite, doomed sooner or later, as we are accustomed to say, to become spent. If we admit that prose is the verbal equivalent of these actions, we have another way of explaining its tragic destiny.

Of course, Valéry refers always to an *ideal* prose; in fact, his whole effort is to establish dialectically, once and for all, the irreducible essence of prose. He would undoubtedly recognize modes of expression intermediate between poetry and prose. But perhaps the greatest value of his definitions is that it helps us understand the sense of discomfiture which most of us experience in the presence of works belonging to these modes —whether it is the poetic philosophizing of a Renan or a Santayana or the poetic narration of the early Melville and Virginia Woolf. We feel that, functionally speaking, this sort of writing is working at cross-purposes.

II

But poetry insists upon or suggests a quite different "Universe": a universe of reciprocal relations, analogous to the universe of sounds

[2] Ezra Pound, in *Make It New*, says much the same thing in a slightly different way: "Most good prose arises, perhaps, from an instinct of negation: in the detailed, convincing analysis of something detestable; of something which one wants to eliminate. Poetry is the assertion of a positive, i.e. of desire, and endures for a longer period."

in which musical thought has its birth and movement. In this poetic universe resonance gets the better of causality, and the "form," far from vanishing into its effect, is ordered back by it. The Idea reclaims its voice.

At first glance this may seem indistinguishable from the formula *de la musique avant toute chose*—another surrender to that "musicalization of literature" which Valéry's brilliant contemporary Julien Benda assailed in *Belphégor*. But Valéry is only making use of an analogy, declaring that, like music, poetry constitutes a whole and self-contained "universe" within which there can occur a multitude of possible relations. As a corollary poetry, which is sufficient unto itself, is not subservient to any extraneous ends. But we can have no doubt that he means us to understand that the "resonance" of this universe which takes the place of the casual order of prose involves a much more complex blending of elements than does music. We know this the moment that he introduces the concept of the Idea—for in music there is no such differentiation between the idea and the form. In poetry there is the ever troublesome consideration that its vehicle, language, happens also to be that of prose. The great question is how it is able to maintain its autonomy in view of this fact.

For Valéry, as we have seen, the question presents itself in terms not so much of language as of metaphysics; that is to say, he is not concerned with the same problems of meaning which occupy I. A. Richards and his school. For example, the former takes almost for granted the important distinctions between the prose statement and the poetic statement made by Richards, whose approach is pretty consistently psychological. He has always been too little concerned with the musical values of language taken as a whole, although he does recognize that sound has something to do with the full value of a word. Valéry brings both his sensibility as a poet and his virtuosity as a thinker to determining precisely the relationship between "meaning" in poetry (its burden of detachable intellectual reference) and its music. But we must first take a look at some later passages in the same preface:

The poetic universe which I was speaking about makes itself known to us by the number, or rather the density, of the images, figures of speech, internal relationships, by the interweaving of phrases and rhythms—the essential thing being to avoid constantly whatever would lead back to prose, whether out of a sense of regret, or in an exclusive pursuit of the idea. . . .

While poetry is constituted of imagery and various musical devices, while these are what first impinge upon the mind's eye and ear, Valéry seems to say, there is something else at work, something which invites temptation and danger. It is this which expresses itself either as a feeling of uncertainty and guilt or as a desire to turn back altogether to prose, to the mode of the purely rational and abstract. And by way of demonstration he tells us what happens when we attempt to translate poetry into prose:

> Lastly, the more a poem conforms to Poetry the less it can be thought out in prose without perishing. Briefly, to put a poem in prose is quite simply to misunderstand the essence of an art. By its very nature poetry is inseparable from its form taken as a whole; and the thoughts articulated or suggested by the text of a poem are not at all the sole and most important purpose of what is being said. But they are the means, competing equally with the sounds, the cadences, the meter and other adornments, by which there is pro-voked and sustained in us a certain tension and exaltation, by which there is engendered in us a "world"—or a "mode of existence"—altogether harmonious.

These are not only the most richly suggestive and original sentences in the whole preface but they provide a reconciliation of all its "danger-definitions" which amounts to a kind of religion of poetry. To begin with, there is a resolution of the great antithesis between prose content and musical effect. The process of the resolution is sharply dialectical: the two are engaged in an intense conflict with each other, on an equal plane, to produce the poem. Or rather this conflict itself is the poem—la forme sensible. (Much depends on our acceptance of the meaning of the adjective sensible to include everything which we take in with our mind as well as with our senses.) It will be noted that there is no real priority between the intellectual substance and the musical effect. Nor is either in itself the sole object of the poem. In fact, they are of relative importance in relation to the final result, for they exist only to make possible in us an experience which transcends either of them. Through the tension which they establish we are translated into the "poetic uni-verse," in which we respire in such a superior atmosphere of harmony that it can even be said that we enjoy a special mode of existence. For it is neither the world of prose, in which we have our normal mode of existence, nor that of pure poetry, which would perhaps be insufferable if it were possible. It is a world that comes into being only through art, in which alone can be achieved a harmonization of the sensory and the rational demands of our being. Also, needless to say, it takes us to a region which is beyond time and space.

In this way, then, Valéry comes round to his definition of poetry in terms of its end or telechy. The end is nothing so simple as the Aristotelian "to give pleasure and instruction." If it is pleasure, it is pleasure of such an exalted kind that the word is scarcely adequate. For the end is the production in us of a state of experience which is indistinguishable from that of ecstasy—in the most literal sense. And this is immediately of course to suggest the mystical and the religious. But one must guard against identifying Valéry too closely with others who have concluded by elevating poetry to the status of a religion. He does not do so, for example, in the manner of Matthew Arnold, who, as T. S. Eliot complained, tried to force poetry to undertake the ethical responsibilities of a systematic religion. For better or worse, there is no allowance for either individual or social ethics in the Valérian scheme of things. Nor is it to be confused with that of Proust, who secures his relief from the discords of time and space by quite different boulevards and alleys. There is actually no quarter given to the claims of the intellect in the Proustian epiphany. If Valéry calls to mind any mystical writer of the past, it is, extraordinarily enough, Thomas Aquinas, providing only that we recall how that most learned of the saints was supposed to have had a vision in which all his philosophy and all his spiritual passion were combined in an irrecoverable harmony. But of course the state to which Valéry directs us is entirely secular and attained by secular means. It is attained through the imagination, which is available to us all. And if it is paralleled in the work of any more recent poets it is in a single stanza of that one of them who alone might be considered his peer:

> Labour is blossoming or dancing where
> The body is not bruised to pleasure soul,
> Nor beauty born out of its own despair,
> Nor blear-eyed wisdom out of midnight oil.
> O chestnut tree, great rooted blossomer,
> Are you the leaf, the blossom or the bole?
> O body swayed to music, O brightening glance,
> How can we know the dancer from the dance?

Alexander Pope

Austin Warren

Neoclassical theory of poetry and neoclassical poetry imperfectly agree. This discrepancy is most simply accounted for by remembering that the period called, in literary and aesthetic history, "neoclassical" is, in philosophical and cultural history, the age of the Enlightenment—the age, that is, of rationalism.

Some bold spirits, impatient of adjustment, were willing to enter heaven at the loss of an eye: in the celebrated quarrel over the relative merits of the Ancients and the Moderns, the modernists firmly took their stand on the achievements of the natural sciences and on social progress, rejecting much ancient literature, notably Homer, as obsolete, childish stuff, compounded of immoral gods, absurd miracles, and primitive manners. The classicists—likely to be either men of letters or churchmen—were necessarily less neat in their position; for, though sharing with their contemporaries the desire to be sensible, enlightened, and modern, they also genuinely admired the achievements of ages unlike their own. Hence their creed often formalizes past moments in literary history, while their practice is very much of their own time.

Thus, while the Enlightenment reinforces the impetus of the *Georgics* and the Horatian epistles toward literature as instruction, the orthodox neoclassical creed still runs: the epic and the tragedy are the highest. Dryden praises the Georgics for showing what virtuosity can do in making poetry out of the most unpromising stuff (*"opus superbat materiam"*); but in his own works he distinguishes between the *sermo pedestris* of such ratiocinative essays as *Religio laici* and his "poetry," a distinction not invalidated by the customary real superiority of his

From *Rage for Order* by Austin Warren. Reprinted by permission of The University of Chicago Press.

"lower" over his "higher" style. When Pope says, I "stoop to truth and moralize my song," he is not wholly ironic.

Neoclassical poems are likely to conform to Cartesian criteria for truth—clarity and distinctness; and the poet is likely to be a well-educated, methodical, and elegant expositor of accepted ethical generalizations. But neoclassical criticism continues to employ a terminology important parts of which are ultimately referable to Plato: words like "invention" (creative imagination), "inspiration," "fire," and "poetic fury." Like Enlightened Christians who, though retaining the word "revelation," are centrally concerned to show that theirs is a reasonable religion, the poet-critics use language difficult to reconcile with their performance or thin down and rationalize the old terms. Thus Johnson dismissed, as mere commonplace, Young's conjectural exhortation to literary originality; and Pope's preface to Homer exalts "invention" and "fire" above all the strategies of literary intelligence; yet neoclassical poetry lacks that large boldness it praises. It praises what it cannot really imitate.

The poets and critics were partially aware of this situation. Unlike the simpler modernists, they found a characteristic adjustment in a double standard of loss and gain, progress and decadence, an advance in refinement, a diminution of vigor. "Our numbers were in their nonage till Waller and Denham" has to be reconciled with the humble acknowledgment of "giant wits before the Flood." Walsh's famous advice to Pope must not be taken too simply; it really means: the great things are done; the age of myth-making is over; what remains to be done is to achieve that "correctness," that nicety of detail, which bolder writers and bolder ages perforce neglect.

Attempting to reconcile Homer and Shakespeare with Hobbes and Locke, the poets found themselves handicapped. The dramatists—Wycherly, Congreve, Dryden (in *All for Love,* which, and not *Cato,* gives us a conception of good neoclassical tragedy)—fared best, though English classicism suffers for want of a tragic genius comparable to Racine's. Milton's epic is not easy to locate in literary history; but, written by a poet versed in the Italian and French critics, praised as well as "tagged" by Dryden, demonstrated by Addison to be a "regular" epic, admired by Pope as well as by Dennis and Gildon, *Paradise Lost* may be regarded as England's neoclassical epic. After *Paradise Lost,* however, epic poetry loses virtue in both France and England, though it is still to be essayed by the ambitions of Blackmore, Glover, and Voltaire. As Pope's ironic recipe for writing an epic implies, a series of technical devices drawn by generalization from the accredited master-pieces is inadequate unless there is an epic spirit—perhaps he would have added, if properly questioned, "and a heroic age."

The idea of the Great Poem, of the Great Genius, of the (often correlated) Grand Style intimidated many Augustan poets, "froze the genial current" of their souls. Only, it seems, if they could say to themselves, "This is of course not poetry, or not *really great* poetry," could they have a fair chance of writing it. Thus Prior, though himself proud of his epic-didactic *Solomon,* his certification that he is a "major" poet, is really sure of his tone, really poetic only in his fables and songs and mock-didactic *Alma.* "Rural Elegance: An Ode" and its companion odes and elegies are negligible exercises; but let Shenstone suppose himself to be writing "levities," and he moves toward poetry. Intending a burlesque of Spenser, he is free to write imaginatively of his childhood. More violent ways of emancipating one's self from the censorship of reason were those of Chatterton and Macpherson, both of whom found pseudonymous personalities through which to express their censorable selves. Chatterton, whose public self held the atheist and republican views of a "man of reason" and wrote able satire ("Kew Gardens"), created, for his more imaginative self, the *persona* of a fifteenth-century Catholic priest. The two kinds of verse written by Christopher Smart, in and out of his mind, instance another split.

The most successful reconciliation of classicism and rationalism, or poetry and philosophy, or the incorrect, great past and the neater, thinner present, took place in terms of burlesque. Burlesque is often mask, often humility. The mock-epic is not mockery of the epic but elegantly affectionate homage, offered by a writer who finds it irrelevant to his age. As its signal advantage, burlesque (with its allied forms, satire and irony) allows a self-conscious writer to attend to objects, causes, and persons in which he is deeply interested yet of which, in part or with some part of him, he disapproves. "Interest" is a category which subsumes love and hate, approval and disapproval; very often it is an unequal, an unsteady mixture. Burlesque covers a multitude of adjustments; and each specimen requires to be separately scrutinized and defined.

Gay's *Shepherd's Week* is one of the clearer cases. Written at Pope's request, it was intended to exhibit the disgustingly crude manners and speech of genuine rustics and so, by reverse, to vindicate Pope's "Vergilian" pastorals against Phillips' wobblingly "natural" ones. Actually, however, it exhibits the unsteadiness of Gay's own feelings. We have Johnson's testimony that contemporary readers felt, like us, that most of Gay's shots had hit an unintended target. Without meaning to betray Pope's cause—indeed imagining that he indorsed it—he discovered in the writing the division of his emotional loyalties and discovered, in that division, his attachment to folkways and rural pieties.

In the mock-genres (as well as in the satire and the epistle) it was possible to escape the stylistic restrictions of Great Poetry—its avoidance of "low" terms, its aim at consistent dignity and elegance. It was possible to shift, honorably, from the Beautiful to the Characteristic.

Pope's development followed, in general, this line—from the elegantly decorative to the richly—even the grotesquely—expressive. His poetry is not so homogeneous as its virtual confinement to couplets has often suggested. We should differentiate the *Pastorals,* the Homer, *Eloisa* (which is not only an Ovidian "heroic epistle" but a soliloquy from tragedy, in the manner of Racine), the essays on *Criticism* and on *Man,* the satires and epistles, and the mock-epics. Pope's contemporaries did not confuse them or like them equally. Joseph Warton was not the only reader to think that in *Eloisa* and the *Elegy* Pope showed himself capable of the Pathetic and to regret his turning from this mode to satire. Nor did Coleridge, in the next "age," fail to distinguish between the Homer (to which he assigned the chief responsibility for the poetic diction of the eighteenth century) and the satires (composed in such words as a Lake Reformer might have used).

The two pieces, early and late, which give the measure of Pope's development are the *Pastorals,* written before he was eighteen, and the *Dunciad,* which appeared in its enlarged and final form the year before his death.

The *Pastorals* once seemed a monument to poetic "progress." In testimony to his admirer, Spence, Pope judged them "the most correct in the versification and musical in the numbers" of all his works; and Warton, in an estimate echoed by Johnson, finds their merit in their "correct and musical versification, musical to a degree of which rhyme could hardly be thought capable, and in [their] giving the first specimen of that harmony in English verse which is now become indispensably necessary." These are technical estimates, specifically of prosody. The *Pastorals* offer evidence of other care and contrivance: they combine as many traditional motifs as possible (e.g., the elegy, the singing match); they profess—in contraction and enrichment of Spenser's precedent—to traverse the four seasons, the four times of day, the four ages of man. Demonstrably superior to Phillips' rival pieces—now turgidly elegant, now rustically English, now plain childish—Pope's stylized pastorals consistently exclude realism.

> See what delight in sylvan scenes appear!
> Descending Gods have found Elysium here.
> In woods bright Venus with Adonis strayed,
> And chaste Diana haunts the forest-shade.

In an early letter Pope explains his prosodic aims in terms suggestive of a "pure" poetry. The principle of delightful variation is conceived of syllabically and as one might conceive of it if one were writing a string quartet. Indeed Pope's initial aim amounts to a precise working within strict quasi-musical forms. Characteristic canons concern the artful shifting of the caesura, the prohibition of the Alexandrine and the triplet rhyme—indulgences which weaken, by relaxing, the triumph of variation within the confines of twenty syllables. The rules sound mechanical; but the poet who wrote them trusted, confidently, to his ear: "One must," he said to Spence, "tune each line over in one's head to try whether they go right or not."

That the "great rule of verse is to be musical" Pope would never deny—assuming, however, that there are more kinds of music than the sweetness of pastoral verse and the majesty of heroic; he could even distinguish "softness" from "sweetness." Whether in blame or praise, eighteenth-century critics often tagged Pope as "sweet" or "smooth," or "melodious," as though his work were all of a texture. But Pope claimed: "I have followed the significance of the numbers, and the adapting them to the sense, much more even than Dryden; and much oftener than any one minds it"—that is, not only in the set pieces. He liked to recollect a showy couplet from his juvenile and discarded epic:

> Shields, helms, and swords all jangle as they hang
> And sound formidinous with angry clang.

Such an instance, however, makes Pope's notion of "representative harmony" appear limited to the stunt-effects of Poe's "Bells" or Lindsay's "Congo" or his own and Dryden's Cecilian correlations of poetry and music. Nor is Pope helpful to a subtle cause in the *Essay on Criticism,* where his four specimens appear to restrict the phonetic expressiveness of verse to the categories of the loud-harsh, the smooth-soft, the slow, and the rapid. Yet it is not onomatopoeia exclusively or primarily which he is commending; in modern terminology, he wants to say that the meaning of a poem is inclusive of its sound as well as its paraphrasable statement. The "echoes to the sense" either are rhythmical (accelerating or prolonging the line, interrupting it into staccato effect, or letting it flow in a legato) or they are phonative (euphonic or cacophonous—according to ease or difficulty of articulation); often these devices work together:

> Behold yon Isle, by Palmers, Pilgrims trod,
> Men bearded, bald, cowled, uncowled, shod, unshod,
> Peeled, patched, and pie-bald, linsey-woolsey brothers,
> Grave mummers! sleeveless some, and shirtless others.

Except for allowing himself the extra syllable in the feminine rhyme, Pope restricts himself to his decasyllabics; but though neoclassical doctrine allows for no further metrical variation than an occasional trochaic substitution, Pope's ear evades the rule by counting, as unstressed, syllables which any intelligent reading (including his own) must certainly have stressed, so permitting himself such a seven-stress line as has been cited. The excess of stressed syllables slow up the lines; the serried syntax gives an irregular, staccato movement; the dominance of plosives helps, with abruptness, in the total intended tone or "meaning" of grotesqueness.

The neoclassical theory of serious diction called for a thinly honorific vocabulary, for adjectives which singled out an obvious attribute implicit in the noun—the "verdant" meadow, the "blue" violet—or were devised as loosely decorative epithets—the "pleasing" shades, the "grateful" clusters, the "fair" fields: all examples from the *Pastorals*. The inhibitions, imposed upon the joint authority of Philosophy and the Ancients, are stringent. Words must not be ambiguous or multiple-meaninged (for then they become puns, and puns are forms of verbal wit, and verbal wit is "false wit"); they must not be homely or technical (since poetry addresses men *as such*—gentlemen, not specialists in science or laborers); they must be lucid (for poetry owes its kinship with philosophy to its universality).

These inhibitions are removed or greatly mitigated, however, when the poet does not profess poetry but only an epistle or a burlesque imitation. The difference is notable in the *Moral Essays*, the *Rape*, the *Dunciad*.

> But hark! the chiming clocks to dinner call;
> A hundred footsteps *scrape* the Marble Hall;

The rich buffet well-colored serpents grace,
And *gaping* Tritons *spew* to wash your face.

Whether the nymph shall break Diana's law,
Or some frail China jar receive a flaw;
Or stain her honor, or her new brocade;
Forget her prayers, or miss a masquerade;
Or lose her heart, or necklace, at a ball.

Zeugma, the joining of two unlike objects governed by a single verb, is of course a form of pun; yet this verbal play constitutes one of Pope's most poetic resources in the *Rape:* it is this device, one might say, which gives the tone to the whole.

Burlesque are both Pope's masterpieces, the *Rape* and the *Dunciad.* Of the mock-epic, we may provisionally say that it plays form against matter, a lofty and elaborate form against a trivial situation or set of persons or theme. But "form against matter" is too simple a naming. The real failure of the post-Miltonic epic lay, surely, in the supposition that the heroic poem could be written in an unheroic age; that a poem which, generically, involved the interrelation of the human and the divine, the natural and the supernatural, could be written in an age when "thinking people" had grown too prudent for heroism, too sophisticated for religion. John Dennis, whose taste among the Ancients was for Homer, Pindar, and Sophocles, and among the Moderns for Milton, was not unsound in his critical contention that great poetry like that of his favorites must be religious. So we might restate the incongruity as between heroic things and refined, between an age of faith and an age of reason. The mock-epic reminds an unheroic age of its own nature: by historical reference, it defines the "civilized" present.

Is Pope, then, satirizing Belinda's world? Yes, but lightly. His intent is rather to juxtapose contrasting modes than to decide how far his aristocracy has gained by its elegance, how far lost by its safe distance from war, politics, poverty, and sin. The poem is in nothing more dexterous than in its controlled juxtaposition of worlds. In another context we should find ominous those brilliant lines which couple by incongruity the worlds of the bourgeoisie and the proletariat with that of the leisure class:

The hungry Judges soon the sentence sign,
And wretches hang that jury-men may dine;
The merchant from the Exchange returns in peace,
And the long labors of the Toilet cease.

The *Rape* owes its richness and resonance to its overstructure of powerful, dangerous motifs. What keeps it from being that filigree artifice which the romantics saw (and praised) is its playing with fire, especially the fires of sex and religion. Though Pope was scarcely a "good Catholic," his parents were devout; and he is writing of an "old Catholic" society; and many of his effects involve the suggestion of blasphemous parallels: the linking of English folklore and the Lives of the Saints, and of both to his gentle mythology of urbane "machines." He links the nurse's moonlit elves and fairy ring with the priest's tales of "virgins visited by Angel-powers"; the visions of the Cave of Spleen are

> Dreadful as hermit's dreams in haunted shades,
> Or bright as visions of expiring maids,

visions which may or may not be reducible to physiological disturbances; the Baron and Belinda have their altars to Pride and Love, their real religions.

What, for religion, is got by parody parallel is, for sexual morality, managed by insinuation. Though it is admitted that nymphs may break Diana's law, we see none do so; the titular *Rape* is but of a lock. The opening of Canto III (a preview for the *School for Scandal*) shows the chorus at work ("At every word a reputation dies"); but we do not hear the death. A characteristic passage of *double-entendre* retails the difficulty of preserving a "melting maid's" purity at such a time and place of temptation as the midnight masquerade, while assuring us that her male companions' Honor, or her sylph, preserves her virtue.

Without doubt the specific perspectives through parody and irony are purposed. But there may be doubt whether these effects are not local and episodic, unsubject to central design and all-governing tone; for, though silly things have been said about Pope's work of composition (as if "closed couplets" must all be equally discrete and unreconciled), he was, of course, so intent on making every verse exciting and finished as to make it difficult for the poem to subordinate them. In the case of the *Rape* he is often in danger but, I think, unvanquished. What organizes the poem is not exclusively the narrative, with its chronological and dramatic sequence of scenes (including two battles); it is yet more its tone—the steadiness with which it holds, against heroic and religious perspectives, to its seriocomic view of a little elegant society.

Not to the manor born, Pope makes the drawing-room seem an achievement. He so treats a woman's day, says Johnson, that "though nothing is disguised, everything is striking; and we feel all the appetite of curiosity for the form which we have a thousand times turned fastidiously away." Pope had not turned fastidiously away; like Proust, another "outsider," he was fascinated by the ritual which gave—or signified—the aristocratic status. He has practiced, on other matter, the Wordsworthian formula of giving to the unmarvelous the light of wonder. Society is a wonder, we are made to feel; convention a triumph of happy contrivance; coffee a luxury; a card game a crisis. This effect is in large measure the result of the "machinery" of sylphs, who not only contrast with Homer's and Milton's "machines" but parallel Pope's women—those coquettes, termagants, dociles, and prudes whose natures they abstract and stylize.

The burlesque of the *Rape* provides, then, an elaborate stratification of attitudes and effects: amusement at trifles taken seriously; delight at elegance; recollections of earlier literature (Homer and Spenser) in counterpoint against the current literary mode; juxtaposition of corresponding worlds (Achilles' shield, the great petticoat); reminders of the economic and political structures which make possible this leisure-class comedy, of the moral and religious structures which make possible a society at all.

In the *Dunciad,* the mock-heroic frame is intermittent. There are frequent local parodies of passages from Homer, Virgil, and Milton; there are classical devices like the Homeric games, the descent into the lower world, the preview of future history from the mount of vision; but there is no plot, no "fable." The loose organization is expressively loose. The poem tenders some recent episodes in a long contest between stupidity and intelligence, anarchy and culture, barbarism and civilization. In this long contest, stupidity and its allies win out, not because of their superior plans, designs, or purposes—for there is no real war of opposed strategies—but because of their sheer multitudinous mass, their dead weight. The poem, a kind of anti-masque, is a series of ritual tableaux and pageants and processions, chiefly sluggish of movement and visually dusky. There are occasional light reliefs, like the episode of the dilettanti, fresh from the grand tour, where (in lines which, for satiric effect, return to Pope's old pastoral "sweetness") one looks back

> To happy Convents, bosomed deep in vines,
> Where slumber Abbots, purple as their wines:
> To isles of fragrance, lily-silvered vales,
> Diffusing languor in the panting gales.

But the general tone, prefigured in the brilliant Canto IV of the *Rape,* is somber and grotesque.

Time has assisted rather than damaged the poem. Though Pope's friends warned him against keeping alive his lampooned enemies, the warning was futile. Outside of literary circles, even in Pope's own time, most of the names must have been meaningless. And today it is certainly not the case that one need master footnotes to understand the poem Pope wrote; for the context provides the categories, which are permanent, while the proper names are annually replaceable. If one is confused by the blur of names, that too serves the purpose: these are not the names of the few masters but of the many applicants. As for the applicants: Pope is satirizing not bad men or poor men as such but bad poets and commercial publishers and undiscriminating patrons and pedantic professors. To relax one's critical standards is to be literarily immoral.

The finale is seriously epic because Pope credits the diabolical power of stupidity. In the myth of Book IV, civilization dies. According to Pope's view of history, brief episodes of enlightenment had all along alternated with far longer sequences of darkness: the primitive golden age gave way to barbarism; Roman civilization yielded to Gothic monkery and mummery; the Renaissance of Leo and Raphael and the Enlightenment of Newton and Locke and Bolingbroke were now threatened by extinction. What there is of the mythic and the dramatic in Pope comes from this sense. He felt the precariousness of civilization.

If this is a comic poem, it is comic only as *Volpone* is comic, by virtue of a grim extravagance, a grim grotesqueness; for it is not without reminder of the *Inferno* with its moral categories, its wry jokes, and its smoky lighting. The method involves not only "representative harmony" but visual imagery of a correspondent sort: the clumsiness and ugliness of the dull, the filthy foulness of their games, in which moral horror turns physical.

> Slow rose a form, in majesty of Mud;
> Shaking the horrors of his sable brows,
> And each ferocious feature grim with ooze.

Pope was not a metaphysician; and it is unlikely that in another age he would have attempted to be, though he might well have been something else—a "metaphysical poet." His "views" are flat and tiresome when he expresses them in general terms, when (as in his letters) he undertakes to moralize like a noble Roman. If he could turn a maxim, it was not this which made him, and keeps him, a poet but his power to see and hear what he felt, to find correlatives for his feelings toward people and doctrines. He images Hervey as a bug, a spaniel, a puppet, a toad; the scholars as grubs preserved in amber; the bad poet as a spider; the virtuosi as "locusts blackening all the land"; he sees Chaos regain its dominion.

> Light dies before Thy uncreating word;
> Thy hand, great Anarch! lets the curtain fall,
> And Universal Darkness buries all.

Poetry and Belief in Thomas Hardy

Delmore Schwartz

I

It is natural that beliefs should be involved in poetry in a variety of ways. Hardy is a rich example of this variety. For that reason, it would be well to distinguish some of the important ways in which belief inhabits poetry.

Some poetry is written in order to state beliefs. The purpose of the versification is to make the doctrine plain. Lucretius is the obvious and much-used example, and Dante is probably another, although there is some dramatic justification for most passages of philosophical statement and discussion in the *Paradiso*.

Some poetry employs beliefs merely as an aspect of the thoughts and emotions of the human characters with which it is concerned. Almost every dramatic poet will serve as an example of this tendency. Human beings are full of beliefs, a fact which even the naturalistic novelist cannot wholly forget; and since their beliefs are very important motives in their lives, no serious poet can forget about beliefs all the time. One doubts that any serious poet would want to do so.

It is not difficult to distinguish the two poetic uses of belief from each other. The first kind is generally marked by the forms of direct statement, the second kind by a narrative or dramatic context. And when there is a shift in purpose, when the dramatic poet begins to use his characters merely as mouthpieces to state beliefs, the shift shows immediately in the surface of the poetry. The poet's use of his medium

Reprinted by permission of the author.

338

and his attitude toward his subject are always reflected strikingly in the looking glass of form.

Between these two extremes, there exist intermediate stages of which Hardy provides a number of examples. It is commonplace, in addition, that a poet may begin with the intention of stating a belief—or perhaps merely some observation which interests him—and conclude by modifying belief and observation to suit the necessities of versification, the suggestion of a rhyme or the implication of a metaphor.

But there is a prior way in which beliefs enter into a poem. It is prior in that it is inevitable in the very act of writing poetry, while the previous two ways may conceivably be avoided. The poet's beliefs operate within his poem whether he knows it or not, and apart from any effort to use them. This fundamental operation of belief can be seen when we consider a Christian poet's observations of Nature, and then compare them to similar observations on the part of a Romantic poet, such as Wordsworth or Keats. The comparison can be made more extreme with ease, if we substitute a Russian or a Chinese poet, using descriptive passages. It should be evident that poets with different beliefs when confronted with what is nominally the same objects do not make the same observations. The same shift because of belief occurs in the slightest detail of language; such common words as *pain, animal, night, rock, hope, death,* and *sky* must of necessity have different powers of association and implication for the Christian poet and one whose beliefs are different. It is a simple fact that our beliefs not only make us see certain things, but also prevent us from seeing other things; and in addition, or perhaps one should say at the same time, our understanding of the language we use is changed.

In Hardy's poetry these three functions of belief all have an important part. Another and equally important factor is at work also. With the tone, the attitude implied by the tone, and often with the explicit statement of his poem, Hardy says with the greatest emphasis: "You see: this is what Life is." And more than that, he says very often: "You see: your old conception of what Life is has been shown to be wrong and foolish by this example."

One hesitates to make a simple synopsis of Hardy's beliefs. It is not that there is anything inherently obscure in them, but that they exist in his poetry so close to the attitudes, feelings, tones, and observations which make them different from their abstract formulation. For the purpose of lucidity, however, it is worth while saying that Hardy believed, in the most literal sense, that the fundamental factor in the nature of things was a "First or Fundamental Energy," as he calls it in the foreword to *The Dynasts*. This Energy operated without consciousness or order throughout the universe and produced the motions of the stars and the long development of the forms of life upon our own planet. Hardy did not hold this view simply, though on occasion he stated it thus. Stated thus, his writing would be an example of philosophical poetry. But this view is only one moment of his whole state of mind and does not by any means exist by itself. It is a view which Hardy affirms in active opposition, first of all, to the view that an intelligent and omnipotent Being rules the universe; second of all, in active opposition to what he knew of the nature of human life as something lived by human beings who in their conscious striving blandly disregarded the fact that they were merely products of the First or Fundamental Energy. Thus Hardy's state of mind is one example of the conflict between the new scientific view of Life which the nineteenth century produced and the whole attitude toward Life which had been traditional to Western culture. Hardy is a partisan of the new view, but acutely conscious always of the old view. He holds the two in a dialectical tension. Indeed there are moments when it seems that Hardy is merely taking the Christian idea of God and the world, and placing a negative prefix to each of God's attributes. The genuine atheist, by contrast, is never so concerned with the view which he has rejected. Or if he is so concerned, he is, like Hardy, a being who is fundamentally religious and essentially possessed by a state of mind in which an old view of Life and a new one contest without conclusion.

There are certain poems in which this conflict is stated explicitly. In the lyric called *A Plaint to Man,* the false God of Christianity is personified and given a voice, and with that voice he addresses mankind, resuming the doctrine of evolution:

> When you slowly emerged from the den of Time,
> And gained percipience as you grew,
> And fleshed you fair out of shapeless slime,
>
> Wherefore, O Man, did there come to you
> The unhappy need of creating me—
> A form like your own—for praying to?

This false God, being told that mankind had need of some agency of hope and mercy, tells mankind that he, God, dwindles day by day "beneath the deicide eyes of seers," "and tomorrow the whole of me disappears," so that "the truth should be told, and the fact be faced"— the fact that if mankind is to have mercy, justice, and love, the human heart itself would have to provide it.

In another poem, *God's Funeral,* the ambiguity of Hardy's attitude becomes increasingly evident. The God of Christianity is being escorted to his grave by a long train of mourners who are described in Dantesque lines and who have thoughts which are overheard by the protagonist of the poem and which rehearse the history of monotheism from the standpoint of a higher criticism of the Bible. Among the funeral throng, however, the protagonist sees many who refuse to believe that God has died:

> Some in the background then I saw,
> Sweet women, youths, men, all incredulous,
> Who chimed: "This is a counterfeit of straw,
> This requiem mockery! Still he lives to us!"
>
> I could not buoy their faith: and yet
> Many I had known: with all I sympathized;
> And though struck speechless, I did not forget
> That what was mourned for, I, too, long had prized.

This confession that Hardy, too, had prized what he was so concerned to deny must be remembered for the light it gives us upon Hardy's poetry as a whole. In other poems, the wish to believe in the dying God is frankly declared. *The Oxen,* a poem which will require detailed attention, tells of an old Christmas story that the oxen kneel at the hour of Christ's nativity, and the poet declares in the most moving terms that if he should be asked at Christmas to come to the pen at midnight to see the oxen kneel, he would go "in the gloom," "Hoping it might be so"! In *The Dynasts,* this desire is given the most peculiar and pathetic form of all. The hope is stated at the very end that the Fundamental Energy which rules the nature of things will continue to evolve until It takes upon Itself the attribute of consciousness—"Consciousness the Will informing till It fashions all things fair!"—and thus, or such is the implication, becomes like the God of Christianity, a God of love, mercy, and justice.

At the same time, there is a decisive moment of Hardy's state of mind which is directly opposed to this one. Hardy works without end to manipulate the events in the lives of his characters so that it will be plain that human life is at the mercy of chance and the most arbitrary circumstances. Hardy not only makes his Immanent Will of the universe an active power of evil, but he engages his characters in the most incredible conjunctions of unfortunate accidents. There is such an intensity of interest in seeing chance thwart and annihilate human life that the tendency of mind seems pathological until one remembers that chance and coincidence have become for Hardy one of the primary motions of the universe. It is Providence, which is functioning in reverse; the poet has attempted to state a definite view of life in the very working out of his plot.

And at the same time also, the older and stronger view of Life inhabited the poet's mind at a level on which it was not opposed. Hardy inherited a substratum of sensibility of a definite character and formed by definite beliefs which denied the scientific view his intellect accepted. He inherited this sensibility from his fathers, just as he inherited the lineaments of his face, and he could as soon have changed one as the other. Hardy was convinced that the new scientific view was the correct one; he was convinced intellectually, that is to say, that Darwin, Huxley, Schopenhauer, Hartmann, and Nietzsche had attained to the truth about Life. But at the same time, he could not help seeing Nature and human life in the light which was as habitual as walking on one's feet and not on one's hands. He could not work as a poet without his profound sense of history and sense of the past, his feeling for the many generations who had lived and died in his countryside before him; and his mind, like theirs, naturally and inevitably recognized human choice, responsibility, and freedom, the irreparable character of human acts and the undeniable necessity of seeing life from the inside of the human psyche rather than from the astronomical-biological perspective of nineteenth-century science. But more than that, he could not work as a poet without such entities as "spectres, mysterious voices, intuitions, omens and haunted places," the operations of the supernatural in which he could not believe.

II

The cosmology of nineteenth-century science which affected Hardy so much has had a long and interesting history in the culture of the last forty years. Its effects are to be seen in the novels of Theodore

Dreiser, in the plays of Bernard Shaw, the early philosophical writing of Bertrand Russell, the early poetry of Archibald MacLeish, and the poetry of Robinson Jeffers. A prime American example is Joseph Wood Krutch's *The Modern Temper,* where it is explicitly announced that such things as love and tragedy and all other specifically human values are not possible to modern man. The example of Bertrand Russell suggests that of I. A. Richards, whose sincerity ritual to test the genuineness of a poem works at least in part by envisaging the "meaninglessness" of the universe which follows or seemed to follow from the scientific view; and the example of Krutch suggests some of the best poems of Mark Van Doren, where the emptiness of the sky, the departure of the old picture of the world, is the literal theme. This array of examples, and the many others which might be added, should not only suggest how modern a poet Hardy is; they should also suggest how variously the scientific view may enter into the poet's whole being, what different attitudes it may engender, and how differently the poet's sensibility may attempt to handle it.

It is nothing if not fitting that I. A. Richards should look to Hardy for his perfect example in *Science and Poetry,* the book he has devoted to precisely this question, the effect of the scientific view upon the modern poet. Mr. Richards is at once very illuminating, I think, and very wrong in what he says of Hardy. It would not be possible for anyone to improve upon the appreciation of Hardy's virtues implicit in the three pages Mr. Richards devotes to him; but it would be equally difficult to invert the truth about Hardy as completely as Mr. Richards does in the interests of his general thesis. He quotes a remark about Hardy made by J. Middleton Murry: "His reaction to an episode has behind it and within it a reaction to the universe." And then his comment is: "This is not as I should put it were I making a statement; but read as a pseudo-statement, emotively, it is excellent; it makes us remember how we felt. Actually it describes just what Hardy, at his best, does not do. He makes no reaction to the universe, recognizing it as something to which no reaction is more relevant than another."

On the contrary, Hardy is almost always bringing his reaction to the universe into his poems. It is true that he sees the universe as something to which no reaction is more relevant than another; but it is just that view of the neutral universe which prepossesses Hardy almost always and gives much of the power to the most minute details of his poems. Perhaps one ought to say not Hardy's beliefs, but Hardy's disbeliefs; whichever term is exact, the fact is that his beliefs or disbeliefs make possible the great strength of his verse. We can see that this is so if we examine some of the poems in which Hardy's beliefs play a direct part.

The Oxen

Christmas Eve, and twelve of the clock.
"Now they are all on their knees,"
An elder said as we sat in a flock
By the embers in hearthside ease.

We pictured the meek mild creatures where
They dwelt in their strawy pen,
Nor did it occur to one of us there
To doubt they were kneeling then.

So fair a fancy few would weave
In these years! Yet, I feel,
If someone said on Christmas Eve,
"Come; see the oxen kneel,

"In the lonely barton by yonder coomb
Our childhood used to know,"
I should go with him in the gloom,
Hoping it might be so.

The belief in this poem is of course a disbelief in the truth of Christianity. The emotion is the wish that it were true. But it must be emphasized that this emotion, which obviously motivates the whole poem, depends upon a very full sense of what the belief in Christianity amounted to; and this sense also functions to provide the poet with the details of the Christmas story which serves as the example of Christianity. It is Hardy's sensibility as the son of his fathers which makes possible his realization of the specific scene and story; this sensibility itself was the product of definite beliefs, to refer back to the point made at the beginning that we see what we do see because of our beliefs. But for the whole poem to be written, it was necessary that what Hardy's sensibility made him conscious of should be held against the scientific view which his intellect accepted. Both must enter into the poem. This is the sense in which a reaction to the universe, if one must use Mr. Murry's terms, is involved in Hardy's reaction to the Christmas story. Hardy, remembering the Christmas story of childhood, cannot help keeping in mind the immense universe of nineteenth-century science, which not only makes such a story seem untrue, but increases one's reasons for wishing that it were true. His sensibility's grasp of the meaning of Christmas and Christianity makes such a choice of detail as calling the oxen "meek mild creatures" likely, perfectly exact, and implicit with the Christian quality of humility. His intellectual awareness of the new world-picture engenders the fullness of meaning involved in the phrase, which is deliberately emphasized by the overflow, "In these years!" A reaction to the universe is involved in this phrase and in addition a reaction to a definite period in Western culture.

If we take a negative example, one in which Hardy's beliefs have operated to produce a poor poem, this function of belief will be seen with further definition. The following poem is as typical of Hardy's failures as *The Oxen* is of the elements which produced his successes:

THE MASKED FACE

I found me in a great surging space,
 At either end a door,
And I said: "What is this giddying place,
 With no firm-fixéd floor,
 That I knew not of before?"
 "It is Life," said a mask-clad face.

I asked: "But how do I come here,
 Who never wished to come;
Can the light and air be made more clear,
 The floor more quietsome,
 And the door set wide? They numb
Fast-locked, and fill with fear."

The mask put on a bleak smile then,
 And said, "O vassal-wight,
There once complained a goosequill pen
 To the scribe of the Infinite
 Of the words it had to write
Because they were past its ken."

Here too Hardy's picture of the universe is at work and Hardy is intent upon declaring his belief that Life is beyond human understanding. But there is a plain incongruity between the vaguely cosmological scene which is declared to be Life in the first stanza and the stenographic metaphor for human life in the last stanza, which, apart from this relationship, is grotesque enough in itself. There is no adequate reason in the poem why a giddying place with no firm-fixéd floor should be beyond understanding, and it is not made so by being entitled: Life. It reminds one rather of the barrel-rolls at amusement parks and by no means of the revolutions of day and night which Hardy presumably had in mind. The masked face is probably intended to designate the Immanent Will; but here again, there is a gulf between what Hardy meant by that Will and any speaking face, and the gulf cannot be annulled merely by the device of personification. Moreover, it is difficult enough to see the human being as a goosequill pen; when the pen complains, the poem collapses because too great a weight of meaning has been put upon a figure which was inadequate at the start.

In poems such as these, and they are not few, Hardy has been merely attempting to versify his beliefs about the universe, and neither his mastery of language nor his skill at versification can provide him with all that he needs. He needs his sensibility; but his sensibility works only when the objects proper to it are in view. When it is required to function on a cosmological scene, it can only produce weak and incommensurate figures. It is possible for a poet to make poetry by the direct statement of his beliefs, but it is not possible for such a poet as Hardy. The true philosophical poet is characterized by an understanding of ideas and an interest in them which absorbs his whole being. Hardy was interested in ideas, too; but predominantly in their bearing upon human life. No better characterization could be formulated than the one Hardy wrote for his novel *Two on a Tower:* "This slightly-built romance was the outcome of a wish to set the emotional history of two infinitesimal lives against the stupendous background of the stellar universe, and to impart to readers the sentiment that of these contrasting magnitudes the smaller might be the greater to them as men."

III

Hardy failed when he tried to make a direct statement of his beliefs; he succeeded when he used his beliefs to make significant the observations which concerned him. This contrast should suggest that something essential to the nature of poetry may very well be in question. It is a long time since the statement was first made that poetry is more philosophical than history; the example of Hardy provides another instance of how useful and how illuminating the doctrine is. The minute particulars of Hardy's experience might have made a diary, history, or biography; what made them poetry was the functioning of Hardy's beliefs. The function of belief was to generalize his experience into something neither merely particular, which is the historian's concern; nor merely general, which is the philosopher's; but into symbols which possess the qualitative richness, as Mr. Ransom might say, of any particular thing and yet have that generality which makes them significant beyond their moment of existence, or the passing context in which they are located. And here again an examination of a particular poem will make the discussion specific:

A DRIZZLING EASTER MORNING

And he is risen? Well, be it so. . . .
And still the pensive lands complain,
And dead men wait as long ago,
As if, much doubting, they would know
What they are ransomed from, before
They pass again their sheltering door.

I stand amid them in the rain,
While blusters vex the yew and vane;
And on the road the weary wain   -
Plods forward, laden heavily;
And toilers with their aches are fain
For endless rest—though risen is he.

It is the belief and disbelief in Christ's resurrection which not only make this poem possible, but make its details so moving. They are not only moving; the weary wain which plods forward heavily and the dead men in the graveyard are envisaged fully as particular things and yet become significant of the whole experience of suffering and evil just because the belief exists for Hardy and provides a light which makes these particular things symbols. *Without the belief, it is only another rainy morning in March or April.* In passing, it should be noted that both belief and disbelief are necessary; the belief is necessary to the disbelief. And both are responsible here as elsewhere for that quality of language which is Hardy's greatest strength. The mere use of such words as *men, doubting, door, rain,* has a richness of implication, a sense of generations of human experience behind it; this richness is created immediately by the modifying words in the context, *pensive, weary, plod, vex, heavily,* and other workings of the words upon each other; but fundamentally by Hardy's ability to see particulars as significant of Life in general. He would not have had that ability without his beliefs and disbeliefs, though it is true that other poets get that ability by other means and other beliefs.

IV

Once we remember that good poems have been produced by the use of different and contradictory beliefs, we are confronted by the problem of belief in the modern sense.

There are good reasons for supposing that this is not, in itself, a poetic problem. But at any rate, it is true enough that many readers are profoundly disturbed by poems which contain beliefs which they do not accept or beliefs which are in direct contradiction to their own. Hardy's beliefs, as presented explicitly in his poems, offended and still offend his readers in this way.

In turn, the poet is wounded to hear that his poems are not enjoyed because his beliefs are untrue. Throughout his long career, both as poet and as novelist, Hardy was intensely disturbed by criticism on such a basis.

In the "Apology" to *Late Lyrics and Earlier,* Hardy spoke out with the tiredness and anger of an author who has suffered from reviewers for fifty years. His answer is curious and defective, however. He points out that the case against him is "neatly summarized in a stern pronouncement . . . 'This view of life is not mine.'" But instead of defending himself by pointing to all the great poetry which would be eliminated if it were judged merely on the basis of its agreement with the reader's beliefs, Hardy concedes the basic issue to his critics by claiming that his beliefs are better than they have been painted. He defends himself by saying that he is not a pessimist, but "an evolutionary meliorist." No one but another evolutionary meliorist could be persuaded by this kind of argument.

On another occasion, in the introduction to *The Dynasts,* Hardy attempts to solve the problem by requiring Coleridge's temporary "suspension of disbelief which constitutes poetic faith." But this formula would seem to provide for no more than the convention of theatrical or fictive illusion. When the curtain rises, we must suspend disbelief as to whether we see before us Elsinore, a platform before the castle. If we do not, then there can be no play. The case seems more difficult, at least on the surface, when we are asked to accept alien beliefs.

Now there are two ways in which we tend to handle alien beliefs.

One of them is to reject those poems which contain beliefs we regard as false. This is an example of judging poetry in terms of its subject, considered in abstraction; and the difficulties are obviously numerous. For one thing, as has been said, we would have to reject most great poetry. Certainly we would have to do without Homer, and without Dante or Shakespeare.

The other alternative, which is in any case preferable to the first, is to judge poetry wholly in terms of its formal character. But this is an act of unjustifiable abstraction also. For it is evident that we enjoy more in a poem, or at least the poem presents more to us, than a refined use of language.

What we need, and what we actually have, I think, is a criterion for the beliefs in a poem which is genuinely a poetic criterion. In reading Hardy when he is successful, in *A Drizzling Easter Morning,* we find that the belief and disbelief operate upon the particular *datum* of the poem to give it a metaphorical significance it would not otherwise have. To repeat, without both belief and disbelief it is only another rainy morning in the spring. Conversely, in *The Masked Face,* the asserted belief, instead of generalizing the particulars of the poem, merely interferes with them and fails to give them the significance they are intended to have.

In both instances, we are faced with a relationship between the belief in the poem and its other particulars. This is a relationship *internal* to the poem, so to speak. It is not a question of the relationship of the poet's beliefs to the reader's. In *The Masked Face,* for example, the inadequacy proceeds from the relationship between the belief that Life is beyond human understanding, and the goose-quill pen which is required to present the human mind.

It might be objected that this internal relationship between the belief and the rest of the poem is in turn good, or not good, in terms of what the given reader himself believes. Thus it might seem that for a reader who shares Hardy's beliefs, the goose-quill pen was an adequate figure for the human mind. Actually this cannot be so, unless the reader is not interested in poetry but merely in hearing his beliefs stated. If the reader is interested in poetry, the poem itself cannot give him the poetic experience of Life as beyond human understanding, which is its intention. The details of the poem, as presented in the context which the belief and the versification provide, do not do the work in the reader's mind which is done by such an element, in *A Drizzling*

Easter Morning, as the weary wain, which plods forward, laden heavily. And one reason why they lack that energy is their relationship, within the poem, to the belief the poem asserts. Whether or not the reader shares Hardy's beliefs, even if he shares them completely, the goose-quill pen is an inadequate figure for what it is intended to signify in the context. The belief in the poem fails to make it adequate, and this is a poetic failure, just as, in *The Oxen,* the kneeling animals are a poetic success because of the disbelief, whether the reader himself disbelieves in Christianity or not.

And again, it might be objected that only valid beliefs, in the end, can operate successfully upon the other elements of any poem. Once more we must refer back first to the fact that poets have written good poetry based upon opposed beliefs, and then to the point made at the start, that there is a basic way in which beliefs have much to do with the whole character of a poet's sensibility, with what he sees and does not see. The subject of poetry is experience, not truth—even when the poet is writing about ideas. When the poet can get the whole experience of his sensibility into his poem, then there will be an adequate relationship between the details of his poem and the beliefs he asserts, whether they are true or not. For then he is getting the actuality of his experience into his poem, and it does not matter whether that actuality is illusory or not; just as the earth may be seen as flat. The functioning of his sensibility guarantees his asserted beliefs; it guarantees them as aspects of experience, though not as statements of truth. The philosophical poet, as well as any other kind, must meet this test. The details of his poem are neither dramatic, nor lyrical, but there is the same question of the relationship between his asserted ideas and the language, tone, attitude, and figures which constitute the rest of the poem.

At any rate, by adopting this point of view, we avoid the two extremes, the two kinds of abstraction, which violate the poem as a concrete whole. And it is especially necessary to do this in Hardy's case, for it is unlikely that many readers will hold Hardy's beliefs as he held them. In the future we are likely to believe less or more; but we will not be in the same kind of intellectual situation as Hardy was.

The important thing is to keep Hardy's poetry, to keep as much of it as we can, and to enjoy it for what it is in its utmost concreteness. And if this is to be accomplished, it is necessary that we keep Hardy's beliefs *in* his poetry, and our own beliefs outside.

Tradition and Modernity: Wallace Stevens

J. V. Cunningham

There is a concern for tradition that is a modern concern, and provoked by something so simple as a sense of alienation from the past, a feeling for history as distinct. It is motivated by the persuasion that tradition has been lost and is recoverable only in novelty. From this arises a corollary concern with modernity in poetry, for which the poetry of Wallace Stevens will serve as an illustration. He himself writes in the poem entitled "Of Modern Poetry":

> The poem of the mind in the act of finding
> What will suffice. It has not always had
> To find: the scene was set; it repeated what
> Was in the script.
> Then the theatre was changed
> To something else. Its past was a souvenir.

To be modern in this sense is not the same thing as to be contemporary, to be living and writing in our time, or to have lived and written within our normal life span. There are many contemporary poets who are not modern. The modern poet writes the new poetry, as it was called some years ago. His poetry is modern in that it is different from the old, the traditional, the expected; it is new. This is the sense in which *modern* has always been used in these contexts: the modern poets in Roman antiquity were Calvus and Catullus, who wrote in new and untraditional poetic forms, in forms borrowed from another language and regarded by the traditionalists of the times as effete and decadent; whose subjects were novel and daring; and whose attitudes

Reprinted by permission of the author.

were in conscious distinction from those of the old morality. Again, the *moderni,* the modern thinkers in the late Middle Ages, were those who advocated and embraced the new logic of that time and whose attitudes were thought to be dangerous to the established order; it was later said that they caused the Reformation.

The modern poet, then, is modern only in the light of tradition, only as distinguished from the old. His forms, his models, his subjects, and his attitudes are different from and in opposition to the customary and expected forms, models, subjects, and attitudes of his own youth and of his readers. Consequently to be modern depends on a tradition to be different from, upon the firm existence of customary expectations to be disappointed. The new is parasitic upon the old. But when the new has itself become the old, it has lost its quality of newness and modernity and must shift for itself.

This is the situation with respect to what is still called modern poetry; it is rapidly becoming the old and the traditional. There appeared some years ago a number of articles in the leading conventional journals of this country in defense of modern poetry. Had the poetry still needed defense, the articles would never have been accepted by the editors of those journals. But modern poetry is, in fact, in secure possession of the field, and its heroes are aged men with a long public career behind them. Wallace Stevens, in fact, died recently at the age of seventy-six, after a public career of forty years. Yet the attitude of modernity still persists. These poets still represent to the young writer of today the new, the adventurous, the advance-guard, the untried. Their names are still sacred to the initiate.

For it is the condition of modernity in art that it appeal to the initiate, that it provoke the opposition of the ordinary reader who has the customary and old expectations which it is the purpose of modern art to foil. Hence it lives in an attitude of defense; is close and secret, not open and hearty; has its private ritual and its air of priesthood— *odi profanum vulgus et arceo,* "I despise the uninitiated crowd, and I keep them at a distance." It is obscure, and its obscurities are largely calculated; it is intended to be impenetrable to the vulgar. More than this, it is intended to exasperate them.

There is something of this in all art that is genuine. For the genuine in art is that which attains distinction, and the distinguished is uncommon and not accessible to the many. It is different, it must be different, and as such provokes the hostility of the many, and provokes it the more in that its difference is a claim to distinction, to prestige, and to exclusion. This claim is diminished by time. Wordsworth is now regarded as quite traditional, quite stuffy and conventional. For the particular qualities of difference in an older body of poetry that has been absorbed into the tradition become part of that tradition, and so something that the reader actually need not see since he does not know it is different. He may then in his early years and through his school days develop a set of social responses to the received body of poetry; he may enjoy that poetry without effort, be pleased by his conditioned responses, and think of himself as a lover and judge of poetry. When the audience for poetry becomes satisfied with a customary response to a customary poem, when they demand of the poet that he write to their expectations, when distinction is lost in commonness, there is need for the modern in art, for a poetry that is consciously different, even if it often mistakes difference for distinction. The poet must exasperate his reader, or succumb to him.

Such was the situation out of which Stevens wrote, at least as it seemed to him and to those of his contemporaries who have become the aged fathers of modern poetry. They sought to appear different, and hence distinguished, and they succeeded perhaps too well. The first thing that strikes the reader of Wallace Stevens, and the quality for which he was for a long time best known, is the piquant, brilliant, and odd surface of his poems. They are full of nonsense cries, full of virtuoso lines, such as

> Chieftain Iffucan of Azcan in caftan
> Of tan with henna hackles, halt!

which unexpectedly make grammar and sense if you read them slowly with closed ears. They are thronged with exotic place-names, but not the customary ones of late romantic poetry; instead of "Quinquereme of Nineveh from distant Ophir" there is "a woman of Lhassa," there is Yucatan. Rare birds fly, "the green toucan," and tropical fruits abound, especially the pineapple. Odd characters appear—Crispin, Redwood Roamer, Babroulbadour, black Sly, Nanzia Nunzio—and are addressed in various languages—my semblables, Nino, ephebi, o iuventes, o filii. And they wear strange hats.

A good deal of this, of course, is simply the unexpected in place of the expected; a new and different collection of proper names, for example, instead of the old collection, but used largely for the same purpose while seeming to deny this by being designedly different.

> Canaries in the morning, orchestras
> In the afternoon, balloons at night. That is
> A difference, at least, from nightingales,
> Jehoveh, and the great sea-worm.

The process is common in Stevens, and can be seen neatly in one of his most engaging stanzas. The theme of the stanza is the traditional one of Tom Nashe's

> Brightness falls from the hair,
> Queens have died young an fair.[1]

But instead of Helen and Iseult there are references to the beauties in Utamaro's drawings and to the eighteenth-century belles of Bath:

> Is it for nothing, then, that old Chinese
> Sat titivating by their mountain pools
> Or in the Yangtse studied out their beards?
> I shall not play the flat historic scale.
> You know how Utamaro's beauties sought
> The end of love in their all-speaking braids.
> You know the mountainous coiffures of Bath.
> Alas! Have all the barbers lived in vain
> That not one curl in nature has survived?

A woman's hair is here used as a synecdoche for her beauty. Have all those who have cared for and cherished her hair, have all the barbers, lived in vain, that though much has survived in art, none has survived in nature? The poet concludes then, expressing the sense of the couplet of a Shakespearean sonnet:

> This thought is as a death, which cannot choose
> But weep to have that which it fears to lose.

in the more specialized terms of his synecdoche, but almost as movingly:

> Why, without pity on these studious ghosts
> Do you come dripping in your hair from sleep?

Much of this is rather amusing, and even, as we say now, intriguing. Sometimes, indeed, it is much more than that, as in the

---

[1] The reading *hair* instead of the customary *air*, here, is justified in my essay, "Logic and Lyric," *Modern Philology*, LI (1953-4), 41.

stanza just quoted, which is poetry of a rare though too precious kind. But Wallace Stevens had a public career in poetry for forty years, and forty years is a little too long for this sort of pepper to retain its sharpness and piquancy. We have to ask, then, what is the motive and purpose in this?

It is usually said that these aspects of Stevens' work derive from a study of the French poets of the latter nineteenth century, the Symbolists and Parnassians, and this explanation no doubt is true enough. But it is not a sufficient explanation. The prestige of that poetry was not so high in Stevens' youth as to serve as a motive, though it might be sufficient now. The motive is rather a more human one. It is disdain—disdain of the society and of the literary tradition in which he grew up, of himself as a part of that society, and of his readers so far as they belonged to it. He sought, he tells us:

> when all is said, to drive away
> The shadow of his fellows from the skies,
> And, from their stale intelligence released,
> To make a new intelligence prevail.

How did he go about it? He celebrated the rankest trivia in the choicest diction. He was a master of the traditional splendors of poetry and refused to exercise his mastery in the traditional way; he displayed it in the perverse, the odd:

> he humbly served
> Grotesque apprenticeship to chance event . . .

He became "a clown," though "an aspiring clown." In his own summary, in the passage that immediately follows the lines quoted above, he explains:

> Hence the reverberations in the words
> Of his first central hymns, the celebrants
> Of rankest trivia, tests of the strength
> Of his aesthetic, his philosophy,
> The more invidious, the more desired.
> The florist asking aid from cabbages,
> The rich man going bare, the paladin
> Afraid, the blind man as astronomer,
> The appointed power unwielded from disdain.

He possessed "the appointed power"—the Miltonic and Scriptural phrasing is blasphemous in this context, and deliberately so—but would not wield it from disdain. The question then is: Why should he have felt such disdain? The answer can be collected from various of his poems but is given full and detailed exposition in the one from which I have just quoted. This is "The Comedian as the Letter C," the show-piece and longest poem in his first book. The poem is sufficiently complex to have several centers of concern. I shall interpret it, however, in terms of our question, and we shall find that this will turn out to be a primary concern of the poem.

The poem consists of six sections, each of a little under a hundred lines of blank verse. It is in form and subject a poem that depicts the growth of a poet's mind, and though the main character is given the fictitious name of Crispin, he may be taken as an aspect of the author, a mask for Wallace Stevens the poet, so that the poem in effect is auto-biographical. It belongs, then, to that literary form of which the model and prototype is Wordsworth's *Prelude*. It is not a wholly easy poem to read, partly because much of it is written in Stevens' fastidious and disdainful manner, partly because its structure is not adequately adjusted to its theme. The hero of the poem makes a sea voyage to a strange and exotic country, in this case Yucatan, and back to his own land. The motive for the voyage is explicitly given late in the poem in the passage already quoted:

> What was the purpose of his pilgrimage,
> Whatever shape it took in Crispin's mind,
> If not, when all is said, to drive away
> The shadow of his fellows from the skies,
> And, from their stale intelligence released,
> To make a new intelligence prevail?

His voyage is a rejection of his society as banal and trite, of its intelli-gence as stale, and his quest is the quest of a new intelligence. His problem was the problem that every teacher of freshman composition sets his better students, the problem of striking through routine phrasing and syntax to the genuine, the honest, the possibly distinguished.

The hero is portrayed as having been before this trip a man who was master of his environment, but he was a little man, "the Socrates of snails," "this nincompated pedagogue," and the environment itself was trivial; it was a land "of simple salad-beds, of honest quilts." It was, in fact, to quote Stevens' own summary of his early environment in an essay of later date, "the comfortable American state of life of the

'eighties, the 'nineties, and the first ten years of the present century."
It was the time and place when the sun

> shone
> With bland complaisance on pale parasols,
> Beetled, in chapels, on the chaste bouquets.

It was that middle-class culture of business, public chastity, and official
Christianity which we often call, with some historical injustice, Vic-
torianism. In this world Crispin wrote the conventional poetry of the
times. He was one

> that saw
> The stride of vanishing autumn in a park
> By way of decorous melancholy . . .
> That wrote his couplet yearly to the spring,
> As dissertation of profound delight . . .

However, he found that

> He could not be content with counterfeit . . .

It was this dissatisfaction with the conventional—in society and in
poetry—"That first drove Crispin to his wandering." He alludes to it
as "The drenching of stale lives," a life of "ruses" that was shattered by
the experience of his voyage.

He found the sea overwhelming; he "was washed away by magnitude." "Here was no help before reality." It was not so much that he
was cut off from the snug land; he was cut off from his old self:

> What counted was mythology of self,
> Blotched out beyond unblotching.

and hence from his environment. He was destitute and bare:

> The salt hung on his spirit like a frost,
> The dead brine melted in him like a dew
> Of winter, until nothing of himself
> Remained, except some starker, barer self
> In a starker, barer world . . .

From this experience he came to Yucatan. The poetasters of that land,
like the poetasters at home, in spite of the vividness of experience
around them

> In spite of hawk and falcon, green toucan
> And jay . . .

still wrote conventional verses about the nightingale, as if their environment were uncivilized. But Crispin's conversion at sea—for it was obviously a conversion—had enlarged him, made him complicated,

> and difficult and strange
> In all desires . . .

until he could reduce his tension only by writing an original and personal poetry, different and unconventional.

The experience at sea is now reinforced by another experience in Yucatan, of the same elemental, overwhelming sort:

> one
> Of many proclamations of the kind,
> Proclaiming something harsher than he learned

from the commonplace realism of home:

> From hearing signboards whimper in cold nights.

It was rather

> the span
> Of force, the quintessential fact,
> The thing that makes him envious in a phrase.

It was the experience that altered and reinvigorated his poetry, the source from which he drew that distinction of style that marks off his published work from the sentimental verses he had printed in the college magazine some twenty years before. The experience was of the type of a religious experience:

> His mind was free
> And more than free, elate, intent, profound
> And studious of a self possessing him,
> That was not in him in the crusty town
> From which he sailed.

The poetry he now wrote issued from this context. It was conditioned by the kind of dissatisfaction that drove Crispin to his wandering, by such an experience as Crispin's on the voyage and in Yucatan, and by its results. This dissatisfaction lies behind a good many of Stevens' poems, which deal, if one looks beneath the distracting surface, simply with the opposition between the aridities of middle-class convention and the vivid alertness of the unconventional, as in "Disillusionment at Ten O'clock." Some repeat in smaller compass and with other properties the subject of "The Comedian": as "The Doctor of Geneva." In others he attempts to deal directly with the experience of the sea, but this was a religious experience without the content of traditional religion. In fact, it had no content at all beyond itself, beyond the intuition of a bare reality behind conventional appearance, and hence was an unfertile subject for poetry since it was unproductive of detail. He treated it in one of his best short poems, "The Snow Man," but when he had stated it, there was nothing more to be done with it, except to say it over again in another place. This he has repeatedly done, though with a prodigality of invention in phrasing that is astounding.

Most of what is interesting in Stevens issues from this problem. It can be put in various terms. It is the problem of traditional religion and modern life, of imagination and reality, but it can be best put for Stevens in the terms in which it is explicitly put in "The Comedian." The problem is the relationship of a man and his environment, and the reconciliation of these two in poetry and thus in life. The two terms of this relationship are really Wordsworth's two terms: the one, what the eye and ear half create; the other, what they perceive. The reconciliation in Wordsworth is in a religious type of experience:

> With what strange utterance did the loud dry wind
> Blow through my ear! the sky seemed not a sky
> Of earth—and with what motion moved the clouds!
>
> Dust as we are, the immortal spirit grows
> Like harmony in music; there is a dark
> Inscrutable workmanship that reconciles
> Discordant elements, makes them cling together
> In one society.

The reconciliation in Stevens is sought in poetry, in

> those
> True reconcilings, dark, pacific words,
> And the adroiter harmonies of their fall.

For poetry is the supreme fiction of which religion is a manifestation:

> Poetry
> Exceeding music must take the place
>
> Of empty heaven and its hymns,
> Ourselves in poetry must take their place . . .

What Crispin is seeking is such a reconciliation, a oneness between himself and his environment. He began in the illusion that he was the intelligence of his soil, but the experience of reality overwhelmed him, and he came to believe that his soil was his intelligence. At this extreme he wrote poems in which a person is described by his surroundings. But he perceived that this too was sentimental, and so he settled for the ordinary reality of daily life, married, had four daughters, and prospered. However, he did not give up poetry entirely; he recorded his adventures in the poem, and hoped that the reader would take it as he willed: as a summary

> strident in itself
> But muted, mused, and perfectly revolved
> In those portentous accents, syllables,
> And sounds of music coming to accord
> Upon his law, like their inherent sphere,
> Seraphic proclamations of the pure
> Delivered with a deluging onwardness.

Such is Stevens' account of the source of his distinctive style and distinctive subjects. But he owed more than he acknowledged to the old and the traditional. He owed "the appointed power" which was "unwielded from disdain."

That he once had the appointed power is clear in his greatest poem, and one of his earliest, "Sunday Morning." The poem is traditional in meter—it is in eight equal stanzas of blank verse—and has as its subject a deep emotional attachment to traditional Christianity and a rejection of Christianity in favor of the clear and felt apprehension of sensory detail in this life, together with an attempt to preserve in the new setting the emotional aspects of the old values.

The poem depicts a woman having late breakfast on a Sunday morning, when of course she should have been at church. She is for the moment at one with her surroundings, which are vivid, sensory, familiar, and peaceful. All this serves to dissipate the traditional awe of Christian feeling, but the old feeling breaks through:

> She dreams a little, and she feels the dark
> Encroachment of that old catastrophe,
> As a calm darkens among water-lights.

Her mood "is like wide water, without sound," and in that mood she passes over the seas to the contemplation of the Resurrection. The remainder of the poem consists of the poet's comment and argument on her situation, on two short utterances she delivers out of her musing, and finally on the revelation that comes to her in a voice.

The poet asserts that Christianity is a religion of the dead and the unreal. In this living world of the sun, in these vivid and sensory surroundings, there is that which can assume the values of heaven:

> Divinity must live within herself:
> Passions of rain, or moods in falling snow;
> Grievings in loneliness, or unsubdued
> Elations when the forest blooms; gusty
> Emotions on wet roads on autumn nights;
> All pleasures and all pains, remembering
> The bough of summer and the winter branch,
> These are the measures destined for her soul.

The truly divine is the human and personal in this world: it consists in the association of feeling with the perception of natural landscape, in human pleasure and pain, in change, as in the change of seasons.

He then argues that the absolute God of religion was originally inhuman, but that the Incarnation by mingling our blood with His, by mingling the relative and human with the Absolute, satisfied man's innate desires for a human and unabsolute Absolute. Certainly, if "the earth" shall "Seem all of paradise that we shall know," we would be much more at home in our environment:

> The sky will be much friendlier then than now . . .
> Not this dividing and indifferent blue.

At this point the woman speaks in her musing, and says that she could acquiesce in this world, that she could find an earthly paradise, a contentment, in the perception of Nature, in the feel of reality, except that the objects of her perception change and disappear. Nature is an impermanent paradise. The poet, however, answers that no myth of a religious afterworld has been or ever will be as permanent as the stable recurrences of Nature:

> There is not any haunt of prophesy,
> Nor any old chimera of the grave,
> Neither the golden underground, nor isle
> Melodious, where spirits gat them home,
> Nor visionary south, nor cloudy palm
> Remote on heaven's hill, that has endured
> As April's green endures; or will endure
> Like her remembrance of awakened birds,
> Or her desire for June and evening, tipped
> By the consummation of the swallow's wings

The woman speaks again, and says:

>   "But in contentment I still feel
> The need of some imperishable bliss."

There remains the desire for the eternal happiness of tradition. The lines that comment on this present some difficulties to interpretation until it is seen that the poet in his answer proceeds by developing the woman's position. Yes, he says, we feel that only in death is there fulfillment of our illusions and our desires. Even though death be in fact the obliteration of all human experience, yet it is attractive to us; it has the fatal attractiveness of the willow in old poetry for the love-lorn maiden. Though she has lovers who bring her gifts—that is, the earth and its beauty—she disregards the lovers and, tasting of the gifts, strays impassioned toward death.

Yet the paradise she would achieve in death is nothing but an eternal duplicate of this world, and lacking even the principle of change, leads only to ennui. Therefore, the poet creates a secular myth, a religion of his irreligion. The central ceremony is a chant, a poem to the sun,

>   Not as a god, but as a god might be . . .

It is an undivine fiction that preserves the emotions of the old religion but attaches them to a poetry in which the sensory objects of a natural landscape enter into a union in celebration of the mortality of men:

>   And whence they came and whither they shall go
> The dew upon their feet shall manifest.

The biblical phrasing creates a blasphemous religion of mortality.

The poem now concludes with a revelation. Out of the woman's mood a voice cries to her, saying that the place of the Resurrection is merely the place where a man died and not a persisting way of entry into a spiritual world. The poet continues:

>   We live in an old chaos of the sun,
> Or old dependency of day and night,
> Or island solitude, unsponsored, free,
> Of that wide water, inescapable.
> Deer walk upon our mountains, and the quail
> Whistle about us their spontaneous cries;
> Sweet berries ripen in the wilderness;
> And, in the isolation of the sky,
> At evening, casual flocks of pigeons make

> Ambiguous undulations as they sink,
> Downward to darkness, on extended wings.

We live, in fact, in a universe suggested by natural science, whose principle is change, an island without religious sponsor, free of the specific Christian experience. It is a sensory world, it has its delights, its disorder, and it is mortal.

The poem is an argument against the traditional Christianity of Stevens' youth, and especially against the doctrine and expectation of immortality, in favor of an earthly and mortal existence that in the felt apprehension of sensory detail can attain a vivid oneness with its surroundings and a religious sense of union comparable to the traditional feeling. The former is undeniably traditional, and much of the deep feeling of the poem is derived from the exposition in sustained and traditional rhetoric of the position which is being denied. In this sense it is parasitic on what it rejects. But the positive argument is almost as traditional in the history of English poetry and in the literary situation of Stevens' youth: it is, with the important difference of a hundred years and the denial of immortality, Wordsworthian in idea, in detail, in feeling, and in rhetoric. Passages comparable to the appositive enumeration of details of natural landscape associated with human feeling, as in

> Passions of rain, and moods in falling snow;
> Grievings in loneliness, or unsubdued elations
> When the forest blooms . . .

are scattered throughout Wordsworth's poetry, especially through the blank verse. I have already quoted a short passage; let me quote another:

> What want we? have we not perpetual streams,
> Warm woods, and sunny hills, and fresh green fields,
> And mountains not less green, and flocks and herds,
> And thickets full of songsters, and the voice
> Of lordly birds, an unexpected sound
> Heard now and then from morn to latest eve,
> Admonishing the man who walks below
> Of solitude and silence in the sky?

The movement of the verse is Stevens', the syntax, and the relation of syntax to the line-ends. The kind of detail is the same. And the idea, if one reads it out of the specific context of Wordsworth's system, is Stevens' idea: for the passage in isolation says, What does man need,

what need he desire, more than a live appreciation of the detail of
natural landscape, for the world beyond, the birds admonish us—or,
Nature tells us—is a world of solitude and silence. This is not precisely what Wordsworth would have endorsed, but certainly what a
young man who was drenched in Wordsworth could make of it. And
as he read on in the poem—it is "The Recluse"—he would come to the
rhetoric of one of his greatest stanzas and the theme of his greatest
poem: he would read in Wordsworth:

> Paradise, and groves
> Elysian, Fortunate fields,—like those of old
> Sought on the Atlantic Main—why should they be
> A history only of departed things,
> Or a mere fiction of what never was?
> For the discerning intellect of Man,
> When wedded to this goodly universe
> In love and holy passion, shall find these
> The simple produce of the common day.

and he would write:

> There is not any haunt of prophesy,
> Nor any old chimera of the grave . . .

The central concern of Stevens' poetry, the concern that underlay
Crispin's voyage and the poet's meditative argument with the woman
in "Sunday Morning," as well as most of the more or less curious
divergencies of his career, is a concern to be at peace with his surroundings, with this world, and with himself. He requires for this an experience of the togetherness of himself and Nature, an interpenetration
of himself and his environment, along with some intuition of permanence in the experience of absoluteness, though this be illusory and
transitory, something to satisfy the deeply engrained longings of his
religious feeling. Now, there is an experience depicted from time to
time in the romantic tradition—it is common in Wordsworth—and
one that has perhaps occurred to each of us in his day, a human experience of absoluteness, when we and our surroundings are not merely
related but one, when "joy is its own security." It is a fortuitous experience: it cannot be willed into being, or contrived at need. It is a
transitory experience; it cannot be stayed in its going or found when
it is gone. Yet though fortuitous and transitory, it has in its moment of
being all the persuasion of permanence; it seems—and perhaps in its
way it is—a fulfillment of the Absolute:

        It is and it
Is not and, therefore, is. In the instant of speech,
The breadth of an accelerando moves,
Captives the being, widens—and was there.

Stevens attempted to will it into being. He constructed a series of
secular myths, like the one in "Sunday Morning," that affirm the traditional religious feeling of the nobility and unity of experience, but
the myths remain unconvincing and arbitrary, and conclude in gro-
tesqueries that betray the poet's own lack of belief in his invention, as
in "A Primitive Like an Orb," in which he evokes:

    A giant, on the horizon, glistening,

    And in bright excellence adorned, crested
    With every prodigal, familiar fire,
    And unfamiliar escapades: whiroos
    And scintillent sizzlings such as children like,
    Vested in the serious folds of majesty . . .

For, as he asks in an earlier poem:

            But if
    It is the absolute why must it be
    This immemorial grandiose, why not
    A cockle-shell, a trivial emblem great
    With its final force, a thing invincible
    In more than phrase?

He has attempted to contrive it by a doctrine of metaphor and
resemblances, which is precisely Wordsworth's doctrine of affinities.
He has sought to present in a poem any set of objects and to affirm a
resemblance and togetherness between them, but all the reader can see
is the objects and the affirmation, as in "Three Academic Pieces," where
a pineapple on a table becomes:

    1. The hut stands by itself beneath the palms.
    2. Out of their bottle the green genii come.
    3. A vine has climbed the other side of the wall . . .

    These casual exfoliations are
    Of the tropic of resemblance . . .

But there is a poem in *Transport to Summer,* one of the perfect
poems, as far as my judgment goes, in his later work, that achieves
and communicates this experience. It is a short poem in couplets entitled "The House Was Quiet and the World Was Calm." There is no

fiddle-dee-dee here. The setting is ordinary, not exotic. It is about a
man reading alone, late at night. The phrasing is exact and almost un-
noticeable. The style is bare, less rich than "Sunday Morning," but
with this advantage over that poem, that none of its effect is drawn from
forbidden sources, from what is rejected. The meter is a loosened
iambic pentameter, but loosened firmly and as a matter of course,
almost as if it were speech becoming meter rather than meter violated.
It has in fact the stability of a new metrical form attained out of the
inveterate violation of the old. It is both modern and traditional:

> The house was quiet and the world was calm.
> The reader became the book; and summer night
>
> Was like the conscious being of the book.
> The house was quiet and the world was calm.
>
> The words were spoken as if there was no book,
> Except that the reader leaned above the page,
>
> Wanted to lean, wanted much most to be
> The scholar to whom his book is true, to whom
>
> The summer night is like the perfection of thought.
> The house was quiet because it had to be.
>
> The quiet was part of the meaning, part of the mind:
> The access of perfection to the page.
>
> And the world was calm. The truth in a calm world,
> In which there is no other meaning, itself
>
> Is calm, itself is summer and night, itself
> Is the reader leaning late and reading there.

Timon's Dog

William Empson

The study of metaphor in Shakespeare would obviously be valuable
if one knew how to do it, but there is a large question as to which metaphors should be taken seriously. The very laborious work of Miss
Spurgeon, in which all the metaphors are counted and classified, leaves
one doubting whether there is any significance in figures that lump
together a descriptive metaphor and a normative one. I don't think
this enough to dismiss her results, because one could make a case for
saying that all metaphors are in part both, but the question is evidently
very complicated. The extreme case of normative metaphor is clear
enough in principle. The thing becomes a "symbol" and involves what
would be called "pregnancy" if free from metaphor—e.g., *man* in "He
was a man; take him for all in all I shall not look upon his like again."
That is, various adjectives are taken as typical of the noun, and there
is an obscure assertion that it ought to possess them; in the case of
metaphor, this gives further obscure assertions about what is typical
or proper for the thing described. One might say that the only metaphors to pick out and examine are those used like this; Miss Spurgeon
would I think claim that even the most careless or conventional metaphors have a kind of statistical total effect, and no doubt both processes
occur though they need to be distinguished. But the most interesting
case, or anyway the difficult one to handle, lies between the two. A
way of making the metaphor a "symbol" is in view, but though the
thought centres round the metaphor, and it is continually used, the
author will not accept its symbolism.

The use of *dog* in *Timon* is a handy and interesting case, and I

Reprinted by permission of the author.

want here simply to discuss that without plunging into a general view of metaphor. Miss Spurgeon had a small triumph over some critic who said that the metaphor of gold was fundamental to the play; her actual count found one doubtful metaphor from gold and a continual protean metaphor from dogs. He could still claim that gold as an implied metaphor is more important than most of the actual ones of her counting; Timon still handling gold in misery is a symbol stronger than most verbal effects, and indeed the metaphor of a golden nature as a noble and magnanimous one raises the whole puzzle of the play—how far Timon's nobility is essentially that of a rich man, even when it becomes sacrificial and suicidal. But the dog too cannot be dealt with by addition. I am indebted to Mr. Wilson Knight for pointing out the extreme subtlety of thought in this uninviting play, but feel sure that he over-simplifies by making Apemantus a mere symbol of Nasty Cynicism and Hate. There is an unusually strong case for his viewpoint here because Shakespeare himself was over-simplifying, but Shakespeare does not cheat Apemantus either of his jokes or of the arguments for his side. I shall try to show that Shakespeare is both presenting and refusing a set of feelings about *dog* as metaphor, making it in effect a term of praise, which were already in view and became a stock sentiment after the Restoration ("you young dog" and so on). It is a popular but tactfully suppressed grievance that Shakespeare did not love dogs as he should, and I think the topic is really a large one; when you call a man a dog with obscure praise, or treat a dog as half-human, you do not much believe in the Fall of Man, you assume a rationalist view of man as the most triumphant of the animals.

Thus for the full possible use of the dog metaphor here one needs a stricter sense of "symbol" than I used at the beginning, or rather needs a new term. Apemantus is continually called "dog" (in a play clearly meant to be taken as symbolic) with the sense "snarling and envious critic," also as "ill-conditioned"—he will "famish, a dog's death." But this kind of critic is a person of recognized value; there is much of him in Jacques and Hamlet as well as in Iago. At one end, as the character who though somehow low will tell the truth, he joins on to the respected figure of the Fool; at another, he is the disappointed idealist. Contrariwise, Apemantus continually calls the courtiers of Timon "dogs" with the sense "flatterers," and puzzles are contrived to include Timon in this as well. But the flattery given by a dog is a type of how you can be foolish and mercenary and yet sincere; the creature shows love to get still more food but is really affectionate. This was an obvious point for instance in *The Praise of Folly* when Erasmus wanted to say that flattery was not mere lying but belonged to the valuable kind of fool—"What is more fawning than a spaniel? Yet what is more faithful to his master?" This would not impress Shakespeare, who found spaniels particularly disgusting because of the way they melted their sweets. But it is clear that the dog so much stressed in *Timon* might have been a very rich symbol. We may compare what Miss Welsford says of Erasmus' *fool*, a symbol in full blast. It could be applied either to the respectable people (scribes and pharisees) who would be fooled at the Judgment Day, or to the unpretending people, failures in the eye of the world, who give sound criticism under the guise of folly; thus it held the crucial positions at the two ends of the scale in hand. Furthermore it implied an escape from the conflict of these criteria—all men are fools in the eye of God; we are dependent on God; it is our nature and he will allow for it. Now the metaphorical *dog* came to give a different escape, one that suited a rationalist individualism; its humour implied that you could start from the rock-bottom low man because he was a decent kind of animal. Shakespeare believed that "there is no worst," and would have no truck with the rock-bottom sentiment. Yet the dog in *Timon* holds the key positions at both ends of a scale; furthermore it gives a hint of escape from the conflict that made the scale important, because there is a hint of liking for dogs in general. Certainly the great majority of the metaphors imply hatred of dogs, and the fact that the dogs *might* have been used to praise both ends of the scale is not relevant. But Shakespeare elsewhere normally made the metaphor from dogs rude. The curious thing is that this play also praises dogs, and apart from the fooling of Launce (who was like a dog himself as a kind of "natural") they are praised nowhere else in Shakespeare.

I shall try to list a paragraph of dog-praises; perhaps only the last is clear, but it affects the interpretation of the others. One may doubt over the first words of Apemantus to Timon:

Tim. Good morrow to thee, gentle Apemantus.
Ape. Till I be gentle, stay thou for thy good morrow;
When thou art Timon's dog, and these knaves honest.

The main point of this is to make Apemantus mention dogs at once and whenever possible, but, however little it means, *dog* is somehow parallel to *honest*. One can read it as dramatic irony—when Timon becomes a cynic (what people call Apemantus a dog for) and the knaves become honest in the sense of showing their villainy, then Apemantus will try to be gentle to Timon before the cave. But the only relevant point is that Apemantus regards becoming a dog as some kind of forward step. Timon himself catches the trick of talking about dogs when he exposes the courtiers at the pretended banquet—"uncover, dogs, and lap"—the "flatterer" sense, but from then on he too can mention actual dogs with an obscure cordiality. Having found one honest man in his old steward (not in Timon or Apemantus) he gives him money on condition he gives none to mankind:

> let the famished flesh slide from the bone
> Ere thou relieve the beggar; give to the dogs
> What thou deniest to men.

Not hearty praise of dogs, but there is something more like it in the crucial scene with Apemantus:

Ape. What man didst thou ever know unthrift that was beloved after his means?
Tim. Who, without those means that thou talkest of, didst thou ever know beloved?
Ape. Myself.
Tim. I understand thee, thou hadst means to keep a dog.

One might think the dog was prepared to love him for such means as he had, therefore was a flatterer, but the paradox admits that in a way he had no means, and that one would expect a dog to be faithful even so.

Ape. I was directed hither; men report
Thou dost affect my manners, and use them.
Tim. Tis then because thou dost not keep a dog
Whom I would imitate. Consumption catch thee.

This retort seems baffling rather than effective. Timon wants, or at any rate proceeds, to deny that he has imitated Apemantus; but if Apemantus is like a dog, and Timon would imitate his dog if he had one, probably he has imitated Apemantus as the nearest thing. Nor is there any clear insult in telling him so. And if Apemantus' dog would be a flatterer (kept dog) he would be a quite different animal to Apemantus, a cynic (pariah dog) with no-one to keep him. Certainly Timon goes on to the paradox of calling the cynic a flatterer, but this seems to be derived from the confusion, and the bewilderment of the two critics on their central issue is already visible in their first words. Finally in a surprising remark of Timon to Alcibiades it is hard to deny that dogs receive obscure but real praise.

> For my part, I do wish thou wert a dog
> That I might love thee something.

The feeling seems to start about metaphorical dogs (men), but these are felt to be somehow unnatural, so the overt praise is given to actual dogs, who therefore take on what good qualities they can—"affectionate," "faithful," and in view of the money hatred in the play "indifferent to money." But this is somewhat grudging, and the first impulse was a fellow-feeling (for metaphorical dogs) gained because contempt for man had extended to self-contempt. Men treat Timon and Apemantus as dogs; men are worse than dogs, reply Timon and Apemantus; Timon and Apemantus notice at last that they cannot escape being men, so that there is some logical puzzle for them in railing against mankind; let them then praise dogs, among whom they are faintly included as cynics, and in rebuking man they may half praise themselves. But the dog from this angle is disgusting rather than cynical, partly because he enjoys smells that we agree to call disgusting; Timon and Apemantus take pleasure in recognizing the worst; they are pleased therefore by dogs' pleasures and view dogs as their allies.

The idea of pleasure in self-contempt goes deep into the Elizabethan theme of the Malcontent, and I do not know where else it has been put so clearly. We are told it about Apemantus in the first scene, before he has appeared. The Poet has described the existing situation in his play:

> yea, from the glassfaced flatterer
> To Apemantus, who few things loves better
> Than to abhor himself, even he drops down
> The knee before him, and returns in peace
> Most rich in Timon's nod.

This need not be unfair to Apemantus. To look to a higher world because of the faults of this world is always to accuse oneself of its faults, so that all divine pleasures might be classed as perverse pleasure in self-contempt; not to see them so would be hubris. Timon himself as a cynic is too little aware of this logical puzzle (thus remaining Renaissance rather than medieval):

Tim.   all is oblique:
There's nothing level in our cursed natures
But direct villainy. Therefore be abhorr'd
All feasts, societies, and throngs of men.
His semblable, yea himself, Timon disdains.
Destruction fang mankind. Earth, yield me roots.

In digging for roots, however far from mankind he may now be, he is trying to keep one man from destruction. We are told clearly that he "disdains himself," but he does not follow this up when railing at other people. Actual pleasure in disdaining himself he avoids recognizing.

The idea that there is nothing direct but villainy is a generalization of the ascetic outlook seen best when it works the paradoxes of *The Fable of the Bees*. What is direct is the satisfaction of a simple appetite (digging for roots); if you take so exalted or insane a view as to call all satisfaction of appetite villainy, on the grounds that it is worldly and self-centred, you are safe in agreeing with Timon. All the less simple satisfactions (meditation on God or pleasure in self-contempt) may at least be paralleled by perversions of appetite and treated as identical with them. The only trouble is that Timon is still wicked to dig for roots, but he could claim that as a minimum. Yet on a similar ground one could claim the pleasure of self-contempt as a spiritual minimum (without it there is hubris). Thus when Timon and Apemantus meet before the cave each has strong grounds for priding himself on his own version of self-contempt and despising the other's. Nobody pretends that *Timon* is a very good play, but given the Malcontent theme this is the cleverest treatment of it ever written.

A main source of their puzzle is that they seem only to have exchanged the senses in which they are dogs; Apemantus has become a flatterer and Timon a cynic. The only effect from their teasing this problem is to suggest that each may always have been both. Yet they are meant of course to be quite opposite characters; the play insists on this by very unfair means, as when Timon finds gold in the desert and can thus go on throwing it away, still more when he turns out to be an important general, the only man who can defend Athens against Alcibiades; unless you have always assumed that they are so far distinct this turns the last scenes into a day-dream of self-justification. But for that matter it is only on this assumption that the puzzles will have seemed impressive before.

In the first scene, with a very delicate irony on the part of his author, the Poet describes how he has written what amounts to the play of *Timon* as a means of flattering Timon and getting money out of him. It is in his list of flatterers that Apemantus (interested in a similar exposure) is described as chiefly enjoying self-contempt. Some such puzzle is necessary to the position of Apemantus in the play, for he has to be brought to the feasts as if he is to comment on them. He himself claims to have come partly to glut his eyes with the falsity of the world (pleasure in contempt) and partly to do Timon good; the Poet would claim that this was itself flattery of Timon, showing that Timon's money could collect even incorruptible philosophers to advise him.

Tim.   Now, Apemantus, if thou were not sullen, I'd be good to thee.
Ape.   No, I'll nothing; for if I should be bribed too, there would be none left to rail upon thee; and then thou wouldst sin the faster.

This claim to goodwill becomes plausible when he follows Timon to the cave, but by an ingenious twist the accusation of flattery is made more plausible as well.

Tim.   . . . Depart.
Ape.   I love thee better now than e'er I did.
Tim.   I hate thee worse.

(Till now they have hidden both love and hatred.)

Ape.   Why?
Tim.   Thou flatterest misery.

Poor Apemantus backs out and claims to have come out of ill-nature, and this again is made to prove him a knave. He flatters Timon's misery as well as his own by the offer of friendship; they are to enjoy railing and self-contempt and thereby feel superior to mankind. Also this has a real likeness to flattery, because Apemantus is a cynic only from the accident of his birth:

Tim.   If thou hadst not been born the worst of men
           Thou hadst been a knave and flatterer.

This is easily retorted; Timon has become a cynic only through "change of fortune." The claim that Timon was always a flatterer is less simple, but Apemantus starts on it as soon as he is rebuffed. At any rate Timon had better become one now:

Ape.   Shame not these woods
        By putting on the cunning of a carper;
        Be thou a flatterer now, and seek to thrive
        By that which has undone thee . . .
          What, thinkst
        That the bleak air, thy boisterous chamberlain,
        Will put thy shirt on warm?

Under cover of the irony or self-protection of this false advice the poetry offers Timon the mood of the exiles in Arden, rejoicing in Nature because she does not flatter. Timon is in no mood to admire anything, certainly not Nature; her use is to provide symbols of the faults of men, and the attraction of a grave by the sea is that it stands for eternal bitterness and infertility. On this view Apemantus is the better dog of the two, and his rudeness has offered the romanticism as tactfully as possible. When this is exposed as "flattering misery" he makes the more searching point:

Ape.   If thou didst put this sourcold habit on
        To castigate thy pride, twere well, but thou
        Dost it enforcedly; thou'dst courtier be again
        Wert thou not beggar. Willing misery
        Outlives uncertain pomp. . . .

Again; he was a courtier when he was holding a court. This is a refinement of money hatred that Marx failed to pick out of the play; Timon's generosity was a way of begging for affection, and it makes him the same kind of dog as the spaniels he could hire. Timon might answer to the main point that he has in fact found gold, and stays in misery from disillusionment about friends or hurt pride; but that would not answer the claim that he was a spaniel.

The answer of the play is no doubt that he has a noble nature, and Apemantus a mean one; but people agree that Timon gets his apotheosis too easily, and it is not only a fidget of logic to complain that the dog theme is unresolved. The most convincing claim for Timon appears when he urges the thieves, in Apemantus' manner, to go on thieving, and gives such profound reasons that one of them decides to stop. No one would pay so much attention to Apemantus; Timon keeps a certain grandeur and generosity which works for good however much he wants to do harm. But the paradox amounts to denying Timon's ascetic posi-

tion, with which Shakespeare seems to identify himself so wholeheart-
edly, and the final arguments against Apemantus are little better than
snobbish.

Tim.   I, to bear this,
          That never knew but better, is some burden.
          Thy nature did commence in sufferance, time
          Hath made thee hard in't. Why should'st thou hate men?
          They never flattered thee; what hast thou given?

The unreason of the question has the pathos of Lear thinking Edgar
had been sent mad by daughters, but he goes on, less like Lear, to exult
over Apemantus for low birth. After a bout of that we have:

Ape.   Art thou proud yet?
Tim.   Ay, that I am not thee.
Ape.   I, that I was
          No prodigal.
Tim.   I, that I am one now.
          Were all the wealth I have shut up in thee
          I'd give thee leave to hang it. Get thee gone.

Apemantus is clearly right in saying Timon cannot claim to be
otherworldly, he is proud of good birth or of being born into money,
and apparently proud of having just found some. But Timon's apparently simple insults amount to a claim for aristocracy, the accident of
birth has saved him from meanness of nature, and the otherworldly life
can be reached only through a sort of success in the world. It is a
splendid answer, but not only to Apemantus, it throws a crucial paradox
into the whole cult of asceticism known to Shakespeare chiefly as Christian. And even here the dog rides the conflict, on the one hand a low
creature which distributes contempt, on the other it is good-humoured
because self-satisfied about its direct pleasures (what else has Timon
felt in generosity and glory?). Yet in the play the only effect of the
idea is that Timon can go off unanswered into neurotic insanity, and
Apemantus is forced for contrast into a reasonable view of life in which
he can cut no figure. They are left with only abuse to entertain themselves:

Tim.   Choler does kill me that thou art alive.
          I swoon to see thee.
Ape.   Would thou wouldst burst.

It seems likely that Shakespeare wrote the scene both in bitterness
of spirit and as a hurried working-over of a play whose somewhat thin

plot was already drawn up. To do that he had to bring out some of his root ideas in a crude form, a process he would find irritating, but this has the convenience of letting us see them clearly. The striking thing, I think, is that the dog symbolism could be worked out so far and yet remain somehow useless. One would not expect it to solve the puzzles any more than "fool" does elsewhere, but it should make us feel better about them. Actually, after all the argument, its parts remain quite separate—the dog does not manage to become a "symbol" that includes cynic and flatterer, flattery and affection, so as to imply a view of their proper relations. It remains a bridge over which they exchange puzzles, and the generalization of it amounts mainly to letting you feel the same kind of distaste for a variety of different people. Yet the range required for the jovial Augustan dog-sentiment, and even the feeling about dogs, are all present; the thing is offered and refused. There is no palliation fit for Timon, and he can find no rock-bottom above the grave—it would be stupid to say that mere full use of the metaphor would have made the play better. But this kind of analysis seems to me to show that the metaphor had a large use, that the refusal was tested, that in an obscure but continuous fashion there was a palliation held in view. And anyone who wants to clear up the very baffling topic of metaphor (perhaps too fundamental to be cleared up) needs I think to hold in mind both cases like this, the most radically complex type, and the fact that machinery like this may be at work even in a metaphor of settled convention and apparently simple form.

Wordsworth's Remorse

Herbert Read

In 1816 Shelley published a sonnet to Wordsworth. Its mixture of admiration and regret expresses an attitude towards that great poet which I still find reasonable:

> Poet of Nature, thou hast wept to know
> That things depart which never may return:
> Childhood and youth, friendship and love's first glow,
> Have fled like sweet dreams, leaving thee to mourn.
> These common woes I feel. One loss is mine
> Which thou too feel'st, yet I alone deplore.
> Thou wert as a lone star, whose light did shine
> On some frail bark in winter's midnight roar:
> Thou hast like to a rock-built refuge stood
> Above the blind and battling multitude:
> In honoured poverty thy voice did weave
> Songs consecrate to truth and liberty,—
> Deserting these, thou leavest me to grieve,
> Thus having been, that thou shouldst cease to be.

Shelley was then twenty-four; Wordsworth forty-six. The older poet had lived through the great days of the French Revolution, and had had some direct contact with the Revolutionary leaders. By the time Shelley had become mentally aware of the issues involved, the Revolution was over and reaction had set in. It is possible to argue that Shelley at this time was an enthusiastic young man who would, like Wordsworth, become sober in his middle age. But six years later, when Shelley died, there was no sign of the process; and the argument is superficial because it avoids the philosophical issues which are involved. There were many contemporaries of Wordsworth—Hazlitt and Leigh Hunt, for

From *A Coat of Many Colors* by Herbert Read. Reprinted by permission of the Horizon Press, Inc.

example—who did not change their attitude towards the principles which inspired the French Revolution. What, then, in Wordsworth's particular case, was the cause of his reaction?

It is a pertinent question because, with this change of political attitude went a change in poetic quality, and a change for the worse. That is a dogmatic statement, but I do not think it would be challenged by any of Wordsworth's admirers. I personally take the view that these two processes of change were connected in Wordsworth's development, and elsewhere I have given my argument full scope.[1] It cannot be argued that the growth of discretion, or of rational judgement, has necessarily an adverse effect on poetic inspiration—there are many examples to the contrary. But was the change, in Wordsworth's case, in any real sense logical or intellectual? Did it not rather arise from deep psychological wounds which he suffered in circumstances only indirectly connected with the political events which were made the excuse for reaction? I believe it did.

We must remember that when Wordsworth decided that all he had written before 1797-8 should be deemed *juvenilia,* he was drawing a line at a point within which many poets have produced their best work. In that year he was already twenty-eight, an age which embraces the whole of Keats's work, and most of Shelley's. Moreover, before reaching that age he had undergone all the vital experiences which were to mould his character and determine the course of his life. He had burned with revolutionary zeal; he had gone to France to participate in the great events which were stirring his imagination; he had fallen passionately in love and become the father of an illegitimate child; and then, still within this period, he had lost his revolutionary zeal, retreating first to Godwinian rationalism and then to his own philosophy of natural piety; and in the process he had renounced his first love, and made of this passionate experience a guilty secret unrevealed to all but a few of his most intimate friends for the rest of his long life. It is one of the strangest transformations in that age of romantic personalities, and the extent to which his poetry can be—or as some would have it, *should* be—interpreted in the light of this experience remains one of the most interesting problems in the history of literature.

The extreme theory which I put forward some years ago seeks to hinge the whole process on what must have been the intensest event—

[1] *Wordsworth.* London (Cape), 1930.

Wordsworth's passion for Annette. The intellectual changes in Wordsworth's mind are regarded as a secondary consequence of the emotional
changes, and as largely determined by them. The fundamental process
is physical or emotional; the rest is a superstructure of rationalization
or sublimation. This theory has not found much favour with academic
critics, least of all with devoted Wordsworthians like Professor de
Sélincourt. But I am bound to say that I find nothing but confirmation
of it in the definitive edition of Wordsworth's works which Professor
de Sélincourt was editing so scrupulously and so objectively up to the
time of his death. That confirmation is to be found, not only in passages and poems which the later Wordsworth suppressed, and which
are now for the first time published, but in a general reconsideration of
the significance of the work done by Wordsworth between his return
from France at the end of 1792 and his mystical rebirth in 1797-8.
Here there is not space to give all the necessary supporting quotations,
but the long poem *Guilt and Sorrow,* the strange tragedy *The Borderers,* and several of the shorter poems included among the *Juvenilia*
and published for the first time in the definitive edition, are bathed in
a morbid atmosphere of guilt and remorse, intense with a feeling which
no merely political disillusionment could justify or explain. The following lines from an early version of *Guilt and Sorrow,* probably written in the summer of 1793, provided the keynote:

> Unhappy Man! thy sole delightful hour
> Flies fast; it is thy miserable dower
> Only to taste of joy that thou mayst pine
> A loss, which rolling suns shall ne'er restore.

From that feeling of inevitable loss he passes to regret for his hasty
passion, then to feelings of guilt and remorse, then to attempts at
rationalistic justification, and finally to more moral and more sublime
feelings of renunciation, resignation and repair. If this process were
not clear enough in the text of the poems, it is revealed with complete
directness and a power of self-analysis of the highest order in a prefatory
essay which Wordsworth wrote for *The Borderers.* This manuscript,
which was only recently discovered, was published by Professor de
Sélincourt in a volume of miscellaneous essays six years ago, but did not
then receive the attention it deserved. Now that it is included in the
canon of Wordsworth's works, it should be studied for what it really
is: a key to the very complex transformation which Wordsworth's mind

underwent in these formative years. The general moral, says Wordsworth, is "to show the dangerous use which may be made of reason when a man has committed a great crime"; but it must be stressed that the final effect of this document, and of the poems we have been considering, is not to involve Wordsworth in a charge of hypocrisy or equivocation. We may regret that he deceived the world and we may believe that this deceit had a blighting effect on his subsequent development; but we know that at least he was uncommonly honest with himself, and that his mind was of a depth and subtlety rarely exceeded among men of genius.

What is this mental activity we call *remorse?* The word comes from the Latin verb meaning *to bite,* and its literal sense is shown by the medieval English mystic who wrote the *Agenbite of Inwit*—the repeated gnawing of the conscience. It arises from the consciousness of some wrong done in the past, perhaps concealed, certainly never expiated. It is a terrible scourge, and the part it has played in the psychology of great writers has always been disastrous. There are many lives from which this truth could be illustrated—Tolstoy's is one, but none is so clear as Wordsworth's.[2]

Wordsworth became so obsessed by this feeling that much of his earlier work, as I have already indicated, deals directly with themes of remorse, as though he were trying to get rid of the burden by objectifying it in a work of art.

In a cancelled scene from *The Borderers,* one of the characters cries:

> . . . ah, teach me first,
> If not to bring back all I've loved, at least
> To rescue my poor thoughts, which now and ever
> Bleed helplessly on Memory's piercing thorn.

In the Preface which he wrote to this play, but which he did not publish (it appeared for the first time in the first volume of Professor de Sélincourt's edition of Wordsworth's *Works*), he makes a very acute analysis of his own case:

[2] "Remorse is not among the eternal verities. The Greeks were right to dethrone her. Her action is too capricious, as though the Erinyes selected for punishment only certain men and certain sins. And of all means to regeneration Remorse is surely the most wasteful. It cuts away healthy tissue with the poisoned. It is a knife that probes far deeper than the evil."—E. M. Forster: *Howards End* (1910), p. 316.

Let us suppose [he says] a young man of great intellectual powers yet without any solid principles of genuine benevolence. His master passions are pride and the love of distinction. He has deeply imbibed a spirit of enterprise in a tumultuous age. He goes into the world and is betrayed into a great crime.—That influence on which all his happiness is built immediately deserts him. His talents are robbed of their weight, his exertions are unavailing, and he quits the world in disgust, with strong misanthropic feelings.

In such a case, said Wordsworth, there would be a tendency for the remorseful mind to seek relief from two sources, action and meditation. If he follows the line of action, he will attempt to build up his own power and to give vent to his frustrated feelings in aggressive violence. "Power is much more easily manifested in destroying than in creating." But if—and here Wordsworth is contemplating his own case—he follows the line of meditation, then he will indulge in what it is fashionable nowadays to call "rationalization"—that is to say, in Wordsworth's words, "having indulged a habit, dangerous in a man who has fallen, of dallying with moral calculations, he becomes an empiric, and a daring and unfeeling empiric. He disguises from himself his own malignity by assuming the character of a speculator in morals, and one who has the hardihood to realize his speculation." The main object of Wordsworth's play was to show "the dangerous use which may be made of reason when a man has committed a great crime."

It is one of the characteristics of remorse that it acts like a slow drug. It calls into existence an antidote to the pain which accompanies it, and when the pain disappears, and the original crime is forgotten, or contemplated with equanimity, it is because the drug has completed its anæsthetic work. Anæsthetic is the right word—it is the feelings that are killed. But the feelings have a unity; they can be dulled only by working upon the whole mind or sensibility. The mind that feels remorse is the same mind that feels the beauties of nature or of human affections. The shell of insensibility which it cultivates is over-all: the victim cannot consciously preserve a sensitive area for the benefit of his poetry, or for any other purpose.

It is for this reason that great artists often seem to despise or evade the code of conventional morality. Shelley is a case in point. His desertion of Harriet Westbrook, his first wife, was a crime against the conventional code of morality as serious as Wordsworth's, and it had far more tragic consequences. But Shelley was not a victim of remorse. In a famous retort to Southey, who had charged him with immorality, he said:

> You select a single passage out of a life otherwise not only spotless, but spent in an impassioned pursuit of virtue, which looks like a blot, merely because I regulated my domestic arrangements without deferring to the notions of the vulgar, although I might have done so quite as conveniently had I descended to their base thoughts —this you call *guilt*. . . . I am innocent of ill, either done or intended; the consequences you allude to flowed in no respect from me. . . .

There are other statements in his letters to the same effect. They do not prove that Shelley had a callous heart: there is, in any case, other evidence in overwhelming quantity which shows how sensitive and affectionate he was. They prove, if anything, Shelley's possession of a moral courage of exceptional strength. There are weak people who have no moral code and there are timid people who conform to a conventional moral code; there are also a few people strong enough to formulate their own moral code, and Shelley was one of these.

But to return to Wordsworth. If we relate his poetic production to the psychological development suggested by the theory I have advanced, we shall find that it divides into four very distinct periods. There is first of all the *Juvenilia*, the poems like *An Evening Walk* and *Descriptive Sketches* which were written before his decisive experiences in France. Then come the poems of Remorse, which I have already mentioned and which fill the next five years. Then in 1797 begins his intimate collaboration with Coleridge. This is the supreme phase of his creative activity, and it lasted about ten years. From about 1800 he composed, not merely with difficulty, but as his sister Dorothy relates in her *Journals,* with a real sense of pain and physical exhaustion. He was fighting against frustration and inhibition. Remorse was completing its deadly work. He was to live for another fifty years, his powers at first swiftly, and then slowly but completely giving out. The dying embers emit an occasional spark, but nothing that in any degree adds to the total impression of his genius.

It may be asked at this point why, if remorse was the active agent of Wordsworth's decline, his greatest period comes, not immediately as a consequence of his decisive experiences, but only some five years later; and why the deadening effects of remorse did not begin to develop until some ten years later. The answer would have to take into account certain rhythms of psychological development (intermittences of the heart, as Marcel Proust called them) of which Wordsworth himself was well aware, and indeed made the basis of his famous theory of poetic composition. We might say, briefly, that from the age of twenty-two to twenty-seven Wordsworth was too near to the events, too inwardly agitated, to compose great poetry; that between the ages of twenty-seven and thirty-two, when he wrote his greatest poetry, he was recollecting his emotions in a state of relative tranquillity, under the immediate personal influence of his sister Dorothy and of Coleridge; and that up to the date of his marriage to Mary Hutchinson, which took place in October, 1802, he had not taken the irrevocable step of finally deserting his French mistress and their child. By then the phase of contending motives was over: the heart was passive and remorse could henceforth do its deadly work without the mitigation of hope or irresolution.

Satan

Arnold Stein

[In *Paradise Lost*] one need not choose between Satan's being a tragic hero or an absurd villain. Either extreme stamps us as a more restricted moralist than Milton the poet. For then we are less able than Milton to admit the test of contradiction into the moral universe of our art. If Satan is a tragic hero, it is because we are not honestly willing to test good by evil. If Satan is merely an absurd villain, it is because we want to ground our art upon too narrow a certainty; it is because we prefer the idea, and the confirmation of our certainty, to the more comprehensive, and therefore more daring, exploration of human experience—the submitting of an idea to a dramatic structure. If Satan is merely absurd, then we are not willing, though Milton is, to test evil by good.

The good in Satan responds to, and struggles toward, the good he encounters outside him. His evil is not pure; it can win the struggle against good only by allying itself with good. The rebellion which leads to the fall is in the name of liberty, and against the name of tyranny. His remorse, pity, tears all pay homage to good, but are perverted. If we do not give Satan his due, we cannot understand the nature of his evil. As Milton expresses it in *Areopagitica:* "look how much we thus expel of sin, so much we expel of virtue: for the matter of them both is the same; remove that, and ye remove them both alike." Even after we have recognized the inadequacy of Satan's tears, we must admit that they provide us with an impressive example of tears such as angels weep. And though Satan's courage before Death must be recognized as a limited virtue, still we should not deny ourselves the pleasure of admiring his courage, nor deny ourselves the tension of seeing a virtue that is magnificent but futile once higher values have been rejected. It is true that Satan is already damned, that he has already felt (and as soon despised) pain; but still his courage is a fact. If we allow ourselves to admire his physical courage we shall have a better idea of what is wrong with his moral courage.

Should we apply strict logic to Satan, as though he were a philosophical position instead of a dramatic character, then of course he could not escape absurdity. Under those circumstances the most he, or any character, might hope for would be logical consistency.

> So farwel Hope, and with Hope farwel Fear,
> Farwel Remorse: all Good to me is lost;
> Evil be thou my Good. [IV, 108ff.]

This is absurd, as C. S. Lewis demonstrates with perhaps more vigor than necessary. But the absurd is not a simple absolute. Above all, it is not static. There is a difference between Dogberry's "write me down an ass" and Falstaff's "they hate us youth." The degree of self-consciousness, and the total situation, determine the quality and the effect of the absurd. Compare, for instance, Lady Macbeth's ignorant "Stop up th' access and passage to remorse" with Macbeth's partly self-conscious absurdities: "But wherefore could not I pronounce 'Amen'?" or "What hands are here?" or "Wake Duncan with thy knocking! I would thou couldst!" Satan, one may well feel, is partly aware of his absurdity, but he is unaware of the total situation, and he cannot master it by means of glib irony. Yet to dismiss him as ridiculous is also to dismiss him as a dramatic character, without allowing ourselves to experience his failure. That is to substitute logical judgment for dramatic experience.

Let us follow the development of one of Satan's failures. His role as leader seems to be a chief dramatic means of expressing his pride. "Faithful to whom?" is Gabriel's taunt after Satan is discovered at Eve's ear practicing his responsibilities as leader. The faith that goes only downward, never upward, exacts its penalties; and Satan is tied to his followers more than he realizes. In his most honest facing of self, at the beginning of Book IV, he goes beyond the trap of his responsibility downward. He cannot repent, he says, because of his "dread of shame" before his followers. That is a real enough barrier for Satan, but he penetrates beyond the active symbol of his pride to the basic mystery of his pride itself. If God should grant him grace, he would only fall again, more heavily. And so he touches the root of his despair, and sees through to the unchanging quality of his fatal flaw. But Satan's vision of himself is not steady. When he pulls back from the desperate realization of what his pride means, it is only to clutch harder the illusions of his responsibility. In the soliloquy that soon follows, after Satan has been touched by the beauty of Adam and Eve, it is "public reason," his duty as leader, that justifies his decision:

> And should I at your harmless innocence
> Melt, as I doe, yet public reason just,
> Honour and Empire with revenge enlarg'd,
> By conquering this new World, compels me now
> To do what else though damnd I should abhorre.   [IV, 388ff.]

The tears and remorse that Satan was able to convert to oratory return to plague him once he is separated from his audience of followers. There seems reason for believing that the main difference between the Satan of the first two books and the later Satan is the difference between a leader making a public appearance and a leader on a solitary mission. That Satan is less magnificent away from his followers hardly proves a falling-off in Milton's creative powers, or a sudden realization that his villain has been getting the best lines. The paradox is true to life: the leader has greater stature when he is before his millions, but partly through being forced to deny his essential solitary self (even while taking self as the standard of measure). When Satan speaks in soliloquy it is the solitary self speaking, still capable of despair and pity; but the relationship holds: the pride that will not submit to superior forces outside itself ends by submitting to inferior forces, also outside itself. It maintains the illusion of pure selfishness by being the will upon which others are dependent, but it cannot escape depending upon their dependence.

And so the evil of selfish pride is tested by the good of selfless devotion. The irony of that situation resides in the necessity of the test; it is also in the dramatic result of the test. But let us see what happens. After the leader's heroic public appearances, and the solitary heroism of his expedition through chaos, some of the first impetus begins to waver, and the solitary unheroic self can bring the conflict to articulation. The despair turns into desperate resolution; true repentance is impossible for him and so he must persevere in the course of action. Still, a little

later the unsubdued good in him responds to the beauty of Adam and
Eve; but evil has allies: pity can slide into self-pity, individual responsibility can be shifted to God, and the best argument of all, selfless dedication to the public cause, can marshal him the way he was going.

This argument helps keep alive the symbolic relationship between
leader and followers. Again in Book IX, after he has returned, "cautious of day," from pacing the dark hemisphere for the sabbath which
precedes his work, he falls into another fit of despair at the beauty of
man's earth. But he comes to terms with his destiny and thinks once
more as a leader, though this time he emphasizes the fruits of responsibility:

> To mee shall be the glorie sole among
> The infernal Powers, in one day to have marr'd
> What he *Almightie* styl'd, six Nights and Days
> Continu'd making, and who knows how long
> Before had bin contriving. [IX, 135ff.]

A little while later, after he has been rendered "stupidly good" by Eve's
beauty, he shifts his pronoun to the plural as a significant self-reminder
of his duty:

> Thoughts, whither have ye led me, with what sweet
> Compulsion thus transported to forget
> What hither brought us. [IX, 473ff.]

But Satan's pious concern for the responsibility of leadership is, as
we have already seen, a complicated attitude, and one he is, perforce,
dependent upon. It is a kind of talisman that he must protect, even at
the cost of speaking truth. To defend the inviolability of his leadership
he will reveal a state secret. When Gabriel taunts him with having
abandoned his legions, Satan promptly drops his lie and reveals his
mission of seeking a better abode for his followers. The language of
defensive pride is significant. It behooves, he says,

> A faithful Leader, not to hazard all
> Through wayes of danger by himself untri'd.
> I therefore, I alone first undertook
> To wing the desolate Abyss. [IV, 933ff.]

From the beginning Satan displays a marked inclination to shift
responsibility. It is all God's fault, he says in his first long public
speech:

> but still his strength conceal'd,
> Which tempted our attempt, and wrought our fall.   [I, 641f.]

This of course is public speech, a fulfillment of his accepted public responsibility; but it serves, we feel, to raise the speaker's own "fainting courage." As a leader, before his followers, Satan shifts the responsibility to God. And alone, Satan will blame God for Satan's vengeance on Adam, and for Paradise's being inadequately fenced. And alone, Satan will use the responsibility of his office as leader to shift the responsibility to his followers, to "public reason." He is dodging his own shadow, on a merry-go-round.

According to Milton's conception of evil, Satan's fate should evolve in two ways: the good he brings to others and the harm he brings to himself. Some passages from the *Christian Doctrine* provide the best commentary:

Nor does God make that will evil which was before good, but the will being already in a state of perversion, he influences it in such a manner, that out of its own wickedness it either operates good for others, or punishment for itself, though unknowingly, and with the intent of producing a very different result.   [Chapter VII.]

Guiltiness, accordingly, is accompanied or followed by terrors of conscience . . . whence results a diminution of the majesty of the human countenance, and a conscious degradation of mind.   [Chapter XIII.]

This death [spiritual death] consists, first, in the loss . . . of that right reason . . . in which consisted as it were the life of the understanding. It consists, secondly, in that deprivation of righteousness and liberty to do good, and in that slavish subjection to sin and the devil, which constitutes, as it were, the death of the will.   [Chapter XII.]

Satan recognizes and rebels against the part of the moral law that may bring good out of evil. His statement, with its clear enunciation of the issue, comes early in Book I:

> To do ought good never will be our task,
> But ever to do ill our sole delight
> As being the contrary to his high will
> Whom we resist. If then his Providence
> Out of our evil seek to bring forth good,
> Our labour must be to pervert that end,
> And out of good still to find means of evil.   [I, 159ff.]

The scope of the epic does not permit Satan ever to realize, dramatically, that good is brought about through his evil. He does envy the beauty of the world and guess that it is a compensation for his fall, but he does not experience, at least in *Paradise Lost,* the truth that Adam inherits blessings through Satan's crime against him. What Satan does experience, and dramatically, is the other part of the moral law, his own failure. The development of Satan's realization begins in Book I, with the evidences of inner conflict. It concludes in Book X with the short-lived triumph of Satan's return to hell—with the histrionic mounting of the throne incognito; with the distorted emphasis of his report, as if it were to his credit to have turned the trick with an absurd apple; with the final mass metamorphosis of all the devils into serpents.

Though Satan comes to realize much of his failure, part of his punishment is the self-punishment, "though unknowingly," of the moral (and dramatic) law. He is so highly self-conscious about some things that the petty lapses of his mind become significant betrayals that he is unaware of what is happening to him. "O indignitie!" he says at the thought that man has angels as his servants, but by the time Satan has rounded out his sentence the real source of the indignity is revealed:

> O indignitie!
> Subjected to his service Angel wings,
> And flaming Ministers to watch and tend
> Thir earthie Charge: Of these the vigilance
> I dread. [IX, 154ff.]

Satan contradicts himself; he was created by God and he wasn't. He is indignant at having to "imbrute" himself as a serpent, apparently forgetting that he has already had this experience before, without indignation. He is the victim (or patient) of his own eloquence, and it is not always magnificent eloquence. At one point he admits that only in destroying can he find "ease." But, in priming himself for the temptation of Eve, he talks as though destroying is more than a passive relief: it is called his only pleasure and joy.

Satan's reasoning, often shaky, suffers most from the kind of sustained naked exposure it receives in Book IX. There is no forensic necessity to cover this:

> O Earth, how like to Heav'n, if not preferr'd
> More justly, Seat worthier of Gods, as built
> With second thoughts, reforming what was old!
> For what God after better worse would build? [IX, 99ff.]

Satan, like Adam after he has decided to eat the apple, is reasoning from a special position—himself. He puts himself in God's place by putting God in Satan's place, and reasoning from there. The passage continues with more of the same:

> hee to be aveng'd
> And to repair his numbers thus impair'd,
> Whether such vertue spent of old now faild
> More Angels to Create, if they at least
> Are his Created or to spite us more,
> Determin'd to advance into our room
> A Creature form'd of Earth, and him endow,
> Exalted from so base original,
> With Heav'nly spoils, our spoils. [IX, 143ff.]

It is a masterly presentation of Satan's psychology, in Satan's terms. And he—"unknowingly"—accepts his own trivial reasoning, or the part that suits his needs; for a few lines further on he states, without reservation or alternative, that man was created to spite the fallen angels. It is like Iago's accepting what he has previously advanced as a tentative possibility.

These examples lead us to the major exhibition of what happens to Satan's mind. We remember his trumpeting challenge, "A mind not to be chang'd by Place or Time." And we see what he cannot see, that he is diminished in mind, and in that important sense changed. But the irony does not stop there, for Satan's mind is both changed and unchanged.

> The mind is its own place, and in it self
> Can make a Heav'n of Hell, a Hell of Heav'n. [I, 254f.]

He is only partly right, but he also speaks truer than he knows. The not-to-be-changed part of his mind cannot prevent him from feeling a kind of terror at the sight of Eve's beauty, and he acknowledges that there is terror in both love and beauty. We understand Satan's fear, and the irony of his situation, when we remember Raphael's lecture on love. Through love, he told Adam, we refine the thoughts, enlarge the heart; love has its seat in the reason, and is the ladder by which we ascend to heavenly love. No wonder Satan backs away, and has to arm himself with hate—to protect the "unchangeable" part of his mind in its program for taking over. What Satan intended as a declaration of mental freedom turns out to be freedom only to pursue the blind impetus of evil action. The true liberty of inward freedom (which is

always "twinned" with right reason) is lost to him: the trap of leadership and the compulsions of the moral law impose upon him the restricted course of action that constitutes the loss of his outward freedom.
It is the "death of the will." Satan is ironically deceived by his ability
to move, and still powerfully; but the power is that of a concentrated
impetus, along a narrow chute, unable to control its rushing speed
toward its own destruction.

"*A mind not to be chang'd by Place or Time*": "*The mind is its
own place.*" Both Belial and Mammon end their long speeches opposing
continued war against heaven with the same argument, presumably
their best: adjust to the environment.

> or enur'd not feel,
> Or chang'd at length, and to the place conformed
> In temper and in nature, will receive
> Familiar the fierce heat, and void of pain;
> This horror will grow milde, this darkness light.   [II, 216ff.]

> Our torments also may in length of time
> Become our Elements, these piercing Fires
> As soft as now severe, our temper chang'd
> Into their temper; which must needs remove
> The sensible of pain.   [II, 274ff.]

It is not an argument that Satan can afford to consider. But it is the
position to which he is, unknowingly, reduced when he is tortured by
the beauty of the earth:

> the more I see
> Pleasures about me, so much more I feel
> Torment within me, as from the hateful siege
> Of contraries; all good to me becomes
> Bane, and in Heav'n much worse would be my state.
>   [IX, 119ff.]

This development could not emerge in hell proper; besides, there his
position required a bold, complete front. But the circle has now closed;
he has adjusted so entirely to the "unchanged" part of his mind, the
hell within, that he *needs* hell.

By way of conclusion let us leave structural analysis and turn to
the style, where we can see in a couple of examples much of the idea
of Satan's failure; for Milton's style is both the medium for dramatic
structure and dramatic structure itself. After his soul-searching solilo-

quy at the beginning of Book IV, Satan proceeds toward the border of
Eden. The verse leaves him for a long description of the beauties of
that place, and then returns to find him apparently still shaken from
the violence of his inner conflict.

> Now to th' ascent of that steep savage Hill
> *Satan* had journied on, pensive and slow.   [IV, 172f.]

The desperate resolution that ended the soliloquy did not, it would
seem, end the conflict. There is no path through the undergrowth, and
only one gate on the other side:

> which when th' arch-fellon saw
> Due entrance he disdaind, and in contempt,
> At one slight bound high overleap'd all bound
> Of Hill or highest Wall, and sheer within
> Lights on his feet. As when a prowling Wolfe,
> Whom hunger drives to seek new haunt for prey,
> Watching where Shepherds pen thir Flocks at eeve
> In hurdl'd Cotes amid the field secure,
> Leaps o're the fence with ease into the Fould:
> Or as a Thief bent to unhoord the cash
> Of some rich Burgher, whose substantial dores,
> Cross-barrd and bolted fast, fear no assault,
> In at the window climbes, or o're the tiles;
> So clomb this first grand Thief into Gods Fould:
> So since into his Church lewd Hirelings climbe.   [IV, 179ff.]

Calling Satan the arch-felon seems like external commentary, or
perhaps only a kind of decorative epithet. But it turns out to be an
anticipation of the imagery. So too is the animal grace of the rhythm
that carries Satan over the barrier to light on his feet. Then we are into
the unfolding imagery. From contempt and ease to hunger and ease,
to the vague itch of "bent to unhoord" and mere skulking trickery:
Satan diminishes in the images. We have three views of him, each one
breaking down the mask of his "contempt" and getting further into
his inner nature—projecting (with the help of the "pensive and slow")
Satan's own real self. It is a kind of counterpoint, the diminishing of
Satan played against the increasing magnitude of the theft. It becomes
the primal theft, in God's house, preparing the way for all subsequent
theft.

Satan's drama continues, though again he disappears from the
verse while the garden and Adam and Eve are described. There is one
mention, a hundred lines further on, of his feelings—the brief "Saw

undelighted all delight." And then, about seventy lines later, we return to him, still shaken:

> When *Satan* still in gaze, as first he stood,
> Scarce thus at length faild speech recoverd sad. [IV, 356f.]

The impetus of the imagery is still working when Satan returns to Eden in Book IX—the ease not lost, but the contempt gone:

> In with the River sunk, and with it rose
> Satan involv'd in rising Mist, then sought
> Where to lie hid. [IX, 74ff.]

Or consider the following passage. The leader has just by the power of his words recalled his falling legions from the burning flood:

> All these and more came flocking; but with looks
> Down cast and damp, yet such wherein appear'd
> Obscure som glimps of joy, to have found thir chief
> Not in despair, to have found themselves not lost
> In loss it self; which on his count'nance cast
> Like doubtful hue: but he his wonted pride
> Soon recollecting, with high words, that bore
> Semblance of worth not substance, gently rais'd
> Thir fainting courage, and dispel'd their fears. [I, 522ff.]

If we fix our attention on what is said about the "high words," we may not observe that Satan, in his role as leader, is being presented dramatically. The key word is the repeated "cast." For Satan's countenance reflects their looks, as his feelings reflect theirs. The relationship between chief and followers is conveyed by the wonderful ambiguity of "Like doubtful hue." And the relationship is extended by the next lines, which are an ironic demonstration of the internal-external mutual relationship between looks and feelings, theirs and Satan's. Satan cannot help himself. Leader-like he subdues his own doubts, which he sees reflected in them (along with their dependence upon him for hope). He *recollects,* with an effort of will, his mainstay, the "wonted pride." (In Book IX, after Satan has been forced, by the beauty and innocence of Eve, to stand abstracted from his own evil, "stupidly good," he regains control of his will by recollecting himself: "Fierce hate he recollects.") He gently raises their (and by implication *his*) "fainting courage." The "high words" are like the pride, recollected by an effort of will. Is it an ignorant effort of will? Unless we are prepared to say so, then we must admit that Satan himself may be aware of the false

worth of his words, and that the commentary may be internal, a projection of Satan's consciousness. Not that we must think Satan coolly
rational about all this, for the irony lies in the trap of leadership: he
may know better but he cannot act better, for he is caught in his own
trap.

Satan's words are not given here, but we are not dependent on this
passage alone for judging his degree of consciousness. After a military
review plainly intended to bolster the morale of both troops and leader
—the band plays in the Dorian mode, the warriors march "Breathing
united force with fixed thought"—the focus returns to Satan. He takes
heart from the sight of them, from their number: *his* strength. He
towers and shines above them. But still, the tone of the passage changes,
as do the details, when we move from the external public appearance of
Satan as leader to his feelings as leader. The "dauntless" courage and
"considerate" pride are there, but so are the scars, and the care, and the
"faded cheek." The passage needs quoting:

> cruel his eye, but cast
> Signs of remorse and passion to behold
> The fellows of his crime, the followers rather
> (Far other once beheld in bliss) condemn'd
> For ever now to have their lot in pain,
> Millions of Spirits for his fault amerc't
> Of Heav'n, and from Eternal Splendors flung
> For his revolt, yet faithfull how they stood,
> Thir Glory witherd. . . .
> Thrice he assayd, and thrice in spite of scorn,
> Tears such as Angels weep, burst forth: at last
> Words interwove with sighs found out their way.   [I, 604ff.]

This is a continuation of our previous insight into Satan's consciousness. In spite of the intervening eighty lines, with what they do
to build up Satan's morale as leader, and to emphasize the external
characteristics of his relations with his troops, the dramatic conflict
within him has been continuing underneath all the surface show of the
military review. The key word, "cast," is repeated. The ambiguity of
Satan's earlier "Like doubtful hue" is resolved, and his feelings made
explicit—remorse, passion, tears. His sense of responsibility as leader,
indirectly conveyed in the earlier passage, becomes admitted guilt here;
he even drops the mask of euphemism (as necessary in private as in
public to the leader), and calls his fellows followers. The Latinate syntax, linking "behold" with "yet faithfull how they stood," perfectly

suits the development of Satan's feelings. This must have been the main impulse of the remorse, but it can find out its way only after his confession of their status as followers, of their loss, of his guilt. The "high words," when he finally can speak them, are those of controlled and self-conscious eloquence, to soothe the emotions and build hope upon calm—by fine sounds and rhythms, by vague optimism, and by the specific assurance that the war will be continued "by fraud or guile" rather than by force. Satan knows that his words have only "Semblance of worth," but he speaks, through an effort of will, what is expected of the leader by his followers. He also speaks what is expected of the leader by the leader.

In the passages just considered the style has been dramatically functional in the fullest sense of that phrase. Only style could have been sensitive and flexible enough to communicate the complex conflict between Satan's internal feelings and the external necessities of his public position. The larger context is the hierarchy of absolute values. The conflict is between the private good within Satan (the remorse, passion, tears, guilt) and the public evil (his position as leader of the forces against good). But the evil is within him too, for his private position has determined his public one. And the private good, which refers to the larger context, also refers to the public evil, for Satan's remorse and guilt are chiefly directed toward his followers and his responsibility for their fall. So his private good is, in the hierarchy of values, a lesser good, for allegiance to his followers is less good than allegiance to God. The responsibility that Satan accepts is, in the scale of values, downward (to his followers) not upward (to God). And so the good which feels remorse and despair within, which struggles with the evil within and the evil without, finds its expression in a secondary good; but once the primary good is rejected, remorse becomes merely a sense of public responsibility, passion and tears become moving eloquence to carry out the public office of removing despair. Guilt gets lost in the shuffle.

Byron's *Don Juan*

Louis Kronenberger

Sooner or later Byron will enjoy a decided vogue again. He will never, of course, be so famous as he once was—he once, after all, intoxicated all England and half of Europe. He carried a sable and self-conscious melancholy to its farthest height; he turned pose into poetry. A dashing hero with some of the glossiest attributes of a villain, he was first swooned over and then hissed, the greatest social success and the greatest social scandal of his age. The whole thing has something excessive about it; there are writers whose careers are an affront to realism, an offense against art. Disraeli's, for example, is too flashy; Beckford's too opulent; Byron's too lurid. Anyone with blood so blue ought not to have blood so black—not kings' and madmen's both. If one is a lord and romantically handsome, need one also walk with a limp? Byron inherited a dank, half-ruined abbey where it was only decent to drink wine from a skull; he could ride like a streak; he swam the Hellespont. He hated and cursed and sobbed over his mother; committed incest with his sister; snarled on his wedding day at his wife. For love of him, titled ladies stabbed themselves with scissors; for love turned hate-wise, had him burned in effigy. After a life of pleasure and excess, he died in squalor fighting for the independence of Greece. And amid all this fame and obloquy, this dandyism and violence, the Lady Carolines and Lady Oxfords and Countess Guicciolis, Byron, before dying at thirty-six, constantly wrote letters, insatiably wrote verse.

It is all too purple for any self-respecting story-teller, let alone real life. That it happens to be true may be the most fantastic part of all, but

From *The Republic of Letters* by Louis Kronenberger. Copyright 1949 by Random House, Inc. and in 1955 by the author. Reprinted by permission of Alfred A. Knopf, Inc.

is not much my reason for recapitulating it here. My chief reason is that for any even brief discussion of *Don Juan* it happens to be immensely revelant. I don't mean in any strictly factual sense; I mean that only someone with the endowments for living so privileged and tempestuous and superbly exuberant a life could have written so worldly and torrential and superbly exuberant a poem. *Don Juan* is not an example of literature compensating for life, of the romantic imagination fleeing mean streets for fairyland. *Don Juan,* to be sure, gallops with imagination; shoots the very rapids of romance. But on that side it hardly bounds more swiftly than Byron's own life did: while, from another side, it is crammed with knowledge of highborn sin and folly, with intimate understanding of the great world. To create Haidée and hymn the isles of Greece it was doubtless enough for Byron to be a poet. But to portray a Donna Julia or Lady Adeline, to move through ballrooms and glide up staircases with so much assurance, Byron needed also to be a peer.

Don Juan is not autobiographical: Byron set down here something better than autobiography, he set down himself. Here at last, after so many studied twitchings of his mantle, here amid a hundred extravagances and excrescences, in a rush of words, a pell-mell of impressions, here where the operatic tumbles sheerly into the farcical, where the beetles of mockery kill the flowers of romance, stands revealed the whole unruly man. *Childe Harold* is in large part Byronism, but *Don Juan* is Byron.

Don Juan is also one of the most staggering performances in literature. So far as I know, there is nothing truly like it—for one thing because no one more of an artist would have dreamed of doing it as Byron did, while no one less of a genius could have contrived to do it at all. In its obstreperous magic, its aristocratic vulgarity, in the eloquence of its praise and far greater eloquence of its abuse, there is such swagger as even Byron never elsewhere attempted; but also such power as he never elsewhere achieved. What he did in *Don Juan* was, fortunately, not portray but express himself.

Than Byron there is in general no stagier actor in our literary history; but the immensely rewarding thing in *Don Juan* is that Byron altogether eschews the leading role, the center of the stage. In return, it is true, he insists on being almost everything else connected with the production: now dramatist and now drama critic; now heckler, now prompter, now minor actor muttering brash asides; frequently stealing a scene, unblushing, by interrupting the show. Hence what we get is as much production as play, as much rehearsal as performance, as much brilliant confusion as clear sense of design. And for Byron it is all wonderfully in keeping and wonderfully liberating: he has found his happiest calling—not actor but showman.

This exchange—of posturing for showmanship—works tremendous good: instead of a personal desire to attract attention, there is the professional ability to command it. And, indeed, filled as it is with such antics and interruptions as no formal work of art could endure, *Don Juan* is most accurately called a show. Nor are we merely hanging on to a metaphor; nothing else—not satire, not epic—so truthfully describes *Don Juan* (which is as often comic as satiric, and less epic than picaresque). Nothing except a show dare be so explosive in its energy, so filled with fireworks and gaudy trimmings, so played in the very lap of the audience; can contain such tossed-off insults, such haphazard profundities. And one of its most showmanlike qualities is that, though episode after episode may be treated tongue in cheek, the episodes themselves are never thrown away, never whittled down to a mere satiric point. Juan's intrigue with Donna Julia is almost as good Boccaccio as it is Byron; the storm and the shipwreck have their quota of excitement, the harem scenes their quota of indecency. Byron deals in meaningless wars but not sham battles; in too lush Mediterranean scenes, perhaps, but never painted backdrops. And writing of Juan and Haidée he can, of course, be genuinely romantic, and chronicle a romance that is genuinely tender and moving:

> Alas! they were so young, so beautiful
> So lonely, loving, helpless . . .

It is the one haunting episode in the poem, its innocence and ecstasy staining our memories more deeply than all the cynicism and worldliness. Nor do the digressions and asides in *Don Juan* come through as mere random frivolities: they not only lend variety, comic vigor, and change of pace, but often help to create suspense: the retardation of Haidée's father's entrance, for example, is managed to excellent effect. For all its waywardness, the story-telling in *Don Juan* is seldom flabby.

But it is for its satire, in the end, or at any rate its elements of laughter, that *Don Juan* must really be praised: for the spectacle it makes of high life, the farce it makes of pretension. Its wars bring nothing about; its lovers (save only Haidée) are all untrue. Juan—an acceptable *jeune premier,* but the least interesting thing in the poem, a merely acquiescent rake, an insipid grandee—is exposed, now in chains, now in triumph, to all the best barbaric society, the most sumptuous misrule, in Europe. But since there's no place, for the satirist, like home, Juan is brought at last—and just when the story needs a complete change of air—to England. In England, Byron's vision narrows but intensifies, his coloring is soberer but his brushwork more expert; we pass out of a world of swashbuckling and opéra bouffe into that of Congreve and Pope. There is no longer any stalking strange beasts through exotic forests with barbaric weapons, but a stiff ride with the hounds after hypocrites and snobs; a long day on the moors bagging philistines and pharisees; a large coaching-party clattering at the heels of politics. The subject being the most nearly "civilized" one in the book, the treatment is, with justice, the most nearly savage: yet the slashing at morals is maintained at the level of manners, with a wonderful accumulation of detail; it is Byron seeking heavy damages for exile, perhaps, but not cheap revenge; and it concludes, in midair, on a wild high note of farce.

A powerfully charged, helter-skelter production, indeed: exhibiting that ebullient gaiety so often twin-brothered by loneliness; that peculiarly magnanimous love of liberty of one who takes inordinate pride in rank; that over-emphasis on sex of one never quite at ease with women: the production of a poet in whom two centuries meet with a great clang but no very deep hostility; the performance of someone versed in English and European and Eastern ways who, if he was in Shelley's words the Pilgrim of Eternity, was also, in Mr. Wilson Knight's, our only cosmopolitan poet.

As with anything so recklessly creative, *Don Juan* has its share of unconscious confession, curious oscillation, odd twistings and turnings. Yet I do not think it superficial to suggest that what the poem *is* enormously outdistances anything it may mean. The critical malady of our age is an indifference to sheer creativeness as a thing—of power and of pleasure—in itself. In its itch to correlate and laminate and explain, current criticism has half lost the instinct to respond and enjoy. Worse, in its obsession over what makes the clock tick, it all too often fails to notice whether it tells the right time. Most great books, it is true, are complex and not lightly mastered; they need to be unraveled and explained. But with something like *Don Juan,* the overwhelming thing is to pitch in, to participate. For you cannot explain inexhaustible energy and high spirits; you can only explain them away. And you lose out if you so concentrate on the targets in *Don Juan* that you only half appreciate the hits; if you care more for Byron's motives than his manner; if you persist in making a laboratory of an amusement park. The motives, to be sure, aren't to be brushed aside; the targets, after 125 years, are still there to shoot at. But what is most exhilarating in *Don Juan* is not so much the satire as what might be called the satiricalness. Obviously what makes any great satirist is much less the occasion for scoffing than the disposition to scoff; for the true satirist, opportunity, so far from knocking only once, knocks all day long. In themselves, ruling classes may or may not be always rotten; but for satire, obviously, they are always ripe. Furthermore, there is about *Don Juan* too great a love of battle for its own sake for us to identify each sideswipe as a blow against tyranny or time-serving, against this vice or that. All the same, the man who wrote *Don Juan* was very far, at bottom, from being either a cynic or a trifler: its cascading poetry, its tumultuous energy cannot consort with the merely cynical and small; and amid the impudences and extravagancies, there sounds again and again the war-cry of the intransigent rebel. Though Byron himself, as Mr. Quennell has remarked, abandoned Juan for Greece out of a "haunting deathwish," *Don Juan* is a very dazzling exhibition of the life-force.

It is difficult, again, to find anything resembling a level of achievement in *Don Juan,* for it dashes up and down the whole ladder of comedy like a monkey. It shows none of the instinct for tone of a satirist like Pope. Pope, for the most part, confines himself to the rapier and the poisoned dart; but Byron (though he worshipped and at times resembles Pope) grasps hold of any weapon, sharp or blunt, subtle or crude; and not guns, swords, arrows only, but stones thrown at windows, firecrackers tossed under chairs, and occasionally a massive field piece, as in the onslaughts against Southey and Wellington. *Don Juan* mingles the wit of the salon with the horseplay of the schoolroom, sensational rhymes with impossible ones, all varieties of facetious nonsense, insult, abuse, pleasantry, unpleasantry. Now it is the buxom widows at the battle of Ismail who wonder despondently why the ravishing hasn't begun; now

> Guests hot and dishes cold . . .

or

> He was the mildest-mannered man
> That ever scuttled ship or cut a throat . . .

or

> And whispering "I will ne'er consent," consented . . .

or

> So for a good old-gentlemanly vice
> I think I must take up with avarice . . .

But it is the profusion, succession, accumulation of jibes, jokes, comments, epithets, apostrophes, the rhymes and running fire throughout sixteen cantos and some sixteen thousand lines that make *Don Juan* the most tumbling and impromptu of epics.

A portrait of a civilization, *Don Juan* is also a kind of pastiche of one. It is immensely "literary"—crammed with poetic tags, critical and biographical tidbits, historical and mythological allusions. In his turning—to sharpen his satire or brighten his narrative—to history, literature, all the compass-points of culture, Byron is like Pope, and achieves a like glitter. For satiric purposes, *Don Juan* is even more a parade and parody of quotations than *The Waste Land;* while it is a virtual anthology of worldly wit and wisdom—Pope and Horace, Chesterfield and Montaigne, Johnson and Swift.

> In her first passion woman loves her lover:
> In all the others, all she loves is love.

> And if I laugh at any mortal thing,
> 'Tis that I may not weep.

Byron has made both these sentiments his endlessly quoted own; but the first of them, of course, is pure La Rochefoucauld; the second, pure Beaumarchais. And of what is entirely Byron's own in *Don Juan,* how startlingly much has passed even beyond common speech into rank cliché: *"Man's love is of man's life . . ."*; *"But words are things . . ."* and so on; even *"Stranger than fiction,"* even—though I fear fortuitously —*"Sweet Adeline."*

We come last to the fact that *Don Juan* is a poem, which is perhaps the most crucial fact of all. Three things, it seems to me, save *Don Juan,* with its prodigious breakneck energy, from coming to grief, from skidding or careening off the road. Byron's great comic sense, which checks his impulse to rant, proves a stout wall on one side; his feeling for tradition, his sensibility for the highbred, the historic, the classical, walls him in on the other. But it is the requirements of verse itself, of rhyme and meter and stanzaic form, that keep a smooth road under him. By virtue of these things indeed, Byron—for all his antics and vulgarities—is an aristocratic poet. As to how decisive such qualities can be, we need only turn to the most democratic of poets, Whitman, who lacked the first quality, never fully acquired the second, and almost wholly rejected the third; and may see how much more impurely and wastefully his genius operated. Byron's sense of the past, of the poetry of history, is much more evident in *Childe Harold,* yet certainly not missing here:

> I've stood upon Achilles' tomb
> And heard Troy doubted: Time will doubt of Rome.

But it is the actual versification, the use of rhyme, meter, touches of poetic diction, stanzaic form, that lifts and liquefies *Don Juan,* that helps give it the "beauty" that Shelley noted. Of immense value is the heightening power of the verse, the regularity that goes with the rush, giving it not an eccentric but a dramatic speed. Or consider the splendid exordiums to so many of the cantos, with their sense not of breaking new ground but of instantly getting *off* the ground: for this, too, we have the élan of the verse to thank.

To perceive the difference—and distance—from prose, we have only to compare *Don Juan* to the long work in English that, all in all, it perhaps most resembles—*Tom Jones.* Certainly both works are in their way first-rate. Both, again, are epical: the one a panoramic entertainment with all England for its stage; the other a kaleidoscopic spectacle, with all Europe. In both the well-placed hero is a youthful rake who comes to know one pure love and countless varieties of lust. In both, the pre-eminent aim is an elaborate satiric survey of manners: in both the author's strongest hate and most frequent target is hypocrisy. In both, conventional morality is regarded with scorn: Fielding and Byron alike forgive many "sins" and castigate many "virtues." Fielding and Byron alike, moreover, deliberately and unceasingly obtrude themselves, interlarding their story with personal comments and confessions, curtain speeches and familiar essays, parodies, denunciations, every variety of obiter dictum. And yet . . . well, I have actually, and understandably, never seen the two compared. For it is somehow like comparing a solid with a liquid, a side of beef with a great bowlful of rum punch, a stagecoach with an Indian canoe—prose, in short, with poetry. As poetry,

Don Juan is disfigured by some slipshod verses and some ghastly rhymes; it is blunted by Byron's sometimes being too busy with satiric weapons to care enough about artistic tools. But as poetry, Byron's masterpiece remains curiously true to itself: it sails off into highfalutin now and then, or nose dives towards bathos, but it never merely dodders into prose.

In Honor of Pushkin

Edmund Wilson

Anyone who has read criticism by foreigners, even well-informed criticism, of the literature of his own country knows what a large part of it is likely to be made up of either banalities or errors. In the case of a novice at Russian like the writer, this danger is particularly great; and I shall probably be guilty of many sins in the eyes of Russian readers who should happen to see this essay. But Pushkin, the hundredth anniversary of whose death is being celebrated this year by the Soviets, has in general been so little appreciated in the English-speaking countries that I may, perhaps, be pardoned for however imperfect an attempt to bring his importance home to English-speaking readers. And Evgeni Onegin, who has played such a role for the Russian imagination, really belongs among those figures of fiction who have a meaning beyond their national frontiers for a whole age of Western society. The English Hamlet was as real, and as Russian, to the Russians of the generations that preceded the Revolution as any character in Russian literature. Let us receive Evgeni Onegin as a creation equally real for us.

It has always been difficult for Westerners—except perhaps for the Germans, who seem to have translated him more successfully than anyone else—to believe in the greatness of Pushkin. We have always left him out of account. George Borrow, who visited Russia in the course of his work for the Bible Society, published some translations of Pushkin in 1835; but the conventional world of literature knew little or nothing about him. Three years after Pushkin's death (and when Lermontov's career was nearly over), Carlyle, in *Heroes and Hero Worship,* described Russia as a "great dumb monster," not yet matured to the point where it finds utterance through the "voice of genius." Turgenev

Reprinted by permission of the author.

struggled vainly with Flaubert to make him recognize Pushkin's excellence; and even Renan was so ignorant of Russian literature that it was possible for him to declare on Turgenev's death that Russia had at last found her voice. Matthew Arnold, in writing about Tolstoy, remarked complacently that "the crown of literature is poetry" and that the Russians had not yet had a great poet; and T. S. Eliot, not long ago, in a discussion of the importance of Greek and Latin, was insisting on the inferior educational value of what he regarded as a merely modern literature like Russian, because "half a dozen great novelists"—I quote from memory—"do not make a culture." Even today we tend to say to ourselves, "If Pushkin is really as good as the Russians think he is, why has he never taken his place in world literature as Dante and Goethe have, and as Tolstoy and Dostoevsky have?"

The truth is that Pushkin *has* come through into world literature —he has come through by way of the Russian novel. Unlike most of the poets of his period, he had the real dramatic imagination, and his influence permeates Russian fiction and theater and opera as well. Reading Pushkin for the first time, for a foreigner who has already read later Russian writers, is like coming for the first time to Voltaire after an acquaintance with later French literature: he feels that he is tasting the pure essence of something which he has found before only in combination with other elements. It is a spirit whose presence he has felt and with whom in a sense he is already familiar, but whom he now first confronts in person.

For the rest, it is true that the poetry of Pushkin is particularly difficult to translate. It is difficult for the same reason that Dante is difficult: because it says so much in so few words, so clearly and yet so concisely, and the words themselves and their place in the line have become so much more important than in the case of more facile or rhetorical writers. It would require a translator himself a poet of the first order to reproduce Pushkin's peculiar combination of intensity, compression and perfect ease. A writer like Pushkin may easily sound "flat," as he did to Flaubert in French, just as Cary's translation of Dante sounds flat. Furthermore, the Russian language, which is highly inflected and able to dispense with pronouns and prepositions in many cases where we have to use them and which does without the article altogether, makes it possible for Pushkin to pack his lines (separating modifiers from substantives, if need be) in a way which renders the problem of translating him closer to that of translating a tightly articulated Latin poet like Horace than any modern poet that we know. Such a poet in translation may sound trivial just as many of the translations of Horace sound trivial—because the weight of the words and the force of their relation have been lost with the inflections and the syntax.

So that, failing any adequate translation, we have tended, if we have thought about Pushkin at all, to associate him vaguely with Byronism: we have heard that *Evgeni Onegin* is an imitation of *Don Juan*. But this comparison is very misleading. Pushkin was a great artist: he derived as much from André Chénier as from Byron. *Don Juan* is diffuse and incoherent, sometimes brilliant, sometimes silly; it has its unique excellence, but it is the excellence of an improvisation. Byron said of some of the cantos that he wrote them on gin, and essentially it is a drunken monologue by a desperately restless, uncomfortable man, who does not know what is the matter with him or what he ought to do with himself, who wants to tell stories about other things or to talk about himself in such a way as to be able to laugh and curse and grieve without looking into anything too closely. Byron's achievement, certainly quite remarkable, is to have raised the drunken monologue to a literary form. But the achievement of Pushkin is quite different. He had, to be sure, learned certain things from Byron—for example, the tone of easy negligence with which *Evgeni Onegin* begins and the habit of personal digression; but both of these devices in Pushkin are made to contribute to a general design. *Evgeni Onegin* is the opposite of *Don Juan* in being a work of unwavering concentration. Pushkin's "novel in verse" came out of Pushkin's deepest self-knowledge and was given form by a long and exacting discipline. The poet had adopted a compact speech and a complicated stanza-form as different as possible from Byron's doggerel; and he worked over the three hundred and eighty-nine stanzas which fill about two hundred pages through a period of eight years (1823-31) and was still, with every successive edition, revising them and cutting them down up to the time of his death.

One can convey a much more accurate impression of what Pushkin's actual writing is like by comparing him to Keats than to Byron. There are passages in *Evgeni Onegin,* such as those that introduce the seasons, which have a felicity and a fullness of detail not unlike Keats's *Ode to Autumn*—or, better perhaps, the opening of *The Eve of St. Agnes,* which resembles them more closely in form:

St. Agnes' Eve—Ah, bitter chill it was!
The owl, for all his feathers, was a-cold;

The hare limp'd trembling through the frozen grass,
And silent was the flock in woolly fold:
Numb were the Beadsman's fingers while he told
His rosary, and while his frosted breath,
Like pious incense from a censer old,
Seem'd taking flight for heaven without a death,
Past the sweet Virgin's picture, while his prayer he saith.

Here is Pushkin's description of the coming of winter:

Already now the sky was breathing autumn, already the dear
sun more seldom gleamed, shorter grew the day, the forest's secret
shadow was stripped away with sighing sound, mist lay upon the
fields, the caravan of loud-tongued geese stretched toward the south:
drew near the duller season; November stood already at the door.

Rises the dawn in cold murk; in the fields the sound of work
is still; the wolf with his hungry mate comes out upon the road;
sniffing, the road-horse snorts—and the traveler who is wise makes
full speed up the hill; the herdsman now at last by morning light
no longer drives his cattle from the byre; at mid-day to their huddle
his horn no longer calls them; inside her hut, the farm girl, singing,
spins, while—friend of winter nights—her little flare of kindling
snaps beside her.

And now the heavy frosts are snapping and spread their silver
through the fields . . . smoother than a smart parquet glistens the
ice-bound stream. The merry mob of little boys with skates cut
ringingly the ice; on small red feet the lumbering goose, hoping to
float on the water's breast, steps carefully but slips and topples;
gaily the first snow flashes and whirls about, falling in stars on the
bank.

If you can imagine this sort of thing, which I have translated more
or less literally, done in something like Keats's narrowy line, you will
get some idea of what Pushkin is like. He can make us see and hear
things as Keats can, but his range is very much greater: he can give us
the effect in a few lines of anything from the opening of a bottle of
champagne or the loading and cocking of pistols for a duel to the spin-
ning and skipping of a ballet girl—who "flies like fluff from Aeolus'
breath"—or the falling of the first flakes of snow. And as soon as we
put *The Eve of St. Agnes* (published in 1820) beside *Evgeni Onegin,*
it seems to us that Keats is weakened by an element of the conventionally romantic, of the mere storybook picturesque. But Pushkin can
dispense with all that: here everything is sharp and real. No detail of
country life is too homely, no phase of city life too worldly, for him to
master it by the beauty of his verse. Artistically, he has outstripped his

time; and neither Tennyson in *In Memoriam* nor Baudelaire in *Les Fleurs du Mal* was ever to surpass Pushkin in making poetry of classical precision and firmness out of a world realistically observed.

I should note also—what I have never seen mentioned—that the passages of social description often sound a good deal more like Praed than like Byron. It is not likely that Pushkin was influenced by Praed, since Praed's poems began to appear in *Knight's Quarterly* only in 1823, the year that *Onegin* was begun, and his characteristic vein of *vers de société* seems to date only from 1826, in which year Pushkin completed his sixth chapter. But the stanza in Chapter Two, with its epitaph, on the death of Tatyana's father might have been imitated from Praed's poem *The Vicar,* and if you can imagine Praed's talent raised to a higher power and telling a long story in his characteristically terse and witty stanzas (Pushkin's measure is shorter than Byron's, a rapid tetrameter like Praed's), you will be closer to Pushkin than *Don Juan* will take you:

> Good night to the Season!—the dances,
>   The fillings of hot little rooms,
> The glancings of rapturous glances,
>   The fancyings of fancy costumes;
> The pleasures which Fashion makes duties,
>   The praisings of fiddles and flutes,
> The luxury of looking at Beauties,
>   The tedium of talking to Mutes;
> The female diplomatists, planners
>   Of matches for Laura and Jane;
> The ice of her Ladyship's manners,
>   The ice of his Lordship's champagne.

To have written a novel in verse, and a novel of contemporary manners, which was also a great poem was Pushkin's unprecedented feat—a feat which, though anticipated on a smaller scale by the tales in verse of Crabbe and several times later attempted by nineteenth-century poets, was never to be repeated. And when we think of *Evgeni Onegin* in connection with *Don Juan* or *The Ring and the Book* or *Aurora Leigh* or *Evangeline,* we find that it refuses to be classed with them. Pushkin's genius, as Maurice Baring has said, has more in common with the genius of Jane Austen than with the general tradition the nineteenth-century novel. It is classical in its even tone of comedy which is at the same time so much more serious than the tragedies of Byron ever are, in its polishing of the clear and rounded lens which focuses the complex of human relations.

But Pushkin is much more vigorous than Jane Austen: the compression and rigor of the verse cause the characters to seem to start out of the stanzas. And he deals with more violent emotions. *Evgeni Onegin* is occupied with Byronism in a different way than that of deriving from Byron: it is among other things an objective study of Byronism. Both in the poem itself and in a letter that Pushkin wrote while he was working on it, he makes significant criticisms of Byron. "What a man this Shakespeare is!" he exclaims. "I can't get over it. How small the tragic Byron seems beside him!—that Byron who has been able to imagine but a single character: his own . . . Byron simply allots to each of his characters some characteristic of his own: his pride to one, his hatred to another, his melancholy to a third, etc., and thus out of a character which is in itself rich, somber and energetic, he makes several insignificant characters; but that is not tragedy." And in *Evgeni Onegin*, he speaks of Byron's "hopeless egoism." Pushkin has been working away from his early romantic lyricism toward a Shakespearean dramatization of life, and now he is to embody in objective creations, to show involved in a balanced conflict, the currents of the age which have passed through him. Evgeni Onegin is presented quite differently from any of the romantic heroes of Byron or Chateaubriand or Musset: when Byron dropped the attitudes of Childe Harold, the best he could do with Don Juan was to give him the innocence of Candide. Evgeni differs even from his immediate successor and kinsman, Lermontov's Hero of Our Time—because Lermontov, though he tells his story with the distinctive Russian realism absent in the other romantic writers, is really involved to a considerable degree with the attitudes of his hero; whereas Pushkin, in showing us Evgeni, neither exalts him in the perverse romantic way nor yet, in exposing his weakness, hands him over to conventional morality. There is, I think, but one creation of the early nineteenth century who is comparable to Evgeni Onegin: Stendhal's Julien Sorel; and the poem is less akin to anything produced by the romantic poets than it is to *Le Rouge et le Noir* and *Madame Bovary*.

Our first glimpse of Pushkin's hero is not an ingratiating one: he has just been summoned to the bedside of a dying uncle, whose estate he is going to inherit, and he is cursing at the tiresome prospect of sitting around till the old man dies. But the scene is shifted at once to his previous life in St. Petersburg. He has been a young man about town, who has had everything society can give him. We see him at the restaurant, the opera, the ball; in one masterly passage we are shown him falling asleep after a round of the pleasures of the capital while the Petersburg of the merchants and cabmen and peddlers is just waking up for the day. But Evgeni is intelligent: he gets tired of his friends, tired of his love affairs. He is infected with the "English spleen" and grows languid and morose like Childe Harold. He shuts himself up to write, but he finds it terribly hard and gives it up. Then his uncle dies, and he inherits the estate and goes to live in the country.

The country bores him, too. Being a man of liberal ideas, he tries to lighten the lot of his serfs, and the neighbors decide he is a dangerous fellow. Then there appears in the neighborhood a young man named Lensky with whom Evgeni finds he has something in common. Lensky has just come back from Göttingen and is saturated with German idealism; and he is a poet in the German-romantic vein. Evgeni thinks him callow and naïve, but tries not to throw cold water on his illusions. He likes Lensky, and they go riding and have long arguments together.

Lensky is in love in the most idealistic fashion with a girl whom he has known since childhood and to whom he has always been faithful. She is pretty but entirely uninteresting: Pushkin tells us that she is just like the heroines of all the popular love stories of the day. Lensky goes to see her every evening—she lives with her sister and her widowed mother on a nearby estate—and one day takes Evgeni with him. Evgeni has sarcastically told Lensky in advance what the refreshments and the conversation will be like—the Larins will be just a "simple Russian family"; and on the drive back home he remarks that the face of Lensky's worshiped sweetheart is lifeless, red, and round "like this silly moon over this silly horizon," and remarks that if *he* were a poet like Lensky, he would have preferred the older sister, who had sat sadly by the window and said nothing.

This older sister, Tatyana, is "wild, melancholy, silent, and shy" and not so pretty as Olga. As a child, she hadn't liked games and hadn't been fond of dolls; she had thought it was funny to mimic her mother by lecturing her doll on how young ladies ought to comport themselves. Now her head is full of Richardson and Rousseau, and she likes to get up before dawn and watch the stars fade and the distance grow bright and feel the morning wind. And now, from the first moment she sees him, she falls furiously in love with Evgeni. She waits for a time in silence; then, as Evgeni does not come to call again, she sits down and writes him a letter, in which, painfully, uncontrollably, innocently, she confesses to him her love. This chapter, which deals with Tatyana's letter, is one of the great descriptions of first love in literature. Pushkin renews for us as we read all the poignancy and violence of those moments when for the first time the emotional forces of youth are released by another human being and try to find their realization through him. All the banal and deluded things that young people say and feel—that Evegni is the one man in the world for her, the man for whom she has been waiting all her life, that he has been appointed by God to be her protector, that she is all alone and that no one understands her—poor Tatyana believes them all and puts them all into her letter; and Pushkin has succeeded in giving them to us in all their banality and deludedness, with no romantic sentimentalization, and yet making them move us profoundly. We enter into the emotions of Tatyana as we do into those of Juliet, yet at the same time Pushkin has set the whole picture in a perspective of pathetic irony which is not in that early play of Shakespeare's: there is nothing to indicate that Shakespeare's lovers might not have been ideally happy if it had not been for the family feud; but, in the case of Tatyana, we know from the first moment that her love is hopelessly misplaced in Evgeni. And the whole thing is set off and rooted in life by a series of marvelous touches—Tatyana's conversation with the nurse, the song she hears the serf girls singing— and saturated with the atmosphere of the country estate where Tatyana has spent her whole life and where—so amazing is Pushkin's skill at evoking a complete picture through suggestion, needing only a few hundred lines where a novelist would take as many pages—we feel by the time she leaves it that we have lived as long as she.

Evgeni does not answer the letter, but two days afterwards he comes to see her. The role of the seducer is *passé:* it went out with periwigs and red heels; and for Evgeni the time for great passions is past: it is too much trouble to do anything about Tatyana. He conducts himself honorably, he talks to her kindly. He tells her that, if he had any desire for family life, she would certainly be the woman he would choose for a wife. But he was not created for happiness, such satisfactions are foreign to his soul. As a husband, he would be gloomy and disagreeable, and he would eventually cease to love her. He makes quite a long speech about it. And he tells her that she ought to learn to control herself: another man might not understand as he does. Tatyana listens silently, in tears. He gives her his arm and leads her back to the house.

But now Evgeni takes an unexpected turn. The Larins give a big evening party to celebrate Tatyana's Saint's Day. Evgeni goes and sits opposite Tatyana and realizes that she is still in love with him and frightened to death in his presence. He thinks that he is angry with Lensky because the party has turned out a bore and Lensky has brought him there on false pretenses. He has for months been watching Lensky moon over Olga with his eternal romantic devotion which treats the beloved object with a reverence almost religious and never makes any practical advances; and he sets out now to annoy the young poet by getting Olga away from him for the evening. Evgeni makes Olga dance with him repeatedly, pays her animated attentions—to which, as she is incapable of saying no, she almost automatically responds. Lensky is deeply hurt and furious; he leaves the party and goes straight home and writes Evgeni a note calling him out.

Evgeni's first impulse, when he receives the challenge, is to set things right with Lensky, not to let the young man make a fool of himself. But then he is moved, as he tells himself, by the fear of public opinion: the second by whom Lensky has sent the challenge, though a thoroughly disreputable individual, is an oldfashioned fancier and promoter of duels. The night before they are to meet, Lensky sits up till morning writing poetry. Evgeni sleeps sound and late; he arrives on the field with his French valet, whom he insolently presents as his second. He and Lensky take their four paces away from one another. But Evgeni, while he walks, is quietly raising his pistol, so that, the moment he turns around, he is able to shoot Lensky before the latter has had a chance to aim. Lensky falls: in a remarkable simile, characteristically realistic and exact, Pushkin tells us how the young man's heart, in which a moment before all the human passions were dwelling, becomes suddenly like an abandoned house blinded and dark and silent, with the windows covered with chalk and the owner gone away. Evgeni has killed in the most cowardly fashion a man whose friend he had believed himself to be and whom he had thought he did not want to kill. Now at last we are sure of what Pushkin, who has always given us Evgeni's version of his own motives, has only so far in various ways suggested: that, for all Lensky's obtuseness and immaturity,

Evgeni has been jealous of him, because Lensky has been able to feel for Olga an all-absorbing emotion whereas Evgeni, loved so passionately by Tatyana, has been unable to feel anything at all. Lensky, the author now tells us, might or might not have become a good poet; but the point is, as he lets us know without telling us, that it is the poet in Lensky whom Evgeni has hated. Evgeni had wanted to write; but when he had sat down with the paper before him, he had found it was too much trouble.

After the duel, Evgeni leaves the countryside. Lensky is soon forgotten by Olga. She says yes to an uhlan, who takes her off when he goes to join his regiment. Tatyana is left alone. She walks over to Evgeni's house and gets the caretaker to let her in; and there she returns day after day and reads the books—so much more up to date than Richardson and Rousseau—which she has found in Evgeni's library. There are a picture of Byron on the wall and a little iron statue of Napoleon; and, for the first time, Tatyana reads Byron, as well as several fashionable novels which reflect the fashionable attitudes of the day. Evgeni has marked them and made notes in the margin: and now his lecture to her after her letter begins to have the sound of an echo of all the things he has read.

But Tatyana contines to languish, doesn't get married. Her mother decides to take her to Moscow. There follows a wonderful description of the Larin family traveling to Moscow. Pushkin, with his infinite sympathy and his equally universal detachment, puts on record characteristics and customs of the Russians which are still striking to a foreigner today. The Larins set several dates to get off, but they never get off on those dates. Then at last they do get off and get there. Now the leafy and mazy and timeless estate is far behind Tatyana, and she sees the gold crosses of the churches and then the people and shops and palaces of Moscow. The shift from country to town is beautifully handled by Pushkin; and there is nothing in fiction more remarkable in its way than the account of Tatyana's first days in Moscow. It is the forerunner of the social scenes in *War and Peace,* and Natasha Rostova and her family seem related to Tatyana and hers, just as Tolstoy's Moscow originals must have been to Pushkin's. The Moscow cousin, to whose house Tatyana and her mother first go and where an old Kalmuck in a ragged caftan and spectacles lets them in, had been in love before she was married with a dandy whom she had thought another Sir Charles Grandison; and now the first thing she says to Tatyana's mother, in whom she had used to confide, is, "Cousin, do you remember Grandison?" "What Grandison? Oh, Grandison!— of course, I remember: where is he?" "He's living in Moscow now; he came to see me at Christmas; he married off his son not long ago."— But the fashion of the younger generation—we are not told whether or not Tatyana makes this reflection—is for Byron instead of Grandison.

Tatyana cannot at first take her place in this world. Her cousins, though urban, are nice; they look her over and decide she is nice. They confide in her, but she cannot return their confidences: she moves among them detached, distracted. She goes to dinner to be shown to her grandparents: " 'How Tanya has grown!' " they say. "Wasn't it just the other day I christened you? and *I* used to carry you in my arms! And *I* boxed your ears! And *I* used to feed you gingerbread!' " And the old ladies in chorus would keep repeating: " 'How our years fly by!' "—But they—in them she could see no change; it was all on the same old pattern: her aunt, the Princess Helena, still had the same tulle bonnet, Lukerya Lvovna still powdered herself just as much, Lyubov Petrovna still told the same lies, Ivan Petrovich was still just as silly, Semen Petrovich was still just as stingy, Pelagya Nikolavna still had the same friend, M. Finemouche, and the same Pomeranian and the same husband; and her husband was just as punctual at his club and just as meek and just as deaf as ever, and still ate and drank enough for two." One night at a ball, her solicitous aunt whispers to her to look to the left. An important-looking general is staring at her. "Who?" she asks. "That fat general?"

When Evgeni returns from his travels and goes into society again, he sees at a ball an extraordinarily smart lady who combines perfect naturalness with great dignity, whom everybody wants to speak to and to whom everybody defers; and he gasps at her resemblance to Tatyana. He inquires who she is of a man he knows. "My wife," the friend replies. It is Tatyana, now a princess; the man is the pompous general. Tatyana meets Evgeni without batting an eyelash: she asks him whether he has been long in St. Petersburg and whether he doesn't come from her part of the world.

Evgeni pays her court, follows her everywhere; but she refuses to recognize him. He writes her a letter, which is the counterpart of hers: now the roles are reversed—it is he who is putting himself at her mercy. She doesn't answer: he writes again and again. Then he shuts himself up in his house, cuts himself off from society and gives himself

up to serious reading: history and moral philosophy. But Lensky gets
between him and the page, and he hears a voice that says, "What,
killed?" and he sees all the malicious gossips and the mean cowards
and the young jilts and bitches whom he has known in Petersburg
society and whom he has wanted to get away from and forget, and he
sees Tatyana in the country house, sitting silent beside the window, as
on the day when he first called.

Suddenly, one day when the winter snow is melting, he gets into
his sleigh and drives off to her house. There is no one in the hall: he
walks in. He finds her reading his letters. He throws himself at her
feet. She looks at him without anger or surprise; she sees how sick and
pitiful he is; the girl who loved him so in the country wakens again in
her heart; she does not take her hand from his lips. Then, after a moment, she makes him get up. "I must be frank with you," she tells him.
"Do you remember in the orchard how submissively I listened to your
rebuke? Now it's my turn. I was younger then, and better. I loved
you, and you were severe with me. The love of a humble country girl
was not exciting for you. Good heavens! my blood still chills when I
remember the cold look and the sermon you gave me. You didn't like
me then in the country, and why do you run after me now? Because
I'm rich and well known? because my husband has been wounded on
the battlefield? because we're in favor at court? Isn't it because my
shame would now be known to everybody, and would give you a reputation as a rake? Don't you think I would a thousand times rather be
back with the orchard and my books and the places where I first saw
you and the graveyard with my nurse's grave, than play this role in this
noisy masquerade? But it's too late to do anything now. From the
moment when you wouldn't have me, what did it matter to me what
became of me? And now you're a man of honor; and although I love
you still—why should I pretend?—I've given myself to another and I
shall always be faithful to him."

She goes; and Evgeni stands thunderstruck, and then he hears the
clank of the general's spurs. And there Pushkin leaves him.

The truth about Evgeni's fatal weakness has for the first time been
fully driven home in Tatyana's speech: he has never been able to judge
for himself of the intrinsic value of anything; all his values are social
values; he has had enough independence, he has been enough superior
to his associates, to be dissatisfied with the life of society, but, even in his
disaffection, he has only been able to react into the disaffected attitude

that is fashionable; his misanthropy itself has been developed in terms of what people will think of him, and, even trying to escape to the country, he has brought with him the standards of society. He had had enough sense of real values to know that there was something in Tatyana, something noble about her passion for him, to recognize in his heart that it was she who was the true unquiet brooding spirit, the true rebel against the conventions, where his quarrel with the world had been half a pose; but he had not had quite enough to love her just as she was: he had only been able to shoot Lensky.

Pushkin has put into the relations between his three central characters a number of implications. In one sense, they may be said to represent three intellectual currents of the time: Evgeni is Byronism turning worldly and dry; Lensky, with his Schiller and Kant, German romantic idealism; Tatyana, that Rousseauist Nature which was making itself heard in romantic poetry, speaking a new language and asserting a new kind of rights. And from another point of view they represent different tendencies in Russia itself: both Evgeni and Lensky are half foreigners, they think in terms of the cultures of the West, whereas Tatyana, who has spent her whole life on the wild old feudal estate, is for Pushkin the real Russia. Tatyana, like Pushkin, who said he owed so much to the stories of his Russian nurse, has always loved old wives' tales and is full of country superstitions. Before the fatal Saint's-Day party and after her conversation with Onegin, she has an ominous dream, which is recounted at length. Tatyana's subconscious insight, going to the bottom of the situation and clothing it with the imagery of folk-tales, reveals to her a number of things which the others do not yet know about themselves: that there is something bad about Evgeni and that there is an antagonism between him and Lensky; in her dream, she sees Onegin stab Lensky. It is the sensitive though naïve Russian spirit, always aware of the hidden realities, with which Tolstoy and Dostoevsky were later on still attempting to make contact in their reaction against Western civilization. Yet with Pushkin, as Gide says of Dostoevsky, the symbols are perfectly embodied in the characters; they never deform the human being or convert him into an uninteresting abstraction. *Evgeni Onegin* has been popular because it has for generations been read by young Russians as a story—a story in which the eternal reasoning male is brought up against the eternal instinctive woman—like Elizabeth Bennet and Mr. Darcy; and in which the modest heroine

—who, besides, is Cinderella and will end up expensively dressed and with the highest social position—gets morally all the best of it.

But there is still another aspect which the characters in *Evgeni Onegin* present. Pushkin speaks, at the end, of the years which have elapsed since he first saw Evgeni dimly, before the "free novel" which was to shape itself could be discerned "through the magic crystal." This magic crystal was Pushkin's own mind, which figures in the poem in a peculiar way. The poet, when he talks about himself, is not willful and egoistic like Byron; his digressions, unlike Byron's or Sterne's, always contribute to the story: they will begin by sounding like asides, in which the author is merely growing garrulous on the subject of some personal experience, but they will eventually turn out to merge into the experience of one of his characters, which he has been filling-in in this indirect way. Yet the crystal sphere is always there: it is inside it that we see the drama. Pushkin, throughout this period, had been tending to get away from his early subjective lyricism and to produce a more objective kind of art. After *Evgeni Onegin,* he was to write principally stories in prose. And in *Evgeni Onegin* it is almost as if we had watched the process—as we can see in the life-cell the nucleus splitting up into its separate nuclei and each concentrating its filaments and particles about it—by which the several elements of his character, the several strands of his experience, have taken symmetry about the foci of distinct characters. Pushkin had finally transfused himself into a dramatic work of art as none other of his romantic generation had done— for his serenity, his perfect balance of tenderness for human beings with unrelenting respect for reality, show a rarer quality of mind than Stendhal's.

Yet *Evgeni Onegin,* for all its lucidity, all its objectification, has behind it a conflict no less desperate than those which the other romantics were presenting so much more hysterically. Though Pushkin had triumphed as an artist as Byron was never able to do, he is otherwise a figure more tragic than the man who died at Missolonghi. For, after all, the chief disaster of *Evgeni Onegin* is not Evgeni's chagrin or Lensky's death: it is that Tatyana should have been caught up irrevocably by that empty and tyrannical social world from which Evgeni had tried to escape and which she had felt and still feels so alien. Pushkin married, the same year that *Onegin* was finished, a young and pleasure-loving wife who submerged him in the expenses of social life; and before he was out of his thirties, he got himself killed in a duel by a man whom he suspected of paying her attentions. It was as if in those generations where Byron, Shelley, Keats, Leopardi and Poe were dead in their twenties or thirties or barely reached forty, where Coleridge and Wordsworth and Beddoes and Musset burned out while still alive, where Lermontov, like Pushkin, was killed in a duel, before he was twenty-seven—it was as if in that great age of the bourgeois ascendancy —and even in still feudal Russia—it were impossible for a poet to survive. There was for the man of imagination and moral passion a basic maladjustment to society in which only the student of society—the social philosopher, the historian, the novelist—could find himself and learn to function. And to deal with the affairs of society, he had to learn to speak its language: that is, giving up the old noble language, he had— as Goethe and Hugo did, and as Pushkin did just before he died—to train himself to write in prose.

Yet Pushkin, who had done for the Russian language what Dante had done for Italian and who had laid the foundations of Russian fiction, had, in opposing the natural humanity of Tatyana to the social values of Evgeni, set a theme which was to be developed through the whole of Russian art and thought, and to give it its peculiar power. Lenin, like Tolstoy, could only have been possible in a world where this contrast was acutely felt. Tatyana, left by Pushkin with the last word, was actually to remain triumphant.

Walt Whitman

"GARRULOUS TO THE VERY LAST"

Irving Howe

Whitman has not been very fortunate in his critics—and, one some-times feels like blurting out, it serves him right! Seldom has a great poet engaged in such adolescent mystifications with regard to himself and his work, seldom has a poet so blatantly promoted a cult of worship in which he served as both prophet and martyr—though toward the end of his life even Whitman, in whom the promoter and the mysta-gogue are closely allied, grew tired of his disciples and began to mock them in a way beyond their capacity to notice. As a result of his need to think of himself in a variety of prophetic roles, Whitman became a victim of his own legend rather than a subject of critical appreciation. People with notions about cosmic consciousness, transubstantiation, in-determinate sexuality and, somewhat later, anti-Fascist unity, soon attached themselves to the roomy dogmas near his books. Academicians wrote studies trying to persuade one another that they really cared whether Whitman was a neoplatonist or a pantheist or a believer in metempsychosis. And many poets and critics of the past few decades, because they didn't write like Whitman, felt they had to keep sticking pins into his reputation until it would collapse.

All this has made it extremely difficult to get at Whitman the poet and almost impossible to get at him directly: too many traps and bar-riers of our culture stand in the way. We have no choice but to begin

A review of *The Solitary Singer* by Gay Wilson Allen and *Leaves of Grass: One Hundred Years After*, edited by Milton Hindus.

with his critics, about whom Whitman once said—and here he was truly a prophet—"I will certainly elude you."

One main line of criticism has stressed Whitman as public spokesman, thereby accepting his claim to embody the collective spirit of American democracy in his rather eccentric individuality. Thereby too it has been forced into the position of placing the greatest valuation upon his more grandiose programmatic poems, a procedure that invites the embarrassment of having to take his formal ideas seriously. A second major line of criticism has exalted Whitman as a sexual champion or liberator, a sort of linsey-woolsey Lawrence—a Lawrence, that is, without the bother of Frieda.

Of inducements and provocations for seeing Whitman in these vatic postures his work offers no lack, but such critical approaches, I am convinced, obscure what is best in the poems themselves and create public images of the poet that, for good or bad, can only estrange him from the audience he deserves. That these approaches to Whitman also happen to be in violent conflict with each other makes for a fine bit of cultural comedy: the nationalist Whitmanites sniff the other way when they get to the sex poems, while the sexualist Whitmanites write as if their hero had never lived in a country.

As a national prophet Whitman now seems inadequate because he so cheerfully lacks, perhaps even refuses, a full sense of social complexity. The Jacksonian mind, admirable as it was and much as one wants to preserve something of its original vigor and bias, seems light-years away from us, almost "pastoral" in its innocence and assurance. For all that Whitman's poems often speak about city life they do not really capture its terrible *newness,* nor do they register that anticipatory awareness of the problems raised by industrialism and the mass society which helps keep the work of other nineteenth-century writers fresh and relevant. To be sure, the fact that Whitman's was a pre-industrial mind would not matter at all (it certainly doesn't matter for innumerable poets before him), were it not that in his later poems one finds frequent signs of incoherence due to his bewilderment before the kind of America coming into existence after the Civil War.

As a sexual prophet, however, Whitman suffers from an opposite difficulty: he has done his work too well, no one is now likely to be shocked by the "Children of Adam" or "Calamus" poems. Some of them charm us, others are troubling because of the abstractness with which they celebrate the need for concrete experience, and after reading

all of them one cannot help wishing that Whitman had indicated some
faint awareness that the sexual liberation he proclaimed might bring
new troubles of its own.

   To say, however, that the dominant modes of Whitman criticism
are not at present very helpful is not to slight a number of fine studies.
An early conservative book like Bliss Perry's has the merit of being
among the first to assess, without hysteria or too great hostility, what
Whitman actually wrote. Van Wyck Brooks' chapter in *America's
Coming of Age,* while presenting Whitman as the American Bard, is a
powerful cultural statement. Basil de Sélincourt's book, for all that it
succumbs to the English fondness for seeing Whitman as the Great
American Naïf, contains many acute remarks on his poetic technique.
D. H. Lawrence in his *Studies in Classic American Literature,* despite
mixed feelings toward a writer close to him in expression but alien in
temperament, finally comes through by hailing Whitman as one of the
great pioneers in transcending the body-mind dualism.

   Yet none of these books will quite do for us now, since none of
them succeeds in getting past Whitman's *persona* and into his poetry.
This task is surely the most challenging that faces American criticism,
but it remains neglected because most American literary people either
are indifferent to Whitman or think of him as a mere loud-mouth. The
extreme version of this latter opinion comes, predictably, from the powerful critic Yvor Winters, who writes that Whitman "a second-rate poet
. . . had no capacity for any feeling save of the cloudiest and most
general kind." As against such admirably direct wrong-headedness,
there are a few signs that Whitman is again being considered by serious
critics, notably a brilliant, wide-eyed essay by Randall Jarrell which
simply points to Whitman's achievements in language, as if to say: *For
God's sake, forget the prophecy, forget the philosophy, just look at these
lines, they're good enough to read, they're poetry!*

   Meanwhile, amidst the pomp and tedium of the Centenary, a new
outpouring of Whitman books has begun. The first, by Gay Wilson
Allen, is one of those over-stuffed biographies that have recently become
fashionable. The book, it can be said without hesitation, is dull enough
to qualify as a definitive study. Mr. Allen manages to avoid a point
of view on almost every controversial aspect of Whitman's life or writings, and this of course helps contribute to the tone of definitiveness.
After having spent a lifetime studying Whitman—the jacket says
twenty-five years—he is unable to write a page about the poems that

has a touch of critical originality or even eccentricity. His credentials as a critic may be tested by his opinion that Whitman's verse lacks irony, a deficiency which turns out, however, to be a virtue since, he tells us, "irony results from self-pity or loss of faith." About Whitman's private life Mr. Allen writes, "he had not made up his mind or did not know whether sex meant primarily an instinctive hunger or responsible paternity"—which indicates that Mr. Allen may have a thoroughly wholesome mind but that a thoroughly wholesome mind is not the ideal qualification for a biographer of Walt Whitman. Well, the book will have to be read by graduate students in American Literature.

Mr. Hindus' collection of essays is another matter: it presents, whether by intention or not, a vivid picture of the schisms, disagreements and cross-currents in recent Whitman criticism. William Carlos Williams, in a characteristic prose rant, writes as if free verse were one of the inalienable rights for which the American Revolution was fought; Middleton Murry invokes the religious sense behind Whitman's democracy, but in terms so vague and grand that it might as well be his own religious sense that is being honored; Kenneth Burke buries himself beneath the grassy debris of free associations on the word "leaves"; Mr. Hindus plumps for Whitman the nationalist or perhaps supernationalist, a Whitman whom he calls "Pan-American" and compares with Dostoevsky the pan-Slavic and Wagner the pan-German. (Mr. Hindus fails to consider how unjust this comparison is, if only because Dostoevsky's pan-Slavism was streaked with rather unattractive elements of anti-Semitism.)

There are, however, two first-rate essays in the book, one by Leslie Fiedler in which he offers a sharp and witty history of Whitman's reputation, ending with a rejection of the vatic Whitman and an acceptance of the Whitman who writes of private experience, and the other by Richard Chase in which he presents the best portrait of Whitman that has yet been composed.

Fiedler's essay points the direction for a revival of serious interest in Whitman, though I think he sometimes runs wild in imposing his favorite critical tags on a writer already stuccoed with everyone else's (e.g., "Whitman's America was made in France, the Romantic notion out of Rousseau and Chateaubriand of an absolute anti-Europe, an utter anticulture made flesh, the Noble Savage as a Continent"—which is bright but hardly verifiable by Whitman's verse).

The Chase essay presents Whitman as a "divided, multiple personality, a shifting amalgam of sycophancy and sloth, of mimetic brilliance and Dionysian inspiration, of calculating common sense and philosophical insight. . . ." His Whitman is neurotic, violently energetic and profoundly indolent by turns, whimsical and witty, given to sharp transitions from manic self-assertion to painful self-doubt. As far as Whitman's sexuality goes, Chase rejects the claim that he was actively and persistently heterosexual, homosexual or both, but sees him instead as a man in whom the sexual impulse did not come to sharp expression but remained latent, diffuse and unfocused. One is reminded somewhat of Turgenev, in whom a large masculine frame was also combined with a maternal fleshiness. And like Turgenev, Whitman is a writer endowed with a curiously impersonal tenderness, a kind of pansexual empathy that is available to all objects, whether sentient or not, in the external world. There is of course no way of "proving" that this is an entirely accurate description of Whitman, and Mr. Chase is wise enough not to try; but his portrait has the positive merit of corresponding rather closely to the sense of Whitman one gains from the poetry, as well as the negative merit of not forcing us to violate or stretch the scant evidence we have from Whitman's life.

II

It is a priceless historical joke that the one poet we accept as the National Bard should lack all the accredited national virtues. Whitman himself knew this, and to recognize how aware he was of the ambiguity of his role is to gain much in reading the poetry, for then it is easier to grasp its half-ridden irony and humor—Whitman staring in amusement at the sheer oddity of his being Walt a *kosmos,* or Whitman announcing that "Having pried through the strata, analyz'd to a hair, counsel'd with doctors and calculated close,/I find no sweeter fat than sticks to my own bones." In his old age he once declared himself to be essentially *furtive,* a description some biographers take, perhaps rightly, to refer to his sexual history; but I think it must be applied to his life and work as a whole, to those strategies and stratagems by which he sends his assumed and hypothetical selves out into the world to discover their possibilities. Almost all American writers tend to be furtive—they have to in this country; but Whitman assumes the role with a greater consciousness of its necessity, its strangeness and its price.

Whitman speaks for the national ethos, the divine average, the *En Masse,* but he is actually a solitary, a secretive watcher. Whitman calls himself "one of the toughs," but the greatest esthetic pleasure of this lonely Bohemian is the opera every American knows to be boring and effete, and his taste in general runs toward the delicate and the rococo. Whitman puffs out his chest with the rhetoric of democracy, but his vision of the democratic life—because it involves a sexual fraternity which can only arouse the fiercest anxieties among Americans, who see in it a threat to their protective code of manliness—must be thoroughly unacceptable to the nation that fancies him its poetic spokesman. It is all a comedy of errors, and if one sometimes feels that Whitman's critics serve him right, one may also indulge the feeling that Whitman serves America right.

I have said that Whitman was a Bohemian, but not with the intention of calling to mind those desperate estrangements and eccentricities the term is likely to suggest when used with regard to writers of our own time. American society in the nineteenth century was sufficiently loose and self-confident not merely to give most people a sense of social possibility but also to allow a margin for the survival and even the health of those who did not accept its dominant values. It was easier to be a Bohemian then, as it was easier to be a political or intellectual dissident, and by that token being a Bohemian in the 1850's did not mean a life as alienated and self-afflicting as it must often mean today. The idea of society had not yet become so overwhelming as it is for us; for long stretches of *Leaves of Grass* it seems a secondary actor, only occasionally providing that resistance to human desire which we have learned to expect from it. The writer who aspired to fulfill Emerson's prescription for the American poet—and who almost succeeded, but for the fact that he became something better—found that between America and himself there were large spaces, perhaps even wastes, and that it was this very spaciousness which allowed him to take chances in his poetry, allowed him to become a furtive experimenter and to test out variant possibilities of the self without having to worry about the pressures of society nearly as much as European writers had to worry.

This freedom, to be sure, also brought unhappy results: it made Whitman much too cavalier toward the past of both Europe and European poetry, it tempted him into discarding literary conventions he had barely tested, let alone understood. And it made him into the first of the many American writers who would try, in the earnestness of their isolation and with the seductive beat of the national music in their ears, to force themselves into the role of folk or tribal poet. In the career of Whitman, as in the careers of Hart Crane and Sherwood Anderson and many others, this effort could lead only to a wearying oscillation between a willed populism and a precious artiness. The price our writers have paid for trying, so to speak, to swallow the idea of America whole has almost always been a series of relapses into the shallowest kinds of estheticism. Scratch an American primitive and you often find an American decadent.

Yet, in the main, Whitman had no choice. Given the disintegrative pressures of his family background; the nature of American life and culture at the time he began to write; a scrappy education, as wide and wooly as the educations of most of our literary autodidacts—given all this, Whitman *had* to try to move back and forth between national and private themes, and the miracle is that all the while he managed to write so much good and even a sizable amount of great poetry.

The most fruitful of his *personae,* the one that corresponds most to the reality of his personal and literary needs, has been described, though not of course with Whitman in mind, by the German sociologist Georg Simmel in an essay called *The Stranger.* "If wandering," writes Simmel

. . . is the liberation from every given point in space, and thus the conceptual opposite to fixation at such a point, the sociological form of the "stranger" presents the unity . . . of these two characteristics. . . . The stranger is being discussed here, not in the sense often touched upon in the past, as the wanderer who comes today and goes tomorrow, but rather as the person who comes today and stays tomorrow. He is, so to speak, the *potential* wanderer; although he has not moved on, he has not quite lost the freedom of coming and going. He is fixed within a particular spatial group. . . . But his position in this group is determined, essentially, by the fact that he has not belonged to it from the beginning, that he imports qualities into it. . . .

Locating the stranger as "a unity of nearness and remoteness," Simmel limits himself to examples based on a clash of cultural styles and does not consider the still more interesting case where the "strangeness" of the stranger derives not from national differences but from a fundamental divergence of outlook and value that has sprung up *within* a culture. It is in the poet-prophet such as Whitman that this divergence is most vividly dramatized, the poet-prophet whose role is made possible by his "unity of nearness and remoteness" and is sanctioned by the readiness of his culture to accept, however conditionally, his ambiguous status.

Does not Simmel's description illuminate Whitman the poet? The man who comes today and stays tomorrow, the potential wanderer whose position in the group is fixed but who imports qualities into it—is this not the author of *Song of Myself,* a poet both remarkably close to everything characteristic and indigenous in our culture and extremely alien and remote from it. The self of the poem is necessarily fluid, defined by its unwillingness to rest in definition, committed with a mixture of ingenuous faith and comic skepticism to that belief in *possibility* which is possible only to Americans. At times this self expands to the condition of a protean demigod who absorbs all creatures into his creative will yet is saved from solipsism by the grace, rather infrequent among demigods, of having a sense of humor. At times the self of the poem sinks to an almost mineral tranquillity, a torpor approaching non-identity, a quasi-mystical dissolution of individual consciousness. The famous "oceanic" impulse which Whitman shares with other romantic poets, the "merging" impulse which disturbs many readers because it seems to blur all distinctions in quality of being, is here made acceptable and often rendered moving by the clear evidence—Whitman seldom tries to deny or hide it—that the self of the poem also acts from a deep anxiety and loneliness, a fear of annihilation which prompts its urge to cosmic identification. This cosmic straining loses much of its apparent pretentiousness once it becomes clear that it is being presented as an emblem of the poet's fears, the very fears we all know and all share. Reduce it from philosophical grandiosity to a common human tremor, and Whitman's possession of all possible selves, as his corresponding withdrawal from them, becomes close and intimate.

What matters, however, is not the variety of postures the self assumes in the poem but the charm and wit and openness of passion with which they are assumed. To be sure, Whitman occasionally succumbs to rhetorical bluster and a kind of inane benignity—and who is he, one asks with an irritation all too human, to pretend to be so assured and reassuring about *our* destiny? Yet between the extremes of his cosmic megalomania and the disintegration to which the fluid self is sometimes subjected, there is the rich substance of the poem, the elegiac gravity that lends it so exquisitely dignified a tone, the quiet comedy that acts as a counter-principle to the poem's surface expansiveness. "I have no mockings or arguments, I witness and wait." "Not words, not music or rhyme I want, not custom or lecture, not even the best/ Only the lull I like, the hum of your valved voice." "Speech is the twin of my vision, it is unequal to measure itself,/ It provokes me forever, it says sarcastically,/ *Walt you contain enough, why don't you let it out then?*" "Agonies are one of my changes of garments." "I am the man, I suffer'd, I was there."

These lines are spoken by a Stranger in the midst, a Stranger who is integral to that from which he moves apart. The poem is in this sense the most American of poems, entirely committed to the idea of freedom as something unfinished and still to be made. The self is seen as an experiment in potentiality, and Whitman, as the freest and gayest of "pragmatists," tries on new "selves" almost as if they were new clothes—I make the comparison partly to suggest an excessively American nonchalance but I hope that after a moment it will also suggest a certain reticence and even shyness.

Meanwhile, a word must be said to explode the common notion that Whitman's language is vague and inflated and pompous. At his best, and in *Song of Myself* he is frequently at his best, Whitman is a master of phrasing, a master of the precise, delicate and epigrammatic statement, a master of the kind of writing which by its combination of unfamiliar elements brings us to the *surprise* of a new insight or observation. I shall not clutter up these pages with examples, but anyone who even glances at *Song of Myself*—anyone who turns to the incredible descriptive power with which Section 5 ends ("And mossy scabs of the worm fence, heap'd stones, elder, mullein and poke-weed") or to the very next section in which the grass is "the flag of my disposition" and then a few lines later "the beautiful uncut hair of graves" or to the final Sections where death ("You bitter hug of mortality") is approached and accepted and yet parried—should see that this is the work of a poet with a great gift for language.

One of the main jobs for the Whitman critic who is yet to appear would be to describe, with scrupulous modesty, the variety of modes and tones in which Whitman writes. Here let me simply say a word about one of them. There are passages in his long poems, and whole shorter ones, in which the struggle of the self to locate a principle of movement, or a place of rest, comes to a momentary stop. A quietness begins; the language becomes hushed and completely controlled; the poet, not Walt the *kosmos* but Whitman the solitary, exposes himself in all his vulnerability. It is the moment after the struggle between the self and everything that resists and hurts and destroys the self, the blessed moment when anxiety has not been suppressed or dispelled but brought to its proper subordination. He reaches such moments in occasional passages of *Song of Myself* and for almost the whole of *Crossing Brooklyn Ferry*, which seems to me his single greatest poem. One thinks of them as moments of twilight, somewhat similar to those shadowy intervals between sleeping and waking, when the unconscious is still active and free yet we are not without some capacity to extricate ourselves from it, and when the will is present to our sense of things yet is relaxed and uncensorious. These are moments of rare psychic balance, everyone knows them in one way or another, but few writers have managed to create verbal equivalents as beautiful as those Whitman has.

It is in these moments that he writes most remarkably of death. At his frequent second best and his occasional worst, Whitman writes of death in the terms of late romanticism, as an adored agony he is waiting to immerse himself in. Yet even as we sense that behind his absorption with death there are pockets of the morbid, we feel that in such chants as *Crossing Brooklyn Ferry* the morbid has been, not exorcised, since it continues to have a claim upon us, but resisted, held in control, and thereby made into something other than itself. It is one of the great creative paradoxes that when Whitman here speaks of death he does so with the accent and breath of life; that when he acknowledges in *Brooklyn Ferry* the certainty of his non-being in the future it is to take on the being of those who like himself will stand and muse upon the continuity and the tragic finality of life; that when he croons his love to death in *Out of the Cradle Endlessly Rocking* it is with the assurance of gained life.

It has become customary to speak of such writings as a reflection of the religious sense. Theologians without theology try to salvage their faith by focusing upon those emotions of awe before the external world and of gratitude for being present in it for a few moments, which all sensitive human beings share. But to speak of such feelings as uniquely religious is arrogantly to pre-empt what is pervasively human. We are concerned here with the poise toward which we strain, the poise that goes beyond the triviality of "accepting" death but consists of a readiness to find a kind of peace in the determination not to accept.

The Whitman I have been presenting is an unorthodox one, and surely incomplete. I would claim nothing more for him than that he allows for a usable strategy for getting into the poems. Once that is done, it will no doubt be necessary to return to the other, the public Whitman.

And a final unorthodox note: It is generally said that Whitman declined in poetic power after the Civil War. This is true in a way, the poems of the later years being obviously more fragmentary and short-breathed than those of the earlier ones. But among the later pieces there are some with the most subtle refinement and humor. In his very old age he wrote a twelve-line poem called *After the Supper and Talk* in which he describes his reluctance to leave—we need hardly be told what it is that he must leave:

Shunning, postponing severance—seeking to ward off the last word,
    ever so little . . .
Farewells, messages lessening—dimmer the forthgoer's visage and
    form,
Soon to be lost for aye in the darkness—loth, O so loth to depart!
Garrulous to the very last.

No praise is needed, nor could any be sufficient, for the frank pathos and relaxed gaiety of that final line. This is the way a man, and a poet, should end.

Notes on the Extinction of Style

Richard Chase

Anyone who admires literature must at some time have been moved by Edward Gibbon's account of the genesis of his great book—how, watching the Christian friars among the ruins of Rome, he had a vision of the revolutions of history, of the transient achievements of men and institutions, of the splendor and pity of the human spectacle.

Surely every successful book must begin with some sort of personal vision, indeed a conversion, more or less like Gibbon's. What shall we expect of a book[1] whose genesis is described as follows:

> At mid-point, the twentieth century may properly establish its own criteria of literary judgment; indeed, the values as well as the facts of modern civilization must be examined if man is to escape self-destruction. We must know and understand better the recorders of our experience. Scholars can no longer be content to write for scholars; they must make their knowledge meaningful and applicable to humanity.

We shall hardly hope to see a fiery vision issue out of this pious, flat, and anonymous language. The vision which bequeaths style and makes the book is in these times mostly confined to novelists and poets. The venturesome mind that once sought to comprehend history has now grown timid and speaks the featureless language of corporate benevo-

Reprinted by permission of the author.

[1] *Literary History of the United States*. Edited by Robert E. Spiller, Willard Thorp, Thomas H. Johnson, and Henry Seidel Canby. (The Macmillan Company, 1948. 3 volumes.) [Volume III, a bibliography by Mr. Johnson, is indispensable to students of American literature.]

lence. *Literary History of the United States* is one of those estimable productions, such as TVA, which are heralded across the land by a general breakdown of grammar and metaphor. In the advertising brochure, an eminent San Francisco reviewer praises the four editors, three associates, and forty-eight contributors to *LHUS* for displaying a "general unanimity in the over-all perspective among all hands" (surely he meant "on the part of all hands"). An eminent professor at Johns Hopkins says that *LHUS* "marks a milestone" (meaning "*is* a milestone"). A Yale tautologist says that it is "inclusive in scope and judicious in its acumen." And a Texan master of truism says that "only once in a generation can such an epochal work as this be produced."

These absurdities would not be worthy of note except for the fact that those who testify to the product of the editors are only somewhat less able to find proper words to describe the book than are the editors themselves. The problem of style in such an undertaking is finally *the* problem. The mixed metaphor on the surface bespeaks an underlying confusion of purpose. The bit of mindless jargon implies more momentous intellectual abdications. The slick "literary" paradox proclaims the writer's readiness to slip with equal facility into some horrific affirmation of the greatness of Carl Sandburg or the coming glorious internationalism of American literature. The style is the book. Here there is no style and no book—or several styles and several books.

That *LHUS* is not a great book *LHUS* itself admits. In his chapter on "How Writers Lived" (in the twentieth century), Malcolm Cowley was unaccountably allowed to write the following subversive words:

Yet there was also a greater timidity among writers, of the sort that develops in any bureaucratic situation; and there was a tendency to forget that, though a great book expresses a whole culture and hence has millions of collaborators, including persons long since dead, in another sense it must finally be written by one man alone in his room with his conscience and a stock of blank paper.

That is the truth. This man alone in his room, this Gibbon or Taine or even this Parrington, is the man we ought to hold out for. The editors of *LHUS* reply that "the United States . . . has produced too much literature for any one man to read or digest." But how do they know? Doubtless a single writer would not be perfectly exhaustive or equitable, but neither is *LHUS* (which, for example, allots less than two pages to the work of Scott Fitzgerald—but more than two each to S. N. Behrman and Clifford Odets). As for digestion, our single writer might not even eat Mrs. Helen Reimensnyder Martin, the author of *Tillie: A Menonnite Maid*. And since some writers, good and bad, are bound to be slighted in *any* history, is it not better to slight them with some illuminating turn of language such as a single writer in control of his style can manage than by some soggy, half-hearted attempt at summation which has probably already been done better in some other book?

The editors are, to be sure, very conscious of style. And by a system of "group conferences" they have tried to achieve a degree of uniformity, to "iron out," as they must have said, obvious discrepancies of statement, and to provide a semblance of continuity by adding a paragraph or two of transition at the end or beginning of the chapters submitted by their contributors. This is what the editors call "relating" the contributions "to one another within a frame." The "frame" of the single writer is formed by the inclusions and exclusions of his point of view and of his style. The "frame" referred to by the editors of *LHUS* may perhaps be defined as "an aspect of an integrated approach channelled at the level of dynamic group collaboration." However it may have happened, there are at least three different styles in *LHUS*.

The first of these is a slickly glamorous style which leaps nimbly from summing up Emily Dickinson as "a breathless, perceptive poet" to such prophetic announcements as "we must recognize that the future of art can only be international." The slick style is affected by contributors both in and out of the academy. Its locus is perhaps the intersection of Maxwell Geismar, Professor Stanley T. Williams, Henry Seidel Canby, and Professor Howard Mumford Jones. Its tone is middlebrow *bravura*:

Emily Dickinson, with a terrible, beautiful intensity, expressed the most aspiring experience of the Puritan soul, sharp-reined in her by a new realism, and released in distilled, gnomic verse; her extraordinary seizure in art of the apexes of despair and ecstasy may well endure.

Captain John Smith is described as "a hard-boiled character" (in an introductory chapter which patronizes colonial America for being religious, aristocratic, and pre-capitalist). In the chapter called "The Discovery of Bohemia" we have alliterations:

The Philistines were reduced by Gelett Burgess to Bromides, by Sinclair Lewis to Babbitts, and by Mencken to the *Booboisie*. The seacoast of Bohemia became the comic opera kingdom of James Branch Cabell's novels, and romantic bookishness was pushed to its illogical conclusion in his *Beyond Life* (1919).

Of Thomas Wolfe, Mr. Geismar writes:

If he was ignorant and superstitious as the hill folks were, and stumbled into many gargantuan pitfalls—some those of his own making too—he had the persistence and cunning as well as the long legs of the hill people, and he walked with the mountain walk.

If he was as ignorant as the hill folks, then let us get on with someone who wasn't and a fig for his legs. Mr. Geismar also writes that "for sheer technical virtuosity Elinor Wylie was to be matched in prose by Katherine Anne Porter, and T. S. Eliot by William Faulkner." The fact that Mr. Geismar can imagine such painfully meticulous writers as Miss Porter (who washeth not her feet in soda water) and Mr. Eliot to be sheer technical virtuosi hints at the limitations of his idea of what literature is. It seems to be mere speciousness of style that leads Mr. Geismar to meaningless assertions.

A second style, appearing in *LHUS* less frequently than the glamorous style, is the jargon of bureaucrats, economists, and graduates of Teachers College. The same writer who speaks of Emily Dickinson's apexes of despair says that "the factor of conscious plan in the poetry of Emily Dickinson is almost negligible." An interesting confusion of styles occurs in the chapter on Emerson:

The resulting unity of approach to living is the key to Emerson's hold on his own and later generations. Henry Adams called it "naif," and others have put it away with childish things.

The following sentence seems to have been written by the editors as a group (unless perchance they called in a major general to do the job) in an attempt to usher the reader with the proper *élan* into the midst of Emerson, Thoreau, Hawthorne, Melville, and Whitman:

In other words, European philosophical theory, acting as a primary catalyst for forces already deeply indigenous to the American mind, had effected and accelerated a reorientation of literature which was tantamount to raising it to a new plane.

The glamorous hyper-metaphoric style of *LHUS* and its jargonistic style are the extremities between which there operates a third style— the featureless combination of both, which is the undistinguished manner of most of the book. It *is* a competent manner. But its competence includes not only the ability to convey useful information but also the ability to evade most of the hard problems posed by that still mysterious phenomenon, American literature. Most people who write about American literature are afraid of it.

The effort of the editors of *LHUS* to achieve continuity cannot help being frequently factitious. The Hawthorne chapter begins with a portentous "Meanwhile." But the "while" in the reader's mind is the present day, wherein (it is said at the end of the preceding chapter) he will do well to cherish Thoreau's sympathy for nature "as the lava flow of our material civilization licks up the natural beauty of earth." Harry Levin's chapter on Ambrose Bierce, Lafcadio Hearn, and James G. Huneker is said to present (apparently) a "further phase" of Henry James's response "to the predicament of a society which did not yet know that it had to be redeemed"—which sounds like the notes an obtuse student might take on the preceding chapter. At the end of Mr. Geismar's chapter we are launched in flight by these words:

These underlying cultural pressures still determined the shape of American life on the brink of another postwar era—and the shape of its literature—and whether the new age would burst in splendor or in terror.

Yet in what follows nothing bursts. Another way of making transitions and giving a single tone to the whole is to send the reader from one chapter to another in such a happy glow that he would feel like a cad to ask for logic. The chapter on "Folklore" ends on this entirely unjustifiable note of optimism:

Phonograph, radio, and sound movie now expand indefinitely the range of oral transmission. At the same time, with universally accessible print intelligible to a literate people, they diminish the need for memory [!]. Folklore may instantly become literature, and literature may speedily travel the road to folklore. Their interaction . . . will be beneficial for both.

The next chapter ends by affirming that American humor "has been democratic; it has made us one," apparently forgetting the lonely muse of Lincoln, Melville, and Mark Twain.

The editors of *LHUS* tend to regard the writers of the past, and especially the great ones, as consciously contributing to a group project sanctioned by the values of a culture which is liberal in politics and conservative-middlebrow in taste. Nevertheless the influence of avant-garde criticism is apparent. The few great writers of the nineteenth century are firmly in the saddle. The avant-garde has won its battle on this point, and with a vengeance. *LHUS* allots one chapter of twenty pages to "The New England Triumvirate: Longfellow, Holmes, and Lowell," fewer pages than are accorded severally to Melville, Henry Adams, and Henry James. "Defenders of ideality," as *LHUS* calls Stoddard, Taylor, Boker, Aldrich, and Stedman, are given the small notice they are now thought to deserve.

The book shows, however, the familiar cultural lag between conservative practice and the new truths proclaimed by the avant-garde. For it is clear that on the whole the editors think more highly of the Longfellows, Holmeses, and Stedmans of today than of the Melvilles, Hawthornes, and Whitmans. The chapter on "Humor," by Harold W. Thompson "with passages by Henry Seidel Canby," praises Dorothy Parker for "mordant wit," says that James Thurber is capable of "deadly satire," and tells us that the wartime editorials of E. B. White are "deeply incisive" and have "powerful emotional undercurrents."

Our literature is neither so great nor so coherent as *LHUS* would have us believe. The book sees our writers as aiming consciously and by duty bound to produce a "world literature," after having overcome the shock of the new American experience and declared their independence of European culture. *LHUS* invites us to see our broken past as a generally blithesome adolescence leading up to a happy one-world of tomorrow.

This is of course the kind of historical-moral vision produced by committees and bureaus—they can produce no other. A single literary historian, even an incorrigible optimist, would not be so bland, so vaguely and happily apocalyptic. Preeminent literary historians, even preeminent anthologists, do not come cheaply or every day. But it would be good for our culture to wait until one does and to deserve him when he appears. V. L. Parrington committed many literary crimes, but better a Parrington than a group conference.

For the time being, *Literary History of the United States* remains a monument to the era of culture which began in this country thirty years ago—the era of Roosevelt, the WPA, the UN, the era, among writers, of social realism and group activity. It was too generally assumed in this era that style in literature and conduct could take care of itself or would automatically issue out of the concerted action of well-meaning men who saw eye to eye on more important questions. It is this assumption which has produced *LHUS;* and the finished product reminds us once again that a humane, personal style in literature, in conduct, and in culture cannot be done without. The enormous labors, the good intentions, the modest successes of the editors should not be allowed to obscure the fact that the invasion of literature by methods more suitable to rural electrification or advertising campaigns is deplorable. Who are the custodians of language and culture if not our literary historians?

Bibiography

The essays in this anthology are drawn from the following books and magazines:

T. S. Eliot, "The Function of Criticism"—*Selected Essays*, Harcourt, Brace and Co.

William Butler Yeats, "Emotion of Multitude"—*Essays*, The Macmillan Co.

Elizabeth Bowen, "Notes on Writing a Novel"—*Collected Impressions*, Alfred A. Knopf, Inc.

Harold Rosenberg, "Character Change and the Drama"—*Symposium*, Vol. III, July 1932.

I. A. Richards, "The Interactions of Words"—*The Language of Poetry*, edited by Allen Tate, Princeton University Press.

Lionel Trilling, "Art and Neurosis"—*Partisan Review*, Winter 1941. *The Liberal Imagination*, The Viking Press.

George Santayana, "Dickens"—*The Works of George Santayana*, Vol. II, Scribners. *Essays in Literary Criticism*, edited by Irving Singer, Scribners.

F. R. Leavis, "The Irony of Swift"—*The Common Pursuit*, Chatto and Windus, Ltd.

Dorothy Van Ghent, "Clarissa and Emma as Phèdre"—*Partisan Review*, November-December 1950, and *The Partisan Reader*.

Yvor Winters, "Hawthorne and the Problem of Allegory"—*In Defense of Reason*, Alan Swallow, publisher.

Virginia Woolf, *"Phases of Fiction"*—*The Bookman*, April-May-June 1929. *Granite and Rainbow*, Harcourt, Brace and Co.

Arnold Kettle, "Thackeray"—*An Introduction to the English Novel*, Vol. I, Hutchinson and Co., Ltd.

Selma Fraiberg, "Kafka and the Dream"—*Partisan Review*, Winter 1956.

R. P. Blackmur, "Crime and Punishment"—*Chimera*, 1, 1943.

D. W. Harding, "Regulated Hatred"—*Scrutiny*, March 1940.

Allen Tate, "Our Cousin, Mr. Poe"—*The Forlorn Demon*, Alan Swallow, publisher.

Philip Rahv, "Dostoevsky in *The Possessed*"—*Image and Idea*, New Directions.

Kenneth Burke, "Caldwell: Maker of Grotesques"—*The Philosophy of Literary Form*, Louisiana State University Press.

Katherine Anne Porter, "On Criticism of Thomas Hardy"—*Southern Review*, Summer 1940. *The Days Before*, Harcourt, Brace and Co.

T. S. Eliot, "Baudelaire"—*Selected Essays*, Harcourt, Brace and Co.

William Troy, "Paul Valéry and the Poetic Universe"—*Quarterly Review of Literature*, 3, 1946.

Austin Warren, "Alexander Pope"—*Rage for Order*, University of Chicago Press.

437

Delmore Schwartz, "Poetry and Belief in Thomas Hardy"—*Southern Review,* Summer 1940.

J. V. Cunningham, "Tradition and Modernity: Wallace Stevens"—*Poetry,* December 1949.

William Empson, "Timon's Dog"—*Shakespeare Survey,* edited by William Empson with George Garrett, Brendin Publishing Co.

Herbert Read, "Wordsworth's Remorse"—*A Coat of Many Colors,* Horizon Press.

Arnold Stein, "Satan"—*Answerable Style: Essays on Paradise Lost,* University of Minnesota Press.

Louis Kronenberger, "Byron's Don Juan"—*The Republic of Letters,* Alfred A. Knopf, Inc.

Edmund Wilson, "In Honor of Pushkin"—*The Triple Thinkers,* Harcourt, Brace and Co.

Irving Howe, "Walt Whitman"—*New Republic,* March 28, 1955.

Richard Chase, "Notes on the Extinction of Style"—*Sewanee Review,* Winter 1950.